Creative Editing
for Print Media

Creative Editing for Print Media

Dorothy A. Bowles
University of Tennessee–Knoxville

Diane L. Borden
University of Washington

William Rivers
Stanford University

Wadsworth Publishing Company
Belmont, California
A Division of Wadsworth, Inc.

Executive Editor: Kristine Clerkin

Editorial Assistant: Patty Birkle

Production: Del Mar Associates

Interior and Cover Designer: John Odam

Copy Editor: Rebecca Smith

Illustrator: Cher Threinen

Cover Photography: © 1992 Walter Bibikow/The Image Bank

Compositor: John Odam Design Associates/Del Mar Associates

Printer: Malloy Lithographing

This book is printed on acid-free paper that meets Environmental Protection Agency standards for recycled paper.

1 2 3 4 5 6 7 8 9 10—97 96 95 94 93

Library of Congress Cataloging in Publication Data
Bowles, Dorothy A.
    Creative editing for print media / Dorothy A. Bowles, Diane L.
Borden, William Rivers.
      p. cm.
    Includes bibliographical references and index.
    ISBN 0-534-19098-7 (alk. paper)
    1. Journalism—Editing.   2. Editing.   I. Borden, Diane L.
II. Rivers, William.   III. Title
PN4788.B75   1993
070.4'1—dc20
                                            92-20488
                                              CIP

Preface

Technology has revolutionized the print media industry during the past 25 years. The conversion from hot-metal typesetting to cold-type (computer) typesetting in the late 1960s and early 1970s eliminated functions performed by the composing room, such as proofreading, and gave editors more control than ever over the finished publication. In the 1980s and 1990s, editor control increased even more with technological changes that allow newsroom personnel to "paste up" the type electronically through the use of pagination computer programs.

Computer technology, the fast-paced lifestyles of today's readers and increasing competition from a vast array of news and entertainment choices challenge the print media to inform, enlighten, fascinate and even intrigue in ways not possible through any other medium. Such challenges bring new opportunities for editors, particularly copy editors, who operate on the cutting edge of these technological and societal changes.

Copy editors are the very heart of the newspaper organization, supplying the lifeblood for healthy existence and serving as gatekeepers of news and entertainment for the public. More than at any previous time in newspaper history, senior editors recognize and appreciate the value of good copy editors. This recognition and appreciation make even better an already excellent employment picture for copy editors, who are rewarded at most newspapers with higher salaries than those of reporters with comparable experience.

Journalists who possess the personal attributes and word and visual skills explained in this book will have no trouble finding stimulating and rewarding work as copy editors. Too, those who aspire to newspaper management will learn that the copy desk is a fertile training ground for learning the intricacies of daily production and a frequent path to management positions.

Creative Editing for Print Media recognizes and addresses the impact that technological, lifestyle and competitive changes have brought to the newspaper industry, particularly as they affect the roles of copy editors. In addition, this book emphasizes traditional news editing skills: using correct grammar, punctuation, style and vocabulary; writing headlines; handling photographs and informational graphics; using typography; designing and laying out pages.

A special feature of this textbook is the extensive collection of exercises, which allows students to test their understanding of the material in each chapter and to practice their editing skills. These exercises and others are also available to instructors on a computer disk.

The organization of *Creative Editing for Print Media* is logical and progressive. Chapter One explains the organization of a typical newspaper staff, the role and importance of newspaper copy editors and career opportunities for copy editors.

Chapter Two focuses on the copy editor's tools: the proper use of language and a working knowledge of standard reference materials. Chapter Three addresses the importance of precision when editing words, sentences and paragraphs.

Chapter Four offers a detailed treatment of legal concerns that affect editors—including libel, invasion of privacy and copyright infringement—and suggests ways that editors can help their publications avoid lawsuits. Chapter Five examines ethical situations of specific concern to editors and suggests ways to frame discussions that should prove useful in ethical decision making. This chapter also offers a sampling of behavioral codes from newspapers around the country, as well as a section on how to edit with good taste and sensitivity.

Chapter Six focuses on the art of writing headlines, discussing the functions and characteristics of headlines and offering rules for writing, counting, placing and styling headlines. Chapter Seven examines the editing of news-service material and explains the anatomy of a breaking news story as it unfolds.

Chapter Eight launches a three-chapter discussion of visual journalism, focusing particularly on editing pictures and infographics. Chapter Nine discusses typography, particularly type sizes, widths, styles, weights and families. Chapter Ten describes newspaper layout and design; examines design principles and elements, forms of layout and tips on laying out a page; and discusses modern technology, such as pagination, personal computers and laser graphics.

Appendices provide an abbreviated style manual and a list of more than 250 commonly misused words and phrases, with clear, easy-to-understand definitions and explanations of proper word usage.

Almost every chapter in the book includes a brief section written by a professional journalist to help students understand the work of copy editors. A short biographical sketch accompanies each of these sections so students can see the career path of the professional.

Throughout the book, we have adhered to the most commonly used newspaper style and have sought to avoid sexism, racism, ageism, homophobia and other discriminatory language.

We would like to express our debt of gratitude to the professional journalists across the nation who helped supply materials and insights for this book. Although they are too numerous to mention individually, we are extremely grateful to them all.

The highly competent editors at Del Mar Associates, particularly Nancy Sjoberg and Rebecca Smith, have been a pleasure to work with. The good people at Wadsworth, known for their excellence in textbook publishing, also deserve our gratitude. Special recognition goes to Kristine Clerkin, editor for mass communications, Patty Birkle, Hal Humphrey and Robert Kauser.

We also offer our special thanks to those who read the manuscript at various stages and gave us many valuable suggestions, including Paul Anderson, University of Tennessee, Chattanooga; Karen Christy, University of Texas at Austin; DeAnn Evans, University of Utah; Sue O'Brien, University of Colorado, Boulder; Howard Seeman, Humbolt University; John Vivian, Winona State University; and Ruth Walden, University of North Carolina.

Finally, a sincere personal thank you goes to Dr. Lisa St. Clair Harvey for her unwavering support during the writing and review process of this textbook. Her love and encouragement helped make this a positive and rewarding experience.

Contents

Five

Six

Seven

Eight

Nine

Ten

Appendix A

Appendix B

Index

The year is 2038. You wake up to the sounds of New Age music on your digital clock/stereo, smell the aroma of freshly ground coffee brewing in your preset coffeemaker, and hear the friendly beep of your personal computer telling you that the morning newspaper has arrived. But not on your doorstep. It has been transmitted through your user-friendly personal computer.

Deadlines do not wait for inspiration.
—Charles M. Schultz, "Peanuts" creator

Quite probably, the newspaper of the 21st century—even if it exists in an ink-on-paper format—will take an entirely different form from those we're used to in the 1990s. If you subscribe to The Washington Post, for example, your newspaper may have a horizontal format, 14 inches wide by 8.5 inches tall. (Old-fashioned newspapers in the 1990s were a quite vertical 13 inches wide by 21 inches tall.) Your Post may be fan-folded, as a brochure would be, and generated by a high-speed printer on one continuous sheet of high-quality paper. Your newspaper is full of color photographs and graphics and combines the best of newspaper design with the best of magazine design for a graphically appealing look (see Exhibit 1-1).

In 2038, if you subscribe to the new USAccess service, your newspaper is customized especially for you and is collated and printed in your home or office. At the time you subscribed, you indicated your news preferences. Now your newspaper selects material from various sources of information to reflect your interests and delivers it to you via your computer.

The Copy Editor's Role in the Newsroom

The importance of good copy editing
The duties of a copy editor
Characteristics of a good copy editor
The copy desk in a modern newsroom
The editing process
A modern editor looks to the future:
Sharon Bibb

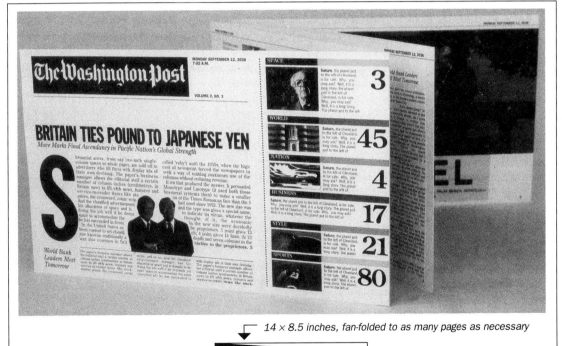

Exhibit 1-1
The future may bring a fan-folded Washington Post, printed in the subscriber's home on a facsimile machine or computer printer. (Reprinted courtesy of the American Press Institute from Newspaper Design: 2000 and Beyond; *used by permission of The Washington Post)*

14 × 8.5 inches, fan-folded to as many pages as necessary

Color indexing, carried throughout

USAccess is colorful, well-designed and easy to read. It also offers you a personal data bank, which lists your portfolio of stocks and their current prices, your checking account balance, your schedule for the day and your exercise routine (see Exhibit 1-2).

If you subscribe to The New York Daily Mail, you obviously are bright, affluent and sophisticated. Your newspaper comes in the mail five days a week, uses only color photographs and offers you computer access to the latest news. As the 21st century opened, most of the big stories of the day were good news: AIDS is curable; Star Wars becomes a space exploration program, with the first all-women team of astronauts; robots boost assembly-line productivity; and a national health plan covers all body part replacements (see Exhibit 1-3).

These newspapers 50 years into the future, imaginative predictions designed by participants in a 1988 American Press Institute seminar called "Design 2000 and Beyond," are not as far-fetched as one might imagine. The 21st century is, after all, less than a decade away. But most newspapers at the turn of the century probably will not look much different from newspapers of today. They simply will be better organized, use more color and attempt to squeeze more information into less space.

Whatever form newspapers take, however, the future of ink on paper,

whether a fan-folded Washington Post or a sophisticated New York Daily Mail, is certainly secure. The printed newspaper is likely to be around well into the 21st century and beyond. However, it may face competition from a medium that blends text, sounds, still pictures and video through technological advances in fiber optics and computers. Such competition will make the verbal and visual skills of good copy editors even more valuable in newsrooms of the future.

Witness the following scenario from a 1989 American Society of Newspaper Editors report on technology and the future. The incident takes place as the closing credits of a movie scroll up the wide screen of the high-definition television set.

The viewer points her remote channel selector at a newspaper symbol in the lower right corner of the screen, and then the movie dissolves into an electronic version of a front page, with typographically attractive headlines and a couple of still photos.

She points to a headline about a surgeon general's warning about the impact of high-salt diets on children's health. The screen fills with a detailed report of the surgeon general's press conference. She begins to read, then moves her pointer to position a small arrow over the first word of the surgeon general's statement. Immediately the text is replaced with a short video showing highlights from the press conference.

Returning to the text, she reads further, until she reaches a reference to the relative risks of sodium and potassium salts. Pointing the arrow to the word "potassium" calls up a listing of brand names for sodium substitutes, as well as a listing of popular packaged foods that have recently replaced sodium salts with potassium salts.

This kind of multimedia product is the future, and the people who produce the newspaper or magazine or multimedia product of the future—editors, reporters, designers, photographers and artists—are the ones who are likely to be affected most by technological changes. Copy editors, key bridges between information gatherers and information consumers, will be called on to perform all the traditional copy editing tasks plus some duties that are now the domain of other news personnel.

The importance of good copy editing

Editors have many functions, but the primary job of an editor is to make writing more precise, concise and meaningful than it was originally. All writers, regardless of experience level, require editing.

Gay Talese, once one of the best reporters for The New York Times, resigned to become a free-lance writer. He was so successful that he was paid more than $1 million to write *Thy Neighbor's Wife*. He took eight years to write that book and came out with sentences that read as if they had been translated badly from Icelandic. For example: "This was when Jim Buckley met Al Goldstein, whose spy piece he helped to edit, and whose expressed frustrations he not only identified with but saw as the compatible essence of a viable partnership—or at least some hedge against the probability that neither of them could ever make it alone." Talese's book also carried ambiguities like this: "After completing high school in 1949, his sister wrote that she had arranged for him an appointment to Annapolis." This sentence was actually about the brother who completed high school in 1949.

Judith Krantz, who also began as a reporter, made millions from writing *Scruples* and *Princess Daisy*. Yet she wrote convoluted sentences like this one: "Thank heaven they'd all be in their staterooms, intently adjusting their resort dinner clothes, caparisoned for the delectation of each other."

David Broder of The Washington Post is generally considered one of the best political reporters and columnists in the country. He wrote a book in 1980 titled *Changing of the Guard*, and the publisher paid him a $40,000 advance against royalties. When the publisher's editor, Jonathan Coleman, saw the manuscript, he left New York for Washington, checked into a hotel, and for a week of 18-hour days reviewed every line with Broder. Broder later remarked of Coleman's efforts: "His fingerprints are on every sentence. This book is as much Jonathan Coleman's as it is mine."

Talese, Krantz and Broder are all famous, successful writers. Yet, although each has been working at writing for more than 35 years, they all still need editors.

Regardless of their experience or expertise, all writers, including reporters, need editors. Theodore Bernstein, for many years chief copy editor at The New York Times and author of several books on word usage, made this observation: "If in a single night each of 40 copy editors saved only a single line in each of, say, 10 stories, the total savings would be almost two columns.

Regardless of their experience or expertise, all writers, including reporters, need editors.

4

Is that piddling? The idea here is not to destroy a writer's style but rather to be alert to word-saving locutions."

Good newspapers, good magazines, good news broadcasts all have one thing in common: They all have good teams of editors. Although bylines give reporters name recognition that copy editors do not have, the strength of the copy editing staff is one of the most important predictors of the strength of the news organization.

Perhaps more than at any previous time in newspaper history, senior editors are recognizing the value of good copy editors, an appreciation that makes even better an already excellent employment picture for copy editors. Linda Grist Cunningham, chair of an ASNE committee that conducted a survey of copy editors, said: "As the literacy skills of even our better writers decline and as the demands of technology complicate our production schedules, editors will be forced to pay attention to the needs of copy editors if we are to improve our newspapers."

Copy editors are a rare breed, and they are scarce. Just ask any editor or publisher trying to hire one. And they are dedicated, intelligent individuals whose love of language and penchant for precision make many reporters look good. Copy editors are the very heart of the organization, supplying the lifeblood for healthy existence and serving as gatekeepers of the news for the public. The importance of copy editors is recognized and rewarded at many newspapers with salaries higher than those of reporters with comparable experience.

Journalists who possess the personal attributes and verbal and visual skills explained in this book will have no trouble finding stimulating and rewarding work as copy editors. In an earlier era, few copy editors were without reporting experience; desk work was seen as a promotion from reporting. However, those in charge of hiring at newspapers today no longer insist that reporting be a prerequisite to working at the copy desk. Also, journalists who aspire to newspaper management will learn that the copy desk is a good place to learn the intricacies of daily production and a frequent path to management positions.

Copy editors are a rare breed, and they are scarce.

The duties of a copy editor

Great reporting alone will produce at best a mediocre newspaper. Good editing is the difference between a great newspaper and a mediocre one.

The chief duties of the copy editor include

- *Improving copy by making dull or verbose copy interesting and concise.* Copy editors can transform halting stories into ones that sing. Creativity is essential. However, as long as the information has been expressed clearly, the aim of the copy editor is to preserve as far as possible the words of the reporter and to retain the tone of the story as it was written.
- *Correcting errors of grammar, spelling and style in all newspaper copy, including informational graphics.* Too many reporters, triumphantly bringing in stories that were difficult to pry loose, refer to minor errors as "just typos." Yet even the smallest error or inconsistency can cause readers to wonder whether that carelessness extends to the reporting as well.
- *Correcting errors of fact and emphasis.* An expert copy editor is invariably a walking compendium. Although reporters are better acquainted with their beats and their sources, the copy editor can supply a context—other stories, the city, the county, the nation, the world—that the reporters, whose single-minded focus is their story, almost in-

evitably fail to comprehend. Copy editors unfamiliar with the context must be adept at using many reference sources for quick research.

- *Judging news value.* Copy editors must be alert to the flow of current affairs and understand how a single item integrates with the stream of news.
- *Guarding against libel and other legal problems.* The copy desk is usually the last line of defense against legal concerns that can cost a newspaper much in money and in lost time.
- *Protecting and enhancing the newspaper's reputation and image.* Every newspaper would like to have a reputation for accuracy and thoroughness in news coverage. It is up to copy editors to build and preserve that reputation. The personality or image of the paper—conservative or breezy, formal or informal, for example—is also largely in the hands of the copy desk.
- *Writing headlines that summarize stories and capture readers' attention.* Copy editors' skill with words and ability to work quickly are especially valuable in this aspect of the job.
- *Selecting, cropping and sizing photographs and other art.* Section editors, along with the photography and graphics staff, handle much of this work, but copy editors also are involved in the process.
- *Writing picture captions.* The idea that "a picture is worth a thousand words" may become meaningless unless the picture is accompanied by a carefully crafted caption.
- *Using computer codes to designate the headline and body type style, size, width and leading.* As newspapers became "computerized" during the 1970s, copy editors assumed many of the production tasks previously performed by others. With expert knowledge of the newspaper's computer system, a copy editor can, with just a few keystrokes, do much of the work that previously was performed by teams of production specialists.
- *Laying out pages.* Many decisions about how the newspaper will look each day are in the hands of copy editors. Designers and other graphics experts determine the basic look of the paper, but copy editors work within the overall design pattern to lay out individual pages. Expert news judgment is also essential as copy editors, working with other editors, make decisions about which stories will go on the front page or an inside page and how much emphasis to give individual stories.
- *Keeping up with the newest technology.* Computer graphics, computer pagination and digital photography are changing rapidly.

Characteristics of a good copy editor

In a recent report from the Associated Press Managing Editors Writing and Editing Committee, William G. Connolly Jr., deputy editor of The New York Times Week in Review section, offered this checklist of the qualities of an outstanding editor:

- *Confidence.* Good editors have confidence in their own intelligence, knowledge and writing skills. They know the newspaper's style, production capabilities and politics. They know the system—and use it.
- *Objectivity.* Editors have an extra obligation to be objective. They must be able to put the material in a broader context and stand back from the person who wrote it. Every newsroom has problem people, but great editors have the ability to look beyond the person.

Computer graphics, computer pagination and digital photography are changing rapidly.

- *Awareness*. Editors must be aware of the readers and of the personality of the publication. Layout, selection of stories, art, graphics and headlines should all come together to reinforce the newspaper's personality. Look at newspapers in trouble, and you'll find a personality problem. Good taste and knowing what's important are the essential elements of personality.
- *Intelligence*. Good editors must have a broad background that enables them to bring to every story a sense of why it is important and what it means in a broader context. They must be instinctively aware of what is right or wrong with a story.
- *Questioning nature*. Good editors know there is no such thing as a stupid question. They question everything. Editors know that if they have doubts, so will the reader.
- *Diplomacy*. Editing is a confrontation. Writing is both an intellectual and emotional experience, and good editors try to minimize the inevitable tension that arises between an editor and a writer. They understand the reporter's problems. Nevertheless, although civility and diplomacy are important, they can't be permitted to overwhelm the need to edit.
- *Ability to write*. Editors should be better writers than reporters are, but they still must be able to retain a writer's style and ideas. A great editor's work is invisible to both the writer and the reader.
- *Sense of humor*. Good editors are able to laugh at the absurdity of some aspects of the business—bad hours, bad tempers, bad deadlines, bad copy—and plunge ahead.

A Dallas Times Herald editor, speaking at a journalism educators' seminar at the American Press Institute, said the following attributes would produce an "almost-perfect" copy editor:

- Have a college education.
- Have newspaper experience, including reporting and editing.
- Be well-read, in both fiction and non-fiction.
- Be familiar with the news and its background.
- Have hobbies, enjoy cultural events and be well-traveled.
- Be quick and thorough when editing copy.
- Have a healthy skepticism that leads to the questioning of information in stories and a desire to release no story with unanswered questions.
- Be familiar with the rules of grammar, with punctuation and spelling, and with style.
- Appreciate good writing and know what to do with it.
- Be able to listen to the rhythm of a story.
- Have a sense of wit and pathos and the ability to discern the difference.
- Have an orderly and well-balanced mind, which implies judgment and a sense of perspective and proportion.
- Know the laws of libel, contempt and copyright.
- Have a team spirit.

The copy desk in a modern newsroom

The fast pace of editing often allows little time for reflection. In today's modern newsrooms, where editors are being asked to perform more and more of the production functions previously handled by composing-room personnel, editors increasingly find that their time is at a premium.

An age of rapid technological advances in the publishing industry has introduced computer-generated copy and computer-activated layout and

Good editors are able to laugh at the absurdity of some aspects of the business.

pasteup (pagination). The copy editor's job, therefore, has become at once more complex, more exciting and more vital to the quality of the final product.

Pagination, some say, is the vital link to a grander scheme for newspaper automation. It calls for the end of the composing room as we know it. Partial pagination, now being introduced at many newspapers, allows editors to create pages on computer terminals with all the text in place. Several companies are testing and manufacturing devices that permit the digitalization of photographs, which would allow editors to produce an entire page on computer terminals. When total pagination is in place—and it will be in the next 10 years—most of the work now done in the composing room, a department that accounts for perhaps 25 percent of the total newspaper payroll, will be unnecessary. (Pagination is discussed further in Chapter 10.)

Clearly, newsroom editors and managers of the future must be ready to meet the challenges of incorporating new technology into newsroom processes. The organizational structure of newsrooms of the future may look quite different. Today most newsrooms are organized in a hierarchical structure like that shown in Exhibit 1-4. That is, the organization looks like a pyramid, with the editor at the apex and the reporters, copy editors and photographers—the workers—forming the base.

Newsrooms of the future may require a more circular structure, in which job functions rather than titles determine the organization and in which jobs are interrelated rather than separated. Copy editors, many believe, will be at the center of this new newsroom because of the breadth of their job functions.

The traditional copy desk physically resembled a horseshoe. The chief copy editor, called the "slot editor" or simply the "slot," sat at the center of the inside curve of a semicircular desk. Copy editors sat along the outside curve of the horseshoe, known as the "rim," and were thus known as "rim editors." Although the terms *slot editor* and *rim editor* persist, the computerization of editing has changed the physical arrangement of the copy desk. Modern copy desks are arranged in a rectangular shape and generally include separate stations with an electronic editing terminal for each editor.

To help speed the flow of copy, many small and medium-sized newspapers have instituted a system of centralized editing called the "universal copy desk." Universal desk copy editors work on copy for all sections of the newspaper. Conversely, most metropolitan newspapers have very specialized desks, which process copy for particular categories of news: local, state, national, international, business, sports, opinion, lifestyle or entertainment.

Some metros also have separate reporting and editing staffs for "zoned" editions, those pages or sections that target news and advertising geographically for a particular circulation area. In many newspaper markets, zoned editions have proved successful with both readers and advertisers. Subscribers receive the individual section containing news and advertising focusing on their neighborhood, along with the rest of the metropolitan newspaper. Some newspapers have published as many as 24 different zoned editions a week; others publish several zoned sections each day.

The editing process

Video display terminals (VDTs) linked to computers have greatly changed the newspaper production process. The computer revolution has simplified some aspects of the copy editor's job but has also added duties. Many production functions are now performed at the copy desk instead of in the composing room.

Pagination . . . calls for the end of the composing room as we know it.

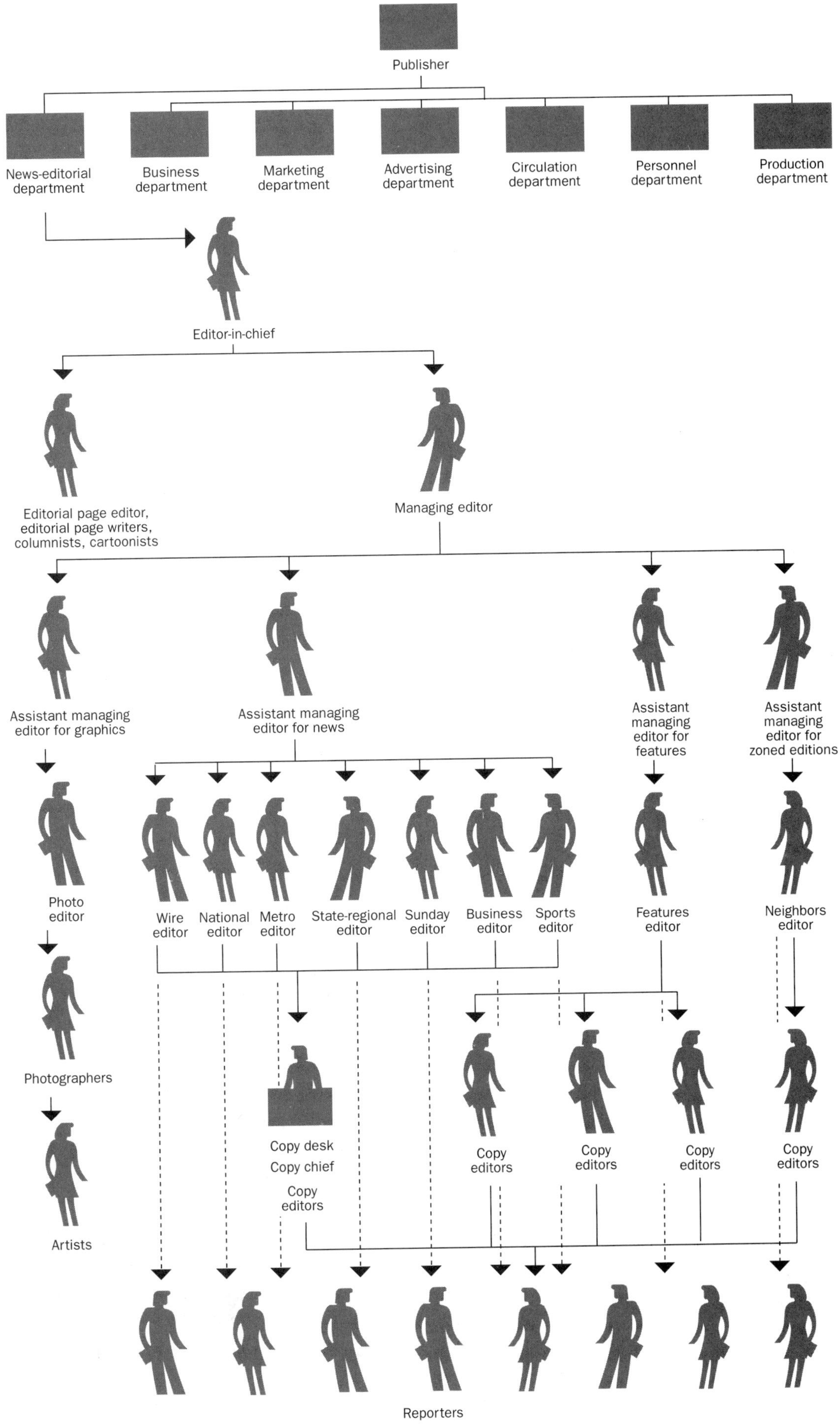

Exhibit 1-4
Today's newsroom is organized hierarchically. This chart illustrates the organizational plan at a large metropolitan daily, which has separate copy desks for general-interest news, business, sports, features and the zoned editions. Many newspapers have a universal copy desk, which edits stories for all sections of the paper.

Publisher

News-editorial department

Business department

Marketing department

Advertising department

Circulation department

Personnel department

Production department

Editor-in-chief

Editorial page editor, editorial page writers, columnists, cartoonists

Managing editor

Assistant managing editor for graphics

Assistant managing editor for news

Assistant managing editor for features

Assistant managing editor for zoned editions

Photo editor

Wire editor

National editor

Metro editor

State-regional editor

Sunday editor

Business editor

Sports editor

Features editor

Neighbors editor

Photographers

Copy desk
Copy chief
Copy editors

Copy editors

Copy editors

Copy editors

Copy editors

Artists

Reporters

Copy editors not only perform more functions but are now also the last people to process copy before the final pasteup stage. Typesetters and proofreaders no longer exist as a final check to prevent errors from being published. Electronic layout soon will eliminate the physical pasteup stage as well.

To demonstrate the editing process, let's track a story from idea to publication (see Exhibit 1-5). First, before a story is assigned to a reporter or accepted from a beat or general assignment reporter, an editor has to decide that the story is newsworthy. A knowledge of the newspaper's audience is the key to determining which news values to emphasize, and many newspapers today periodically conduct sophisticated surveys to help editors stay abreast of readers' interests. In exercising news judgment, editors evaluate the extent to which each individual story contains one or more traditional news criteria, such as timeliness, importance, proximity, uniqueness, unusualness, conflict, emotion, prominence and impact on the audience.

Thus, the editing process begins before a story is ever written. It is not a copy editor, however, who is involved at this stage. Rather it is an editor, sometimes called an *assigning editor*, in charge of a newspaper section or category of news. Types of assigning editors vary with the organization and size of the paper, but typical examples are city, state, sports, lifestyle and entertainment editors. Whether the assigning editor conceives the idea for a story or accepts an idea generated by a reporter, he or she then helps direct the

Exhibit 1-5

As copy flows through a newsroom, several people help give it form. After assigning editor or reporter conceives story idea, reporter gathers information and writes story. (1) Reporter types it on VDT and files it into computer system. (2) Assigning editor calls up story on VDT screen and reads it for content, perhaps making layout decisions and specifying headline. Story (3) goes back to reporter for more work or (4) goes to copy desk chief. Copy desk chief loosely edits story and may make layout and headline decisions, depending on story's page placement. (5) Story goes to copy editor for editing and headline writing, (6) then goes back to copy chief for approval. Copy chief (7) may return story to rim editor for more work or (8) may send story to assigning editor for a final look or (9) may give computer command to have story set in type. (10) Story, now set in type, goes to composing room personnel and is pasted into position on specified page according to editor's dummy layout. (Photo by Kerric Harvey/courtesy of the Seattle Times)

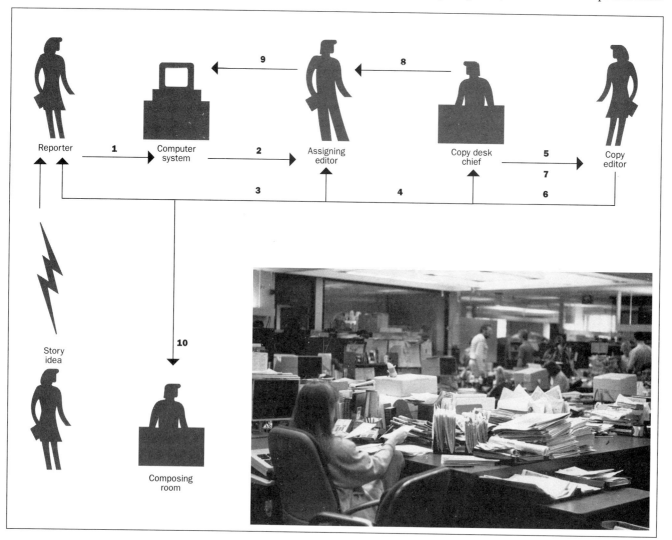

reporter's work by suggesting angles that the story might examine, sources to interview and questions to ask. The assigning editor, often in consultation with other editors or with the reporter, also determines whether the story should be accompanied by photographs or other artwork. If so, a photographer or graphic artist is assigned to begin working on the story.

Once the story is written, the assigning editor reads it, primarily for content rather than style or tone. If substantial content changes are needed—for example, if obvious questions remain unanswered—the editor generally sends the story back to the reporter for additional work. If the editor is satisfied with the overall content of the story, he or she decides where it will be placed in the newspaper, how long it will be, and what size and style of headline will accompany it. Sometimes a story is sent to the copy desk with an *HTK* ("headline to come") notation, meaning that the headline form has not been determined yet. Decisions about story placement and headline specifications are made by the person who lays out the page, which may be the assigning editor, the copy desk chief, a copy editor or perhaps a layout editor or graphics specialist.

The story is then sent to the copy desk chief, who may edit it loosely before passing it along to one of the copy editors sitting on the rim. In assigning copy, the copy desk chief often considers the special knowledge or ability of each rim editor. Like reporters, some copy editors are experts in certain fields, and this expertise can be useful in editing particular stories. Others are especially talented at handling stories of a statistical nature, writing bright or clever headlines for feature stories, or editing stories of exceptional difficulty or length.

In modern newsrooms, all of this shuffling of stories is done electronically from computer terminal to computer terminal. But as recently as the mid-1970s, many newspapers still edited paper copy with pencils, used scissors and glue for reorganizing paragraphs, and moved copy from person to person physically.

A rim editor edits the story carefully, perhaps cutting it to fit a specified length for the page layout. Copy editors, even experienced ones, should read each story at least three times. During the first reading, the copy editor analyzes the thoroughness of the content and the appropriateness and effectiveness of the lead and organization of the story. The copy editor should make few, if any, changes during this first reading.

Next the copy editor rereads the story to make changes where needed. For example, a buried or uninteresting lead may be rewritten, the overall organization of the story may be rearranged, facts are verified, and style, grammar, punctuation and spelling errors are corrected. In addition, the copy editor addresses questions of ethics, taste and sensitivity, as well as legal problems with the story.

Finally, the copy editor reads the story a third time to be sure that all errors have been corrected and that everything possible has been done to produce a clear, concise, accurate and well-organized story. During the copy editing process, the editor may need to talk with the reporter about unclear passages or ask for details. Often the copy editor uses standard reference books or makes telephone calls to verify information or fill in gaps in the story.

When the copy editor is satisfied with the story, he or she writes the headline according to the specifications assigned by the editor. Computer codes are inserted so the body and headline type will be set (or "output," as it is expressed in computer jargon) in the desired style, size, width and leading (space between the lines of body type). If an informational graphic or

Copy editors, even experienced ones, should read each story at least three times.

photograph is to accompany the story, the copy editor edits it and writes a caption for it (processes that are discussed in Chapter 8).

Then the copy editor sends the story back to the chief copy editor for approval. If the copy chief finds fault with the editing or the headline, the story may be bounced back to the copy editor to make still more changes. If the copy and the headline meet with the copy chief's approval, the computer command is given to send the story or to output it.

The story, printed on a long strip of photosensitive paper, then emerges from the computer in the composing room. Following a sample layout prepared by an editor, composing room personnel trim excess paper and paste the type onto a page. Most newspapers today use offset printing. In this process, after all elements for the page are pasted into position, the entire page is photographed, and a printing plate is made from the resulting negative. This plate goes onto the printing press.

Most metropolitan daily newspapers print several editions of each day's issue. A good newspaper, not satisfied with merely rearranging stories or rewriting headlines, continually updates its editions to reflect the latest developments in the news. New page layouts may require that stories be edited and headlines be written as many as three or four times.

As the editions are updated, copy editors assume responsibility for rechecking material from earlier editions. Although practices vary from paper to paper, the job of reading a story already in print differs markedly from the job of handling a story before it is set in type. Between editions, copy editors read to update old information and to correct errors of fact or omission rather than read for grammatical and stylistic errors. Updates are handled quickly by making the required changes on the computer screen and outputting the entire story again. In addition to saving time, this method reprocesses the new version of the story in one clean piece and reduces the chances of error.

The copy editor's work, day or night, is usually marked by roller-coaster fluctuations in activity. At newspapers, most of the action comes in the last few hours before deadline, regardless of whether the newspaper is distributed to readers in the morning or in the afternoon.

It is no longer enough to inform.

A MODERN EDITOR LOOKS TO THE FUTURE

By Sharon Bibb

Like it or not, the newspaper industry is more a bottom-line business than the labor of love I believed it to be when I enlisted years ago. The newspaper is more and more an entertainment product, competing directly with television, radio and home movies for attention within the constraints of our harried lives. And what the newspaper is about has as much to do with marketability as it does with what the public wants and needs to know.

However distasteful the connotations of marketing and promotion may be to some, the stark reality is that readers—the consumers—need news and information in a new way. Newspapers have adapted to the new market, but we as newspeople have adapted too slowly, either unwittingly or unwillingly, to our own detriment. If consumers are finding radio and television news more desirable, more accessible, more suitable to their lifestyles, we can't blame anyone but ourselves. Worse, no matter how clever and enterprising we think we are, we cannot hope to serve and inform an absent public. Our challenge is to respond to the new age of accelerated, mobile lifestyles. If we can't show vivid, moving video images as does TV or conveniently provide audio information as does the car radio in rush hour, we must somehow create a product consumers still can't live without.

It is no longer enough to inform. We must enlighten and fascinate and even intrigue—and in ways not possible through any other medium. What USA Today set out to do in the 1980s wasn't visionary so much as it was the right thing at the very right time. Six million readers a day can't be all wrong. Now papers across the nation try to mimic what USA Today does so well, but the concept has eluded most. The point is not to have simply more graphics or more color or more sidebars (separate stories related to the main story). The point is to understand the consumer. And today's reader needs news quickly, succinctly and in a digestible form for today's workaday world.

That is where editors, particularly copy editors, enter the picture. No newspaper that intends to survive will be content to invest in copy editors who are simply the best professional proofreaders money can buy. The editor of the '90s (and of the next century) will have a vision—not of the future, but rooted in the here and now, with a clear and precise view of what's important to everyday people in everyday affairs.

SHARON BIBB

Editor Sharon Bibb received her bachelor's degree in 1975 and her master's degree in 1977, both in communications from the University of Washington in Seattle. She interned as a reporter and as a copy editor at the Tacoma (Wash.) News Tribune, where she discovered that she preferred copy editing. She enjoyed the challenge of polishing stories and writing the kind of headlines that would sell those stories. She was hired as a full-time staff member by the News Tribune and performed such copy-desk duties as slotting, layout and makeup.

Three years later, Bibb was hired by the Oakland (Calif.) Tribune, where she served as the night Lifestyle section editor, Sunday Lifestyle section editor and Travel section editor. She saw a need for more newsroom efficiency and sold her editors on a job description that allowed her to write the newspaper's stylebook, redesign the Sunday TV magazine, and improve systems formats and guides.

Her increasing interest in new technology took her to the Philadelphia Inquirer, where she served as an assistant news editor and where she became involved in paginating the News, Style and Sunday sections of the newspaper.

Later, Bibb was hired by USA Today as a Life section layout editor. Her interest in new technology continued, and she eventually moved into the systems editor role at USA Today, training other editors in pagination.

She recently returned to the Bay Area, where she serves as the night news editor for the San Francisco Examiner. She also has served as a co-coordinator and lecturer at the Howard University High School Urban Journalism Workshop.

The editor who survives, I think, is one who can be what I call an "anti-journalist." In these hard times, when events are sometimes too ominous to ponder, readers are becoming more average, more ordinary in the sense that what's most important to them is how to survive. We editors must identify with that need and relate to everyday survival as they do.

It sounds simplistic, but too frequently we edit stories that serve only to showcase how much our reporters know rather than what readers need to know. Have you ever heard reporters talking about a story they're working on? They often share with each other and with their editors interesting anecdotes and little-known facts, yet little of what was so interesting gets written into the story. It happens all the time, as if reporters are prisoners of some archaic newswriting regimen they learned in school—as if journalists aren't allowed to talk to people normally, neighbor to neighbor.

Editors who survive and who become indispensable in the newsroom will be anti-journalists; they will be crusaders for readers. They will be able to spot what is missing in stories. They will be able to find what words are best as *words* and what words are better understood illustrated. They will ask the questions that transcend mere reporting of an event, questions readers will ask. For example, "Now that I know this fact, what can I do about it? What *should* I do about it? How can I get help? Where can I find out more?"

If a story is about the closing of a popular store, agency or service, the editor must ask what consumer alternatives still exist. If there *are* other alternatives, even if they already are named in the story, the editor must ask if the reader would be further served with a sidebar listing specific names, addresses, phone numbers and hours of operation.

If a story is about a major bridge that has collapsed, the editor must ask whether the obligatory map of where the collapse took place is enough—or whether the reader might be even better served by a map (and text) outlining alternate routes.

If the story is about a child drowning in a backyard pool, the editor must ask what supplemental elements can be provided to arm readers against such tragedies in their own homes.

If the subject of any story is complicated, the editor must ask how it can be broken down in terms that can be understood or how it can be put into perspective. A story about a state's budget crisis can seem complete on the surface; a sidebar comparing that state's budget crisis to similar crises in other states can be enlightening. In one case, the reader has been duly informed; in the latter, the reader has a truer understanding.

As an anti-journalist, the editor thinks like an average citizen. There is no need to worry about wearing the journalist's hat; the editor does that on instinct. The editor who also is an anti-journalist sees to it that—by words and photos and illustrations and lists—she or he has helped answer the kind of questions a brother or sister or aunt or neighbor would ask.

The editor of the future will see the big picture—not the single story to be edited, but all the stories in the edition and which ones connect to others. The successful editor will see news as packages of information, tied together for the reader's convenience. The successful editor will be the *instigator* of information rather than a passive conduit through which seemingly unconnected news passes.

The editor with the big picture will take an ordinary story and find ways to make it extraordinary, without changing words or tone, but perhaps by suggesting a different presentation. One of the nicest compliments a reader can pay is to clip a story for safekeeping. It means the reporters and editors have done something right. It is not always the copy editor's job to see that quality first. But the copy editor can resolve to read each story as a person on the street would and wonder what is missing or what could be better.

Packaging not only helps readers connect events and trends, it also can help make the most efficient use of shrinking news holes. How most papers have failed to successfully copy USA Today is by delivering graphics and sidebars that virtually duplicate information in stories—for the sake of having graphics and sidebars. USA Today editors, however, rightfully see *all* the story's elements as part of the whole. In other words, what readers find in a chart is *in* a chart because it better delivers the data or better illustrates a point than words do. And a sidebar is just that: a related but separate angle on the same story, not words that recap news in the mainbar.

At USA Today, it is as much the reporters' as the editors' responsibility to suggest how stories could be packaged with the various elements. It is no less the copy editor's job to do the same.

New technology has compelled editors to learn new methods and master new machines. It hasn't been without resistance. When pagination (electronic dummying of pages) arrived at USA Today, one editor resorted to wearing a hard hat with the letters EPUP, for "electronic paste-up person." Many editors working with pagination believe their jobs indeed have been reduced in some way to the role of pasteup people. On top of editing, they now have to know elaborate coding for stories and be user-friendly with Macintoshes and other layout terminals.

Pagination is a fact of newsroom life now for newspapers that can afford the technology (most can't afford *not* to have it). There is an overwhelming benefit: precision. Editors should welcome any new methods that allow them to see stories and pages exactly as they were designed. Any editor who uses this opportunity to become an expert in emerging technological systems can guarantee a secure future as a newsroom pioneer and leader.

Pagination (and other methods of precision, such as area composition) rewards us with more control over the final product. What journalists produce is what is published.

In many ways, the new technology has not changed the copy editor's job very much. But in a few profound ways, it has. Copy editors remain the "last line of defense." For the newspaper of the future, copy editors must also take the offense to turn ordinary stories into neatly packaged information that connects with readers—and connects them to the larger world.

Suggestions for additional reading

Bernstein, Theodore M. *The Careful Writer: A Modern Guide to English Usage.*
　　New York: Atheneum, 1978.
Cappon, Rene J. *The Word: An Associated Press Guide to Good News Writing.*
　　New York: Associated Press, 1982.
French, Christopher W. (ed.). *The Associated Press Stylebook and Libel Manual.*
　　Reading, Mass.: Addison-Wesley, 1988.
Gordon, Karen Elizabeth. *The Well-Tempered Sentence: A Punctuation Handbook for
　　the Innocent, the Eager, and the Doomed.* New Haven, Conn.: Ticknor & Fields,
　　1983.
Kessler, Lauren, and Duncan McDonald. *When Words Collide: A Journalist's Guide to
　　Grammar and Style,* 3rd ed. Belmont, Calif.: Wadsworth, 1992.
Newman, Edwin. *Strictly Speaking: Will America Be the Death of English?*
　　New York: Warner Books, 1975.
Newspaper Design: 2000 and Beyond. J. Montgomery Curtis Memorial Seminar.
　　Reston, Va.: American Press Institute, 1988.
The Next Newspapers. Future of Newspapers Report. Washington, D.C.: American
　　Society of Newspaper Editors, 1988.
Rogers, James. *The Dictionary of Cliches.* New York: Ballantine Books, 1987.
Strunk, William Jr., and E. B. White. *The Elements of Style,* 3rd ed.
　　New York: Macmillan, 1979.

1. Observe the copy editors at your campus newspaper. How does their work compare with the work of professional copy editors, as described in this chapter? Make notes on the differences so you can discuss them in class.

2. Draw a chart to explain the copy desk arrangement at your school or local newspaper.

3. Discuss the relationships of, and explain the differences in job duties performed by, assigning editors, slot editors and copy editors.

4. Try to get an interview with a copy editor at your local newspaper and ask about his or her role and responsibilities in the newsroom. From your discussion, develop your own list of the virtues of a good copy editor.

5. On weekends, large metropolitan dailies contain inserts that are not produced locally but are transported in and inserted in the mailrooms as newspapers come off the presses. Find a Sunday edition of the largest daily in your region and identify inserts that were not produced by the newspaper's regular staff. What characteristics suggest that these are out-of-town products? Does this Sunday edition also contain inserts that were produced by the newspaper's regular staff? How can you tell?

6. Review the news values listed in this chapter. Applying those news values, plus others that your instructor may add to the list, consider whether each of the following items is suitable for publication in the news section of your hometown newspaper. Tell which news values apply for each item.

   a. After a successful run on Broadway, the cast of an award-winning musical is beginning a tour of the United States. The nearest performance to your hometown will be in a city 200 miles away. (wire story)

   b. Scientists working in Washington, D.C., think they may have made a breakthrough in cancer research. The National Science Foundation awarded them a $2.5 million grant this week. (National Science Foundation press release)

   c. This is the right time for gardeners in your area to get their tulips and other bulbs into the ground. (material from local agricultural agent)

   d. Business analysts expect a bullish market for mining stocks in the next few months. (business wire story)

   e. "Tiger," a German shepherd owned by a local woman, won "best in show" yesterday at the annual dog show in Madison Square Garden. (wire story)

   f. A student from the local junior high school placed second in the national spelling bee, conducted yesterday in Washington, D. C. (story from education beat)

   g. A train derailed 30 miles away. Emergency rooms at local hospitals were crowded with injured passengers. (story from police beat)

   h. Fashion designers say that women's skirts will be shorter than ever next year. (wire story)

   i. The local school board decided last night to build a new high school in town. (story from education beat)

j. A city official says that property taxes will increase dramatically to pay for the costs of building a new high school in town. (story from city government beat)

k. A 75-year-old man was the first customer at a new bungee jumping attraction that opened yesterday on the outskirts of town. (story from business beat)

Copy editors, just like doctors, lawyers, carpenters, landscape painters and architects, must master the tools essential to their work. It has been said that the ideal copy editor knows everything about something and something about everything.

Language, the basic and most important tool for copy editors, is the "something" that a perfect copy editor would know "everything" about. Reference materials, either in traditional book format or stored in computerized data banks, provide copy editors with the information they need for knowing "something about everything," so copy editors also need to have a librarian's working knowledge of standard reference materials.

Computers are another essential tool for copy editors. By the '90s few, if any, newspapers were being produced without computers. However, journalists editing books, public relations materials or magazine copy often continued to use traditional paper-and-pencil copy editing methods, so knowledge of copy editing symbols is still important.

Editing should be, especially in the case of old writers, a counseling rather than a collaborative task.
— *James Thurber*

The Copy Editor's Tools

Computers
Traditional copy editing symbols
The importance of careful writing
Common pitfalls in grammar and usage
Consistency of style
Reference materials
On careful writing: B. H. "Bud" Liebes

Computers

Reporters and editors at most U. S. newspapers and magazines today write and edit copy at video display terminals (VDTs) linked to a central computer or at personal computers that are part of a newsroom network. In this modern process, a reporter enters a story into the computer system. Then editors retrieve or call up the story from the computer files.

Once the story is on the VDT screen at the copy editor's desk, changes are typed directly into the system (see Exhibit 2-1). The copy editor "formats" the copy by entering computer codes for the type style, size, leading (the amount

Exhibit 2-1
An editor works at a video display terminal. When she finishes editing the story and writing a headline for it, she will insert computer codes that specify the desired type style, size, width and amount of leading. Production personnel will paste the computer-generated type into place, according to an editor's layout. (Photograph by Kerric Harvey/ courtesy of the Seattle Times)

of space between lines of type) and column width. The copy editor types the headline at the top of the story and codes it for type style and size.

Finally, the copy is sent electronically to a phototypesetter, which produces a "hard" copy that can then be pasted onto a page. In the 1980s a few newspapers were experimenting with electronic layout, or pagination, which eliminates manual pasteup. Pagination will probably become widely used during the 1990s.

Computerized typesetting eliminates the retyping of stories to set them in printer's type, a redundancy that allows new errors to be introduced. Because rekeyboarding is unnecessary, the proofreader's job no longer exists at most newspapers. Nor does electronic typesetting require some of the copy editor's old tools: reams of copy paper, soft-lead pencils, scissors and glue.

In addition to helping with typesetting, computers provide reporters and editors almost instant access to information stored in data bases. Without leaving their desks, reporters and editors can use personal computers to search the newspaper's own morgue (files of previously published stories) or to get information from commercial or academic data bases anywhere in the world. By the early 1990s, fax machines, personal computers for data gathering and analysis, electronic news libraries, data base searching and online access to public records were becoming routine at the largest newspapers. Medium-sized and smaller papers will incorporate this technology into their news operations as financial resources permit, opening the way for new career opportunities for journalists who are facile with the new technology.

Traditional copy editing symbols

By the end of the 1990s, it is likely that journalism schools will no longer teach the use of traditional copy editing symbols. At the beginning of the decade, however, knowledge of the symbols continues to have some practical application because not all journalism schools, publications, public relations firms and advertising firms are fully computerized. Some editing jobs still are done the old-fashioned way, and occasions for proofreading still arise.

When preparing copy that is to be rekeyboarded by a typist, writers should always double- or triple-space. Such wide spacing allows copy editors to write corrections between the lines of type.

Copy editors write parallel to the lines of type, instead of writing in the margins, to avoid causing confusion and difficulty for the typesetter. If there is insufficient room between lines of type to write a correction, copy editors use scissors and paste to insert clean paper on which corrections can be written. If the correction is long, copy editors type it and then paste the correction in its proper place.

All notations on the copy that are not to be set as part of the story—such as indications of column width, typeface, point size and other instructions to the typesetter—are circled. Copy editors avoid using lines and arrows to vertically transpose paragraphs or sentences within a story. Such markings are difficult to follow, so copy that needs rearranging is cut and pasted into the story at the proper place.

An experienced copy editor never blacks out, pastes over, or destroys a word, phrase or guideline. To delete the copy, the editor simply draws a line through it, in case the information is needed later for checking purposes or needs to be restored to the copy.

Copy editing symbols (see Exhibit 2-2), which indicate changes in copy without using words, are easy to learn. Lack of consistency in the use of copy editing symbols may confuse the typist and slow the rekeyboarding process.

Proofreading symbols, on the other hand, are used after the copy has been

Some copy editing jobs still are done the old-fashioned way.

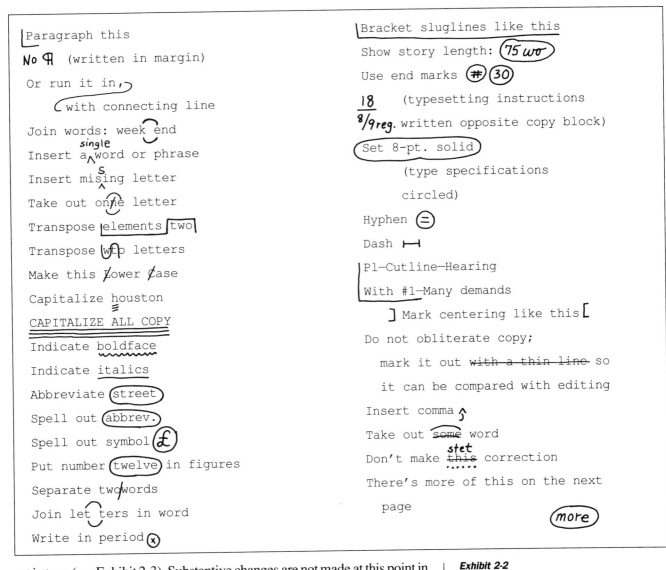

Exhibit 2-2
Copy editing symbols are written within or above a line of copy that has not yet been typeset.

set in type (see Exhibit 2-3). Substantive changes are not made at this point in the production process, because the purpose of proofreading is to catch typographical errors. There isn't room on the typeset version, or pasteup copy, for errors to be marked within the line or paragraph, so proofreading symbols are placed in the margins of the copy, with a line drawn to indicate the exact place of the error.

The use of copy editing symbols is illustrated in Exhibit 2-4, which shows how a simple news story looked after it was edited. Exercise 1 at the end of this chapter tests your knowledge of copy editing symbols.

The importance of careful writing

Students often enter beginning newswriting courses with the mistaken idea that they are embarking on a kind of writing that bears little resemblance to what they have been taught in English courses. This is a false notion. Proper word usage and correct grammar and punctuation are just as important to newspapers as they are to books and other forms of communication. The inverted-pyramid organization of news stories differs from the traditional narrative pattern, and paragraphs are kept artificially short in news stories, but most other conventions of good writing are unchanged.

Some claim that the constant stress on proper English usage is merely a form of snobbery and has no place in the fast-paced, widely circulated daily press. But a newspaper or magazine cannot be casual about language usage,

PROOFREADER'S MARKS

Because newspaper galley proofs are narrow compared to book proofs, a simplified system of marks is possible. These symbols should not be confused with those used in editing copy.

In marking proofs two basic marks are made for each error: (a) a pencil line running from the point of the error and (b) a correction at the end of that line. Corrections should be made in margins at right or left of the error, exactly opposite the type line in which the error occurs. If there are two errors in a line, corrections should be made in the margin nearest each. In no case should the penciled lines cross.

Corrections should be so neatly made that the compositor will waste no time reading them.

Wrong font letters should be reported to the composing room foreman immediately.

No proofreading is properly done without comparing copy with proof. If several lines are omitted by the compositor, return copy to him and mark "See Copy" at the point of the "leave out."

Proofreaders should a-l-e-r-t-l-y watch for errors in end-of-line word divisions, substitutions of words, omissions of letters or words, transpositions, and errors in fact. Fact errors should be reported to the copy desk.

Editing on proof is expensive and, when done, should be done by the copy desk. Sometimes words can be juggled in 2 lines enough to avoid resetting a paragraph.

In checking a page proof, look particularly for headline errors, wrong heads over stories, transposed cutlines, errors and in date lines.

Proofs should be read promptly to prevent necessity for railroading—using type before corrections are inserted.

for precision of language sharpens the meaning of fact. In addition, improper usage damages credibility. Readers will question the accuracy of information in a publication containing frequent errors in spelling or use of the language.

Newspaper stories, in general, are directed to all readers, whatever their level of education. Because of the extremely diverse audience, simplicity and clarity are important. Newspaper writing must convey its message to a wide range of readers, from the fringes of illiteracy to maximum literary competence. English used in newsrooms, therefore, should be the language familiar to all educated persons. Of the four basic types of language—literary, common, colloquial and slang—common is preferred.

The idea of "math phobia" has received attention in recent years, and quite

1 (Actress)

When actress Lisa Jacobson, 20, auditioned
for her first off-broadway show, she could not
give a prepared monologue like the 400 other
women trying for the part.

2 "I didn't have one ~~(a monologue)~~ or even
know what one was," she said.

She got the lead.

3 The play was "Spring Awakening," by Frank

4 Wedekind. Lisa's role ~~that was to be her~~

5 ~~first acting experience ever~~ was that of an
innocent, but wise, 14-year-old girl who had
long, black hair.

"She was me. I felt it," Lisa said as she

6 pushed back her own long, *curly* black hair and lay

7 on the floor, ~~to continue her story.~~

8 Lisa ~~decided~~ *said* ~~to try acting only 15 months
ago.~~ The part in "Spring Awakening" came ~~only~~ *soon*
~~weeks~~ after ~~Lisa~~ *she* "decided to try acting
because I didn't have a passion for anything
at the time," ~~she said.~~

9 Dressed in a too-big sundress, dark red
socks and hiking boots, ~~her face enveloped in~~
~~naturally curly hair,~~ *the* 5-foot-2, inch Lisa
seemed to be the ~~little girl~~ *teen-ager* of her first role
-- laughing ~~as she spoke~~ and rolling from side
to side on the floor.

1. *The word* Actress *is the slugline, which is used to guide the story through the production process. It will not be part of the published story, so it is circled.*

2. *A* monologue *is redundant. Clearly, one refers to* monologue *in the preceding paragraph.*

3. *Verify the playwright's name. He's not that well known.*

4. *Lisa or Jacobson? Many style books insist on using last names after a person has been introduced to the readers. But in "light" stories, feature stories or stories in which children play a prominent role, the rule is relaxed.*

5. *Delete* that was . . . experience ever. *The phrase is redundant. The body of the story makes it clear that she is a beginning actress.*

6. *Inserting the adjective* curly *adds a good detail and proves to be a word saver in the last paragraph.*

7. *Delete* to continue her story. *The attributive verb* said *indicates that she's continuing her story.*

8. *A time problem haunts this paragraph. The first sentence indicates that Lisa decided to become an actress 15 months ago. The second sentence says she decided to try acting weeks before she won the role. Unless the writer can clarify this discrepancy, the adverb* soon *at least guarantees accuracy.*

9. *This sentence is tripped up by a dangling participle. Lisa's face is not dressed in a sun dress, dark red socks and hiking boots. Any editing that eliminates the dangler is acceptable.*

Exhibit 2-4
Copy editing symbols indicate how a story is to be rekeyboarded. This sample was edited by B. H. Liebes, a former newspaper editor.

a few people have said they don't understand math, have never understood it and don't really think an understanding of math is essential to their lives. "Grammar phobia" hasn't been discussed as much, but it does exist. Some students attribute their grammar phobia to inadequate or unskillful instruction in grammar during grade school or high school.

Some English-speaking people say they never understood English grammar until they studied the grammar of a different language. Perhaps that is because little can be accomplished in learning a foreign language without careful attention to its grammar rules and conventions. People who grow up in an English-speaking home or country can write and speak the language with some skill without ever giving careful attention to its grammar. Their understanding of grammar just seems to come naturally, although it is accompanied, in many cases, by incorrect usage, colloquialisms and slang. Most people can get by with this casual knowledge of English grammar, relying to a great extent on "what sounds right," but one who aspires to become a professional writer or editor needs more specific knowledge.

A professional writer or editor uses language to enhance communication. Journalists aren't particularly interested in being able to label the parts of speech or to diagram sentences. But to use grammar, punctuation and words correctly, they need to understand the parts of speech and how sentences are constructed. Trying to get by on what sounds right is insufficient in the world of professional journalism. So put aside your grammar phobia or, at the other extreme, the notion that you already know everything you need to know about English grammar.

Exercises 2 through 4 at the end of this chapter test your knowledge of the parts of speech and of how sentences are constructed. If necessary, consult one or more of the basic grammar books listed at the end of this chapter.

Common pitfalls in grammar and usage

Eugene T. Maleska, crossword puzzle editor of The New York Times, often told this story about himself:

As a junior high school teacher in the inner city of New York, I was expected to build the vocabulary of the youngsters. One Monday, an assistant principal arrived at my classroom door. "Mr. Maleska," he said, "once a week you are ordered to distribute these dictionaries and base a lesson upon them."

To my students, the dictionary was the dullest of books, and they told me so. What to do?

Finally, I hit upon a solution: a game I called Stick the Teacher. I asked the students to scour their dictionaries for unusual words and then call them out. If I couldn't give a satisfactory definition, then the class scored a point. If I knew the word, a point was recorded in my favor. The students gave me toughies like *xebec, prolix, xyloid, comestibles* and *funicular.* The scores were always close.

Not long ago, I received a letter from a former student who said that the game had given him his initial interest in exploring dictionaries. He is now a playwright.

Such stories may remind some readers of what the famous writer James Thurber said when someone asked where he had been that day: "I've been reading my dictionaries over and over." Like some other writers, Thurber developed knowledge of grammar, spelling and word usage from reading dictionaries.

English is not a simple language, and unfortunately, many of those who deal with it as a daily profession have never mastered it. Mistakes common to all copy—from a beginning reporter's weather report to a nationally syndicated column—are those of grammar, punctuation, spelling, word usage and style.

Some of these common pitfalls are listed and explained in the following pages. The items are numbered consecutively so you and your instructor can refer to the numbers as you work on the exercises at the end of this chapter.

Subject and verb agreement

The basic rule is that the subject and predicate (or main verb) must agree in number. To apply this rule, first determine the subject of the clause, and then

Of the four basic types of language— literary, common, colloquial and slang— common is preferred.

determine whether the subject has a singular or plural meaning. Here are some rules concerning subject-verb agreement:

1. When two or more subjects are connected by the conjunction *and*, use a plural verb:

```
An introvert and an extrovert rarely  make
good partners.
```

Use a singular verb, however, when two parts of a compound subject refer to a single person or thing:

```
His friend and partner  is very patient.
```

2. A noun or pronoun joined to the subject by phrases that act as prepositions rather than conjunctions is not part of a compound subject. Examples of such phrases are *with, together with, accompanied by, as well as, including, in addition to* and *no less than.* Identify the subject and then apply the basic rule that the subject and predicate must agree in number:

```
John, as well as Jim,  is going to play on the
team.
```

```
The order form, in addition to a money order,
is required.
```

```
Mary, as well as her mother,  is on the guest
list.
```

3. When two or more subjects are joined by *or* or *nor*, the verb should agree with the nearest subject:

```
Mary or her sisters  are going to keep the ap-
pointment.
```

```
Mary or her sister  is going to keep the ap-
pointment.
```

```
Neither John nor his children  are required to
attend.
```

```
Neither John nor his son  is going fishing today.
```

If both subjects are singular, the verb is singular:

```
Either Jim or Jack  is to be at the stadium by 1
p.m.
```

If both subjects are plural, the verb is plural:

```
Neither the boys nor the girls  are doing well
on the agility test.
```

4. Don't let words before or between the subject and the verb mislead the reader. First find the sentence's subject, then make its predicate agree:

```
The last two innings of the game  were dull.
```

In this sentence, the prepositional phrase *of the game* comes between the plural subject *innings* and the predicate *were.*

5. The prepositional phrase between fractions and percentages used as subjects influences the verb:

```
Three-fourths of the students  are prepared for
college.
```

```
Three-fourths of a cup of water  is needed in
the recipe.
```

6. These pronouns, when used as a subject, always take singular verbs: *it,*

English is not a simple language, and unfortunately, many of those who deal with it as a daily profession have never mastered it.

each, either, anyone, everyone, much, no one, nothing, someone, such. For example:

```
Each student has lunch money.
Everyone has lunch money.
No one has money for lunch.
Much has been written about grammar.
Someone is going to meet us at the airport.
It seems like years since we last met.
```

Pay special attention to the placement of *each* in a sentence. As a subject it takes a singular verb. But as an adjective in apposition with a plural subject, it needs a plural verb:

```
John and Mary each are scheduled to meet with
the president of the company.
```

7. Collective nouns take a singular verb when used in the sense of a single unit operating in agreement but take a plural verb when the collective operates as individual units or in disagreement. These are some collective nouns: *jury, team, army, audience, family, faculty, couple, group, staff, club, class, committee, crowd.* Treat the names of organizations as collectives as well: *National Association for the Advancement of Colored People, National Council of Churches, National Organization for Women.* For example:

```
The team is going to compete for the champion-
ship.
```

The individuals are working together as a single unit operating in agreement, so you would use a singular verb.

The combination of a plural verb with a singular-sounding noun sounds unnatural, although it is technically correct:

```
The team were arguing about their individual
playing assignments and the selection of a cap-
tain.
```

The plural verb is used because the team is in disagreement; the individuals are not working as a unit. To avoid the strange sound, most people would probably write or say "The team members were arguing . . ." or "Members of the team were arguing . . ."

8. *Number, couple, majority* and *total* are singular if preceded by *the* but plural if preceded by *a*:

```
The number of convictions is increasing.
A number of people were convicted on those
charges.
The majority has voted for Jones.
A majority of citizens agree that the laws
should be enforced.
```

9. Deciding whether a collective noun is singular or plural is relatively easy, but no similar rule consistently applies for "non-countable" nouns. Most of the non-countable nouns end in *s*, which makes them appear to be plural, but they are not all plural.

These non-countable nouns ending in *s* always take singular verbs: *apparatus, aesthetics, athletics, civics, economics, linguistics, mathematics, measles, mumps, news, shambles, summons, whereabouts.* Some other non-countable nouns that take singular verbs are *advice, courage, fun, health, information, jazz and remainder.*

These non-countable nouns need a plural verb: *assets, earnings, goods, kudos, manners, odds, pants, proceeds, scissors, shears, tactics, thanks, wages.*

These non-countables are either singular or plural, depending on context: *politics, series, gross, headquarters, statistics, ethics, species.* As a study or a science, *politics, statistics,* and *ethics* take singular verbs:

```
Statistics is a required course for business ma-
jors.
```

```
Politics is not an exact science.
```

When in doubt, consult a dictionary to see which words ending in *s* need a singular verb or can be either singular or plural.

Exercise 5 at the end of this chapter tests your understanding of subject and verb agreement.

Noun and pronoun agreement

The basic rule concerning noun and pronoun agreement is that pronouns agree with their antecedents in person, number and gender. Let's consider each of these ideas separately.

10. Pronouns are substitutes for nouns or other pronouns, their antecedents. Be sure that every pronoun has an antecedent and that, if other nouns or pronouns come between the pronoun and its antecedent, readers are not confused: "John introduced Mary to his mother, whom he planned to marry." In this example, the clause beginning with *whom* is misplaced, because John planned to marry Mary, not his mother. The sentence should be written this way:

```
John introduced  Mary, whom he planned to marry,
to his mother.
```

11. Pronouns should agree with their antecedents in person (first, second, third):

```
I asked for my money.
```

```
He asked for his money.
```

12. Pronouns should agree with their antecedents in number. Singular nouns take singular pronouns (*he, she, it, him, her, his, hers*):

```
John lost his books.
```

```
The woman said she would compete in the race.
```

Plural nouns take plural pronouns (*they, them, their, we, us our*):

```
The men said they would go on strike.
```

```
John and Mary received their new bicycles today.
```

```
The women asked that they be given equal pay for
equal work.
```

Pronouns and collective nouns that take singular verbs (see Rules 6, 7 and 8) also take singular pronouns:

```
The team defended its championship.
```

```
The National Organization for Women  announced
its position on the proposed legislation.
```

```
Either of the boys should receive  his prize.
```

```
The faculty expressed its displeasure with the
salary proposal.
```

```
Each of the girls received  her invitation in
the mail.
```

Pronouns agree with their antecedents in person, number and gender.

The position of *each* in a sentence determines whether a later noun is singular or plural (see the comment about *each* in Rule 6). If *each* is in apposition with a plural subject, the later noun is plural. But if *each* is the subject, the noun should be singular. For example:

```
The girls each receive invitations.
Each of the girls receives an  invitation.
```

Pronouns and collective nouns that take plural verbs (see Rules 7 and 8) also take plural pronouns:

```
All of the students have  their pencils.
A majority of voters cast their votes for Jones.
```

13. Pronouns should agree with their antecedents in gender. If the antecedent is male, the pronoun should be masculine (*he, him, his*); a feminine pronoun (*she, her, hers*) is used for female antecedents; a neuter pronoun (*it, its*) is used for neuter antecedents.

This rule is straightforward, but problems arise with *either . . . or* and *neither . . . nor* constructions where one subject is masculine and one is feminine. In that situation, the pronoun should agree with the antecedent that follows *or* or *nor*:

```
Neither Mary nor John has applied for his visa.
Neither John nor Mary has applied for her visa.
```

In this example, the plural pronoun *their* would be incorrect, because *neither* is singular. However, the phrase *for a visa* would be better in both cases.

Another consideration in choosing pronoun gender is to attempt to avoid sexism in journalistic writing. Traditionally, masculine pronouns have been used to refer to a singular antecedent that included both males and females, but most newspapers now try to avoid sexist terms (as well as racist and ageist terms). One way to avoid excluding women is to use the expressions *he or she* and *his or her*. A better way is to use plural forms and plural pronouns. Compare the following:

```
A journalist should edit his or her copy care-
fully.
Journalists should edit their copy carefully.
```

Reflexive and intensive pronouns

Reflexive and intensive pronouns, the *self* pronouns, are used when a noun acts on itself or when a noun must be emphasized.

14. Reflexive pronouns should not be used alone without referring to a noun or pronoun earlier in the sentence:

```
The store manager himself waited on customers.
I myself don't mind working hard.
John injured himself.
```

The following usage is incorrect: "Sarah and myself will work hard"; "He divided the work between John and myself."

Pronoun case

Case refers to the use of a pronoun in a sentence. Nominative case is used for subjects of sentences and as predicate nominatives. Objective case is used for objects, such as direct objects, indirect objects, objects of prepositions,

In choosing pronoun gender . . . attempt to avoid sexism in journalistic writing.

Exhibit 2-5

The choice of
personal pronoun
depends on the
person, number
and gender of the
antecedent and on
the case indicated
by the pronoun's
position in the
clause.

| | Case | | |
Person	Nominative	Objective	Possessive
Singular			
First	I	me	my, mine
Second	you	you	your, yours
Third			
Masculine	he	him	his
Feminine	she	her	her, hers
Neuter	it	it	its
Plural			
First	we	us	our, ours
Second	you	you	your, yours
Third	they	them	their, theirs

participles, gerunds and infinitives. The objective case is also used as the subject of an infinitive. Possessive case shows ownership.

15. Pronouns agree with their antecedents in person (first, second, third), number (singular, plural) and gender (masculine, feminine, neuter), but they take their case from the clause in which they stand.

Exhibit 2-5 shows the person, number, case and gender of personal pronouns. The relative pronoun *who* also has a different form for each case: *who* is nominative case, *whom* is objective case, *whose* is possessive case.

People have little problem distinguishing the proper case in simple sentences. But as sentence structure becomes more intricate, more effort is required to determine the role of each pronoun in each clause. The relative pronouns *who, whom* and *whose* are generally the most troublesome. In the following example, the relative pronoun is used as the subject of the sentence and thus needs the nominative case:

```
Who is coming?
```

In this example, the object of the preposition takes the objective case:

```
To whom should we address the letter?
```

The following example is more complicated:

```
He gave advice to  whoever asked for it.
```

The subject of the dependent clause is *whoever,* although the entire dependent clause is used as the object of the preposition *to.* Here, again, the nominative case is correct:

```
Jones, who I always thought was unapproachable,
gave me advice.
```

Who is the subject of the dependent clause *who was unapproachable; me* is used as an indirect object in the main clause.

In this case, *whom* is the object of the preposition:

```
We tried to discover to  whom the gun belonged.
```

The final example clearly calls for the possessive case:

```
Whose gun is this?
```

Exercise 6 at the end of this chapter tests your understanding of the pronoun cases.

16. Unlike all other subjects, which are in the nominative case, the subject of an infinitive is in the objective case. Doubt about the correct form usually can be erased by transposing the sentence. In the first example, the pronoun *him* is the subject of the infinitive *to be*:

```
They declared the culprit to be  him.
```

If you transpose the sentence, you can clearly see that *him* is the direct object:

```
They declared him to be the culprit.
```

17. Do not confuse *who's*, the contraction for *who is*, with the possessive form *whose*. The contraction for *it is* is *it's*; the possessive form is *its*. For example:

```
Who's going to ride in our car?
```

```
It's unusually warm today.
```

An analysis of how the relative pronoun is used is the best way to be sure that the correct case is used. However, you can also try substituting *he* for *who* and *him* for *whom* to see whether the substitute sounds right. With intricate sentences, this system is not foolproof.

Exercise 7 at the end of this chapter tests your understanding of noun-pronoun agreement and pronoun case.

Essential and non-essential clauses

Both *that* and *which* are relative pronouns used to introduce clauses that refer to an inanimate object or an animal without a name. The use of *that* or *which* depends on whether an essential or a non-essential clause is being introduced. A non-essential clause gives additional information about the noun or pronoun it modifies. Because a non-essential clause could be eliminated from the sentence without altering its meaning, the clause is set off with commas. An essential clause, on the other hand, is necessary because it gives the sentence the intended meaning; thus, it is not set off from the rest of the sentence.

18. *That* should be used to introduce an essential clause; *which* is correct for non-essential clauses. In the following example, the clause is essential because it restricts or identifies the car:

```
This is the car that won the race.
```

In the next example, the clause adds non-essential information:

```
John Smith's 1991 Ford,  which won the race last
weekend, is for sale.
```

The car that is for sale is sufficiently identified or restricted by the modifiers *John Smith's 1991 Ford*. Note that commas set off the non-essential clause.

Exercise 8 at the end of this chapter tests your understanding of essential and non-essential clauses.

Possessive nouns

The possessive form of a noun is used to show ownership.

19. Most nouns form their possessive by adding an *'s* to the singular form:

```
girl's book, John's glove, horse's saddle
```

20. If a noun ends in an *s* sound and is followed by a word that begins with *s*, form the possessive by adding an apostrophe alone:

```
for appearance' sake, for conscience' sake
```

21. If the singular form ends in *s*, add *'s* unless the next word begins with *s*, in which case just add an apostrophe to the singular form:

An analysis of how the relative pronoun is used is the best way to be sure that the correct case is used.

the <u>hostess's</u> invitation, the <u>hostess'</u> standards

the <u>witness's</u> testimony, the <u>witness'</u> story

22. To form the plural possessive, first make the noun plural; then add an *'s* if the plural noun does not end in *s*:

<u>woman</u> (singular), <u>women</u> (plural), <u>women's</u> (plural possessive)

23. If the plural form ends in *s*, add only an apostrophe:

<u>boy</u> (singular), <u>boys</u> (plural) <u>boys'</u> (plural possessive)

24. For compound words, add an *'s* to the word closest to the object possessed:

the <u>major general's</u> decision (singular), the <u>major generals'</u> decisions (plural)

25. To show that two people own something jointly, use a possessive form after only the last word. If the objects are individually owned, use a possessive form after both nouns:

<u>John and Mary's</u> home (joint ownership), <u>John's</u> and <u>Mary's</u> projects (individual ownership)

26. For descriptive phrases, no apostrophe is needed for a word ending in *s*. To determine whether the word or phrase is used in a descriptive sense, try using *for* or *by* rather than *of*. The following is correct:

<u>New York Yankees</u> pitcher

In this case, the phrase *New York Yankees* is descriptive, meaning that the person is a pitcher for the New York Yankees.

27. Use *'s* for a plural word that does not end in *s:*

<u>women's</u> hospital, <u>men's</u> team

28. For corporations or organizations with a descriptive word in their name, use the form that the group uses:

<u>Writer's</u> Digest, the <u>Veterans</u> Administration, <u>Diners</u> Club

Journalistic style cautions against excessive personalization of inanimate objects. Often a phrase referring to an inanimate object is clearer if an *of* construction is used instead of a possessive form:

<u>mathematics'</u> rules, the rules <u>of mathematics</u>

Personal pronouns and relative pronouns have separate forms for the possessive and do not need an apostrophe: *my, mine, our, ours, your, yours, his, her, hers, its, theirs, whose.* The exception is *one's*, the possessive form for *one.*

Exercise 9 at the end of this chapter tests your understanding of plurals and possessives.

Sequence of tenses

The tense of a verb describes the time of the action. Newswriting commonly uses past tense to report what has already happened. But confusion about the proper verb tense often arises when journalists paraphrase and attribute information.

29. The basic rule is to select the verb tense that describes the time of the action and to stick with that tense unless a shift is needed to show a change in time. Do not shift tenses unnecessarily. In this example, all actions are in the past tense:

The tense of a verb describes the time of the action.

```
The Senate passed the tax bill, defeated the
food stamp proposal and sent the defense measure
back to the appropriations committee.
```

Now let's shift the tense from past to past perfect to indicate that the House action took place before the Senate action:

```
The Senate defeated the food stamp proposal,
which had been approved by the House of Repre-
sentatives.
```

A shift from past to future tense again indicates different timing of the action:

```
The Senate sent the defense measure back to the
committee, where it will be amended.
```

30. Grammarians agree on the basic rules for consistency in verb tenses, but neither grammarians nor newspaper editors agree on the importance of a rule governing the sequence of tenses in reported speech. That rule states that when reported speech is used, the verb of attribution governs subsequent verbs in the sentence.

To a great extent, journalistic work involves reporting what has happened in the recent past and what sources have said, so journalists commonly use reported speech, which can be distinguished from direct speech and parenthetical speech:

```
"I disagree with the mayor's policies, but I
don't confront him about them," Jim said. (di-
rect speech)

Jim disagrees with the mayor's policies, he
said, but he doesn't confront him. (parentheti-
cal speech)
```

Note that, in parenthetical speech, the quote is paraphrased and the attribution is in the middle of the paraphrase. In reported speech, in contrast, attribution is at the beginning of the sentence:

```
Jim said he disagreed with the mayor's policies,
but he didn't confront the mayor about them.
(reported speech)
```

In this example, the verb of attribution is in the past tense, so other verbs are in the past tense as well.

It can be argued convincingly that reported speech confuses readers. Does Jim still disagree with the mayor, or is the disagreement a thing of the past? Strict proponents of following the sequence of tenses in reported speech can argue that the job of the newspaper is to report what the source said at the time the reporter received the information ("Jim disagrees with the mayor") rather than being concerned about whether the source changed his mind between the time he said it and the time the article was published. Of course, one way to avoid the problem is to use a present-tense verb of attribution ("Jim *says* he disagrees"), but typical usage in news stories calls for past-tense attribution.

The rule for sequence of tenses in reported speech requires that the verb used in direct speech should be changed one degree: from present to past (*disagrees* to *disagreed*), from past to past perfect (*disagreed* to *had disagreed*), from future to future perfect (*will disagree* to *would disagree*).

Some grammar books omit entirely the sequence-of-tenses rule for reported speech, and many editors pay no attention to it. Other editors are rigid in their adherence to the rule. The late Theodore M. Bernstein, for many years a wordsmith at The New York Times, devoted six pages to an explanation of

It can be argued convincingly that reported speech confuses readers.

sequence of tenses in his book *Watch Your Language*. He ended his discussion with this suggestion: "Normal sequence of tenses is desirable except when it produces obscurity or ambiguity." So even Bernstein, who stood firmly by the rules of sequence of tenses for reported speech, would allow a variation for perpetual truths, referred to as "exceptional sequence." Thus, this sentence would be correct:

```
She said that the earth revolves around the sun.
```

Irregular verb forms

Irregular verbs change the middle of the word to get the past tense instead of adding *ed, t* or *en* at the end, as is the pattern for regular verbs.

31. Check a dictionary when you are uncertain about forming the past and past participle forms of a verb. These are the principal parts (present, past, past participle) for some of the irregular verbs that are frequently misused:

awake, awoke, awakened
be (am, is, are), was (were), been
bear, bore, born
bite, bit, bitten
broadcast, broadcast, broadcast
burst, burst, burst
catch, caught, caught
cling, clung, clung
do, did, done
drink, drank, drunk
drove, drove, driven
drown, drowned, drowned
eat, ate, eaten
find, found, found
fly, flew, flown
fly, flied, flied (for a baseball)
forsake, forsook, forsaken
get, got, got (gotten)
go, went, gone
hang, hanged, hanged (as in "execute someone")
hang, hung, hung (as in "hang a picture")
hide, hid, hidden
hit, hit, hit
know, knew, known
lay, laid, laid (transitive verb meaning "to place")
lead, led, led
leave, left, left
lie, lay, lain (intransitive verb meaning "to recline")
mean, meant, meant
pay, paid, paid
ring, rang, rung
rise, rose, risen (not to be confused with transitive verb raise*)*
say, said, said
set, set, set (transitive verb meaning "to place")
shake, shook, shaken
shine, shone, shone
show, showed, showed (shown)
shrink, shrank, shrunk

Check a dictionary when you are uncertain about forming the past and past participle forms of a verb.

sit, sat, sat (intransitive verb)
spring, sprang, sprung
steal, stole, stolen
strive, strove, striven
swear, swore, sworn
swim, swam, swum
swing, swung, swung
tear, tore, torn
weave, wove, woven
wring, wrung, wrung
write, wrote, written

Pay particular attention to the correct meanings and principal parts of *lie/ lay, sit/set* and *rise/raise. Lie* and *lay* are particularly troublesome because the past tense of *lie* is the same as the present tense of *lay. Set, lay* and *raise* are transitive verbs and need direct objects.

Exercise 10 at the end of this chapter tests your understanding of troublesome verb tenses.

Subjunctive mood

Some usage experts (Rudolf Flesch, for one) argue that the subjunctive mood is dead or is dying and has little practical use. Other grammarians (Theodore M. Bernstein, for example) say that the subjunctive mood is alive and necessary.

32. Use the subjunctive mood to express a condition that is either contrary to fact or is purely hypothetical:

```
If I were president of the company, I would give
workers a salary increase.
```

Were is used instead of *was* because the condition is contrary to fact; I am not president of the company.

Except for forms of *to be*, the present tense of the subjunctive mood is the infinitive without the *to*. That verb form is the same as the indicative mood, for the first and second persons but not for the third-person singular:

Indicative	**Subjunctive**
I run	*I run*
you run	*you run*
he runs	*he run*

```
If Bill were in shape to run faster, the coach
would not have asked that I run the final leg of
the relay.
```

Misplaced and dangling modifiers

Modifiers are used to make writing more descriptive and interesting. To avoid confusion, modifiers should refer clearly and logically to some specific word in the sentence. Modifiers that aren't attached grammatically are called "misplaced" or "dangling" modifiers. They can bring a humorous picture to mind, as in this example:

```
Running down the road, my nose got cold.
```

You have a couple of options for correcting this dangler:

```
Running down the road, I felt my nose getting
cold.

As I ran down the road, my nose got cold.
```

Modifiers are used to make writing more descriptive and interesting.

33. Modifiers must be attached grammatically to the word they modify to avoid reader confusion. Consider this sentence: *"To grow strong, good diet is important."* What is to grow strong? Not the diet. The infinitive phrase has no word to modify in this sentence. Give it a logical noun or pronoun to modify:

> <u>To grow strong, children</u> need a good diet.

Prepositional phrases often cause problems when misplaced or left dangling. Here's an example of the problem: *"As a member of Congress,* I want get your views on alleged ethics violations by some of your colleagues." The reporter is not a member of Congress. The sentence could be written correctly in several ways. Here are two:

> <u>Because you are a member of Congress,</u> I want to get your views on alleged ethics violations by some of your colleagues.

> I want to ask <u>you, a member of Congress,</u> about your views on alleged ethics violations by some of your colleagues.

The word *only* as a modifier is frequently misplaced in sentences, leading to ambiguity. An omitted article (*a/an* for indefinite reference, *the* for definite reference) often causes the confusion with *only*. In these examples, the placement of *only* has a considerable effect on the meaning:

> She was only a lawyer.
> She was the only lawyer.
> He gave the hungry children only money.
> He gave only the hungry children money.
> He gave the hungry children the only money.

Double negatives

A negative word is one that expresses *no*. The rule prohibiting the use of double negatives, two negative words in a row, has been drilled into us since elementary-school days. It is so fundamental that the Associated Press stylebook does not even include it.

34. Avoid double negatives. "He *don't* know *nothing*" is a construction that no journalist would use. Still, a double negative sometimes slips past, particularly in long sentences and especially when the adverbs *hardly, rarely* and *scarcely* are used. Consider the following pairs of examples:

> She <u>never hardly</u> studies.
> She <u>hardly ever</u> studies.
> The store <u>doesn't</u> have <u>but</u> one brand.
> The store <u>has but</u> one brand.

But, when used as an adverb, is also a negative.

Negative adjectives (those with the prefixes *im, in, ir, non* and *un*) may be used with negative adverbs. Therefore, the following are correct:

> It is <u>not impermissible</u> to use negative adjectives with negative adverbs.
> It is <u>not incorrect</u> to say it this way.

Authorities have mixed opinions on usage of the phrase *cannot help but*, as in

> Workers <u>cannot help but feel</u> the effect of the wage freeze.

Bernstein, Flesch and the American Heritage Dictionary accept this usage;

the Random House Dictionary says it is common usage but frowned upon. To avoid the argument, omit *but* and use the present participle:

```
Workers cannot help feeling the effect of the
wage freeze.
```

Exercise 11 tests your understanding of misplaced modifiers and double negatives.

Parallel construction

Lack of parallel construction is another common pitfall in writing. Parallelism helps give a sentence balance, rhythm and symmetry.

35. Use the same grammatical patterns to express equal ideas in a sentence. Here, along with improved versions, are examples of sentences that hinder understanding because they lack parallel construction. The first set demonstrates that the objects of a preposition should both be either gerunds or nouns:

```
Cardiovascular health is promoted by exercising
frequently and a good diet. (not parallel)
Cardiovascular health is promoted by frequent
exercise and a good diet. (parallel)
Cardiovascular health is promoted by exercising
frequently and eating a good diet. (parallel)
```

Don't mix two kinds of verbals:

```
Velcro is popular for fastening shoes and to
keep compartments in handbags shut. (not paral-
lel)
Velcro is popular for fastening shoes and keep-
ing compartments in handbags shut. (parallel)
```

Avoid shifting from active to passive voice; consistency in voice speeds reading and aids comprehension:

```
Congress passed the tax-reform legislation, but
the minimum-wage increase was defeated. (not
parallel)
Congress passed the tax-reform legislation but
defeated the minimum-wage increase. (parallel)
```

In a series, don't mix verbals and nouns:

```
He was charged with drunken driving, carrying a
weapon, resisting arrest and possession of co-
caine. (not parallel)
He was charged with drunken driving, carrying a
weapon, resisting arrest and possessing cocaine.
(parallel)
```

Not only should be followed by *but also*:

```
She not only sold some of her possessions, she
took a second job to earn money to pay the hos-
pital bills. (not parallel)
She not only sold some of her possessions, but
she also took a second job to earn money to pay
the hospital bills. (parallel)
```

Don't mix nouns and a dependent clause in a series:

36

```
They elected him because of his  knowledge, hon-
esty and because he was personally appealing.
(not parallel)

They elected him because of his  knowledge,
honesty and personal appeal. (parallel)
```

Punctuation

Punctuation guidelines are listed in the Associated Press Style Primer in Appendix A. Exercises 12 through 15 at the end of this chapter test your understanding of the uses of various marks of punctuation.

Consistency of style

Frank Norris, a wonderful writer and editor of his own work, said this about simplicity:

Once I had occasion to buy a silver soup ladle. The obliging salesman brought forth an array of them, including ultimately one that was as plain and unadorned as the unclouded sky—and about as beautiful. But the price! It was nearly double any of the others.

"You see," the salesman explained, "in this highly ornamental ware the flaws don't show. The plain one has to be the very best. Any defect would be apparent."

There, if you please, is a final basis of comparison of all things: the bare dignity of the unadorned that may stand before the world all unashamed, in the consciousness of perfection.

Like the maker of the ladle, you should aim at perfection of your style. It's not likely you or your classmates will reach perfection, but all of you can come close.

Consistency is important in communication, so the print media have adopted style guidelines for reporters and editors to follow. Research indicates that readers are irritated when they find, for example, *advisor* in one paragraph and *adviser* in another or *street* spelled out in one address and abbreviated in another. Carefully edited publications, including newspapers, magazines and materials designed for public relations purposes, adopt consistent style.

Most newspapers use either the stylebook published by the Associated Press or the one published by United Press International. In addition, newspapers commonly develop a supplementary style guide to spellings, titles and other matters peculiar to their circulation area.

Thomas W. Lippman, director of personnel/news of The Washington Post, writing in an issue of The Washington Post National Weekly Edition, said this about style:

We are a medium of mass communication. The need to communicate clearly and quickly with a vast and diverse audience imposes its own restrictions. We have little room for Joycean experimentation or 800-word, punctuation-free Faulknerian paragraphs. We strive for consistency of presentation not because we adhere pedantically to inflexible rules, but because we want to enlighten our readers without confusing them or diverting their attention from the material at hand. In addition, we recognize that the newspaper is read every day by educated people who expect us to uphold a high standard of English usage. Consistency of style is part of the high quality they have a right to demand.

A primer of Associated Press style is in Appendix A of this book. Exercise 16 at the end of this chapter tests your understanding of newspaper style.

Consistency of style is part of the high quality readers have a right to demand.

Sydney J. Harris, one of the most thoughtful of columnists for nearly 30 years, said:

When a baseball player makes an error, it goes into the record and is published. How many of us could stand this sort of daily scrutiny? Or are we willing to admit an error before we are called on it?

Most of us are protective and defensive, from the chief of staff down to the janitor's assistant. Our aim is not to do right so much as not to be perceived as doing wrong.

Yet all the decisive people in the world have made waves, and sometimes they have been swamped by them. But no waves, no progress. The only way to avoid mistakes is to be totally passive, which is to say, dead. You won't get any blame that way—nor will you get anything else.

Copy editors must always be alert to errors, discrepancies and illogical statements in copy. Much of the skill in checking facts exists in knowing what to doubt. The most frequent errors in a story are in names, dates, locations and descriptions of past events.

When copy editors question the facts in a story, four courses are open to them:

- If the question can be answered by a reference book, the story can be fixed rather easily.
- If the reporter is available, the question can be referred to that person.
- If it is a question of policy, taste or consistency, copy editors should know. If they do not know, they must consult the chief copy editor.
- If the fact is not vital and cannot be checked by deadline time, it can be deleted from the story. Of course, this is the last resort, not merely an easy way out of a difficulty. A fact that is essential to the story must be checked at all costs.

Exhibit 2-6 lists some reference books helpful for fact checking. Exercises 17 and 18 test your ability to use some standard reference books.

Much of the skill in checking facts exists in knowing what to doubt.

Exhibit 2-6
Copy editors often find these reference books helpful.

Current events sources

Congressional Record. The daily Record is set into type a few hours after the House and Senate complete the legislative day and is available the next morning.

CQ (Congressional Quarterly) Weekly Report. This weekly summary of the actions of the U.S. Congress includes lists of legislation voted on or under consideration and of Senate and House votes.

Facts on File. Published weekly, this source gives a summary of international information on news events and domestic developments.

Urban Affairs Abstracts. This is a weekly abstracting service of the National League of Cities. It includes abstracts of articles related to urban affairs. Topics range from aging to solid waste disposal.

Factual data, including statistics

American Statistics Index. This is a master guide and index to statistical publications of the U.S. government. Publications are listed by title, subject and other categories.

Census of Population: Characteristics of the Population. Published for each general census period, this multivolume set summarizes census data for the nation.

City and county directories and official publications. Cities and counties publish a wealth of data.

Columbia Encyclopedia. This one-volume edition contains a wide range of information.

County and City Data Book. This provides statistical information on counties and cities throughout the country, including such data as income, health care, welfare data, employment.

Demographic Yearbook. The United Nations publishes this volume, which gives world population data and statistics on topics such as mortality, marriage and divorce.

The Guinness Book of World Records. This book is the final authority on world records in a variety of fields. It is updated each year.

Historical Statistics of the United States. This publication gives comparative historical statistics for the country in areas such as agriculture, labor, migration and population.

Standard Education Almanac. This book includes statistics on education in the United States.

Statistical Abstract of the United States. Published by the Government Printing Office, this is a digest of data collected by all the statistical agencies of the U.S. government and by some private agencies. It has been issued since 1878. Similar statistical abstracts are available for individual states.

Statistical Yearbook. It includes world statistics on population, manpower, agriculture, industry, communications, health, culture and many other areas of economic and social affairs. A shortcoming is that no index is included.

Survey of Current Business. Published biannually by the U.S. Department of Commerce, this book gives data on national income and production.

World Almanac and Book of Facts. This handbook of miscellaneous information includes such subjects as copyright law, presidential elections, weights and measures, and flags of the world.

Biographical information

American Men and Women of Science. This volume contains information about the lives and professional activities of the people most instrumental in shaping science in America.

Biographical Dictionary of Musicians. This contains short biographical pieces on musicians of the past and present.

Biography and Genealogy Master Index. This indexes more than 350 Who's Who and other current works of collective biography. It's a good place to begin a biographical search.

Congressional Directory. This is a good source for biographical information on members of Congress, their committee assignments, addresses and names of press representatives.

Contemporary Authors. Restricted to living authors, it includes those who have written relatively little and those who have written in obscure fields.

International Yearbook and Statesmen's Who's Who. This has information on international and national organizations, including brief biographies of world leaders in commerce, education, industry, government and religion.

Who's Who. This biographical dictionary, published annually, gives sketches of prominent people.

Who's Who Among Black Americans. This is a biographical dictionary of notable living African-Americans. It includes a geographical and occupation index.

Who's Who in America. This is another biographical dictionary of notable living people.

Who's Who in American Art. This dictionary includes living artists, critics, dealers and other people active in art.

Who's Who in American Politics. This includes biographical sketches and current addresses of people in national, state and local government.

Who's Who in Rock Music. This volume contains biographical data on popular rock musicians, including both individuals and groups.

Exhibit 2-6
(Continued)

Who's Who in Television and Cable. This work includes information about more than 2,000 people in the field.

Who's Who in the Theatre. This gives biographical sketches about those involved with the modern theater, including players, dramatists, composers, critics, managers, scenic artists, historians and biographers.

Book reviews

Book Review Digest. This publication condenses published reviews of fiction and nonfiction. It also is an index to reviews published in selected British and American periodicals.

Technical Book Review Index. Reviews of new books dealing with technical, scientific and medical subjects are indexed in this monthly publication.

Directories of newspapers and magazines

Directory of Publications. This reference book lists newspapers and magazines by state and city and gives addresses, subscription prices, circulations and information about commerce in the cities.

Directory of the College Student Press in America. This information is similar to that in the Editor and Publisher International Yearbook, except that it pertains to college newspapers and magazines.

Editor and Publisher International Yearbook. This annual reference provides information about U.S. and foreign newspapers as well as other information about the industry.

Ulrich's International Periodicals Directory. This is a subject guide to periodicals published throughout the world.

Dictionaries and manuals of language and style

The American Thesaurus of Slang. This book covers general slang and colloquialisms.

The Dictionary of Bias-Free Usage: A Guide to Nondiscriminatory Language. Author Rosalie Maggio provides advice on how to avoid language bias concerning race, gender, sexual orientation, ethnic background, religion or belief system, age, and class.

A Dictionary of Modern English Usage. This classic by Henry Watson Fowler provides definitions, pronunciations, spellings of plurals, and essays on the use and misuse of words in the English language.

The Elements of Style. Generations of journalists have learned the rules of usage and composition from studying this guide by William Strunk and E. B. White.

The Handbook of Nonsexist Writing. Written by Casey Miller and Kate Swift, this book is valuable for writers and speakers who are trying to free their language from semantic bias.

The Nonsexist Communicator: Solving the Problems of Gender and Awkwardness in Modern English. This book by Bobbye D. Sorrels provides help for eradicating sexist communication.

The Nonsexist Word Finder: A Dictionary of Gender-Free Usage. This is another reference book that promotes gender-free speaking and writing. The author is Rosalie Maggio.

Oxford English Dictionary. The most authoritative English language dictionary, a 13-volume work, attempts to show the history of each word in the English language.

Roget's Thesaurus of English Words and Phrases. This aid to word selection can be especially valuable to headline writers. It provides categories of words classified by ideas.

Business and advertising

Business Periodicals Index. This is a subject index to magazine articles in advertising, public relations, marketing, management and other areas of business.

Leading National Advertisers Multi-Media Report Service. This work compiles statistics about advertisers and is indexed by brand name, product class and company.

Simmons Study of Media and Markets. This multivolume set provides data about buying habits in the United States.

Standard Directory of Advertisers. Included are more than 17,000 companies that use national or regional advertising. The amount of money spent on advertising is broken down by media type.

Standard Rate and Data Services. Advertising rates, specifications and circulation data about mass media are included in separate monthly publications for each type of media, including business publications, consumer magazines, direct-mail lists, newspapers, radio and television.

Broadcasting and film

Broadcasting Yearbook. This directory to the broadcasting industry includes current information about the Federal Communications Commission, advertising, equipment and many other aspects of the industry.

Television Factbook. This guide for the advertising, television and electronics industries covers television organizations, market rankings, cable television, manufacturers and educational opportunities.

Exhibit 2-6
(Continued)

Television News Index and Abstracts. Published by Vanderbilt University since 1972, this monthly volume is a summary of the evening news broadcasts of the three major television networks.

Religion

The Bible. This is the sacred book of Christianity, and the Old Testament portion of the Bible comprises the Holy Scriptures of Judaism.

A Dictionary of Comparative Religion. This volume defines religious terms and examines their variations in meaning from one religion to another.

Encyclopaedia Judaica. This book gives comprehensive coverage of aspects of Jewish life, learning and history.

Encyclopaedia of Religion and Ethics. This volume contains articles about world religions, the great systems of ethics, philosophical ideas and religious customs.

New Catholic Encyclopedia. This work contains information about the history and activities of the Roman Catholic Church from its beginnings to the present.

Government, politics and law

The Almanac of American Politics. This gives state-by-state political background, census data, voter characteristics, election results, and information about senators, representatives and governors.

America Votes. This contains election statistics for all U.S. states in presidential, gubernatorial and congressional races.

Black's Law Dictionary. Now in its fifth edition, this legal dictionary has been considered a standard for almost a century.

Congressional Quarterly Almanac. This annual publication gives a survey of U.S. congressional legislation, divided into subject areas.

Dictionary of American Politics. This book contains concise definitions for political terms and also includes political slogans, slang and nicknames.

Index to Legal Periodicals. Articles from legal periodicals published in the United States, Canada, Great Britain, Ireland, Australia and New Zealand are indexed.

Political Handbook of the World. This volume gives information about world politics and lists newspapers with political affiliations.

Public Affairs Information Service Bulletin. It indexes books, documents, pamphlets and periodicals relating to public policy issues.

United States Government Manual. The official handbook of the U.S. government describes most governmental agencies and their programs and lists key officials.

Maps and geographical information

Commercial Atlas and Marketing Guide. This work, which is revised annually, provides extensive state-by-state coverage of the United States, including basic business data. Coverage of the rest of the world is more limited.

The National Atlas of the United States. This atlas includes detailed information on the physical features, resources and social activities of the United States. Thematic maps present statistics.

World Atlas. In this basic atlas of the world, the United States is covered by region rather than state by state. Other maps focus on language, climate, agriculture and politics.

Quotations

Bartlett's Familiar Quotations. This famous source lists sayings and writings from 2000 B.C. to the present. It includes a key-word index.

The Oxford Dictionary of Quotations. This collection has more than 70,000 entries and includes a key-word index.

Science

A Dictionary of Agriculture and Allied Terminology. This book provides definitions for both general and technical words in agriculture and related fields.

McGraw-Hill Dictionary of Scientific and Technical Terms. This dictionary defines scientific and technical terms more thoroughly than a general dictionary would.

McGraw-Hill Encyclopedia of Science and Technology. This covers every area of modern science and technology. Survey articles written for the general reader give introductions to basic scientific concepts.

McGraw-Hill Yearbook of Science and Technology. This is an annual update of the McGraw-Hill Encyclopedia of Science and Technology.

ON CAREFUL WRITING

By B. H. Liebes

As a writing coach for several newspapers, I've found that the key is listening, then asking questions of the reporters and nudging them. Serving as a writing coach has reaffirmed what I've learned from my days as reporter and editor: that a story can never be stronger than the reporting that supports it. Therefore, I emphasize the reporting as well as the writing, trying to help the reporters sharpen their questions and research and to keep asking questions if the answers they receive are unsatisfactory.

The same basic idea was central to the first editorial in Feed/back: The California Journalism Review:

The press of Northern California is free of the kind of scrutiny it's supposed to provide free of charge to public servants, corporate executives, topless dancers, school musicians, sidewalk philosophers, fire chiefs, and unclad children on hot afternoons.

We will review the press of Northern California on a regular basis, but our scope is limited only by the concerns and interests of those who report and edit the news.

We'll apply to ourselves the standards we expect from the working press. We'll try to be constructive, not vindictive, and we will not wear blinders.

B. H. "BUD" LIEBES

B. H. "Bud" Liebes' career includes 18 years as a journalist on daily newspapers and 23 years as a professor of journalism at San Francisco State University. He has worked as a reporter, copy editor, a telegraph editor, a chief copy editor and a news editor. In addition to teaching in a classroom, Liebes is a writing coach for several newspapers.

He started his newspaper career on the Illinois State Journal, diploma fresh in hand from the School of Journalism at the University of Missouri. Other papers he worked for were the Stars & Stripes in Germany, Milwaukee Sentinel, San Francisco Chronicle and San Francisco Examiner. Gaps in his newspaper career were filled by studies at the University of Grenoble in France and Stanford University, where he earned a master of arts degree.

Liebes was also co-founder and co-editor of Feed/back: The California Journalism Review. This remarkable publication lasted for 11 years and gathered plaudits from many journalists.

In his academic career, Liebes took three leaves of absence: to help found a department of communication at Hong Kong Baptist College; to serve as a Fulbright teaching professor at the Institute of Mass Communication, University of the West Indies in Jamaica; and to teach in China in the International Journalism Program at Shanghai International Studies University.

As for Liebes' career as a journalist, he says, "I've had rough days, but never a dull day."

Suggestions for additional reading

Berner, R. Thomas. *Language Skills for Journalists*, 2nd ed. Boston: Houghton Mifflin, 1984.

Brooks, Brian S., and James L. Pinson. *Working With Words: A Concise Handbook for Media Writers and Editors*. New York: St. Martin's Press, 1989.

Kessler, Lauren, and Duncan McDonald. *Uncovering the News: A Journalist's Search for Information*. Belmont, Calif.: Wadsworth, 1987.

Kessler, Lauren, and Duncan McDonald. *When Words Collide: A Journalist's Guide to Grammar and Style*, 3rd ed. Belmont, Calif.: Wadsworth, 1992.

Lippman, Thomas W. (ed.). *The Washington Post Deskbook on Style*, 2nd ed. New York: McGraw-Hill, 1989.

McCormick, Mona (ed.). *The New York Times Guide to Reference Materials*, rev. ed. New York: New American Library, 1971.

Rubin, Rebecca B., Alan M. Rubin and Linda J. Piele. *Communication Research: Strategies and Sources*. Belmont, Calif.: Wadsworth, 1986.

Ward, Jean, and Kathleen A. Hansen. *Search Strategies in Mass Communication*. New York: Longman, 1987.

1. Use the correct copy editing symbols to make changes in this story:

While performing such simple tasks as brushing-teeth or tossing back a drink, Young adults have suffered strokes by causing trauma to one of 4 main arterys supplying blood to the brain doctors reported.

A 32 year old woman recently suffered a stroke after playing a drinking game in which she tossed back several shotsof whiskey, according to a lettter published today by the New England Journal of Medicine. "It was not only the alcohol but the manner in which she consumed it said Dr. Richard Trosch, a neurology resident at the yale university School of Medicine. Knocking back a shot of whiskey shouldbe include among a list of potential stroke-causing "trivial traumas," including old whip lash injuries, child birth, lifting heavy, brushing teeth and diving into water Trosch wrote.

Trosch said young adults was particularly prone to damageing the extracranial carotid artery a vein through which bloood is pumped from the heart to teh brain

2. Label each word in the following sentences according to its part of speech.

a. Marty Hudson has not eaten since Monday.

b. Hudson is on a hunger strike in the Roanoke City Jail.

c. Hudson, 32, is a United Mine Workers of America strike organizer.

d. The study found that teachers want to receive broadcasts from other networks.

e. Completing the story about the council meeting moments before deadline, the reporter took a break to get a cup of coffee.

f. Stop! You can't go in there.

3. Identify the subject, verb, direct object or complement in each clause in the following sentences. Draw one line under the subject, two lines under the verb, and three lines under the direct object or complement. Mark whether the verb is completed by a direct object, predicate nominative or predicate adjective.

a. In some rural areas, people believe the devil makes them sick.

b. They dose themselves with turpentine to cure worms and tie a dirty sock around their neck to treat a sore throat.

c. Doctors should know about these cultural and religious beliefs of their patients.

d. The American Bar Association has said it will not rate future judicial candidates on ideology or politics, but the ABA's critics say the advisory group could still kill the nominations of qualified conservatives.

e. A young woman wanted to tell the invading soldiers that they were unwelcome in her city.

f. Thinking they wouldn't shoot a woman, she walked fearlessly toward their lines.

g. They fired. She fell. A bullet wound turned her white shirt scarlet.

h. Although some people buy three or four pairs of sunglasses at a clip, the average number of sunglasses purchased per person is 1.3 pairs, according to Ray-Ban research.

i. Thomas Edison had 400 species of plants in the garden of his winter home on the Caloosahatchee River in Fort Myers, Fla.

j. With intentions of revising his travel book annually, Arthur Frommer tells of travels that are politically oriented, vacations on campuses and at dance camps, and digs with archeologists.

4. Label each of the sentences in Exercise 2 according to sentence type: simple, compound, complex, compound-complex.

5. Choose the correct verb in these sentences. To show that you under-stand the rules of subject-verb agreement and are not relying only on what sounds right, write the number of the rule (as numbered in this chapter) that applies to each choice.

a. Five passengers on the plane and a farmer working in the field [was, were] killed.
b. Like other produce wholesalers on the three-block-long market, she [know, knows] the ultimate fol-lower of seasons [is, are] the farmer.
c. Each of the children [is, are] enrolled in music lessons.
d. Neither John nor his brothers [know, knows] what to expect when election day [come, comes].
e. The final hours of the legislative session [was, were] chaotic.
f. Two-thirds of the protesters [was, were] arrested before noon.
g. Club members [was, were] scheduled to vote for new officers.
h. The committee, composed of three members of the board of directors, [is, are] going to plan the annual convention.
i. A number of animals [was, were] trapped in the burning barn.
j. The majority [is, are] in favor of the legislation limiting immigration, which [is, are] to be voted on today.
k. Politics [was, were] interesting when I studied it in college, but the courses [has, had] little ef-fect on my personal politics, which [was, were] firmly fixed.
l. Good manners [is, are] best learned when young.
m. The mayor's delegation, as well as several Chamber of Commerce members, [was, were] scheduled to meet with the executives visiting from Japan.
n. Everyone [hope, hopes] that the contract will be awarded to this company.
o. The National Council of Churches [is, are] plan-ning a convention in Washington, D.C., this year.
p. The company's earnings [was, were] greater this year than last year because new products [was, were] popular.
q. The total sold [was, were] 450, but a total of 10 [was, were] returned because of faulty construc-tion.

6. Mark each pronoun in the following sentences, and tell whether it is in the nominative, objective or possessive case.

a. An offshore intake pipe sucked up a scuba diver and pulled him 1,650 feet through the duct before depositing him at a nuclear power plant.
b. "I thought I was dead," said William Lamm, 45, who was spearfishing when he was pulled into the 16-foot diameter, barnacle-studded pipe off Florida

Power & Light's St. Lucie nuclear plant on the Atlantic Coast.

c. Lamm said the suction pulled off his mask and diving gloves and ripped his mouthpiece out several times as he moved through the pipe at 7 feet per second.

d. Lamm, a scuba diver for five years, says it will be a long time before he dives again, if at all.

7. Indicate correct noun and pronoun agreement by crossing out the incorrect pronoun choices in these sentences.

a. Jeff Mayer bills [hisself, himself, themselves] as the most expensive maid in the nation. Business executives pay [his, him] $1,000 so [he, him] will tell [they, them, it] how to clean off [they, them, their, there, its] cluttered desks.

b. Some financially strapped cities can't make across-the-board purchases of semiautomatic pistols, [that, which] cost from $350 to $550. But police departments frequently permit officers to buy [they, them, there, their] own sidearms.

c. Each male officer was required to buy [his, him, its, their, them] own uniforms.

d. Uniforms were expensive, but [they, them, it] lasted for several years if [they, them, their, its] owners kept [their, its] weight constant so the uniforms fit properly.

e. Listen carefully to those [who, whom, whose] you have reason to believe know how to express [theirselves, themselves] well.

f. I will exchange letters with [whoever, whomever] writes.

g. [Who, Whom] shall you choose as captain?

h. The company needs to know [who, whom] it is insuring.

i. I thought [she, her] to be my friend.

j. [Who, Whom] do you suppose [he, him] to be?

k. Between you and [I, me], I think [she, her] previous boyfriend was friendlier.

l. None but [I, me] was able to complete the work.

m. Some of [we, us] editors think students need to know much more about grammar.

n. The editors decided to hire the student [who, whom] scored highest on the English usage test.

o. The newly married couple went to a resort in the Smoky Mountains on [their, its] honeymoon. [They, Them] will return home next week.

p. The women's basketball team is in [their, its, it's] first season of competition.

8. Cross out the incorrect pronoun choices in the following sentences. Add commas where needed to set off non-essential clauses.

a. Three victims were members of a Delaware Army National Guard unit [that, which, who] had just completed [their, its] first week of training.

b. Officer Glenda Jones [who, whom] has been coordinating police patrols in housing developments plagued by drugs, gangs and gambling said most of the problems stem from non-residents.

c. Widely publicized safety breakdowns at the government's nuclear weapons plants are rooted in a perverse devotion to secrecy and poor management, congressional investigators said in a report issued Sunday. The safety problems [that, which] came to light during the past two years were aggravated by a lack of outside scrutiny and effective oversight from the Energy Department [that, which] pays private companies to run the facilities, the report said.

d. He criticized the students [who, whom, that, which] led the demonstrations [that, which] were crushed by army assaults.

e. Eight-year-old Chad Brenner said he would have liked to use the $39,541.55 tax refund check [that, which] was mistakenly mailed to him to buy a new bicycle.

9. Complete this list of nouns and pronouns to show the plurals and possessives:

Singular	Singular possessive	Plural	Plural possessive
a. Smith			
b. girl			
c. man			
d. attorney general			
e. church			
f. Jones			
g. army			
h. monkey			
i. mouse			
j. piano			
k. oasis			

10. Use the correct verb and verb tense in each of the following sentences.

Lie or lay

a. The gun _____ in the street.
b. The gun had _____ in the street for several hours before it was recovered by police.
c. The police officer _____ the gun on the table.
d. The officer thought that he had _____ the gun on the table, but his supervisor could not find it.
e. The woman _____ on the beach to get a suntan.

f. She had _____ there for several hours before she noticed that she was getting sunburned.

g. _____ the baby in the crib.

h. The twin babies were _____ in the crib.

i. _____ her books aside, she spoke to him.

Sit or set

j. We were _____ on the swing when Bill began crying.

k. She _____ the books on her desk.

l. The fat man _____ on the chair and broke it.

m. She had _____ the alarm clock for 6 a.m.

n. They had _____ in the car for two hours.

Rise or raise

o. Please _____ the flag.

p. He _____ from the water and surprised me.

q. The dough has _____ sufficiently.

r. The student _____ her hand.

s. He had _____ his hand several times, but the teacher did not call on him to respond.

t. The stage was designed to allow the orchestra to _____ from the orchestra pit.

11. Rewrite or edit the following sentences to correct misplaced or dangling modifiers and double negatives.

a. Police described the suspect as a burly, white, middle-aged male with brown hair and a beard, more than 6 feet tall. _____

_____

b. Accused of making errors on telephone bills for the past four months, students living in residence halls will receive a refund from the phone company for long-distance calls. _____

_____

c. AIDS in New York City is becoming the most common cause of death for women under the age of 35. ____

_____

d. An anti-government coalition staged the protest march in an attempt to force the ouster of Panama's Gen. Manuel Noriega yesterday afternoon.

_____

_____

e. After training the tiger cub to walk on a leash, it could be used in the zoo director's presentations to schoolchildren. _____

_____

f. Still searching for an incinerator site, a previously rejected location is getting a second look by the city council. _____

_____

g. The baby kitten doesn't have scarcely any hair.

_____

h. The jail is the first in the state to be operated by a private management firm that accommodates 100 inmates. _____

_____

i. A Manchester woman, on the pretense of searching for someone, allowed a man to enter her home and was assaulted. _____

_____

j. The zoo doesn't have but one gorilla, but the director says another one will be added next year.

_____

_____

12. Edit the following sentences to punctuate them correctly. Use correct copy editing symbols. Pay particular attention to the correct use of apostrophes, colons and commas.

a. Down's syndrome has been linked to a defect on a tiny slice of one of the human chromosomes an important step toward prevention and treatment of the disorder researchers said Saturday.

b. "By mapping a gene you can find it isolate it and develop new means of therapy" said Dr. Frank Ruddle of Yale University one of the organizer's of the conference.

c. At the Ninth International Gene Mapping Workshop two years ago in Paris scientist's had mapped about 1000 human gene's.

d. The announcement of 400 new genes Saturday brings the total to nearly 2000 an increase of more than one-fourth over what it was two weeks ago.

e. Meanwhile the Immigration and Naturalization Service has proclaimed the law a clear success but the current administration has yet to put it's own stamp on immigration policy.

f. "The legislation bought time for everyone and made the problems more manageable for a while" said Leonel J. Castillo former INS commissioner.

g. The law offered legal status to aliens who had lived in the United States continuously since before Jan. 1 1982 and imposed penalties on employers who knowingly hired illegals.

h. He said that he had but one thing on his mind sleeping.

i. Gardeners who wear broad brimmed hats, coveralls, and heavy duty gloves while using an electric hedge clipper to trim bushes are displaying common sense—but not enough of it says the American Optometric Association.

j. The garb protects the face from the sun and clothing and hands from the wear and tear of yard work but the eyes are left exposed and vulnerable to flying twigs leaves and other debris.

13. Edit the following sentences to punctuate them correctly. Use correct copy editing symbols. Pay particular attention to the correct use of dashes, exclamation points and hyphens.

a. She announced that newly developed tests would be used during the upcoming tournament to detect drug using athletes.

b. A 4 foot boa constrictor a scary tarantula and a baby Bengal tiger gave Joey Black a front line education about zoos.

c. "Bring back tax incentives" Jones [headline]

d. Every state has reported influenza activity except New Hampshire and Rhode Island with three states

New York Connecticut and New Mexico listing widespread outbreaks.

   e. Bob Woodward wrote "VEIL The Secret Wars of the
CIA, 1981-1987.

   f. Gosh It will be a 15 to 20 minute procedure and I
don't think I can lie still that long.

14. Edit the following sentences to punctuate them correctly. Use correct copy editing symbols. Pay particular attention to the correct use of parentheses, periods, question marks, quotation marks and semicolons.

   a. "We don't know how much longer we can wait before
beginning it (the Dexter Bridge project the mayor
said.

   b. It was identified as a USSR plane but US planes
were in the area also Maj Gen Larry Jones said.

   c. Did the Maryville Tennessee Daily Times win the
photography award.

   d. Dustin Hoffman won an Oscar for Rainman he also
appeared in Midnight Cowboy.

   e. The inmate said to the parole board "Jones should
not be released from prison. He is a dangerous
man. He has told me several times, I will kill
again if I get a chance.

15. Punctuate these sentences:

   a. Davis who is usually soft spoken talked in loud
tones yesterday.

   b. Eisenhower who was commander of the national force
refused to attack.

   c. The 1000 word story had a pro American tone and a
definite anti Communist slant.

   d. The Manning who used to live here was returned to
England.

   e. The Iron Building which is a 40 story structure is
owned by Pat Maffery Jr.

   f. The home office is in Los Angeles which is one of
Americas largest cities.

g. The 25 member board held a five day conference.

h. Headlines which are fashioned to summarize the
   stories are also used to display the news.

i. Citizens who voted for the new law now are regret-
   ting their lack of knowledge about its impact.

j. Durham shot his father in law with a 12 gauge
   shotgun and received a 15 year sentence when the
   12 man jury recommended mercy.

16. Circle the correctly styled item in each of the following sets. All are the
first reference, unless otherwise noted.

   a. Cumberland Avenue
      Cumberland Ave.

   b. 123 9th St.
      123 Ninth St.
      123 9th Street
      123 Ninth Street

   c. 455 California
      455 Calif.
      455 California St.
      455 Calif. St.

   d. 4th and Iowa streets
      4th & Iowa
      Fourth and Iowa streets
      Fourth and Iowa Streets

   e. Captain Mary Brown
      Capt. Mary Brown
      Mary Brown, Captain

   f. Chancellor Jack E. Reese
      Dr. Jack Reese
      Jack E. Reese, Chancellor
      Dr. Jack Reese, chancellor
      Chancellor Dr. Jack E. Reese
      Jack E. Reese, the chancellor
      Chanc. Jack E. Reese

   g [second reference]
      Chancellor Reese
      Chan. Reese
      Reese
      Dr. Reese

   h. Phil Scheurer, Vice-Chancellor of Student Affairs
      Vice Chancellor for Student Affairs Phil Scheurer
      Phil Scheurer, vice chancellor for student affairs
      Phil Scheurer, vice-chancellor of academic affairs

   i. [second reference]
      Vice Chancellor Scheurer
      Scheurer

j. [second reference]
   Attorney General Bromley
   Att. Gen. Bromley
   A. G. Bromley
   Bromley

k. [second reference]
   Smith
   Miss Smith
   Ms. Smith
   Mary

l. from Jan. 22–25
   from January 22 to 25
   from Jan. 22 to Jan. 25
   from Jan. 22 to 25

m. Marilyn Jones, dean of law
   Law School Dean Marilyn Jones
   Marilyn Jones, dean of the School of Law

n. 5 cents
   five cents
   5¢
   $.05

o. the English Department
   the Department of English
   the department of English

p. the History Department
   the Department of History
   the history department
   the department of History

q. Grade Point Average
   GPA
   grade point average
   g.p.a.

r. [second reference]
   Grade Point Average
   GPA
   grade point average
   g.p.a.

s. The Supreme Court ruled eight to one.
   The Supreme Court ruled 8-1.
   The Supreme Court ruled 8 to 1.

t. Tuesday at 7 p.m. in 127 University Center
   In 127 University Center Tuesday at 7 p.m.
   7 p.m. Tuesday in 127 University Center
   7 p.m. Tuesday night in University Center room 127

u. [news story]
   She is 5 feet 8 inches
   5-8
   five feet eight
   5 feet 8

v. Paul Ashdown., professor of journalism
Prof. Paul Ashdown, journalism
Professor of Journalism, Paul Ashdown
Paul Ashdown, prof. of journ.
Prod. Dr. Paul Ashdown

w. [second reference]
Prof. Ashdown
Professor Ashdown
Ashdown
Paul
Dr. Ashdown

x. Susan Jones, asst. prof. of history
Asst. Prof. Susan Jones, history
Susan Jones, assistant professor of history
Susan Jones, assistant professor in history

y. [second reference]
Prof. Jones
Professor Jones
Asst. Prof. Jones
Jones
Ms. Jones

z. Gov. Ned McWherter
Governor Ned McWherter
Ned McWherter, Governor

aa. [second reference]
Governor McWherter
McWherter

ab. 7 a.m.
7 A.M.
7:00 a.m.
7:00 A.M.

ac. 12 noon
noon
12:00 p.m.
12:00 noon

ad. 8 p.m. tonight
8 P.M. tonight
8 tonight
8:00 tonight

ae. 1990 A.D.
1990 AD
A.D. 1990
AD 1990

af. Number One choice
Number 1 choice
No. 1 choice
No. one choice

ag. National Organization for Women
National Organization of Women

ah. Joe Jones, 7
    Joe Jones, seven
    seven-year-old Joe Jones

ai. Detroit, Michigan
    Detroit, Mich.
    Detroit, MI.
    Detroit

aj. Nome, Alaska
    Nome, Aka.
    Nome, AL
    Nome

ak. the '60s
    the '60's
    the 60's
    the 60s

al. The odds were 5-4.
    The odds were 5 to 4.
    The odds were five to four.
    The odds were five-four.

am. the 1st Amendment
    the First Amendment
    the first amendment
    1st Am.

an. The boy is nineteen.
    The boy is 19.
    The man is 19.
    The man is nineteen.

ao. The girl is nineteen.
    The girl is 19.
    The woman is 19.
    The woman is nineteen.

ap. "Time" magazine
    Time Magazine
    Time magazine
    "Time"

aq. Tennessee River
    Tennessee river
    the Tennessee

ar. 17th century
    Seventeenth Century
    17th Century
    seventeenth century

as. Chief Justice of the Supreme Court
    Chief Justice of the United States
    chief justice of the United States
    chief justice of the Supreme Court

at. Feb.
    February

au. Aug. 26
August 26
26 Aug.
August 26th
8-26
August, 26

av. Head Coach Patricia Smith
coach Patricia Smith
Patricia Smith, Coach
Coach Patricia Smith

aw. [second reference]
Coach Smith
Smith
Coach
Patricia

ax. They traveled through the West Coast states.
The oil spill was along the East Coast.
Shrimp were once plentiful along the Gulf Coast.
He lived on the Virginia Coast.

ay. The flag is red and white and blue.
The flag is red, white, and blue.
The flag is red-white and blue.
The flag is red, white and blue.

az. I had juice, toast, and ham and eggs.
I had juice, toast and ham and eggs.
I had juice, toast, and ham, and eggs.
I had juice toast ham and eggs.

ba. three dollars
$3.00
$3
3 dollars

bb. We will play this Saturday.
We will play next Saturday.
We will play Saturday.

bc. We played last Saturday.
We played Saturday week.
We played Saturday.

bd. 26 to 27,000
26–27 thousand
26,000 to 27,000

be. U.S. Congress
U.S. congress
United States Congress
United States' Congress
United States congress

bf. 8th Congressional District
Eighth Congressional District
8th congressional district
eighth congressional district

bg. Corp.
   corp.
   corporation
   Corporation

bh. Knox County District Court
   Knox County district court
   District Court
   district court of Knox county

bi. Knox County Courthouse
   County court house
   Know County Court House

bj. United States Supreme Court
   U.S. Supreme Court
   U.S. supreme court

bk. the Mississippi and Ohio Rivers
   the Mississippi and Ohio rivers

bl. daylight-saving time
   daylight savings time
   DST
   daylight-savings time

bm. deans list
   deans' list
   dean's list
   Dean's List
   Dean's list

bn. Defense Attorney John Jones
   Def. Atty. John Jones
   John Jones, defense attorney
   John Jones, Defense Attorney

bo. the 9-by-12 rug
   the nine-by-12 rug
   the 9 by 12 rug
   the nine by 12 rug

bp. He drove northwest.
   He drove north west.
   He drove Northwest.

bq. She has arthritis.
   She has Arthritis.

br. District Attorney Jill Jones
   Dist. Atty Jill Jones
   Jill Jones, District Attorney
   D.A. Jill Jones

bs. 62 degrees Fahrenheit
   62F.
   62 Fahr.
   Fahrenheit 62
   F 62

bt. Philippine islands
Aleutian islands
Pacific islands
Islands of Florida
Mediterranean Islands

bu. They drove west.
They drove West.

bv. U.S. Government
United States government
United States Government
U.S. government

bw. Department of Defense
defense department
department of Defense
Defense department

bx. Western Texas
western Texas
W. Texas
West Texas

by. Knox County jail
Knox County Jail
Knox Co. Jail

bz. Knoxville Fire department
Knoxville fire department
KFD
Knoxville Fire Department
Knoxville Fire Dept.

ca. The town has no Fire Department.
The town has no fire department.
The town has no Fire Dept.

cb. Flags ashore sometimes fly at half-mast.
Flags ashore sometimes fly at half mast.
Flags ashore sometimes fly at half-staff.
Flags ashore sometimes fly at half staff.

cc. The dentist committed suicide; he hung himself.
The dentist committed suicide; he hanged himself.
The dentist committed suicide; he was hanged.
The dentist committed suicide; he was hung.

cd. hydrogen bomb
H-Bomb
H-bomb
Hydrogen Bomb

ce. newsman
newswoman
reporter

cf. U.S. House of Representatives
United States House of Representatives
US House
the House of Reps.
U.S. House of Reps.

cg. catsup
ketchup
catchup
Ketchup

ch. Queen Elizabeth II
Queen Elizabeth 2nd
Queen Elizabeth Two
Queen Elizabeth the Second

ci. [second reference]
Queen Elizabeth
Elizabeth
Windsor
HRH
Queen

cj. K Mart
K-Mart
K mart
K-mart
Kmart

ck. held High Mass
Held high mass
sung High Mass
sung high Mass

cl. mid-semester
mid-term
mid-life
mid-America
mid-wife

cm. Middle West
Mid-West
mid-West
middle west

cn. 12 midnight
12:00 midnight
midnight
12 a.m. midnight
12 p.m. midnight

co. 35 m.p.h.
35 mph

cp. General Sid Bostic
Gen. Sid Bostic
general Sid Bostic
Sid Bostic, General

cq. [second reference]
    General Bostic
    Gen. Bostic
    Bostic
    the General

cr. Admiral Earl Jones
    Adm. Earl Jones
    admiral Earl Jones
    Earl Jones, Admiral

cs. [second reference]
    Admiral Jones
    Adm. Jones
    Jones
    Earl
    the Admiral

ct. $1,200,000
    1.2 million dollars
    1,200,000 million dollars
    $1.2 million

cu. Fifth Armored Division
    5th Armored Division
    Fifth Armored Div.
    5th Armored Div.

cv. He left an estate worth from $6 to $7 million.
    He left an estate worth from $6–$7 million.
    He left an estate worth from $6 million to $7 million.
    He left an estate worth from six to seven million dollars.

cw. Mount Everest
    Mt. Everest

cx. National Anthem
    National anthem
    national anthem
    national Anthem

cy. National Guard
    National guard
    national Guard
    national guard

cz. 10 knots
    10 knots per hour
    ten knots
    ten kph

da. U.S. Navy
    U.S. navy
    U.S.N.
    United States Navy
    USN

db. The team is ranked No. 1.
    The team is ranked number one.
    The team is ranked Number One.
    The team is ranked #1.

dc. King George III
King George 3d
King George 3rd
King George the Third

dd. first base
First Base
1st base
1st Base

de. Her sons are 15, 12, and seven.
Her sons are 15, 12 and 7.

df. They have 12 chairs, nine tables and four lamps.
They have 12 chairs, 9 tables and 4 lamps.

dg. Pacific Ocean
Pacific ocean
pacific ocean

dh. OKs
okays
OK's
okay's

di. We will meet in Knoxville Saturday.
We will meet in Knoxville on Saturday.

dj. Page 7
page seven
page 7
Page Seven

dk. The team has a 20-2 record this season.
The team has a twenty to two record this season.
The team has won twenty games and lost two games this season.

dl. 10 persons were killed.
10 people were killed.
Ten persons were killed.
Ten people were killed.

dm. 1 1/2%
1.5%
1 1/2 percent
1.5 percent
1 1/2 per cent
1.5 per cent

dn. 1st Ward, 10th Precinct
First Ward, 10th Precinct
First ward, 10th precinct
first ward, tenth precinct

do. She is a pom-pom girl.
She is a pom pom girl.
She is a pompom girl.
She is a pompon girl.

dp. He is the Pope.
He is the pope.
He is the Pontiff.

dq. The Rev. James Jones
Rev. James Jones
the Rev. Mr. James Jones

dr. [second reference]
Reverend Jones
Rev. Jones
Jones

ds. Act 1, Scene 3
act 1, scene 3
Act One, Scene Three
Act I, Scene 3

dt. the State of Tennessee
the state of Tennessee
The State of Tennessee

du. the television show "The Cosby Show"
the television show The Cosby Show

dv. Temperatures fell 5 degrees.
Temperatures fell five degrees.
Temperatures fell 5°.

dw. the Ten Commandments
the 10 Commandments
the 10 Comm.

dx. 9 a.m. this morning
9 A.M. this morning
9 a.m.
9 A.M.

dy. Former Gov. Lamar Alexander
former Gov. Lamar Alexander
former Governor Lamar Alexander

dz. T-shirt
Tee-shirt
t-shirt
T shirt

ea. Smith beat King 11,101 to 9,706.
Smith beat King 11,101–97,706.
Smith beat King 11.1 thousand to 9.7 thousand.

eb. The Senate vote was 63–32.
The Senate vote was 63 to 32.
The Senate vote was sixty-three to thirty-two.

ec. The baby weighed 8 pounds, 13 ounces.
The baby weighed 8#13.
The baby weighed 8 lbs., 13 oz.
The baby weighed eight pounds, 13 ounces.
The baby weighed eight lbs., 13 oz.

ed. U.S. Senator Nancy Kassebaum
Sen. Nancy Kassebaum
Nancy Kassebaum

17. Use standard reference books to answer the following questions. Answer in complete sentences, as though the information were part of a story you are editing. Cite your source for each answer.

a. What is the latest figure on population in your county? How does this figure compare with the state's other counties (first, 14th, etc.)?

_____

_____

b. How many total crimes against persons were there in your county in 1989? How many total crimes against property were there in 1989?

_____

_____

c. What are the communities that make up your county? What are the populations of the five largest of these communities? _____

_____

_____

d. How many school districts are there in your county? What is the total enrollment of each of these school districts? _____

_____

_____

e. How many residential units are in your county? How many are single-family homes or condos, and how many are apartments? _____

_____

_____

f. What recognized political parties are operating in your county? How many registered voters does each of these parties have? _____

_____

_____

18. Use standard reference books to answer the following questions. Answer in complete sentences, as though the information were part of a story you are editing. Cite your source for each answer.

a. You are editing a story on the first ladies of the White House. In one or two sentences, give Martha Washington's full name, age and marital status at the time she married George Washington. Include the date of their marriage. _____

_____

b. You are editing a story about U.S. department store chains. Give a brief description of Sears, Roebuck and Co., including the number of stores and approximate annual gross sales figures. Where does Sears rank among department store chains? _____

_____

c. A group of local high school students has been working to build a house of playing cards. The group has built the house 33 stories tall so far. How much higher would the house have to be for a world record?

_____

_____

d. How many people have immigrated to the United States since 1820?

_____

_____

e. Give the full names of the U.S. senators from your home state and the names of the Senate committees they serve on in the current session of Congress.

_____

_____

f. Who won the Pulitzer Prize for fiction in 1991? _____

_____

_____

g. Use information from Who's Who in America to write several sentences about the winner of the Pulitzer Prize for fiction in 1991. _____

_____

_____

h. Who won the Nobel Prize for physics in 1991? _____

_____

_____

i. Has the number of farms in your state increased or decreased since 1960? Give the specific figures for the number in the current year (or the last year that figures are available) and in 1960. _____

_____

_____

**Editing Words,
Sentences and
Paragraphs**

Using the right words
Shaping sentences
Shaping paragraphs
Altering story length

An editor at work: Michael Molyneux

Precision means exactness, and reporters are always in danger of drifting into imprecisions of speech. If they are careless about word meanings, then the editor has a big job to do.

Confucius, the ancient Chinese philosopher, when asked what he would do first if he were in charge of a national government, answered:

*Simple, short
sentences don't
always work.*

—*Theodore Geisel
(Dr. Seuss)*

It would certainly be to correct language. If language is not correct, then what is said is not meant, then what ought to be done remains undone. If this remains undone, then morals and arts deteriorate. If morals and arts deteriorate, justice will go astray. If justice goes astray, the people will stand about in helpless confusion. Hence, there must be no arbitrariness in what is said. This matters above everything.

The lofty practices Confucius wanted to protect—morality, art and justice— suffer when what is written is not what is meant. Many lesser practices—such as carrying on the everyday business of living, relating experiences, describing people or places, expressing emotions and ideas—also suffer because of failure to use the right words.

Using the right words

J. D. Salinger, author of *Catcher in the Rye* and other stories, sometimes sits for hours making lists of words, searching for those that will precisely shape the meaning of a sentence. Truman Capote, author of *In Cold Blood,* also wrote slowly, largely because he weighed and tested each word. Robert Ruark, who was a fast and slovenly writer, one evening boasted of his own speed to Capote. "Truman, I'll bet you spent all day writing one word," Ruark said. Capote responded, "Ah, but it was the *right* word, Robert."

Editors with large vocabularies must resist two strong temptations in editing: showing off words and trying to make reporters' writing seem important by clothing it richly. The true measure of vocabulary is not the number of words used but the number used effectively.

Editors must be alert to correct usage of even ordinary, simple words. For example, a writer used *since* for *because* like this: "Since it rained Sunday, the ground was too wet for our picnic." If you think of *since* as a time-sequence word, when you hear "since it rained Sunday" your inner ear is tuned for words that will tell what happened later ("we've had nothing but sunshine"). The writer meant "*because* it rained Sunday."

Meaningless words and phrases

Phrases such as *needless to say* and *remains to be seen* are widely used but meaningless. If something really is needless to say, why say it? Aside from events that already have run their course, everything remains to be seen.

To become discriminating, editors should think about individual words. For example, in a story about broadcasting, a student wrote, "The daily news has become one of television's largest productions." If he had thought about *largest,* surely he would not have used the word in that context. The scope of daily news production in television can be measured in number of employees, dollars spent or hours of broadcast time, but by none of these measurements is news one of the *largest* productions.

Another example is the term *well-known.* Thoughtless writers use it without thinking, as in "Michael Jordan is a well-known athlete." The term means that Jordan is known well by a great many people. A more precise

65

expression is *widely known,* meaning that he is known to a great many people who do not actually know him well.

Careless writers may drift into using words such as *area* to refer to almost anything. An area is geographic. Like most words, *area* can be used in other ways, but it should not be substituted for a specific word that neither the writer nor the editor can think of at the moment. "Learning to play an instrument is an area that . . . ," one student wrote. Learning to play a musical instrument can be a hated chore, a happy experience, a drudgery or a torture, but it is not an area. It is an activity. But *activity* is another word that is often used thoughtlessly. *Situation* is another frequently misused all-purpose word. *Situation* and *activity* are rarely used by writers who care about what they are writing.

Precision vs. pomposity

A plumber once wrote to the National Bureau of Standards to say that he had found hydrochloric acid useful in cleaning drains and asked whether it was harmless. An official wrote in reply: "The efficacy of hydrochloric acid is indisputable, but the chlorine residue is incompatible with metallic permanence."

The plumber replied that he was happy to hear that hydrochloric acid was all right. The official responded again in pompous language, and the plumber wrote back that he was still happy that the official agreed. Then the official wrote: "Don't use hydrochloric acid. It eats hell out of the pipes."

This story may be fiction, but it illustrates the problem of writing and editing pompously, a problem not limited to bureaucrats. It has been noted that some students become afflicted with pomposity during their graduate studies. At the beginning of their studies, they write precise and concise prose like this:

To determine the molecular size and shape of A and B, I measured their sedimentation and diffusion constants. The results are given in Table 1. They show that A is a roughly spherical molecule of molecular weight 36,000. The molecular weight of B remains uncertain because the sample seems to be impure. This result is being investigated further.

To scientists who know about such things as sedimentation and diffusion constants, this writing is clear and direct. However, after two years in graduate school, students often write something like this:

In order to evaluate the possible significance of certain molecular parameters at the subcellular level, and to shed light on the conceivable role of structural configuration in spatial relationship of intracellular macromolecules, an integrated approach (see Table 1) to the problem of cell diffusivity has been revised and developed. The results, which are in a preliminary stage, are discussed in some detail because of their possible implementation in mechanisms of diffusivity in a wider sphere.

Prospective editors and reporters need not become graduate students to write so pompously. The more expert one becomes about a subject, the greater the danger.

Cliches

A cliche is more than a phrase that has been used often over many years. *Beautiful woman* and *handsome man* have been written billions of times by millions of writers, but those words in that order are as useful now as they were the first time they were written. The same is true of most phrases; they merely give information and can be used endlessly.

A cliche is a phrase that calls attention to itself. Because it was expressive

A cliche is a phrase that calls attention to itself.

when used the first time, it was borrowed again and again by other writers and finally became exhausted. How wonderful it must have been to be the first to write *light as a feather, heavy as lead* or *hot as the hinges of hell.*

How can editors turn a literary junkyard into something creative? First, they should consider the antiquity of borrowed phrases. One who is tempted to write "The proof of the pudding is in the eating" should know that its first recorded use was by Joseph Addison in 1714.

The writer who uses "Don't look a gift horse in the mouth" should know that Saint Jerome wrote: "Do not, as the common proverb has it, scrutinize the teeth of a gift horse." Note that Saint Jerome considered this a common proverb when he wrote it in A.D. 400.

As for "One man's food is another man's poison," Lucretius wrote in 45 B.C.: "What to one man is food, to another is rank poison."

The writer who wants to lure readers must shun cliches. And one who hopes to write unforgettably will try to create phrases that live beyond the writer. Editors must help writers move beyond cliches, but doing so calls for the most demanding kind of work: mental effort.

Vague modifiers

David Niven, award-winning actor, heard his long-time friend, producer Garson Kanin, refer to himself as middle-aged. When asked his age, Kanin said he was 57. Niven responded, "And you call that middle-aged? How many people do you know who are 114?"

Because writers often don't know exact figures, they use general words like *few, several* and *many* in their sentences. Unfortunately, vague words lead to vague meanings, which hinder readers' understanding of the writer's real intentions.

When 65 college students read the statements in the left column below and then responded to the questions in the middle column, their answers covered a wide range, as shown in the column on the right:

"The senator was elected by an overwhelming majority."	What percentage did he receive?	Lowest: 54 percent Highest: 75 percent
"My 17-year-old son is of average height."	How tall is he?	Shortest: 5 feet 8 inches Tallest: 6 feet 1 inch
"Uncle Ned is a moderate smoker."	How many cigarettes does he smoke a day?	Least: half a pack Most: one and a half packs
"Jane isn't a 'brain,' but she makes good grades."	What is her scholastic average in percentage terms?	Lowest: 75 percent Highest: 90 percent
"Although my friend isn't wealthy, he makes a comfortable living."	How much does he make a year?	Least: $8,000 a year Most: $30,000 a year
"I read several books last summer."	How many books did I read?	Least: 2 Most: 13
"Mrs. Jensen is middle-aged."	How old is she?	Youngest: 35 Oldest: 55

Obviously, such words as *average, moderate* and *several* are vague and open to interpretation. The respondents in this study were college students and

The writer who wants to lure readers must shun cliches.

were all about the same age. Imagine the scattershot responses that would come from a cross-section of the population.

Controlling tone

Occasionally the copy editor will receive instructions to "tone down" a story, "clean it up" or "brighten it." Stories that need to be toned down have been worded too strongly. Toning down often means eliminating adjectives (using *murder* rather than *brutal murder*), exchanging strong verbs for milder ones (using *said* rather than *admitted*) and striking out words that characterize or describe in a distasteful manner (deleting such stereotypical adjectives as *swarthy, mellow* and *spry*).

Stories that need to be cleaned up have a misleading perspective. They are usually crime or similar stories with details that are too explicit.

Stories that need brightening up can be fixed by judiciously using adjectives or transferring a phrase or sentence from the detail of the story to the lead. The goal is to transform a dull story into an interesting one.

Accuracy in numbers

Copy editors must check the arithmetic on stories containing numbers, so a calculator is another copy editing tool that should be handy. Some computer systems include calculators.

Do the numbers in the story add up to the total given by the reporter? If the story reports that five people received awards, editors should count the names listed. If only four names are listed or if six are listed, the point should be clarified.

Make numbers easy for readers to understand. For example, a city budget in the millions of dollars means little to readers. The story should provide a breakdown by budgetary categories and report percentages allocated for major items. In reporting sources of revenue for the budget, show how these numbers affect individual residents: How much are property taxes increasing? What is the percentage of increase? Are automobile registration fees increasing? If so, how much?

Stories often need to report raw numbers, but those numbers will be more easily understood if the percentage of increase or decrease is also reported. Percentages are derived this way:

$$\% \text{ increase or decrease} = \frac{\text{New figure} - \text{Original figure}}{\text{Original figure}}$$

For example, if enrollment in the school district was 30,200 students last year and 33,100 students this year, enrollment has increased 9.6 percent:

$$\frac{33,100 - 30,200}{30,200} = \frac{2,900}{30,200} = .0960 = 9.6\%$$

Another example: If the number of burglaries decreased this year from 3,196 to 3,005, the percentage of decline is 5.97 (which may be rounded off to 6 percent):

$$\frac{3,005 - 3,196}{3,196} = \frac{-191}{3,196} = -.0597 = -5.97\%$$

Percent and *percentage points* do not mean the same thing. If interest rates increase from 10 percent to 12 percent, they have increased 2 percentage points, but it is an increase of 20 percent:

$$\frac{12 - 10}{10} = \frac{2}{10} = 20\%$$

Make numbers easy for readers to understand.

Copy editors should be especially alert in handling stories that include ages, box scores, infographics, results of opinion polls and information about taxes.

- *Ages.* Use common sense in editing stories that include a person's date of birth, dates of accomplishments and ages. An alert copy editor should spot the inconsistencies, for example, in an obituary published in 1992 that reports the age of the deceased as 60 if the birthdate is listed as 1922 or that reports this person graduated from a university in 1932. Was he 70 when he died, or was he born in 1932? Did he graduate from the university at age 10, or is the graduation date a typographical error?
- *Box scores.* Add the number of points scored by each player to be sure that the totals for each team equal the final score.
- *Informational graphics.* Check the numbers. Do they add to the total reported in the graphic? Check that the percentages add to 100. If they don't, an explanation should be included in the graphic.
- *Opinion polls.* A story about a public opinion poll should include the margin of error and an explanation of what it means and how it applies to the results being reported. The margin of error refers to the difference between the results if the entire group (for example, all students at your university or all voters in the country) had been questioned rather than a sample of the group. As long as the sample is carefully and randomly selected to be representative of the population as a whole, a survey administered to several hundred people can yield results that accurately reflect the opinion of the entire population of the United States within 3 percent, plus or minus. A margin of error of plus or minus 3 percent means that, if the entire population had been surveyed, the results could have been as much as 3 percentage points higher or lower. Thus, a 3 percent margin of error for a poll showing Jones leading Smith 53 percent to 47 percent means that the election is too close to predict the outcome, because 53 minus 3 is 50 percent and 47 plus 3 is 50 percent. Copy editors should make sure that reporters have included the margin of error in all stories about public opinion polls.
- *Property taxes.* Property taxes are expressed as mill levies. A mill is 0.1 cent (1/10¢), and the mill levy for a community is generally expressed as the number of cents or dollars for each $100 in assessed valuation. Stories about property taxes should include an example of how much tax will be levied on a representative home in the community. For example, if the mill levy is 1.50, property owners will pay 1.5 cents tax for each $1 of assessed value or $1.50 for each $100 of assessed value or $15 for each $1,000. For a home assessed at $50,000 (note this is assessed value, not market value), the tax would be $750 ($15 × 50). If several governmental units within the community have taxing power, a story about the city tax rate should not mislead readers into thinking that this will be their total property tax bill. The story should include the rates that other governmental units have levied or note that the budget is not complete and thus the mill levy has not been determined.

Frequently misused words

Appendix B lists words that often are misused in both written and spoken English. A few are homonyms that are unlikely to be confused except by people uneducated in the language. Others are word substitutions that literate people commonly but erroneously make. A few of these words have fallen into common misusage to the extent that even the experts debate the merits of

A story about a public opinion poll should include the margin of error and an explanation of what it means.

maintaining the original distinctions. To professional writers and editors who want to say exactly and concisely what they mean, the distinctions are important.

Exercises 3 through 8 at the end of this chapter test your knowledge of the frequently misused words in Appendix B.

Shaping sentences

Good reporters review their own work and delete repetitious words and phrases, but it is the copy editor who reads the stories carefully, deflating language and breaking long, difficult-to-comprehend sentences into two or more sentences. At the same time, the copy editor must preserve the writer's voice.

Such revising requires balance and taste, and it depends on purpose and audience. Is the writer trying to inform readers who differ in knowledge and interest? If the writer's main purpose is to transfer facts, as in most news stories, sentences should be short. Is the writer trying to explain and inform? With explanation, the sentences may be longer. The editing task is more complicated if the writer is trying to create a reading experience.

The following experience illustrates how taste, purpose and individuality create variety in writing: During the first meeting of a composition class, the teacher emphasized the need for direct, concise writing. An hour later, a student attended the first meeting of her American literature class and was assigned to read some of the works of Thomas Wolfe and William Faulkner. That evening, the student began to read Faulkner and was understandably confused. If direct, concise writing is the ideal, she thought, why didn't William Faulkner practice it? How could one teacher applaud concise writing and another applaud Faulkner?

The contradiction might be explained by saying that people's preferences differ. In addition, complex phrasings and structures fit some kinds of writing better than others. Writing that appeals to the emotions can sometimes be best expressed by the rich, the complex, the unusual. Writing that appeals primarily to reason is best expressed by simplicity.

Conciseness and complexity

The work of some of our most noted writers might be even better if it were simpler. For example, when Thomas Wolfe originally submitted manuscripts to his publisher, some passages were dense thickets of words. Only laborious editing by Maxwell Perkins, who worked for Wolfe's publisher, made them comprehensible.

Not all writers should imitate Ernest Hemingway, George Orwell and E. B. White, who wrote far more simply. Wolfe often affected the emotions of his readers with long, cadenced sentences whose roll and rhythm were almost as important as their substance. This sentence from *Look Homeward Angel* indicates the power and complexity of Wolfe's prose:

He knew the inchoate sharp excitement of hot dandelions in young spring grass at noon; the smell of cellars, cobwebs, and built-on secret earth; in July, of watermelons bedded in sweet hay inside a farmer's covered wagon; of cantaloupe and crated peaches; and the scent of orange rind, bittersweet, before a fire of coals.

The rhythm is almost as important as the sense of the words. Likewise, the length and complexity of some of Faulkner's sentences are themselves meaningful: the form is an echo of the sense. But Faulkner and Wolfe achieved a high level of artistry, and beginners who try to reach it usually fail.

Every writer should master simple expression. Not only should it be the

---

Every writer should master simple expression.

beginning strategy, but many of the greatest writers have made it the end as well. Leo Tolstoy is a prime example. His novel *War and Peace* has a complex structure, with many plots, subplots and characters, but the prose is simple.

Tolstoy's experience suggests yet another reason to work for simplicity. Toward the end of his life, Tolstoy became obsessed with the need to write for the peasants of Russia in the simple language they understood. The lesson is to remember the audience. Communicating complex ideas and paradoxical facts simply enough for any literate person to understand enables writers to address the largest possible audience.

Length and conciseness

Conciseness means using as few words as possible to achieve the intended meaning or effect. It does not mean reducing graceful expressions to choppy sentences.

Grace should be sacrificed, however, if the extra words serve no purpose, as in the following sentence: "Throwing modesty aside, he claims to be the world's greatest musician." The editor deleted the first three words, reasoning that the rest of the sentence made it clear that the man threw modesty aside. The student writer argued that, because the sentences immediately before and after the edited sentence were both short and were both in subject–verb–direct object order, the deletion destroyed the balance of the passage. To his credit, the student had learned the value of variation but not that sentences must be balanced with substance, not ballast. Reporters and editors should seek variety by using sentences structured differently, not sentences carrying dead words.

Sometimes one can condense too much. Consider this sentence: "He is heterozygous for curly hair." Not all readers will understand without more explanation: "He has received a gene for curly hair from one parent and a gene for straight hair from the other." The 20-word sentence is better because most readers don't know the meaning of *heterozygous*.

Does it make any difference to readers that in a 1,000-word story an editor has left in 75 words that serve no purpose? Yes. Those wasted words, especially when multiplied in every story, occupy space that could be devoted to other stories or pictures, perhaps attracting more readers. In addition, superfluous words and phrases slow reading and comprehension. Here's an example: "The past experiences of the future prospects for employment in the city of Indianapolis were brought out in interviews that were conducted throughout the entire day of June 12 in the year of 1992." The sentence could be rewritten as follows: "Job seekers in Indianapolis described their experiences during interviews June 12, 1992."

It may be more difficult to delete modifiers. The copy editor must decide whether a modifier helps emphasize, color or round out meaning. If it does not, it is expendable. In this sentence, a writer tries to describe how a rich man protected the wealth of his company: "An elaborate and payrolled watchdog system was set to safeguard his interests should any ambitiously piratical executive attempt a personal seduction of organizational assets." The sentence is bad because the reader must work to determine its meaning. The most obvious flaw is that the sentence is drunk with adjectives. The force of each is reduced because readers must give their attention first to one adjective, then to another. The modifiers drown the nouns and verbs. When editing sentences that are loaded with modifiers, search for more precise and meaningful modifiers or cut them.

If a sentence causes you to stumble, even slightly, it probably will make

Superfluous words and phrases slow reading and comprehension.

readers stumble as well. Any sentence that you must read more than once for understanding probably will not be clear to readers. Any sentence that begins *in other words, that is* or *that is to say* probably follows a sentence that you should rewrite.

Alert copy editors will spot the most frequently used redundancies. Here is a list published by the Minnesota Newspaper Association:

absolutely necessary	important essentials
advance planning	necessary requirements
ask the question	open up
assemble together	other alternative
at a later day	patently obvious
attached hereto	plain and simple
at the present time	postpone until later
canceled out	reasonable and fair
carbon copy	redo again
city of Chicago	refer back
close proximity	right and proper
consensus of opinion	rise up
continue on	rules and regulations
each and every	send in
enclosed you will find	small in size
fall down	still remain
first and foremost	temporarily suspended
friend of mine	totally unnecessary
gathered together	true facts
honest truth	various and sundry

Shaping paragraphs

Editors and editing instructors advise reporters to keep paragraphs short—one or two sentences—because newspaper style must be suited to the format of small print and narrow columns. A single sentence can fill several lines in a newspaper column. Lengthy, multisentence paragraphs turn the page into an uninviting blur of gray.

The concept of the paragraph has changed somewhat in recent years. More than 50 years ago, Henry W. Fowler wrote *Modern English Usage,* which is considered by many writers and teachers of writing to be the best book of its kind. "The purpose of a paragraph is to give the readers a rest," Fowler wrote. The kind of rest provided by the end of a paragraph does not slow the pace of reading but quickens it. Instead of feeling as though a paragraph will never end, readers become aware of frequent intervals and move swiftly toward them—or think they do.

Before publication of Fowler's book, and among some teachers and writers even today, the paragraph was conceived as a well-defined structure. A topic sentence set the direction and the boundaries, followed by sentences that developed it so that the whole paragraph was a small essay, a well-defined part of the entire piece. The concept has not disappeared, but it is no longer so widely used, especially for newspapers.

Transitions

A well-written story with good transitions flows smoothly from sentence to sentence and from paragraph to paragraph, in a logical fashion. The parts of the story stick together. Some stories unfold in a natural order. They hold together without the glue of the traditional transitional devices that are necessary for most event-centered stories written in inverted-pyramid fashion.

In some stories readers are taken on a journey, and the trip itself gives the story continuity. Others unfold according to time, and readers are moved through the story as one event follows another. Transition also seems to come naturally in stories that pose a problem and take readers along in search of the solution.

All of these transitional techniques—chronology, journey, problem solving—move readers along in this story by Don Williams, a staff writer for the Knoxville, Tenn., News-Sentinel. The story, published on the 20th anniversary of the beginning of the first manned space flight to the moon, develops a local angle on that momentous event.

```
Joan Trolinger waits for a rocket engine to speak
thunder and roll a brand new cloud into the sky.
    Few rocket tests are conducted here at the
Redstone Arsenal, where Wernher Von Braun brought
a ragtag band of scientists and a few left-over
German V-2 rockets after World War II and launched
America toward the stars.
    Ever since Trolinger was a child she wanted to
be part of that movement into space, a movement
rife with glamor, but also with tedium and terror,
as she would discover.
    Growing up in Morristown, the daughter of Jim
and Sarah Gose, she was 6 years old when she
watched Neil Armstrong take his small step/giant
leap onto the moon.
    Later she made spacesuits for her dolls and
suspended rocket models from her ceiling. Children
were doing much the same thing throughout America.
    These days, at 26, Trolinger drives daily past
real rockets on display in Huntsville—rockets
named for gods—Jupiter, Atlas, Titan, Saturn.
    Trolinger still has a model of the Starship
Enterprise hanging from her ceiling, but her
interest in space has matured.
```

The story continues, describing Trolinger's path to becoming a rocket engineer and working in the space program on the specific problem assigned to her: the space shuttle rocket nozzle, composed of hundreds of tubes, side by side. Icy cold liquid hydrogen is pumped through the nozzle so it can withstand the inferno it is built to control.

In addition to using chronology, time and problem solving to move a story along, a writer can achieve continuity by

- Repeating a key word of the preceding paragraph
- Using a synonym to refer to a key word in the preceding paragraph
- Referring to a fact or idea in the preceding paragraph
- Elaborating details in logical sequence
- Using words and phrases as transitional devices

The first several paragraphs of this news story by Eric Vreeland of the Knoxville News-Sentinel staff illustrate the first three methods of achieving transition:

```
The Knoxville Food Policy Council last week waded
into the fray over where to locate a farmers'
market. The council lobbied Gov. Ned McWherter to
pick Knox County over Sevierville or White Pine.
```

In some stories readers are taken on a journey, and the trip itself gives the story continuity.

However, the <u>council</u> added a new wrinkle—advocating that, regardless of where the main <u>market</u> is built, <u>inner-city</u> Knoxville should be developed as a retail satellite <u>market</u>.

The idea is that poor <u>inner-city</u> residents suffer by not having adequate food outlets near them. Since 1979, eight super<u>markets</u> and about 30 independent grocers have closed in the <u>inner city</u>, says Bill <u>Powell</u>, a staff member with the <u>council</u>.

<u>Powell</u> is a Mechanicsville resident and die-hard historical preservationist. He thinks he has the perfect candidate in mind for housing that retail <u>market</u>: the Western Avenue Market.

The technique of elaborating details in logical sequence was also evident as the reporter described the details of Powell's proposal for refurbishing and promoting the old market.

Writers can use a variety of words and phrases as transitional devices:

- To show time: *then, meanwhile, shortly, thereafter, now, later, soon, all this time, formerly, previously, at last, finally*
- To cite examples: *for instance, thus, for example, to illustrate, an illustration*
- To indicate emphasis: *indeed, moreover, in particular, especially, in addition to, similarly, furthermore*
- To show change of viewpoint: *however, but, nevertheless, of course, also, seriously, in another way, in a lighter view, in addition, in general, on the other hand*

Quotations

Careless handling of attribution in quotations can result in cluttered, ambiguous and awkward sentences.

One guideline is to grammatically join a direct quotation to the speaker. Don't make the reader guess about the source of the quotation:

<u>Wrong:</u> Jones praised the workers. "You have exceeded our expectations, and I plan to give everyone a party."

<u>Right:</u> "You have exceeded our expectations, and I plan to give everyone a party," Jones said.

Attribution is important, but it can be overdone. A continuous quotation needs only one attribution within the same paragraph:

<u>Wrong:</u> "Our quota was 10,000 units," Jones said. "This month the company produced 50,000 widgets," he continued. "I plan to give everyone a party," he added.

<u>Right:</u> "Our quota was 10,000 units," Jones said. "This month the company produced 50,000 widgets. I plan to give everyone a party."

When two or more sentences of direct quotation run continuously in a paragraph, the speaker should be identified in the first sentence. Don't make the reader wonder who is talking. In the preceding example, the attribution is placed after the first sentence instead of at the end of the three-sentence paragraph.

Don't make the reader guess about the source of the quotation.

What the speaker said is generally more interesting and important than who said it, so put the quotation first, followed by the attribution:

> Wrong: Jones said, "I plan to give everyone a party. Our quota was 10,000 units. This month the company produced 50,000 widgets."

> Right: "I plan to give everyone a party," Jones said. "Our quota was 10,000 units. This month the company produced 50,000 widgets."

This rule cannot be followed if a second speaker is quoted, because readers will be misled into thinking that the original speaker is continuing:

> Wrong: "I plan to give everyone a party," Jones said. "Our quota was 10,000 units. This month the company produced 50,000 widgets."
>
> "I wish the company would give everyone a pay increase instead of a party," Joe Smith, president of the union, said.

> Right: "I plan to give everyone a bonus," Jones said. "Our quota was 10,000 units. This month the company produced 50,000 widgets."
>
> Joe Smith, president of the union, said, "I wish the company would give everyone a pay increase instead of a party."

Start a new paragraph when a different speaker is quoted, as in the previous example. Direct quotations from two different speakers should not be included in the same paragraph, even if the quotations are extremely brief.

Do not bury the direct quotation within the paragraph; start the paragraph with the direct quotation. Inexperienced reporters sometimes write in "stutter" quotes; that is, they paraphrase what the speaker said and then use a direct quotation that says the same thing:

> Wrong: Jones said that the workers exceeded their quota this month and had earned a party. "Our quota was 10,000 units," Jones said. "This month the company produced 50,000 widgets. I plan to give everyone a party."

> Right: "I plan to give everyone a party," Jones said. "Our quota was 10,000 units. This month the company produced 50,000 widgets."

Rarely is it necessary to tell the reader what question was asked. The question generally is obvious from the phrasing of the answer in either a direct or an indirect quotation:

> Wrong: When asked about the company's production this month and whether workers would be rewarded, Jones said, "I plan to give everyone a party. Our quota was 10,000 units. This month the company produced 50,000 widgets."

Just give the quotation.

In general, avoid fragmentary quotes. If a speaker's words are clear and concise, favor the full quotation. If cumbersome language can be paraphrased fairly, use an indirect construction, reserving direct quotations for sensitive or controversial passages that must be identified specifically as coming from the speaker. Unless a particular word or phrase has special

Do not bury the direct quotation within the paragraph.

significance or is used in an unusual or colorful sense, do not enclose it in quotation marks as a partial quotation:

Weak use of partial quotes: To conserve energy, Americans began "turning off" lights and "turning down" thermostats, the official said.

Good use of partial quotes: Referring to his quick pitching style, the major leaguer said he pitched "like my hair is on fire."

Punctuate direct quotations correctly. Refer to The Associated Press stylebook, a grammar handbook or Appendix A for rules on punctuating direct quotations.

Should a reporter or editor correct grammatical errors in direct quotations? Most newspapers have the policy of making such corrections, unless, of course, the source's speech patterns are important to the story. The AP stylebook notes that quotations should be corrected to avoid the errors in word usage that often occur unnoticed in speech but are embarrassing in print. Do not routinely use abnormal spellings, such as *gonna,* in attempts to convey regional dialects or mispronunciations. Such spellings are appropriate, however, when they are relevant or help to convey a desired effect in a feature.

Space limitations usually preclude extensive use of direct quotations from an interview or speech. However, reporters should paraphrase and use sufficient background information to preserve the context of direct quotations, especially startling remarks. It isn't always possible for editors to detect out-of-context quotations that distort the speaker's meaning, but editors should question reporters about context when especially surprising or strong quotations are used. In addition, the manner of delivery sometimes is part of the context. Reporting a smile or a deprecatory gesture may be as important as conveying the words themselves.

Copy editors should pay careful attention to verbs of attribution. *Said* is the most common verb of attribution and usually the most appropriate. But reporters, in their reluctance to repeat *said,* often resort to other verbs of attribution. Note that terms such as *pointed out, noted* and *claimed* are not synonymous with *said* and convey editorial opinion. *Stated* and *declared* are too stilted for informal speech.

Pointed out and *noted* should be reserved for attribution when the speaker said something that is a fact: " 'New York City is the largest city in the United States,' she *noted.*" It would be incorrect to use *pointed out* or *noted* as the verb of attribution if the speaker said "New York City is the best city in the United States," because that statement is arguable, not generally accepted as fact. *Claimed* as a verb of attribution connotes doubt of the speaker's credibility. Reserve *claimed* for an assertion of legal rights by the speaker: " 'Roger is innocent of the crime,' he *claimed.*" Or "He claimed that the property belonged to him."

Verbs that describe the speaker's tone or mood more specifically than *said* may be used: " 'The house is on fire,' he *yelled.*" " 'I wouldn't do that for all the money in the world,' she *snapped.*" " 'I love you,' she *whispered.*" But use such verbs accurately. A copy editor should question a reporter who has someone whispering that the house is on fire or hissing a greeting or groaning a profession of love.

Remember, reporters can report what sources said, not what they thought or believed or felt. Reporters aren't mind readers. They know only what the source said or did:

Copy editors should pay careful attention to verbs of attribution.

<u>Wrong:</u> `The convicted murderer felt remorse.`

<u>Right:</u> `The convicted murderer said he felt`
`remorse.`

Another way to handle this idea would be to describe the convicted murderer's actions or comments that would indicate a feeling of remorse.

Altering story length

The desire among editors and readers for economy of language has produced some tight, fast-paced writing in today's newspapers. The most notable example is USA Today, a national newspaper whose use of short stories and high-impact graphics has brought changes in the ways newspapers are edited. The copy editor often finds it necessary to reduce a story because of excess verbiage or space limitations. An order to cut 2 or 3 inches from a 10-inch story is not uncommon on today's copy desks.

Estimating story length

Before copy editors begin cutting a story to fit a desired length for layout purposes, they must first estimate its present length. In most modern newsrooms, VDTs, or editing terminals, are programmed to provide story length with a tap on the right key on the keyboard. Programs vary from newspaper to newspaper because the width of columns varies. Copy is measured in column inches.

Those whose electronic editing systems do not display story length can determine story length relatively easily. The copy editor measures at random several inch-long samples from stories that have already been printed in the newspaper, then counts the number of words in each sample. Averaging these word counts gives a fairly accurate idea of the number of words in an inch of body copy.

Until a copy editor becomes accustomed to judging the number of words in a typewritten or computer-generated line, he or she should count the number of words in the first several lines to establish the average number of words per line for each story. To arrive at a close estimate of the length of a story, in column inches, the editor need only divide the estimated total number of words in a story by the estimated number of words in an inch of body copy.

Editing with precision

The reduction of story length generally falls within three broad categories: trimming, a tightening of the story; "boiling," a more drastic process of paring most of the sentences and sacrificing minor facts; and cutting, which eliminates all but the most important facts. Copy editors should be careful when reducing any story's length to ensure that elimination of facts or descriptions does not leave readers with a false or misleading impression.

Trimming. A mark of good writing is economy of language. This maxim is most eloquently stated in *Elements of Style* by William Strunk and E. B. White:

Vigorous writing is concise. A sentence should contain no unnecessary words, a paragraph no unnecessary sentences, for the same reason that a drawing should contain no unnecessary parts. This requires not that a writer make all his sentences short, or that he avoid all detail and treat his subject only in outline, but that every word tell.

The duty of the copy editor is to delete all words and phrases that do not

𝔄 *mark of good writing is economy of language.*

contribute to the clarity and conciseness of the news story. A carelessly written story must be pulled together to be compact and readable. By deleting non-essentials, the copy editor artfully turns an overwritten piece into a story with impact.

Strong writing depends on nouns and verbs. Deleting unnecessary adjectives and avoiding redundancies can help strengthen the story's message.

Boiling. In boiling a story with more than one angle, copy editors may be forced to remove one or more angles completely and to concentrate on developing the remaining angles fully. When a story presents two sides of an issue, however, both sides must be represented fairly.

When boiling a story already set in type, copy editors should remember that the paring of paragraphs is more economical mechanically than the paring of sentences or words. And deleting an entire sentence causes fewer complications in the production process than deleting a word here and there.

Cutting. Most of the time, stories are cut because they need to fit a specified space, usually determined by a layout editor. Because surveys have shown that newspaper readers prefer short news stories and because the space devoted to news each day is limited, today's copy editors are often asked to cut a few long stories to accommodate more short ones.

When cutting a story, the copy editor should try to preserve the essential facts and enough detail to answer the reader's pressing questions. The copy editor should never assume that a story can be chopped off anywhere; cutting a story requires a great deal of skill. The broad outline of the story should be preserved when the story is not written in the routine inverted-pyramid style. The flavor or tone of the story should be maintained.

After the copy editor completes the cuts, he or she should read the new version with care, making certain transitions are clear and the copy flows past the cuts. For routine stories written in the inverted-pyramid style, chopping the story from the bottom up is usually the easiest and quickest way to get the desired length. However, bad editing can result. The copy editor must make sure no newspaper story ends with a line like this: "In other action, the council decided . . . ."

Copy editors must use common sense, as well as good judgment, in cutting stories for publication.

Paring of paragraphs is more economical mechanically than the paring of sentences or words.

AN EDITOR AT WORK
by Michael Molyneux

People often ask me what we copy editors really do. I tell them that we are the ones at the newspaper who put the stories into publishable shape. We're not proofreaders, fact checkers or rewrite people, but we are a bit of each.

The copy editor does the final editing of a story, which is assigned by the head of the desk, known as the slot editor. The copy editor also writes the headline and sends it and the story back to the slot. The slot scrutinizes the story and makes further changes or asks the copy editor to make them. The slot also ponders the headline and says yea, says nay or tries to write a better one.

Monday through Friday, from about 11 a.m. to 7 p.m., I am the slot editor on the Living/Style desk at The New York Times. Our desk, with six copy editors, handles all the stories each week for a fashion page, a consumer page, the Living section, the Home section and a Sunday package that includes dozens of weddings and engagements. Sitting next to me is the production editor, who works with the art directors to create the fancy arrangements of type that newspapers are doing more and more.

Sometimes I feel like the needle's eye through which stories, some as ungainly as camels, pass. Other times, I feel like a soccer goalie who is peppered with shots, making great saves on some and letting others go by.

Like New York City, the Times is large, fast-paced and competitive. It is filled with incredibly talented people. Whatever the subject, there's probably an expert in the building. Copy editors, however, tend to be generalists. Some play a mean game of "Trivial Pursuit."

The Times has separate desks for editing foreign, national, metropolitan, business, sports, science, culture and living/style news. Some editors develop a specialty and stay on a desk for years; the Times also believes good editors can be shifted to unfamiliar areas.

At the Times, each story is read first by a "backfield" editor who does the preliminary work, making sure, for instance, that the lead paragraph is in line with what the reporter promised the story would be. Most stories at the Times are read by several other editors, all of whom can funnel their questions through the copy desk.

These are some of the things that copy editors at the Times do:

1. *Help the reader.* We make the stories precise and concise. We often trim them to fit a limited space. We make them as readable as possible and typographically attractive. We clarify the ambiguous and make sure the ideas follow coherently. We fix grammar, spelling and punctuation. We're supposed to know the difference between *sensuous* and *sensual* and *Episcopal* and *Episcopalian*. We make sure there is enough background for a reader who is new to the story. Any reasonable question should be answered.

The Times' tradition of strong editing adds to our authority in dealing with the writers. We have questions for them on nearly every piece. Most full-time reporters at the Times are resigned to being edited heavily, although some of the free-lancers aren't.

2. *Uphold standards of completeness, accuracy and fairness.* These are strong traditions at the Times. We watch for libel and for imbalance of any kind. Any pejorative statements should have a response from the subject. A copy editor will occasionally challenge, successfully, a story's being in the paper at all.

MICHAEL MOLYNEUX

In 1977 Molyneux, then a graduate student, asked his journalism professor, "Do writers make a lot of money?"

The response he got was, "Well, even Hemingway had to catch his own fish."

Although Molyneux took the professor's words to heart, he decided that a career in journalism was a way for him to make his mark on society.

Molyneux, who now lives in Stamford, Conn., graduated from Princeton University in 1976 with a degree in history and American studies. After earning a master's degree in journalism, he was a reporter for a year and then spent four years on the editing desks of several small newspapers before landing a job as a copy editor on The New York Times metropolitan desk in 1982. The talented journalist remained there until 1988, when he became slot editor, or copy chief, of the Times' Living/Style section. He shifted to the *Times Magazine* as its chief copy editor in late 1989.

Explaining the role of a copy chief, Molyneux says, "A slot editor has some of the tasks of any low-level manager: making up schedules, writing memos, going to meetings. The slot also hears complaints from all sides and mediates some of them.

"The slot editor feels some responsibility for everything about how the section is presented. That is particularly true when editing corrections occur, which is another part of my job," Molyneux says.

Although much of the reading public overlooks the work of Molyneux and his fellow copy editors, reporters and writers rely on their abilities. Reporters have seen how editors can create new angles, add spice to a story or save the paper from printing incorrect information. Copy editors play as important a role in putting together the final product, if not a more important one, as anyone else associated with the paper.

"It's nice to look over a section of the paper and see your mark, however anonymous, on each story," Molyneux says. "It's an imprint, I hope, of grace."

Sexism has become more and more of a concern: no more home computer stories with Dad making up the Little League roster and Mom storing recipes.

We can't check every fact, but copy editors develop a sixth sense about what might be wrong. We always recalculate any arithmetic and check quotations, say, from the Bible or Shakespeare.

A Times reporter once told me, "This is not an exact science, you know." He was right, but we come as close as we can.

3. *Enforce style rules.* The Times has stylistic concerns that have been forgotten by most American newspapers, like courtesy titles. Does he prefer Mr. or Dr.? Does she prefer Miss or Ms.? The reporter has to find out, and the copy editor has to make sure it's right.

The Times has very precise rules about language. For instance, *fund-raiser* is used for people, not for events. *Massive* is reserved for things that literally have a great mass, like a uranium nucleus.

The paper has its own stylebook (that's one word, not two), which is our bible, backed up by other standard reference works and what I call "the official dictionary of The New York Times," Webster's New World dictionary. It's supplemented by frequent memos, daily "post mortems" and periodic issues of *Winners & Sinners,* the Times' own "bulletin of second guessing." Winners' names are mentioned; copy editors are usually commended for a good headline. Sinners are unidentified, mercifully.

With the Times' high value on tradition, precedent means a lot. We check what we've done in previous stories, either from our morgue or, through the miracle of electronic data retrieval, on our computer screens. It sometimes seems like Talmudic scholarship to find the rule that applies to the case at hand and to decide when a rule is prudently to be broken.

4. *Respect the writer's work.* Copy editors often have to rewrite sentences or insert artfully written paragraphs of background culled from out-clips. We also might suggest a solution when a reporter says, as one did to me, "This is too complicated for words." The job is not, however, to rewrite a story as we would have written it. In columns, which we run more than ever, we are particularly sensitive to the writer's style.

The story may have the writer's name on top, but the copy editor assumes some responsibility for each word in it. The word may not be the best one, but it shouldn't be a wrong one.

At the Times, we try to avoid the pretentious and the trite. We sometimes walk a fine line between being too ponderous and too breezy.

5. *Write right, sharp headlines.* For the copy editor, the question of tone comes up most acutely with headlines. We can't also use some of those short, punchy words like *tot* or *prez* that some papers do. Creative wordplay is desirable, as in the headline about Dan Quayle when he was selected as candidate for vice president: "Baby Boomer With the Right Credentials." (Must check *baby boomer* though. Do we hyphenate it? No.) But obvious puns like "Tire Industry Bounces Back" wouldn't make it.

There are other strict headline rules. On hard-news desks, the heads must fit precisely, without a lot of white space at the end of the line. And in most of our heads, we can't break a phrase from one line to the next, as in "Man Bites Dog in / Central Park."

There's concern about who is a "headline name." The mayor's name might be recognizable in a headline, but the budget director's might not be. And as our readership becomes more regional and national, we can't sound too parochial, in heads or stories.

6. *Apply quality control.* Copy editors coordinate many parts of a product that is made anew every day, with the blueprint drawn up as it goes along. The copy editors ensure that stories, headlines, captions, summaries, maps, graphics, index lines and floating quotations all form a harmonious package. As newspapers display information in more varied and graphically attractive ways, copy editors are becoming more and more involved with the production side. Computer literacy is becoming more important, especially with the advent of pagination, which arranges all the stories and headlines on an editor's computer screen.

7. *Work on deadline.* Steps 1 through 6 are performed with one eye on the clock.

Reporters have deadlines, and backfield editors have deadlines, but copy editors' deadlines are particularly pressing. Production schedules are the reason. The Times' metro desk, where I worked for five years, handles a lot of breaking news, and most of the copy editing is done between 5 p.m. and 9 p.m., when the paper locks up. Copy editors work in gears. There's one way to edit a story at 5 p.m., another way to edit at 8 p.m. And the 8 p.m. stories are often the most sensitive, the ones that have been through the hands of the editors.

Steps 1 through 7 apply not only to the copy editors but also to the slot editor, sometimes more intensely. Deadlines are an example.

The slot editor has much of the responsibility for "closing" the paper on time, making sure that the composing room can put every page together by deadlines. If the last page isn't pasted up by 9 p.m., the whole New York Times is delayed. Trucks and airplanes may sit idled.

In the Living/Style section, most stories are sent to the desk well in advance, and we are expected to close early. If we don't do that by 6 p.m., everyone else's production schedule is delayed. It's a domino effect.

A metro copy editor's day might go from 4 p.m. until 11 p.m., with a chance to fix things for the second edition, which closes at 11:30. Some editors must stay until the newsroom shuts down, at 2:45 a.m. Living/Style copy editors might work from noon to 7 p.m. Pages can be adjusted for the late editions, but we're expected to pretty much get it right the first time.

Suggestions for additional reading

Berner, R. Thomas. *Language Skills for Journalists,* 2nd ed. Boston: Houghton Mifflin, 1984.

Bernstein, Theodore M. *Dos, Don'ts and Maybes of English Usage.* New York: New York Times Books, 1977.

Bernstein, Theodore M. *Watch Your Language.* New York: Atheneum, 1965.

Brooks, Brian S., and James L. Pinson. *Working With Words: A Concise Handbook for Media Writers and Editors.* New York: St. Martin's Press, 1989.

1. Supply the missing numbers in this exercise. Use the style primer in Appendix A to express your answers unless your instructor directs you to use a different style guide.

a. The number of faculty members increased from 752 in 1991 to 767 in 1992, an increase of _____ percent.

b. The number of students receiving scholarships was 1,520 last year, as compared with 1,432 this year, a decrease of _____ percent.

c. During his career, the coach has had a record of 405 wins and 110 loses, a win-loss ratio of _____ to _____.

d. The United Way campaign has raised $136,000, _____ [fraction] of its goal of $185,000.

e. The number of companies contributing to the United Way campaign increased _____ percent, from 67 last year to 82 this year.

f. He deposited $3,260. At an annual interest rate of 6.4 percent, his deposit will earn _____ during the next 12 months, giving him a total of $_____.

g. The grade distribution this term for freshmen at the university was 157 A's, 203 B's, 436 C's, 179 D's and 124 F's. The percentage of freshmen making A's was _____; B's, _____; C's, _____; D's, _____ and F's, _____.

h. The monthly subscription rate for cable television went from $11.95 for basic service to $13.97, an increase of _____ percent.

i. Among football players at the university who had been in school for four years, four of 18 graduated last year and three of 20 graduated this year, a decrease of _____ percentage points.

j. Census data indicates that 578 women in the county said they had been sexually assaulted last year, but the number of sexual assaults reported to all law enforcement units in the county was 265, indicating that _____ [fraction] of the alleged sexual assaults went unreported to police agencies.

k. Here are the mill levies for three taxing units: city, 42.2; county, 32.5; school district, 75.7. Property is assessed at 8.6 percent of market value. The owner of a house with a market value of $70,000 would pay property taxes on an assessed value of $_____ for a total of $_____. The city would receive $_____, the county would receive $_____, and $_____ would go to the school district.

2. Edit this story. Be on the lookout for errors in numbers as well as grammar, punctuation and spelling.

The state Bureau of Investigation released crime statistics yesterday which cover the first six months of 1991. According to those statistics, crime in the state dropped 5.7 per cent during the first six months of 1991 from the same period during the previous year but 9.2% more rapes were reported.

Violent crimes (murder, rape, robbery, aggravated assault) decreased over all 3.6% from the first half of 1990. Property crimes, including burglary, larcany, motor-vehical theft and arson dipped 5.7%.

Crime bureau statistics that were released yesterday indicate violent and property crimes in the state dropped for the tenth consecutive quarter. Rape is the only violant crime on the upswing in the last 5 quarters bureau director J. A. Kelly said.

Among violent crimes, rapes (at least those reported) increased from 276 in the first half of 1990 to 304 during the comparable period in 1991.

Homocides showed the biggest drop at 47.6%. 62 murders were recorded in the first half of 1990 but only 42 murders through June of 1991.

Robbery dropped 16.1 per cent while aggrevated assault was up less than one per cent.

Arson was down 12.5% with 392 cases reported in the first half of 1991, compared with 441 in 1990.

The most frequent crime commited was larcany, with 31,756 cases reported during the first half of 1991.

Exercises 3 through 8 are based on the list of frequently misused words in Appendix B.

3. Cross out the incorrect choices in the following sentences:

   a. [A while, Awhile] before he came to the party, refreshments were served.
   b. As mayor, she hoped to [affect, effect] change.
   c. Because of the [adverse, averse] weather conditions, we must [altar, alter] our plans.

d. Her status as a celebrity was an [allusion, illusion].

e. It is [alright, all right] for you to paint it green.

f. My dream of becoming a film star was an [allusion, illusion].

g. She [alluded, eluded] to her past glory as an actress.

h. The fall [aggravated, irritated] his knee injury.

i. The new drug has a powerful [affect, effect], but it may not be [affective, effective] for treating cancer.

j. Has he been [appraised, apprised] of the situation?

k. The teacher's [advice, advise] to her was to study harder.

l. We mailed 150 invitations [all together, altogether].

m. Were you able to get her to [ascent, assent] to our proposal?

n. He didn't seem to understand the [affect, effect] of his actions.

o. A [burro, burrow] has sure footing on mountain trails.

p. After all the monthly bills were paid, the family had a [balance, remainder] of [fewer, less] than $50.

q. After careful consideration, I [believe, feel, think] I should accept the job offer.

r. Beef [bouillon, bullion] was used in the recipe.

s. She retired to her [birth, berth] on the train.

t. He enjoys going to the horse races, and he is a big [better, bettor].

u. She seemed reluctant to [broach, brooch] the subject with her boss.

v. His explanation sounded like [baloney, bologna] to me.

w. I don't like [baloney, bologna] sandwiches.

x. It was a [bazaar, bizarre] situation.

y. Members of labor unions voted as a [bloc, block] in the spring election.

z. Please [boar, boor, bore] holes in this piece of lumber.

aa. She could hardly catch her [breath, breathe].

ab. He froze the [balance, remainder] of the meat.

ac. He gave his mother a beautiful [broach, brooch] for Christmas.

ad. She placed the ball [beside, besides] the tennis racket.

ae. The [biannual, biennial] event is in April and October.

af. The game was canceled [because of, due to] rain.

ag. The judge set his [bail, bale] at $10,000.

4. Cross out the incorrect choices in the following sentences:

a. The papers must be in a [bail, bale], or the recycling plant will not accept them.

b. The room was filled with smoke, making it difficult to [breath, breathe].
c. The tennis player was a [boar, boor, bore] with
   his frequent complaints about the referee's
   calls.
d. To raise money, the church sponsored a [bazaar,
   bizarre.]
e. We used the bucket to [bail, bale] water from the
   leaking boat.
f. While they were on vacation, a [burglar, robber]
   broke in and stole their television set.
g. This would be a good [cite, sight, site] for a
   picnic.
h. Although she was in her mid-30s, her [childish,
   childlike] mannerisms made her a popular elementary-school teacher.
i. He had thick [callouses, calluses] on his feet.
j. He was [censored, censured, censered] for his unethical behavior.
k. She learned to play [chords, cords] on the guitar.
l. The [climactic, climatic] moment was when Jim met
   his birth mother for the first time.
m. Some National Football League players receive
   salaries that are not [commensurate, commiserate]
   with their playing abilities.
n. How do NFL salaries [compare to, compare with]
   those of the National Basketball Association?
o. His behavior at the party shows that he is a
   [callous, callus] person.
p. It was [childish, childlike] for him to pull such
   a stunt at a formal occasion.
q. We were unable to catch [cite, sight, site] of
   her in the huge crowd.
r. It was a [cement, concrete] driveway.
s. The tent was made of [canvas, canvass].
t. The truck [collided with, hit] a fence.
u. They went to the [cemetary, cemetery] to visit
   the grave site.
v. To [censor, censure, censer] in that manner was a
   violation of the First Amendment, the court
   ruled.
w. We admired the murals on the walls of the [capi-
   tal, capitol].
x. He seemed embarrassed by her [complement, compli-
   ment].
y. When editing copy without a VDT, use a [carat,
   caret] to show insertions.
z. I think he is too [complacent, complaisant] to be
   the team leader. In his eagerness to please everyone, he is [reluctant, reticent] to make decisions.
aa. How many sources did you [cite, sight, site] in
    your term paper?
ab. While in the army, he was assigned to [calvary,
    cavalry] duty.
ac. We received [complementary, complimentary] tick-
    ets to the play.

ad. This policy provides [comprehensible, comprehensive] coverage.
ae. Although the foreign student had an excellent grasp of formal English, she sometimes did not understand the [connotation, denotation] of words.
af. Mammals, reptiles and birds [compose, comprise] the zoo.
ag. The local city [council, counsel] meets every week.

5. Cross out the incorrect choices in the following sentences:

a. He [councilled, counselled] the students.
b. The red tie is a good [complement, compliment] to your new suit.
c. Ask the treasurer to [disburse, dispense, disperse] payment for these bills.
d. Was she [conscience, conscious] after the accident?
e. A synonym for *intermittent* is [*continual, continuous*].
f. His story did not seem [creditable, credible, credulous] to me.
g. Because the judge seemed biased, I thought that she would not give a(n) [disinterested, uninterested] decision.
h. Salmon [croquet, croquette, coquette] was the main dish.
i. Don't talk; you might [detract, distract] the golfer.
j. I asked the real estate agent whether she [felt, thought] the property would [deprecate, depreciate] during the next two years.
k. In the movie two men fought a [dual, duel].
l. She hit her attacker with a [cue, queue].
m. We spent a wonderful vacation in [Cypress, Cyprus].
n. The scientist spent much of his career trying to [disapprove, disprove] Einstein's theory.
o. The room has a [distinctive, distinguished] odor.
p. The [desert, dessert] was a perfect [complement, compliment] to the meal.
q. The car has [dual, duel] mufflers.
r. He hurled [epithets, epitaphs] at his opponent.
s. The new law makes a jail term mandatory for [drunk, drunken] drivers.
t. She always feels [eager, anxious] on the night before a big test.
u. The scene [evoked, invoked] memories of his boyhood home.
v. [Fliers, Flyers] were placed throughout the campus to announce the meeting.
w. After many years as a successful newspaper reporter, he became a [flack, flak] for a politician.
x. In his dealings with children in the neighborhood, he was an [erasable, irascible] old man.

y. The mother told her child to be careful at summer camp, [especially, specially] when swimming.

z. They chose this camp [especially, specially] for its musical activities.

aa. As part of her physical training program, she walked at least a mile [farther, further] each week.

ab. He [figuratively, literally] hit the ceiling when he heard about the ruling.

ac. He [flaunted, flouted] his wealth.

ad. It was a [flagrant, fragrant] foul, but the referee did not see it.

ae. Please cook some [flounder, founder].

af. Please study the matter [farther, further] before deciding what to do.

ag. Two [fewer, less] candidates filed for office this year.

6. Cross out the incorrect choices in the following sentences:

a. His colleagues did not think his [factious, factitious, facetious] remarks were amusing.

b. His presence seemed to [ferment, foment] trouble.

c. Jim is her [fiance, fiancee].

d. The 400-pound wrestler was a [forbidding, foreboding] opponent.

e. To accomplish the task on time, workers had to [forego, forgo] vacations.

f. He was a [gorilla, guerrilla] in Nicaragua.

g. The reporter became [nauseated, nauseous] when he saw the [grisly, gristly, grizzly] crime scene.

h. [Hopefully, I hope] it will not rain on July 4.

i. If your mother marries my father, we will become [half sisters, stepsisters].

j. He was an [inapt, inept] carpenter.

k. The Bible is a [holey, holy] book.

l. The city wanted to erect a [historic, historical] marker at the site.

m. The commander ordered that all flags on the naval fleet should fly at [half-mast, half-staff].

n. The temperature today will be [lower, cooler] than yesterday.

o. After the discussion, the marriage [counselor, councilor] had a better [incite, insight] into the couple's problems.

p. Grease is [insoluble, insolvable, insolvent] in water.

q. Did you [elicit, illicit] a promise from the child?

r. Have you decided [if, whether] you will attend this university?

s. He was [impassable, impassible] during the funeral.

t. She was [incredible, incredulous] about the sales representative's claims for the product.

u. This was the [cite, site] of a World War II [interment, internment] camp.

v. You should be polite to John, [irregardless,

irrespective] of your dislike for him.

w. It was an [ingenious, ingenuous] solution to the problem, and she wondered why no one had tried it earlier.

x. The [eminent, imminent] scientist was born in Germany but [emigrated, immigrated] to the United States.

y. He brought [elicit, illicit] drugs into the country.

z. The teachers did everything they could to [insure, ensure] the students' safety.

aa. The doctors had no explanation for the higher [incidence, incidents] of cancer in that county.

ab. The family [emigrated, immigrated] to the United States in 1945.

ac. The county commission has the power to [levee, levy] property taxes.

ad. The paint had the [affect, effect] of [lightening, lightning] the wood.

ae. He was [judicial, judicious] in his handling of money.

af. I don't like him because he is a [leach, leech].

ag. I am [loath, loathe] to go to the dentist.

7. Cross out the incorrect choices in the following sentences:

a. The president of the United States nominated her to the [Interstate, Intrastate] Commerce Commission.

b. When you talked to him, did you mean to [imply, infer] that you were unhappy?

c. The sky is dark; it looks [like, as though] it will rain.

d. Newspaper advertising [linage, lineage] has increased 10 percent this year.

e. He [lay, lain, layed] in the sun too long.

f. The recipe called for [leaks, leeks].

g. He was selected parade [marshal, marshall].

h. Newspapers are an example of (a) [mass media, mass medium].

i. The challenger was able to [marshal, marshall] his strength to defeat the reigning champion.

j. [May be, Maybe] she will run for office next year.

k. The car [motor, engine] overheated.

l. The commander asked that someone volunteer for the [odious, odorous] duty.

m. The experienced driver won the race with a [masterful, masterly] display of racing ability.

n. After taxes, her salary increase was [negligent, negligible].

o. He became [nauseated, nauseous] on the plane.

p. The parents were [negligent, negligible] in their treatment of the child.

q. [More than, Over] 2,000 attended the performance.

r. He could not get the company to honor the [oral, verbal] promises made by the sales clerk. Only written warranties were valid.

s. An artist uses a [palate, palette, pallet].

t. He bit into the pizza, burning his [palate, palette, pallet].

u. She hoped to [parlay, parley] her fame into fortune.

v. The [burglar, robber] gained entry to her home on the [pretense, pretext] of coming there to repair the telephone.

w. The district attorney will [persecute, prosecute] the murder suspect.

x. The [councilor, counselor] was able to [persuade, convince] the students that a college education is important.

y. The senior class will [proceed, precede] the junior class.

z. He sent his son into town to [pedal, petal, peddle] the wooden toys.

aa. She wanted to uphold the [principal, principle] of equality, although doing so would cost her company more money.

ab. He wore a [pendant, pendent].

ac. I was flattered when the boss asked for my [perspective, prospective] on the situation.

ad. My bicycle [peddle, petal, pedal] is broken.

ae. Students who engage in [prescribed, proscribed] behavior will be expelled from this university.

af. The [principal, principle] shareholder spoke at the annual meeting.

ag. The child slept on a [palate, palette, pallet].

8. Cross out the incorrect choices in the following sentences:

a. The company announced its [perspective, prospective] earnings at the annual meeting today.

b. The fancy car was a [perquisite, prerequisite] that came with his new position.

c. The guest speaker climbed the stairs to the [podium, lectern] and placed her notes on the [podium, lectern].

d. The doctor [prescribed, proscribed] medicine for my illness, but she seemed [quiet, quite] [reluctant, reticent] to do so.

e. The politician was [reluctant, reticent] during the interview.

f. We will finish the project [irregardless, regardless] of our financial situation.

g. You have made some serious errors, but I think the situation is [remediable, remedial].

h. He is a [reckless, wreckless] driver.

i. Although the pay was good, the work was [seasonable, seasonal], and he wanted to work throughout the year.

j. The baker wanted the dough to [raise, rise].

k. The veterinarian suggested that the dog be [spade, spayed].

l. The barber used a [strap, strop] to sharpen the razor.

m. She ordered new [stationary, stationery] for the company.

n. Magicians engage in [sleight, slight] of hand.

o. Police erected a [stationary, stationery] barrier.
p. She is a [tackful, tactful] person.
q. It was a [tenant, tenet] that guided him in his business dealings.
r. It was a [tort, torte] that could have been avoided with careful copy editing.
s. Stained-glass windows are [transparent, translucent].
t. She wore a [shear, sheer] blouse.
u. Bob Hope is a [trooper, trouper].
v. She hoped to join the state highway patrol as a [trooper, trouper].
w. Here is the book [which, that] I ordered.
x. This version of the computer program will [supercede, supersede] the one issued two years ago.
y. Unexpected expenses will [wreak, wreck] havoc on my budget.
z. Her argument was [tortuous, torturous].
aa. He used a special batter to make shrimp [tempera, tempura].
ab. He said it was a [venal, venial] sin.
ac. It is a [viral, virile] disease.
ad. Having gone without food for two days, the hunters had [veracious, voracious] appetites.
ae. He said he would [wangle, wrangle] an invitation.
af. Let's not [wangle, wrangle] about this matter.
ag. The recipe called for three egg [yokes, yolks].

9. Edit the following sentences to eliminate redundancies:

a. The humane society director said she would postpone her decision about computer identification for pets until later.
b. The car skidded a total distance of 100 feet before the driver managed to resume control.
c. College students sometimes think editing exercises are totally unnecessary and the answers are patently obvious.
d. When we break camp, we must promise to assemble our lively little group together again next summer.
e. At 6 a.m. yesterday morning, the networks broadcast the first news reports that Prince would begin a national tour in the fall.
f. The decision to increase funding for education became clear after the mayor asked the council for a consensus of opinion.
g. Suddenly the lawyers began to argue over whether the testimony referred back to the original crime or to the pretrial hearing.
h. The freshness of the spring rain still remains, although each and every cloud has disappeared from the morning sky.
i. A happy song advises that if you fall down, you should pick yourself up and start all over again.

    j. The football player said he wouldn't turn pro at
       the present time but might consider the option
       next year.

10. Combine each pair of sentences into one sentence. Make certain each
new sentence has the same meaning as the sentences you made it from.

    a. Music shouted from a stereo.
       Music drifted out to the dark garden and quiet
       street.

    _____

    _____

    b. Brownies had been baked.
       Brownies had been stacked high on paper plates.

    _____

    _____

    c. An awkward couple lazed to the center of the
       floor.
       An awkward couple disappeared in a clump of
       bodies starting to dance.

    _____

    _____

    d. The soft drink seeped into the carpet.
       The soft drink dried to a sticky patch on the
       floorboards.

    _____

    _____

    e. The sound of a ringing telephone cut through the
       blend of music and voices.
       The sound of a ringing telephone continued and
       continued until someone picked up the receiver.

    _____

    _____

11. Edit the following story by deleting at least 15 words:

Educators throughout the Sunshine State will keep a

close watch on a unique experiment as four northern

Floridian counties try to establish a joint voca-

tional school district.

    One of the major aims of this ambitious venture,

which will offer vocational programs that are not

currently available at the high schools the students

now attend, will be to act as a deterrent to the

dropout problem besetting schools in this area.

12. Correct any errors you find in these sentences:

a. She lost her sister Beths dress and it has not yet been found.

b. Salingers story is better than anyone elses. It's theme is common to everybodys experience. The others have poor plots.

c. Ms. Handy accompanied by her brothers are flying to Mexico.

d. Mayor Driver said county-owned property including the the 50 room hotel will no longer be tax-exempt if the innocent sounding law is passed.

e. Theres absolutely nothing I can do Cindy said. Absolutely nothing I can do. Its just one of those things she said apologetically.

13. If you were one of the editors of a newspaper, how would you react to the following lead?

He is the freshest thing to blossom in New York since chopped liver, a mixed metaphor of a politician, the antithesis of the packaged leader, irrepressible, candid, impolitic, spontaneous, funny, feisty, independent, uncowed by voter blocs, unsexy, unhandsome, unfashionable and altogether charismatic, a man oddly at peace with himself in an unpeaceful place, a mayor who presides over the country's largest Babel with unseemly joy.

This 65-word lead about Edward Koch, the former mayor of New York City, was written by Saul Pett, an outstanding writer for the Associated Press. Although it is longer than the usual 18 or 20 words, it is acceptable. Note especially that the subject and verb come first, followed by a long series of modifiers. The lead reads simply despite its length.

Here's another example of how Pett uses sentence length:

Clearly an original. Asked once what he thought his weaknesses were, Ed Koch said that for the life of him he couldn't think of any. "I like myself," he said.

 The streets are still dirty. The subways are still unsafe. The specter of bankruptcy is never further away than next year's loan. But Edward Irving Koch, who runs the place like a solicitous Jewish mother with no fear of the rich relatives, appears to be the most popular mayor of this implausible town since Fiorello LaGuardia more than a generation ago.

The writer first used 65 words in the lead sentence, then only three words in the next sentence. That is followed by a 22-word sentence, then a five-word sentence. Pett begins the third paragraph with two five-word sentences and a 12-word sentence and ends the paragraph with a 39-word sentence.

Are these paragraphs too difficult for the many millions who read AP stories? Discuss the beginning of Pett's story in class. How many of your classmates object to the lengths of the sentences?

14. In hard news stories, reporters try to make their leads as simple and as short as possible. Some of the following leads contain unnecessary attribution, redundancies, opinions of the reporter, excess wordage, unimportant quotations, too many statistics or imprecise information. Tighten the following leads:

a. Blue-collar rocker Bruce Springsteen won three American Music Awards yesterday for his 18-month-old *Born in the USA* album, and nine other artists or groups won two awards each at ceremonies that ended with a stirring anniversary salute to "We are the World."

b. The space shuttle Challenger's solid-fuel rockets were not equipped with sensors that could have warned of trouble because designers thought the boosters were "not susceptible to failure," William Graham, acting administrator of the National Aeronautics and Space Administration, said yesterday.

c. A 14-year-old boy fired three shots into a third-floor apartment at 91 Monmouth St. yesterday to climax an argument with a 39-year-old mother who had defended her 9-year-old daughter against an attack by the boy.

d. Four French and two Canadian women have started a ski trek from Norway's Spitsbergen Island about 690 miles across the Arctic, aiming to reach the North Pole by Jan. 1, the Norwegian NRK television reported yesterday.

e. A federal grand jury indicted former Philippine President Ferdinand Marcos and his wife, Imelda, Tuesday in a racketeering case that includes charges he embezzled more than $100 million from the Philippine government and used the money to

buy millions of dollars' worth of New York real
estate.

15. Imagine that you are a copy editor for a metropolitan newspaper. You are given a story written by a historian for the op-ed page, and you find that one page is divided into only one paragraph. The copy chief said that each page of copy must have at least three paragraphs. Edit the following copy so that it has three paragraphs:

This observation indicates the essential difference between the layperson and the professional historian. Although a layperson may develop either a personal or a professional interest in some aspect of the past—and may then study it thoroughly and become an authority—the historian's work consists entirely of analyzing the past. Because the past can be examined only through its traces, historians devote themselves to them: coins, stamps, art objects, buildings and especially documents. How the historian examines the past is indicated in part by the sketch of Professor Anderson's work. We can discover that a particular detail in a document is false by comparing that detail to facts established in other studies. Those facts, in turn, were first examined to determine whether they corresponded to other facts that had previously been established by careful examination. It is not oversimplifying to say that the writing of history is based on correspondences, on the degree to which purported fact corresponds to established fact. Essentially, historians assert probabilities, although many are so little in doubt that their factual basis is unquestioned. We cannot know in the sense of experience and observation, for example, that the members of the Continental Congress signed the Declaration of Independence on the second of August, but the other facts that make this date probable are so well established that it is not to be doubted.

16. After reading the following story and comments, go beyond what the copy editor has done by editing the story again. You may need to retype the story so it will be clear to the production staff.

1. *This quotation pulls the reader into the story, but you don't really need "(American)" because "America" and "our" make the identification clear. Always aim at using exactly as many words as you need. Using many superfluous words exhausts the reader.*

2. *The edited version seems smoother.*

3. *Newspapers customarily require that paragraphs be shorter than these because long paragraphs in narrow columns confront the reader with a sea of type. It has been demonstrated over and over that readers avoid long patches of type.*

4. *Again, use only the words you need; "who also" is crisper than "both of whom have."*

1 "65% of the recruits of the Communist Party are drawn from the youth movement in America" and what's more, the Communists "plan to achieve their objectives with

2 our (American) children." These were just two of the *many*

3 startling facts revealed by F.B.I. counter-spy Mrs. Marion Miller in her talk to students in Dinkelspiel

4 Auditorium yesterday. Mrs. Miller, accompanied by her husband Paul, *who also* both of whom have worked for the

5. *Moving "Paul Miller" into the sentence has two values: (1) it removes one comma-halt, making the sentence more graceful; (2) it provides variation. Note that all the preceding sentences began with the subject.*

6. *"Before World War II" says "during the pre-World War II era" more crisply. Using the colon after "II" and deleting "He said" may seem minor, but this is an important technique for adding pace. This rockets the reader into the next sentence.*

7. *The period at the end of "F.B.I." also ends the sentence.*

8. *"Gave up spying" seems to say all that's needed here.*

9. *When you find yourself using two words that mean the same in a short space, you can almost certainly revise to good advantage ("both . . . they").*

10. *(The diagonal lines through capital letters make them lowercase.)*

11. *As in the above deletion of "decided," a writer can make it clear that the decision was made simply by reporting the action.*

12. *Does the original version say anything more than the revision? It merely uses more words.*

13. *The words circled seem to have little value, saying merely that she told her audience why Americans join the party. For this to be valuable, the writer should recount the speaker's points.*

14. *How did the audience make clear its concern?*

15. *"Of the nation" isn't needed (and one might delete "American"); the meaning is clear.*

16. *"She, it would seem, was (and is)" is halting and hard to follow:*

17. *Make words say exactly what you mean. You cannot use "in a word" unless you use a word ("In a word, yes"; "In a word, no." etc.). (By the same token, never use such loose language as "Needless to say." If it really is, why say it?)*

18. *Indeed, this last paragraph has no value. If the reporter has adequately reported the speech, the fact that the speakers hate the party and try to lure the audience into the same attitude will be clear. And, of course, showing is always better than telling.*

F.B.I. against the Communists, told of her ~~entry~~ ~~into and~~ work for the Party.

5 ~~Paul Miller, while~~ introducing his wife, ^Paul Miller^ capti-

vated the audience with his own history of counter-

6 spy activity ~~during the pre-~~ ^before^ World War II: ~~era. He~~

~~said,~~ "I played the part of a good Communist and fi-

nally became Party Secretary on the East Coast, all

7 for the sake of gaining information for the F.B.I.["]

8 After the War, however, Mr. Miller ~~decided to give~~ ^gave^

up ~~the~~ spy^ing^ ⊗ ~~activity and settle down with his wife.~~

Mr. and Mrs. Miller moved from the East Coast to

9 Los Angeles ~~and both felt~~ ^believing^ they were finished with

the Party and the F.B.I. One afternoon, however,

10 Mrs. Miller was invited to join a Communist ₣ront

₲roup, "The Committee of Protection for Foreign

11 Born"⸗ and ~~she decided to~~ resume^d^ her husband's spy

work for the F.B.I.

12 ~~In the~~ ^During^ five years ~~she spent~~ in the Communist

Party, Mrs. Miller learned many of its secrets and

13 grew to hate its methods and motives. She ⟨pointed

out her explanation for Americans' joining such an

organization and⟩ stated that the party, by its very

make-up, attempts to bring the young, disillusioned,

14 and curious into its fold. Mrs. Miller and the audi-

ence seemed to be especially concerned with^American^ students

15 and ~~the~~ adolescents⊗ ~~of the nation~~. She ~~it would seem~~

16 was (and is) trying to gain ~~the~~ support ~~of the stu-~~ ^student^

~~dent body~~ in the fight against Communism.

17 ~~In a word,~~ both Paul and Marion Miller, through

their experience in the Party, have learned to hate

it, and in their speaking try to make the entire au-

dience do the same.

-30-

17. A student reporter turned in the following story. Correct the misspelled words, and rearrange the paragraphs as needed so the story will sound smoothly written. For example, note that near the middle of the story, "Bivins also lashed back at critics." Why didn't the reporter place that paragraph and the next three paragraphs near the lead (perhaps beginning right after the lead)? Edit this story closely.

The American preoccupation with technical analysis and usefulness must be balanced with humanistic vision, Gilmore University President Don Bivins urged the Gilmore University graduating classes, June 15, during his cammencement address.

Americans need a humanistic vision which, Bivins said, "extends beyond utility."

"That vision includes the values and convictions that underly alll of the more utilitarian, more proffessional, more technique oriented things we have to spend so much time learning to do," the freshman president expostulated.

Bivins warned that the United States is endangered by a "national infatuation" with the effectiveness of utilitarian analysis-cost/benefit ratios, tradeoffs, and all the rest."

Many policymakers "may not quite undersatnd that a framework of social justice theory should always underly and often limit that kind of analysis."

Bivins, the former statistician of the federal government in Washington, D.C., also cautined against America's "disproportionate faith in new technology."

"We Americans are disposed to to have to much faith in the quick technological fix-to expect repairs to 'take' instantly. Because of this "over-expectation," Americans "view of the past efforts to reshape society is skewed." Too many Americans are mistakenly "now prepared to conclude that social improvement cannot be sought through social and personal effort."

Although there have been some proninent failures in "efforts" to engineer social improvement, Bivins pointed out, the great, great social movements of the 1960s produced some extraordinary "successes."

Citing environmental, racial and educational advances, Bivins concluded, "These are momentos human triumphs. Rather than deny them, we should note them with pride."

Bivins also lashed back at critics who have characterized today's college students as being conformist, materialist and conerned more about caers than about ideals.

Bivins told the graduates: "The criticism you are hearing from most analysts of your generation is, I suspect, a form of projection. It is always more conenient to blame the failures of service in our society on the choices you make than on the quality or opportunity they have provided."

It would be surprising if the United States economic ills did not have student more concerned about the security of their futures," Bivins explained while adding, "but that is not proof of a corresponding loss of idealism."

In fact, Bivins said to the graduates, "I regularly advertise you . . . as being, below the the surface, as concerned with the state of the world, and your fellows as your predecessors."

In his closing words, Bivins advised the graduates to sieze "the abundant opportunities to make the world better."

"Human service matters and one person can make a difference," Bivins said.

18. Cut the following news story by at least 24 lines. Remember to read all of the story thoughtfully before you begin editing. Try to preserve as much news value as you can.

The body of a large elderly man, which had been shipped across the country in a sealed trunk, was discovered in San Francisco yesterday.

He had been murdered: A single bullet had pierced the heart. But who he was and how he met death were not known.

The victim, according to police inspectors, was shipped here from Newark, N.J., by a woman. The big black trunk, carefully sealed with tape, left Newark on April 1 and arrived at the Railway Express Agency's warehouse early Tuesday morning.

Newark homicide inspectors would give no details, but they said that "some progress had been made" in tracing the identity of the shipper.

The trunk, 38 inches by 21 by 23, was addressed to a specific person in San Francisco and was marked *Will Call.* The cost of $57.40 had been prepaid. Local inspectors would not reveal the name of the person. There was speculation, however, that the name might be phony.

The fact that the Railway Express Agency's modern headquarters at 1815 Egbert St. had received a shipment of more than usual morbidity was first discovered by the agency's acting foreman, Dirk Van Denakker.

He said that he noticed a slight odor but initially was not alarmed by it, because "biological specimens are often shipped this way." But the odor got stronger.

At 10:30 a.m. yesterday, Van Denakker opened the big steamer trunk. "It was kind of a shock," he said. "I could see an arm." (The body was wrapped in a sheet and a pillow case, and extra space in the trunk had been stuffed with brightly colored sofa pillows.)

Van Denakker closed the lid immediately, and he and the agency's chief security guard, Hugh Smith, called the police.

Homicide Inspectors Gus M. Coreris and John Fontinos arrived on the scene soon after. So did San Francisco Coroner Henry W. Turkel.

Dr. Turkel said later that the body was in very bad condition, having been dead for "10 days or more." The body was that of a Caucasian weighing about 185 pounds. Decomposition had wiped out all facial characteristics.

After the body was taken to the coroner's office for autopsy and attempts to get fingerprints, Dr. Turkel said the lead slug had penetrated the heart, nicked a rib and lodged just under the skin.

The slug was of medium caliber, "perhaps from a .32 revolver."

A Chronicle reporter and photographer were the first members of the news media to arrive at the Railway Express Agency's offices. They asked for, and were met by, the agency's manager, E. P. Buskirk, who was visibly distressed by their presence.

"There's no story," he said emphatically. "There's no story. This is private property, and I can't let you back there" (to the loading zone where the body was).

When he was told that one of his subordinates had already confirmed the body's existence, Buskirk repeated that there was no story and invited the Chronicle team to sit in his office. Then he proceeded to lock the doors that led from his front office to the loading dock.

Asked later if this was the first time that the

local Railway Express Agency had ever received a body, Buskirk said: "To my knowledge, yes."

Asked if his superior could be questioned about the case, he said: "That won't be necessary."

Even before the bullet wound had been found, Lieutenant Barnaby O'Leary, in charge of homicide, said it was reasonably certain that the man was a murder victim.

19. This is another cutting assignment, this time with a feature story. Edit it, preserving as much of the tone and flavor of the feature as you can. Cut this one by at least 18 lines.

Today is World Meditation Day. The goal of World Meditation Day is world peace.

All of this sounds grandiose, even formidable. It sounds less formidable when you get to know its source: a slip of a girl, age 24 years, name of Darlene Owsley, with an address that is, in a vague and itinerant sort of way, Omaha, Neb.

Miss Owsley is, along with Gerald Thatcher (writer, musician and publisher of the Omaha Press), co-founder of World Meditation Day and, she hopes, of many more "days" that will be cosmic and benign.

Miss Owsley insists that Thatcher, who is older than she is, get all the credit ("Please be sure and put Gerald in the story first"); but it was she who walked into the Bulletin office wearing very long, straight blond hair, an open blue-eyed gaze, a blue miniskirt and shiny black shoes that look much too expensive for someone who is more concerned with spiritual than with material things. So it is she who must bear the burden of this report on World Meditation Day.

When she arrived, Miss Owsley was carrying a small cardboard box. It contained a collection of orange buttons that said "World Meditation Day—June 6" and pictured a world superimposed on a yellow daisy.

Miss Owsley smiled brightly and offered a button, which was accepted. Would you kindly explain, Miss Owsley, what you are about?

"Well, World Meditation Day is non-denominational and non-political, and you can take part in it wherever and whoever you are. We just thought it would be nice if everybody meditated on their personal peace on a certain day, and we made it June 6, which is the anniversary of D-Day.

"And we purposely made the buttons so they didn't give the year, and if we have some left over we can do it next year, and maybe it'll become an annual thing.

"What we want is for everybody to have a common vision of peace.

"Also we've sent out hundreds of cards saying 'World Meditation Day is June 6. Pass it on.' We sent them to Pope Paul and to the White House and to the Beatles and even to the Maharishi Mahesh Yogi. The Maharishi sent us a form letter offering a one-week course in meditation for $35. Be sure and point out that $35 bit in your story. I think that's a gas.

"What I do, I travel around giving out these buttons. Only I get an awful lot of parking tickets, and I can't pay for them. That's my problem right now. I've given out maybe 400 buttons.

"I don't give them all out. I sell enough, at 25 cents, to make $2 a day, and that's what I live on. Every day I eat a tuna fish sandwich. And I crash with friends.

"We hope the buttons will help people think peace. Not just in relation to wars but within themselves. Like maybe they'll stop getting mad and kicking the dog."

When Miss Owsley stopped talking—and she talks quite a bit—she was asked to say a few words on her own background.

She did. It would be just as wrong to pin down Miss Owsley's lifestyle as it is to pin down a butterfly. But some of its components are a childhood in Seattle, a degree in psychology from the University of Washington, study at the Zen Buddhist Center in San Francisco, a temporary job with the Esalen Institute in Omaha, and the study of yoga with the Cultural Integration Fellowship.

The one characteristic that distinguishes Miss Owsley, above all others, is optimism. She glows.

Before Miss Owsley left, a Bulletin employee purchased four World Meditation buttons for a dollar. Miss Owsley was delighted.

"Tonight," she said, "I'll eat a ham sandwich instead of a tuna fish sandwich."

20. Edit this story, which has a variety of problems.

wild pigs

Titusville, Florida—AP—The wild pigs which have been giving Kennedy Space Center officials headaches for years are now ending up on the menu at the Bravard County jail.

Sheriff Jake Miller says the pigs are "goodies from heaven". "I'm constantly looking for food sources for that jail Miller said.

The plan to trap the animals is the latest of several ideas by Miller to cut down on the food bill for the jail's two hundred and fifty inmates. His efforts are apparently paying off.

The jails meal budget for the up-comming fiscial year is $260 thousand dollars, the same as in 1989-1990. Its the first time anyone can remember the food bill not going up. The National Auronautics and Space Administration gave Miller permission about 2 months ago to trap the porkers whose population was estimated recently at over 5000 and multiplying fast.

NASA officials are afraid the pigs could threaten the space shuttle and other craft by wandering onto the space center's runway. In addition, the porkers cause traffic accidents dig near under ground cables and endanger other wild life by hogging food supplies.

The piggs began multiplying after they were abandoned by home owners displaced in the 1960's when NASA bought their property to build the space center. At first Millers traps came up empty when he tried baiting them with corn which the wild pigs barely noticed. Once trappers switched to leftovers from the jail and other goodies to give the bait an odor the hogs couldn't resist the sheriff said. About 6 hogs were slaughtered last week and are in the jails freezer waiting to be cooked. Jail Administrator Frank Billings says he hopes eventually to keep about twenty-five or thirty porkers at the prison farm to serve as a constant suply of meat.

21. Edit this story, which has various sorts of problems.

mouse trap

HIPASS, Ca (AP)—A sound so shrill that it drives rodents wild, flattens cock roaches, and sends fleas flying is whistling up a fortune for Bob Brown, a guitar player disabled by polio who retired in 1980 on a $235 a month social security check.

In his garage one day 6 years ago Brown was putting together a electric guitar when he tangled some wires. He saw rats scatter. He crossed the wires again and the rodents ran again.

Brown, 51 built what he called a "rat repellant box". Since then 18000 of the boxes have been produced in Los Angelas and TiJuana Mex

A chicken farmer North of San Diego bought the first repellant box when according to Brown "about 10000 mice were bothering the chickens every night".

"It cleared his place in 4 or 5 days" Brown said.

The Venezualan government recently bought three hundred of the boxes to kill cock roaches in food stores in Caracus and 1000 were sent to spanish graneries in Barcelona.

Brown plans to fly to New York city next week to talk to Department of housing and urban Development officials about placing 9000 units in government housing.

"The box'es frequency is over a million cycles per second Brown said. The human ear can hear up to about 20000 cycles per second.

"We're jaming the sensory systems of rats, cock roaches, and even ants" Brown said. "We've got a vibration high enough to jam 'em like a foreign broadcaster jams our radio Brown said. We discovered that the antenna on roaches just folds up when they hear that sound he said. "They're on there backs, out of touch, and without any balance"

The First Amendment to the U.S. Constitution pro-
vides, among other things, that the people may speak
and write free of censorship from the federal government. Colonial history and subsequent Supreme Court
interpretations of the First Amendment make it clear,
however, that the First Amendment is not an absolute.
Competing societal interests limit the unbridled exercise of free expression.

*Congress shall
make no law
respecting an
establishment of
religion, or
prohibiting the free
exercise thereof; or
abridging the
freedom of speech,
or of the press; or
the right of the
people peaceably to
assemble, and to
petition government
for a redress of
grievances.*

*—First Amendment,
Constitution of the
United States*

The press must abide by the lesson of the old
saying that "your right to throw a punch ends where
my nose begins." That is, the press's practice of its
right to free expression must accommodate competing rights of the public, including the right to the
reputation that one has built, the right to be left alone
if one wishes to be left alone, the right to a fair trial for
a criminal defendant, the right not to have obscene
material forced upon one, the right to profit from
one's intellectual or artistic creations, and the right
not to be cheated by unfair or deceptive advertising.

Newsroom personnel are expected to understand legal topics that directly concern the editorial process: prior restraint, libel, privacy, copyright
and other issues. These topics are discussed in this
chapter.

Prior restraint

The Supreme Court has held that raw governmental
censorship in the form of *prior restraint,* or telling the press what types of
information it cannot publish, is inconsistent with the guarantees of the First
Amendment. Nevertheless, the court has ruled that the government, in the
interests of national security, has a right to protect its secrets. Therefore, the
press can be restrained from publishing information that will cause direct,
immediate and irreparable harm to national security.

Determining what information falls into that category is not always clear-
cut. The result is judgment calls by the highest arbiter in the land, the U.S.
Supreme Court. The 1971 Pentagon Papers case is an example. The court
held in that case that The New York Times and other newspapers could
publish the secret Pentagon study of U.S. involvement in the war in Vietnam
because the government was unable to prove that publication would cause
direct, immediate and irreparable harm to the national security.

Freedom of expression is now guaranteed protection from abridgment by
state laws, but it was not always protected. Earlier in U.S. history, state
legislatures were not bound by the limits that the First Amendment placed on
Congress. The states often passed laws that punished people for saying or
printing information that might upset the prevailing social order. For example, some states in both the North and the South passed statutes punishing
those who advocated the abolition of slavery. Many states had laws on the
books that punished people who criticized certain government policies, such
as drafting men into military service, or who advocated a different system of
government, such as socialism or communism. In a 1925 ruling (*Gitlow v.
New York*), the Supreme Court held that freedom of expression was among
the liberties protected from state infringement by the due-process clause of
the Fourteenth Amendment.

The First and Fourteenth amendments do not grant the press special privileges that are unavailable to other businesses. Communication companies, like other businesses, are subject to laws governing such matters as antitrust, labor, contracts, taxation and postal services. Reporters and copy editors are not expected to have specific knowledge of these matters, which are generally handled by corporate attorneys.

Competing personal interests

Our society places high value on freedom of expression, guaranteed by the First Amendment. But society likewise values other personal rights, such as the right to enjoy a good reputation once it has been earned and the right to be left alone. Also of value are property rights, including the right to profit from intellectual creations. As noted above, the First Amendment is not an absolute, so laws concerning libel, privacy and copyright are not considered inconsistent with First Amendment guarantees.

Sometimes these interests clash. That is, the media may publish information that they think is protected expression, but individuals may think the published statements infringe on personal rights. Individuals who think their reputations have been damaged may choose to "suffer in silence," doing nothing to correct the perceived wrong. Or offended people may seek redress by asking the media to publish a clarification, correction or retraction.

A retraction is not a libel defense, but it may be sufficient to ward off a lawsuit or, if a lawsuit is successful, mitigate damages. A conversation with the newspaper editor or publisher or perhaps with the newspaper's attorney may persuade upset people that they would be unlikely to prevail in a libel or privacy lawsuit.

If informal attempts to resolve a conflict over rights are unsuccessful, a civil lawsuit may result. The party with the complaint files a lawsuit and becomes the plaintiff. The party being sued becomes the defendant. One of several things might happen at this point. For example, the parties might decide to settle out of court, in which case the defendant might pay some agreed-on amount of money for damages. However, most defendant news organizations are extremely reluctant to take this approach, because it could invite frivolous lawsuits.

Once the lawsuit is filed, both parties engage in discovery proceedings to prepare their cases. Attorneys for each side question the other party to ascertain the facts of the situation and to gain information about evidence that will be presented during the trial. The discovery process can involve many hours of expensive legal work. Copy editors may edit several stories about a newsworthy case during the discovery phase.

The defendant might file a motion for summary judgment on any of several grounds, and this action may also be worth a news story. In a motion for summary judgment, the defendant argues that no legal wrong has been committed. For example, in the case of a libel or privacy lawsuit, the defendant might argue that the offending statements did not constitute libel or invasion of privacy. Or the motion for summary judgment might be based on the argument that the plaintiff will be unable to meet the required burden of proof.

If the judge agrees, a summary judgment for the defendant may be granted, eliminating the need for a trial. This decision ends the lawsuit, unless the plaintiff appeals the judge's ruling to a higher court, arguing that the summary judgment was improperly granted.

If the lawsuit survives preliminary motions and goes to trial, the plaintiff will try to prove the elements necessary to the case, those elements varying with the nature of the complaint. The media defendant will argue that the

Our society places high value on freedom of expression.

plaintiff has not been damaged or is otherwise unable to meet the burden of proof. In addition, the defendant will advance one or more legal defenses.

The following sections look at the elements that the plaintiff must prove, and the legal defenses, for libel, invasion of privacy and copyright infringement lawsuits.

Libel

Libel is a false statement that exposes people to hatred, ridicule or contempt, lowers them in the esteem of their colleagues, causes them to be shunned, or injures them in their business or profession.

Generally, libel falls into one of two classifications: libel per se (pronounced per say), words that are defamatory on their face and thus presumed to damage reputation; and libel per quod, words that are not ordinarily defamatory but that become damaging by facts or circumstances extrinsic to the story. Some states recognize a third category: statements susceptible to two meanings, one defamatory and the other not defamatory.

Examples of words that are defamatory on their face include those that falsely accuse someone of committing a crime or of having a loathsome disease.

An example of libel per quod would be to publish an incorrect date for the granting of a divorce so it appeared that someone had remarried before the divorce became final.

The Supreme Court ruled in 1974, in *Gertz v. Robert Welch, Inc.,* that states could not impose liability without fault on the part of the defendant. Since then, the distinction between libel per se and libel per quod has become less important, but many courts continue to make the distinction.

Plaintiff's burden of proof

A person who sues a newspaper for libel must prove the following:

- The statement was published.
- The plaintiff was identified in the statement.
- The statement was defamatory.
- The statement caused injury.
- The publisher was at fault in publishing the statement.

Publication is usually obvious in cases involving the mass media. Strictly speaking, publication has occurred when at least one person other than the defamed person has received the material. In media cases, courts have usually held—but not always—that publication has not occurred until the material reaches its intended audience. In other words, media personnel can discuss a potentially libelous item during the production process without fear of a successful libel lawsuit. However, in 1980 an Illinois jury found the Alton Telegraph liable for material that was never published in the newspaper. Publication resulted, the jury decided, during the news-gathering stage. In an attempt to verify accusations of wrongdoing by a local building contractor, reporters wrote a memo about the wrongdoing to a government official.

Identification may be established even though the plaintiff is not named in the story if people reasonably understand that the statement referred to the plaintiff. An address or title might be sufficient for people to identify the plaintiff.

Individuals cannot sue successfully just because they are members of a large group that has been defamed. For example, the statement "All lawyers are crooks" would not be sufficient identification for an individual lawyer to

Individuals cannot sue successfully just because they are members of a large group that has been defamed.

bring a lawsuit. But an attorney might be able to prove individual identification and harm by the statement "All lawyers at the XYZ Law Firm are crooks." No exact number exists for deciding how small a group must be before any single member can claim to have been libeled. A "rule of 25" grew out of a libel case during the 1950s, but subsequent court decisions allowed members of groups larger than 25 to sue when individuals were closely identified with the group.

Although published statements may identify and damage the memory of a deceased person, the dead cannot sue, and relatives may not sue on their behalf.

Defamation is another part of the plaintiff's burden of proof. The plaintiff must persuade the court that the offending statement carried a "sting," meaning that it harmed the plaintiff's reputation. Evidence about a plaintiff's reputation before and after publication is admissible. In a few instances, courts have decided that plaintiffs were "libel proof" because their reputations were already tarnished beyond the possibility of further damage.

In most cases involving the mass media, the plaintiff must also prove that the offending statement was *false*. True statements that harm someone's reputation are not actionable as libel, although they may be actionable as an invasion of privacy. Thus, the accurate claim that someone has been arrested and charged with murder is not actionable, even though the person may subsequently be acquitted of the charge. Minor inaccuracies will not defeat the defense of truth so long as the part of the statement that carries the sting is true. For example, a libel case would not be decided on inaccurately reporting the place of arrest of the murder suspect so long as the suspect was accurately identified and the charge accurately reported.

Copy editors should be particularly alert when dealing with copy containing any of the following "red flag" words and expressions:

has AIDS	liar	fraud
adulteration of products	mental disease	illegal gambling
adultery	Nazi	graft
altered records	peeping Tom	hypocrite
atheist	perjurer	illegitimate
attempted suicide	corruption	illicit relations
bad moral character	coward	incompetent
bankrupt	crook	infidelity
bigamist	deadbeat	Jekyll-Hyde personality
blackmail	double-crosser	sold out
bribery	drug addict	spy
brothel	ex-convict	stuffed the ballot box
buys votes	scoundrel	suicide
cheats	shyster	swindle
collusion	sneak	unethical
criminal	sold influence	unprofessional
kept woman	fool	villain
Ku Klux Klan		

Fault joined the list of elements that a libel plaintiff had to prove following the 1964 Supreme Court ruling in *New York Times v. Sullivan*. The court determined that the U.S. Constitution protects defamatory statements published without fault. Before then, once a libel plaintiff had established publication, identification and defamation, the burden of proof shifted to the defendant, who then had to offer a defense.

The dead cannot sue, and relatives may not sue on their behalf.

Defenses against libel

Media defendants attempt to persuade the court that they should not have to pay damages for a libeling statement because its publication was protected by the Constitution or by one of the traditional common-law defenses.

The constitutional defense. A full-page advertisement in The New York Times in 1960 led to a case that profoundly altered libel law. A group of civil-rights leaders placed the ad, which criticized tactics used by police and public officials in several Southern cities to disrupt the civil-rights movement. The ad asked for contributions to pay bail for Martin Luther King Jr. and other movement leaders who had been jailed for their protest activities. The accusations made in the advertisement were true for the most part, but the copy also contained several minor factual errors. L. B. Sullivan, police commissioner in Montgomery, Ala., sued the Times for libel. Sullivan won $500,000 for damages in the state courts of Alabama, but in 1964 the Supreme Court of the United States overturned the damage award.

In *New York Times v. Sullivan,* the Supreme Court reasoned that public officials must live with the risks of a political system in which there is "a profound national commitment to the principle that debate on public issues should be uninhibited, robust, and wide-open, and that it may well include vehement, caustic, and sometimes unpleasantly sharp attacks on government or public officials." Further, the court said that "erroneous statement is inevitable in free debate, and . . . it must be protected if the freedoms of expression are to have the breathing space that they need to survive." In effect, the Supreme Court was saying that the U.S. Constitution protects false, defamatory statements about public officials as long as the defendant does not recklessly or knowingly publish them. On the basis of that ruling, public officials accusing the media of libel became obligated to prove that a media defendant published with actual malice. Malice was defined by the court as knowledge of falsity or reckless disregard for truth.

Soon after the decision, the court determined that public figures, in addition to public officials, should have to prove that the defendant published with knowledge that the defamatory statements were false or with reckless disregard for truth.

In 1974, in *Gertz v. Robert Welch, Inc.,* the Supreme Court extended to all libel plaintiffs the burden of proving some measure of fault on the part of the defendant. The court held that state laws could no longer impose liability without proof that the defendant was at fault in publishing the offending statement. States were free to set the standard of fault to be met in their individual jurisdictions, with negligence being a minimum degree of fault. A finding of actual malice would be necessary to award punitive damages, the *Gertz* court specified.

Several states, including Colorado, Indiana, New York and Alaska, have decided that all libel plaintiffs must meet the actual malice standard for stories that are a matter of public interest. Other states allow private figures to show negligence on the part of the publisher, a less difficult standard of fault than actual malice.

Negligence is defined somewhat differently from state to state. In some states the "reasonable publisher" definition of negligence is used: whether a reasonable publisher in the same community or a similar community under existing circumstances would have published the defamatory statement. Other states use a "reasonable person" definition: Would a reasonable person have published the statement under existing circumstances? In New York, if

Malice was defined by the court as knowledge of falsity or reckless disregard for truth.

the case concerns a public matter, a private individual has to establish that the publisher "acted in a grossly irresponsible manner without due consideration for the standards of information gathering and dissemination ordinarily followed by responsible parties."

Here are examples of situations where state courts have ruled that the press was negligent: relying on a source whom local police described as not having been reliable in the past; failing to examine a public court record when writing about a criminal case; publishing a negative, one-sided story about a teacher, based primarily on complaints of parents who had ill will toward the teacher.

In most states, the fault standard to be used in the case depends on the status of the plaintiff. Thus, the outcome of a libel case often hinges on whether the plaintiff is considered a public official, a public figure or a private person. That determination is not always easy to make, and many libel verdicts have been overturned by appeals courts because the wrong fault standard was imposed on the plaintiff. In a series of cases debating this issue, the courts have set down guidelines for deciding the status of the plaintiff.

A *public official* is one who has, or who the public perceives to have, substantial responsibility for or control over the conduct of governmental affairs. A government employee does not necessarily meet this definition. Candidates and applicants for public office are also considered public officials in the context of a libel suit because the public is interested in their qualifications for the job.

The Supreme Court has distinguished two different types of public figures:

- *All-purpose public figures.* These are people who achieve such pervasive fame or notoriety or who occupy a position of such pervasive power and influence that they are considered public figures for all purposes and in all contexts. An all-purpose public figure would be someone with a high degree of name recognition in the community.
- *Limited public figures.* These people, by their public statements and actions, have projected themselves into the arena of public controversy and into the vortex of a question of pressing public concern in an attempt to influence the resolution of an issue.

Few public figures are "all-purpose" public figures, involved in all aspects of public life. Instead, most are limited public figures; they voluntarily become involved in just a few, perhaps only one, controversy. For example, someone who becomes involved in the public debate about whether abortion should be legal in the United States would be a public figure in a libel lawsuit concerning that controversy. However, if that same person filed a libel lawsuit about a private matter or about a public controversy in which he or she had not become involved voluntarily, that person would be classified as a private person. Depending on the state, such a plaintiff might be able to argue that the publisher acted with negligence rather than actual malice, which is more difficult to prove. Another example: A person involved in a highly publicized divorce case was held to be a private person in a libel case that originated when a magazine misstated the grounds for granting the divorce. The court held that divorce was a private matter, not a public controversy.

Finally, a *private person* is one who may be widely known in the community but who has no authority or responsibility for the conduct of governmental affairs and has not thrust himself or herself into the middle of an important public controversy. Elmer Gertz, the plaintiff in *Gertz v. Welch*, was a prominent lawyer who was widely known in several contexts in Chicago. As a lawyer, he had represented defendants in highly publicized cases; he was an author and an amateur actor and had served on various citizens' committees in Chicago. The famous libel case that bears his name arose after Gertz took a case to represent a family in a civil lawsuit against a Chicago police officer who had been found guilty of murder in the shooting of a youth. The John Birch Society magazine then published an article falsely accusing Gertz of having a criminal record and being a "Leninist" or a "Communist fronter." Despite his prominence, the Supreme Court ruled that Gertz was a private person for the purposes of his lawsuit because he had done nothing to inject himself into the controversy surrounding the shooting and subsequent criminal trial of the police officer, which was the focus of the magazine article. In representing the family in a civil action, the court held, Gertz was just practicing his profession and acting in the capacity of a private person.

Reporting and writing techniques are examined during the discovery process and during the trial to determine whether the defendant acted with fault. Before and during the trial, copy editors, reporters and other newsroom personnel might have to give information about procedures used in producing the story. These are among the factors about which they may be interrogated:

- The number and credibility of sources
- Deadline pressures involved in gathering information, writing and editing the story
- The reasonable probability that the information was accurate
- News personnel's doubts about the story's truth

Neutral reportage is recognized in a few jurisdictions as having constitutional protection in a libel action. Neutral reportage is the practice of accurately and disinterestedly reporting that a responsible, prominent person or organization has made false, defamatory statements about a public official or public figure. Most courts have not considered a case dealing with this defense or have refused to recognize it, and the Supreme Court has not decided the issue.

The several courts that have recognized neutral reportage as a libel defense have accepted the argument that such accusations are newsworthy and that the First Amendment does not require the press to ignore newsworthy statements just because the press cannot verify them or just because the reporter has doubts about their truth.

It is important to note that in cases in which the doctrine of neutral reportage has been accepted, the stories included denials or explanations from the defamed parties. Both legal and ethical concerns require careful adherence to this practice. Such stories should also alert readers to the fact that the defamatory charges are debatable and have not been independently verified. Copy editors working for a newspaper in a jurisdiction that recognizes neutral reportage should insist that such information be included in this type of story. Neutral reportage is not recognized as a libel defense in most parts of the country, so editors in those states should not allow such a story to be published if no other libel defense is available.

Common-law defenses. Defendants in both criminal and civil cases typically argue every defense that potentially applies. Libel defendants advance the constitutional defense if the published statement is false but was

Libel defendants advance the constitutional defense if the published statement is false but was published with insufficient fault on the part of the publisher.

published with insufficient fault on the part of the publisher. In addition, one or more common-law defenses—fair comment, qualified privilege or truth—might be argued.

Fair comment protects opinion about matters of public interest or things that have been put on public display. The doctrine of fair comment allows reviewers, for example, to publish scathing reviews of plays, movies, books, restaurants and the like.

Copy editors should ensure either that opinion in a story is based on generally known facts or that the factual basis for such opinion is stated in the story. The Supreme Court reinforced this principle in a 1990 decision, *Milkovich v. Lorain Journal*. The Supreme Court held that the Constitution does not provide a "wholesale defamation exemption for anything that might be labeled opinion."

Copy editors must eliminate opinion that relies for its support upon the existence of undisclosed information unless the editor knows that such information is accurate. For example, it is protected opinion to say that an actor gave a poor performance in a play, but to falsely imply that the poor performance can be attributed to the actor's use of drugs is an unprotected statement of fact. Copy editors must edit editorial page material with the same care as other stories. Expressions of opinion can often imply the existence of facts that may turn out to be false and defamatory and thus actionable.

A newspaper is responsible for what it publishes, including letters to the editor. Like editorials, the letter writer's opinions are protected, but the facts that underpin opinions are not protected if they are false and defamatory. This letter, which actually appeared in a newspaper, should not have left the copy desk (identifying names have been changed for the purposes of this illustration):

To The Sentinel:

I was stopped at the corner of Victoria and Water Streets when Officer Smith's cruiser hit my vehicle.

He hit me. The dent and blue paint on the driver's side door proves it. (He can't drive.)

Because of one cop's stupidity Jonesville just lost another cruiser (myself a car). This is his sixth cruiser he zeroed, and I don't drive with my lights off.

Smith is a Wyatt Earp who likes to assault perpetrators (allegedly).

He muscled me with both hands handcuffed, lying in a hospital bed (a real man). He's done it before, and will do it again to you.

Assistant City Attorney John Doe has numerous complaints on the matter of Smith.

Eh, what's happening Jonesville? Go to sleep. Don't get involved.

[Signature]
[Address]

EDITOR'S NOTE: Attorney Doe denies he has received complaints about Patrolman Smith, except from Dr. ____ with regard to his recent arrest.

The editor's note did little to remedy the situation. And the "letters policy" statement, which the newspaper published with its letters column, increased the potential for a libel lawsuit in connection with the letter: "The reader's column is for your opinions. . . . We do not publish letters we feel to be libelous . . . or that make allegations we are unable to verify independently."

Ed Williams, editorial page editor for the Charlotte, N.C., Observer, gives these instructions to editorial page writers and editors at his newspaper:

- Get the facts straight.
- Be sure facts are facts and opinions are opinions.
- Read it on the page proofs.
- Talk with the paper's lawyers before publication if the subject matter is touchy.

Qualified privilege, another common-law defense, allows the media to cover privileged situations. But the privilege is conditioned upon an accurate and fair account of the proceedings. Usually, to be considered privileged, the proceeding must be open to the public, or the information must be available for public inspection. Public meetings and public records are examples of privileged situations.

It is this common-law defense that allows the media to cover damaging and false statements that are made during trials, for example. Even if it is later revealed that a witness lied during testimony, the media are not held liable for repeating those lies. Copy editors must keep in mind, however, that the privilege applies only to those comments made during the proceedings, not to comments made by public officials or other parties outside the proceedings.

The reporter's account of what happened during a privileged proceeding must be a fair and accurate account. It would not be fair to report only one side of a controversy if conflicting viewpoints were presented during the meeting. To rely on the qualified privilege defense, journalists must make sure that records used as sources are indeed public records. Because reporters sometimes gain access to information that is not considered a public record, copy editors should be on guard against non-public information that is the basis for a potentially actionable story.

Truth is the best common-law defense against libel because falsity is an integral part of the definition of libel. Unfortunately, truth is not always easily proven. Where the offending statement concerns public matters, the plaintiff has the burden of proving falsity—certainly a heavy burden—but the defendant will try to convince the jury that the published statements were true.

The truth must be as broad as the charge. To support a published charge that the plaintiff is a crook, it is not enough to prove, for example, that the plaintiff once shortchanged someone. Likewise, it is not sufficient to prove that the plaintiff was convicted of a misdemeanor shoplifting charge if the published statement said the plaintiff was a convicted felon. Again, copy editors must be especially alert when handling stories that make accusations against someone.

Courts usually allow truth to stand as a defense even though the story contains minor inaccuracies that do not carry the "sting" of the statement. For example, to publish that someone was arrested on Aug. 1 instead of Aug. 2 is unlikely to defeat the truth defense unless other circumstances make the exact date important to the case.

The reporter's account of what happened during a privileged proceeding must be a fair and accurate account.

Privacy

Privacy has been defined as the right to be left alone, the right to be free from unwarranted publicity. The information explosion, the increasing amount of personal information that the U.S. government collects about its citizens and the ease with which computers allow access to that data have all contributed to legal and ethical problems for the mass media.

Many journalists have ethical qualms about publishing some information that they have a legal right to publish. Opinion polls in recent years indicate a decline in media credibility, and to some extent the decline of public approval can be traced to the public perception that the media sometimes use unethical news-gathering techniques and often publish information about individuals that should remain private.

Difficult ethical questions arise as responsible journalists attempt to perform their "watchdog" function: How much does the public need to know about the private lives of candidates for public office in order to make wise voting decisions? Should people know that a co-worker suffers from AIDS or any other disease? Should the public know that the man who thwarted an assassination attempt on the president was a homosexual? Ethical dilemmas posed by such questions are dealt with in Chapter 5; this section discusses the legal aspects of invasion of privacy.

Unlike libel laws, privacy laws do not protect reputational interests. Instead, they are meant to give legal redress for mental anguish and suffering caused by an invasion of personal privacy. Most states recognize four distinct legal wrongs under the broad heading of invasion of privacy:

- Intrusion into a person's physical solitude
- Publication of private information that violates ordinary decencies
- Publication of information that places a person in a false light
- Appropriation of some element of a person's personality—the person's name or likeness—for commercial purposes

Intrusion upon physical solitude can occur in several forms, such as trespassing upon private property and using hidden cameras or microphones to eavesdrop on private conversations. Unlike libel actions, publication is not a prerequisite for an intrusion lawsuit. The act of trespassing constitutes the legal wrong.

If the defendant observes the plaintiff in an embarrassing situation in public, no intrusion has occurred. But the defendant who invades the plaintiff's "zone of privacy," either physically or with mechanical or electronic devices, shows intent of intrusion. For example, it would be legally permissible to photograph or report that a public official engaged in adulterous behavior in a public place, but it would be intrusion to hide in a bedroom closet or to use hidden cameras to gather information about the public official's behavior in a private place.

Courts have held that property owners have the legal right to request that journalists leave public places such as restaurants when the journalists' purpose does not coincide with the primary purpose of the public place—to dine, for example.

Publication of private information involves publicizing a private matter that would be highly offensive to a reasonable person and also is not of legitimate concern to the public. Published information that is embarrassing or upsetting to a plaintiff is not sufficient to support a privacy claim; the information must be highly offensive to a reasonable person in the community. This type of privacy is not designed to protect the "overly sensitive" person, and community mores may be considered in determining whether the information was highly offensive or lacking in newsworthiness. A jury would make that determination should an invasion of privacy lawsuit go to trial.

The information must be private, not public. If embarrassing and offensive information becomes a matter of public record, then a privacy action will not succeed. Embarrassing information like that sometimes published in "looking back into history" columns—for example, that a person with good standing in the community served a prison sentence years ago—usually is not actionable if based on information available in public records.

Published information that is embarrassing or upsetting to a plaintiff is not sufficient to support a privacy claim.

Unlike the law of defamation, truth is not a defense for this type of privacy lawsuit if the offensive information is indeed private and not newsworthy.

"False light" is like defamation in that it it involves falsity and requires showing the publisher's knowledge of falsity or reckless disregard for truth if the matter is of public concern. As in libel law, truth and privilege are defenses for this aspect of privacy. However, no damage to reputation is required. Some courts have required that the "false light" statement must be highly offensive to a reasonable person.

Picture captions and file photographs used to illustrate stories can be particularly troublesome. For example, a couple filed a "false light" privacy lawsuit against a magazine that published a picture showing their child being hit by a car. The use of the picture in the newsworthy context of an accident would have been permissible if the caption had been accurate. However, the magazine used the picture to illustrate a story titled "They Ask to Be Killed," which concerned careless or negligent actions through which people cause themselves harm. Because the accident had involved no carelessness or negligence on the part of the child or the parents, the family won the lawsuit.

Appropriation is the unauthorized use of a person's name or likeness for commercial gain—for example, using someone's name or picture in an advertisement without permission. The argument is made that such use causes the plaintiff mental anguish. A better argument may be that a "right of publicity" is involved and that unauthorized use deprives people of the right to decide how their name or picture will be used and the right to profit from such use.

It is not considered appropriation for a newspaper or magazine to solicit subscriptions by using copy or pictures that ran in earlier issues of the publication. As long as the ad does not imply that the person named or pictured is endorsing the publication, such an ad is considered a sample of the contents.

Appropriation usually concerns the advertising department of a newspaper or magazine more than the editorial department. Permission is not needed to use people's name or picture for news purposes, assuming that no illegal news-gathering techniques were used. Written consent should be obtained from people whose name or picture is used for advertising purposes.

The legal defense in invasion of privacy lawsuits varies. Truth, for example, is a defense for "false light" invasion of privacy but not for any of the other three categories of privacy cases. If truth cannot be established in a "false light" case, the defendant can try to establish that the falsity was not published with actual malice.

Consent, either explicit or implied, is the only legal defense for trespass.

Consent is the defense for appropriation.

Faced with a lawsuit claiming publication of private information, a defendant can argue newsworthiness and claim that the published material is not highly offensive to a reasonable person.

Consent, either explicit or implied, is the only legal defense for trespass.

Copyright

Copyright law provides the right to control or profit from a literary, artistic or intellectual production. In preventing material from being copied without permission of the copyright owner, copyright law both protects and restricts the mass media.

A key principle of copyright law is that facts and ideas cannot be copyrighted. No person or news organization can "own" the facts concerning a newsworthy story or the idea of covering a particular subject. But the manner of expression used to tell the story or discuss the idea—the specific patterns of words and the pictures—can be copyrighted and thus protected from infringement by others. Plagiarism is both illegal and unethical.

Many publications may use the same article through contractual agreements with news services and other suppliers of syndicated material. Members of the Associated Press, for example, agree to send to the AP all spontaneous local news stories, and AP members have the right to use such "spot news" stories verbatim.

The AP contractual agreement specifies that stories resulting from individual enterprise and initiative and copyrighted by the originating news organization cannot be used by fellow AP members without permission. For example, the collapse of an overhead walkway into a crowded hotel lobby in Kansas City, Mo., which killed more than 100 people, was a major news story. No single publication or news service owned the rights to that story. The Kansas City Star and Kansas City Times and other AP members in that metropolitan area furnished AP with much of the spot news coverage of the disaster and rescue efforts. AP members throughout the world could publish those stories and photos.

In the days and weeks after the disaster, the Times and the Star, morning and afternoon papers owned by the same company, invested time, energy and money in an investigation of the cause of the walkway collapse. The company hired consulting engineers and architects to study the blueprints and construction methods, and reporters and editors investigated the city's building inspection procedures, examined public records and conducted interviews. The series of stories produced by that initiative won a Pulitzer Prize for the Star Co. Those stories, unlike news about the initial collapse, could not be used without permission of the copyright owner, the Star Co.

Current copyright law protects original works of authorship fixed in any tangible medium of expression, now known or later developed. Categories of such works include literary works; musical works, including any accompanying words; dramatic works, including any accompanying music; pantomimes and choreographic works; pictorial, graphic and sculptural works; motion pictures; and other audiovisual works and sound recordings. Under the most recent revision of U.S. copyright law, enacted in 1976, a copyright lasts for the lifetime of the owner plus 50 years, after which the work becomes part of the public domain.

Under the work-made-for-hire doctrine, unless specific contractual agreements establish otherwise, the newspaper, rather than an individual newsroom employee, owns the copyright on material published in the paper. Reporters and photographers who work for a publication do not own work done as part of their employment. Unless the employer gives permission, reporters or photographers cannot sell or give away copies of their work or authorize some other publication to use it.

Free-lance journalists retain ownership in their work unless they expressly sign away such rights. A free-lancer can agree to give or sell specific rights to a work and retain all other rights. For example, an author can sell "first serial rights," which allow a publication to publish the work one time anywhere in the world; "first North American rights" allow publication of the work one time in North America only.

The defense against copyright infringement is *fair use*. This defense allows publications to use brief quotations from a copyrighted work for the purposes of critical reviews or scholarly work. Key ideas behind the fair use doctrine are that the one who copies must add substantial independent work and that such copying should be in the public interest. Despite the protests of

Reporters and photographers who work for a publication do not own work done as part of their employment.

producers of television shows, the Supreme Court ruled that the copying of off-the-air television shows for non-commercial use is "time shifting" for the convenience of viewers rather than copyright infringement.

Because no formula exists for determining how much copying is permissible under the fair use doctrine, copy editors should give careful scrutiny to stories that contain verbatim passages from copyrighted material. Several paragraphs may be acceptable in some circumstances, whereas a single line from a poem or song may be grounds for a successful infringement lawsuit. Much depends on the amount and nature of the material that the copier adds to the original work.

These are factors that courts generally consider when deciding whether copyrighted material has been used fairly:

- The purpose and character of the use, including whether such use is of a commercial nature or is for not-for-profit educational purposes
- The nature of the copyrighted work
- The amount and substantiality of the portion used in relation to the copyrighted work as a whole
- The effect of the use on the potential market for or value of the copyrighted work

Techniques for avoiding lawsuits

A copy editor reviewing a story for libel, privacy or copyright problems has four choices:

- Publish the story because it has no legal problems.
- Kill the story because it is libelous, invades privacy or infringes copyright.
- Skillfully edit the story to remove offending passages.
- Expect a lawsuit, but publish the story because we'll win if we're sued.

The decision to publish a dangerous-but-defensible story must not be made lightly and must not be made by a copy editor acting alone. As noted elsewhere in this book, the copy desk is the last line of defense at most publications today. No typist will retype the copy. No proofreader will read the copy after it is in type. If the copy editor lets a dangerous story leave the computer terminal, the story is very likely to be published. If a dangerous story has made it through the reporter and the assigning editor to the copy desk, it is up to the copy editor to notify a supervising editor. The story may then be subjected to review by the whole chain of command at the newspaper, and attorneys may become part of the decision-making process.

Cost of a lawsuit

Most journalists would applaud the publisher who publishes an important story in the face of an expensive lawsuit, and most would have little respect for the timid publisher or the one who places greater emphasis on the bottom line of the balance sheet than on the social responsibility of the press. However, the tremendous cost of a lawsuit—even one that the publisher can win—is a factor in deciding whether to publish. Is the story worth the cost of a lawsuit? It might not be, especially for a small publication or a company with few financial reserves.

A lawsuit is an immense drain on the time and energy needed to go about the business of publishing. A small staff will be unable to meet deadlines if

The decision to publish a dangerous-but-defensible story must not be made lightly.

personnel are occupied with planning sessions with lawyers and then with sitting in a courtroom day after day during pretrial motions, jury selection, the trial itself and perhaps the appeals process.

In addition to time and energy, costs are a tremendous burden. A 1986 report issued by the Gannett Center for Media Studies (now The Freedom Forum Media Studies Center) put the average cost of defending a libel lawsuit at $95,000 to $150,000. That is for legal costs alone and does not include money for damages if the publisher loses the lawsuit. The average damage award for libel now exceeds that for medical malpractice or product liability. In 1985, the average medical malpractice damage award was $650,000, and the average product liability award was $750,000, as compared with $2 million for libel.

Libel insurance isn't a complete solution either, because libel insurance premiums have tripled during the past several years. Further increases are expected, and insurance companies are now writing contracts that exclude the costs of defending lawsuits.

Complaints from the public

The most desirable outcome for the publication is to publish the important, dangerous-but-defensible story without being sued. Assuming that the story is fair and balanced, the publisher may be able to persuade the would-be plaintiff that a lawsuit is a waste of time and money.

Unfortunately, the publisher or publisher's representative may never get an opportunity to placate an angry person if newsroom personnel fail to exercise common courtesy. Anyone who calls the newsroom with a complaint, with a story tip or for any other reason should never be passed around from one person to another or treated with the "Hey-we've-got-a-crazy-on-the-line" approach.

Three professors at the University of Iowa interviewed more than 700 people who had sued the media on libel claims from 1974 to 1984. The majority of these libel plaintiffs told the researchers that they were upset about harm to their reputation and about emotional distress, rather than financial damage. They said that they sued to seek restoration of their reputation and to punish the media, not to get money.

The plaintiffs told researchers that a lawyer was not the first person they called after they became upset about something read in a newspaper or magazine or heard in a broadcast. First the distraught person contacted the offending publisher or broadcaster—either with a personal visit to the newsroom or, usually, with a telephone call. After that initial contact, however—after being treated rudely—the person was no longer just upset and hurt. The person was angry. Then came the call to a lawyer. What could have been a golden opportunity to head off a lawsuit became a golden opportunity for an attorney.

The media can't be expected to satisfy all agitated complainers, even if the publisher or station manager were willing to yield to every demand. But media personnel can be expected to refrain from rudeness. The Iowa researchers recommended that newsroom managers take the following actions:

- Insist that everyone in the newsroom understand the great power that the press has to hurt people and that everyone give courtesy a high priority.
- Make one person responsible for dealing with complaints. Be sure that person has good human-relations skills. If financially possible, select someone who is not responsible for news coverage, because editors

Libel insurance premiums have tripled during the past several years.

don't have time to handle complaints and because often the qualities and skills that make a person a good editor or news director are not the same qualities that make for good people skills.

- Develop policies and procedures for addressing complaints. Put those policies and procedures in writing, and make sure that everyone in the newsroom knows what they are.
- Deal harshly with any employee who stifles a complaint and doesn't direct it to the designated person.

Two trends during the past few years show that newspapers treat reader complaints seriously: More papers regularly publish corrections columns, and more newspapers have created the position of ombudsman or reader representative. At one time, newspaper editors did not want to admit that their paper made mistakes, but now many papers of all sizes publicly correct errors that have appeared in print.

Readers can talk back to their newspapers through letters to the editor, of course, but the majority are not motivated to spend time and effort writing letters. Many readers will take the time to phone the paper and report errors, and those who do seem to appreciate the opportunity to talk with someone specially designated as the reader representative. Where questions of news judgment and standard journalistic practices are concerned, the reader representative often can satisfy angry readers simply by explaining why journalists do certain things.

Smaller newspapers rarely have someone on the payroll to serve solely as a reader representative, but small papers, like their larger counterparts, often publish a regular corrections column. Newspapers vary in their policies about what kinds of errors they acknowledge and the prominence they give to corrections columns. Some papers give the corrections column prominent treatment in the front section; others relegate the column to a less noticeable spot in a back section.

Along with the corrections, some papers tell readers how each error was made, such as "incorrect information supplied by a source," "a reporting error" or "a copy editing error." Some papers, in addition to correcting the error, go a step further by apologizing. Regardless of specific policies on the content of regularly published corrections columns, they serve as one more quality-control device for newspapers and can help enhance papers' credibility with readers.

Prepublication cautions at the news-gathering stage

The work of avoiding clearly libelous stories or ones that invade privacy or infringe on copyright should begin at the reporting stage, so that such stories never reach the copy editor. That's the way it should be. But in a "real-life" newsroom, the copy editor must aggressively question reporters about their news-gathering techniques and about the credibility of their sources.

Reporters must understand that they can defame someone at the news-gathering stage, even before a story is written. Making a defamatory statement about someone to a third party constitutes slander, so the old reporter's ploy of pretending to know more than he or she does in order to gain information can be dangerous. A reporter who has no proof and is just fishing for information shouldn't tell a source, "We already know that Jones is a dishonest cop. We just want your comments." A statement like "We're looking into Jones' conduct as a police officer, and we'd like to get your comments" is far safer.

Privacy also can be invaded during the news-gathering stage. Being in hot

Newspapers treat reader complaints seriously.

pursuit of a story does not excuse intrusion or trespassing. Reporters have no legal right to enter private property without consent, even if the purpose of the story is to expose wrongdoing on the part of the property owner.

Journalists have no legal right to accompany protesters onto private property—a nuclear power plant, for example—to get a story. The power plant operators may legally restrict reporters and cameras to a particular "viewing" area, even though the view from that area might not result in pictures that are as good as those the photographer could get from the vantage point of the protesters.

Likewise, in some jurisdictions it is considered trespassing for a reporter or photographer to accompany public officials onto private property. Court decisions are mixed on this question. To be safe, news personnel should have permission from the property owner, preferably in writing or with witnesses to oral consent. If the property owner is present, observes the reporter or photographer, and doesn't object, then "implied consent" could be argued. But journalists have little recourse if the owner asks them to leave the property. The general rule is that anything that can be seen from a public place is not private, so it is permissible for a photographer to stand in a public area to take pictures of something happening on private property. Yet it would be hard to defend a photographer who climbed a seldom-scaled cliff to take pictures with a telephoto lens of activities in a fenced yard.

Another form of trespass or intrusion is surreptitious taping. Most states allow one-party consent; that is, the reporter may record an interview or telephone conversation without telling the source, but a dozen or so states require both parties to give consent for taping. Know the law in your state. Many journalists and news organizations, however, question the ethics of such news-gathering procedures. Even where surreptitious taping is legal, a reporter who has no ethical qualms about using hidden recorders should talk with supervising editors about organizational policy on the matter.

Prepublication cautions at the copy desk

Generally, an assigning editor reads stories before sending them to the copy desk, but copy editors must not assume that the assigning editor was alert to all potential legal problems. As always, accuracy is essential. In addition, copy editors should take special care to ensure that stories are fair and balanced. Stories involving reluctant sources or confidential sources, as well as stories about lawsuits, can be particularly dangerous.

Accuracy, fairness and balance. Accuracy cannot be stressed too much, and attention to accuracy must start at the very beginning of the news-gathering process: when the idea for a story is conceived. The copy editor must be alert to stories that reporters approached with preconceived notions—for instance, that the subject of the story was a good guy or a bad guy; that corruption existed in the police department; that the school superintendent was incompetent. Copy editors shouldn't hesitate to question reporters about whether they examined all angles of a story and relied on the most credible sources.

To head off lawsuits, the copy editor must check the story for fairness and balance, ensuring that the reporter has included evidence from interviews and from record searches to support generalizations. The copy editor should ascertain that the reporter has contacted those who might be damaged by the story. Denials, if made, should be included in the story.

Remember that truth is a defense for libel but not a defense for three of the four types of privacy cases. Private information that is highly offensive to a

Being in hot pursuit of a story does not excuse intrusion or trespassing.

reasonable person is actionable as an invasion of privacy, even though the information is true. Also, truth is often difficult to prove in a libel lawsuit. Although the plaintiff has the burden of proving the falsity of a story, the publication will also present arguments to support the accuracy of the story, because the burden of proof is a distinction that is difficult for juries to make.

Literal accuracy is not always enough to defend against a libel lawsuit, because literal accuracy is not necessarily the same as truth. One newspaper was hit with a libel lawsuit when it published a story stating that a woman shot her husband when she found him in the company of another woman. The statement was literally accurate, but it wasn't entirely true, because it falsely implied adultery. The truth was that the woman entered a residence where her husband was sitting in the living room in the company of several other people, including the "other woman's" husband.

A story that accurately reports that someone made a false and defamatory statement about someone else may also be grounds for a successful libel action. Unless the charge is made during a privileged situation, like a city council meeting, it is not safe to republish defamatory statements. For example, to publish someone else's statement that a local merchant was dishonest would be dangerous unless the newspaper had independent proof of, say, embezzlement or was published in one of the few jurisdictions that recognizes neutral reportage as a libel defense. The general rule is that anyone who republishes a defamatory quotation is just as guilty of libel as the original defamer.

Double-check even routine facts and stories, because those are often the basis for a lawsuit. The University of Iowa study showed that more than half the libel lawsuits against newspapers were based on stories that appeared on inside pages. About 45 percent of the lawsuits were for front-page stories.

Reluctant sources. If a person who might be damaged by a story is reluctant to talk to a reporter and is avoiding phone calls, the copy editor should not let the story go with a simple "Jones was unavailable for comment."

The copy editor should work with the assigning editor to make sure that the reporter goes to extra lengths to talk with the person. Have the reporter make several calls to Jones' business, home, lawyer, family, usual hangouts. In talking to people at all these places, the reporter also may gain important information for a better story. Leave messages for the reluctant source.

Establish a record of attempts to get the source to talk. These extra efforts may be important if the publication is sued for libel. Repeated attempts to reach the person and information from sources close to him or her may help show a lack of fault on the part of the press.

If conditions were imposed on an interview and the reporter agreed to those conditions, the copy editor should be prepared to honor them. Should the news organization decide to violate agreements that the reporter made with a source, such a decision should be the responsibility of supervising editors rather than a copy editor.

Confidential sources. Anonymous sources should be avoided in most instances. Some news organizations have adopted a policy of allowing their use only in exceptional circumstances, arguing that the public is better served if it knows the source of information. Also, the story is stronger when the source is named, and the publication has a better legal case if the story becomes the basis for a lawsuit.

Many states do not have shield laws to protect confidentiality if the

Double-check even routine facts and stories, because those are often the basis for a lawsuit.

defendant in a libel lawsuit uses information from a confidential source. Source credibility is one of the factors used in determining actual malice. If the jury does not know the identity of the source, credibility cannot be judged.

When a newspaper is faced with a story of Watergate magnitude, an anonymous source may be the only way to get the story. So go meet "Deep Throat" in the parking garage in the dark of night. But too often the use of anonymous sources seems to readers to be an excuse for "weasel" journalism and sloppy, lazy reporting. The use of anonymous sources can be an invitation to exaggerate, embellish, slant or take a cheap shot.

Information supplied by an anonymous source should be verified independently by at least one other source, preferably more than one. If the decision is made to use an anonymous source in a story, explain to readers why the identity is being withheld. Give readers enough information to establish the source's authority to speak on the subject. Of course, this is sometimes difficult to do without revealing the source.

Stories about lawsuits. Be especially alert to libel and privacy dangers when copy editing stories about civil or criminal lawsuits. Never let a story leave the copy desk saying that someone "may" or "plans to" file a civil lawsuit. Be sure that the lawsuit has been filed and, depending on the laws of the state, that some action has been taken on the lawsuit. Make sure that the complaint is accurately quoted or paraphrased once the lawsuit is filed.

In criminal cases, double-check all key facts: the name of the accused, address, specific charge. Use middle names or initials for the suspect to avoid confusion with someone who has a similar name. Be aware that manslaughter and murder are not the same charge.

Let the court, not your publication, judge the guilt or innocence of the defendant. The word *alleged,* as in "alleged ax murderer John Jones," does not always get the publication off the libel hook. Grammatically, the description *alleged ax murderer* can be understood to mean that Jones is an ax murderer who also happens to be accused, which is hardly what the writer meant, unless the writer does not accept the innocent-until-proved-guilty principle of American jurisprudence.

Don't let defamatory out-of-court statements by police or attorneys find their way into print. If the police chief says, "We've got an airtight case against this killer John Jones," don't go to press with the statement unless the police chief says it in a privileged, public situation. When reporting what was said during an open court session or other privileged situation, be sure to restate it accurately and to present a fair account of what happened during the privileged proceeding.

In the interest of fairness, the outcome of both civil and criminal cases, especially if the criminal defendant is acquitted, should be published as prominently as the story about the defendant's arrest or indictment.

Headlines and quote boxes. The copy editor's task doesn't end with the story. Once the story is "lawsuit-proof," the editor must take care not to libel someone or invade privacy in the headline. Quote boxes can be problematic also, because quotations taken out of context may be damaging.

The use of anonymous sources can be an invitation to exaggerate, embellish, slant or take a cheap shot.

Suggestions for additional reading

Bezanson, Randall P., Gilbert Cranberg and John Soloski. *Libel Law and the Press: Myth and Reality.* New York: The Free Press, 1987.

Carter, T. Barton, Marc A. Franklin and Jay B. Wright. *The First Amendment and the Fourth Estate,* 3rd ed. Mineola, N.Y.: Foundation Press, 1985.

Denniston, Lyle W. *The Reporter and the Law: Techniques for Covering the Courts.* New York: Hastings House, 1980.

Forer, Lois G. *A Chilling Effect: The Mounting Threat of Libel and Invasion of Privacy Actions to the First Amendment.* New York: W. W. Norton, 1987.

Gerald, J. Edward. *News of Crime: Courts and Press in Conflict.* Westport, Conn.: Greenwood Press, 1983.

Kane, Peter E. *Errors, Lies, and Libel.* Carbondale, Ill.: Southern Illinois University Press, 1992.

Nelson, Harold L., Dwight L. Teeter Jr. and Don R. LeDuc. *Law of Mass Communications: Freedom and Control of Print and Broadcast Media,* 6th ed. Westbury, N.Y.: Foundation Press, 1989.

Smolla, Rodney A. *Suing the Press.* New York: Oxford University Press, 1986.

Stevens, John D. *Shaping the First Amendment: The Development of Free Expression.* Beverly Hills, Calif.: Sage Publications, 1982.

1. Shortly after the Three Mile Island nuclear plant in Pennsylvania was shut down because of an accident, a newspaper reporter was told by a former security employee at the plant that plant security was inadequate and lax. To observe firsthand the security precautions, the reporter used the name and credentials of a former college roommate to apply for a job as a guard at the plant. The reporter was hired, and after two weeks of training, he started working full time as a guard.

The reporter worked two weeks at the plant, during which time he made notes about the facility and took photographs of the control room. He told no one there about his affiliation with the newspaper.

After quitting the security guard job, the reporter returned to his newspaper and wrote a series of articles about his experiences and observations at the nuclear plant. Before the stories were published, the reporter revealed his true identity to his former employers and asked to interview them. They refused to be interviewed.

Metropolitan Edison, operator of the plant, went to court seeking an injunction to prohibit publication of the articles. A spokesperson for the company told reporters that the company did not want the reporter to divulge anything that could be detrimental to the security of the plant and the community. The spokesperson said that publication of the articles might expose the plant to terrorist attacks.

Answer these questions about this situation:

a. This case involves prior restraint. What is meant by prior restraint?

b. If the court follows the precedent of the Pentagon Papers case discussed at the beginning of this chapter, what legal test will the court use to decide whether to grant the injunction?

c. Briefly describe the argument that Metropolitan Edison would use to try to persuade the court to issue the injunction.

d. Briefly describe the argument that the newspaper would use against the granting of the injunction.

e. Given your knowledge of precedent, which argument do you think the court will accept?

2. For each of the following statements, tell whether the elements of libel are present and what, if any, defense is available if the item sparks a libel lawsuit.

    a. The Community Theater production of "Dear Old State University" is three hours of sheer boredom. Instead of buying a ticket to this masquerade of a play, spend your $10 on something worthwhile.

    b. Jane Playwright denies that she is an addict, but she must have written "Dear Old State University" during one of her frequent bouts with booze and drugs.

    c. A woman, who asked that her name not be revealed, said in an interview that John Politician, local mayor, raped her last year after the Christmas party for city employees. She said that she did not report the rape to police because she was afraid that she would lose her job at city hall.

d. Sarah Bitter, who testified yesterday, told reporters that the prosecutor did not ask the right questions when she was on the witness stand. "If he had done his job right, I could have told the jury enough to convict that murdering John Smith," Bitter said.

e. In passing sentence on John E. Smith yesterday, Judge James Hangman said, "You are a sorry excuse for a man. The lowest animal known to humankind deserves more mercy than you gave your victim. I wish this state gave me the authority to pronounce the death penalty on such dregs of humanity as you."

f. Jane X. Doe, 2468 Kingston Ave., was drunk when she raced her car through the red light at Green and Main streets and struck the pedestrian, police on the scene said.

g. Jane X. Doe, 2468 Kingston Ave., was arrested and charged with driving under the influence of alcohol after an accident at Green and Main streets last night.

h. "You are a murderer!" Sarah Bitter screamed from the witness stand as she pointed at the defendant, John E. Smith.

i. "All sorority girls are whores," the evangelist told a campus crowd yesterday. "State universities shouldn't condone the sinful activities of sororities and fraternities."

j. At a meeting of the city council yesterday, a social worker told council members that Mayor John Politician was "charging big money to poor people who rent his rat-infested hovels."

k. The Coffee Cup Cafe was ordered closed yesterday by the county health department. Records indicate that the cafe has scored below the "acceptable" rating at each of the last three inspections by health officials.

l. Unless you're in the mood for a middle-of-the-night visit to the hospital emergency room, don't eat at the Country Style Delights restaurant. The desserts are pretty good, but the rest of the food isn't fit for a dog to eat.

3. Show that you understand the legal distinction between a limited public figure and a private person by naming two people in your town and the contexts for which each would be considered a limited public figure.

4. Describe a situation in which the president of the city council would be considered a private person in a libel lawsuit.

5. Consider each of the following situations in terms of privacy. Tell which privacy category, if any, and what defense, if any, apply. Which side is likely to win if a privacy lawsuit is filed?

a. Suzy Goodtan, movie celebrity, was sunbathing nude in her backyard, which is surrounded by an 8-foot privacy fence. A photographer stood on a 10-foot ladder to look over the fence and take Suzy's picture. The picture was never published.

b. Mark Jones was shopping at the Super Save Supermarket yesterday when a big display of tomato soup cans fell on his head. He is now in the hospital, suffering from a head injury. A photographer who happened to be in the supermarket at the time of the accident took a picture of Mark lying on the floor awaiting the ambulance. The local newspaper published the picture with a tagline reading "Freak Accident," and the caption included Jones' name and address.

c. If the picture caption mentioned in item b included the name and address of the Super Save Supermarket, would the owner of the market have a good chance to win a libel or privacy lawsuit? Explain.

d. In the same edition of the newspaper that ran the picture of his accident, Mark Jones was surprised to see an advertisement with a picture of him and his cute six-year-old daughter entering the store. Copy for the ad reads: "Mark Jones and six-year-old Heather enjoy shopping at Super Save, where they can buy at the lowest prices in town."

e. A famous actress is in town to appear in a play. The local newspaper publishes a picture of a prominent local executive, who is married, embracing the actress in a hotel lobby. The picture caption identifies both the man and the actress.

f. The caption for the picture of the actress and the prominent executive embracing implies that the two have a romantic relationship.

g. A magazine reveals that 25 years ago Stephen Goodman was released from prison after serving a 10-year term on a conviction of molesting children. During the past 25 years, Goodman has been an outstanding citizen in town and has been honored for his volunteer work with children. Goodman's family, friends and business associates were unaware of his past criminal conviction.

h. A magazine reveals that 25 years ago Stephen Goodman was arrested and charged with molesting children but was acquitted after a trial.

i. A magazine publishes a story revealing intimate, graphic details about the sex life of a famous Hollywood actor. The story is based on interviews with two long-time employees at the actor's home.

j. To attract subscribers, a newspaper uses direct-mail advertising to all non-subscribers in town. The ad includes a page reprinted from the newspaper, showing a color picture of the star quarterback at the state university.

6. You are a photographer for a local newspaper and specialize in sports photography. A nationally circulated sports magazine contacts you about buying some of your pictures that have appeared in the newspaper. Discuss this situation in terms of copyright.

7. A local woman is the author of a new book. The newspaper wants to condense the book and publish it as a series of newspaper stories during the next month, along with a feature story about the author. Is such a series likely to qualify as fair use? Explain your answer.

I

The domain of the mass media today is an ethical jungle in which pragmatism is king, agreed principles as to daily practice are few, and many of the inhabitants pride themselves on the anarchy of their surroundings.

—Hodding Carter III

n his book *On Press,* Tom Wicker, now a columnist for The New York Times, describes a significant lesson he learned at age 23:

As a correspondent for the Sandhill Citizen in Aberdeen, N.C., I covered a divorce case that involved one party who had futilely chased the other with an ax. It was the human comedy at its most ribald, and the courtroom rocked with laughter. I wrote a humorous account for Page 1.

The next day I had a visitor: a worn-out woman whose haggard eyes were blazing. "Mr. Wicker," she said, "why did you think you had the right to make fun of me in your paper?"

I have never forgotten that question. My story had exploited unhappiness for the amusement of others. I had made the woman something less than she was—a human being. Seeing that, I saw, too, that I had not only done her an injury but had missed the story that I should have written.

Wicker's story amounted to ridicule, which is not illegal but which raises ethical questions, the topic of this chapter.

We know, from research conducted by the chief media organizations in this country, that a credibility gap exists between the media and their audiences. For journalists in the 1980s, a lack of credibility was a serious enough problem to warrant action. Some began to respond by remembering the basics: Practice the journalistic principles of fairness, accuracy and completeness; respect people's feelings; become aware of sensitive topics; broaden issues of coverage.

But many believe the credibility gap, among other factors, has had a negative effect on the media's financial health. At the end of the 1980s, for example, newspaper circulation rates, although increasing in raw numbers, had failed to keep up with population growth. Network news ratings also continued to slip.

Nationwide surveys taken in the mid-1980s revealed that the public did not appreciate or like what reporters and editors did, how they did it, or the explanations they offered for their actions.

In 1985, the American Society of Newspaper Editors released the results of an important research study, called "Newspaper Credibility: Building Reader Trust." The survey indicated that, among other things, 75 percent of all adults in the United States questioned the credibility of the media. Many people thought the media were arrogant, biased and sensationalistic; that they invaded people's privacy; and that they emphasized bad news. Many questioned the honesty and ethical standards of reporters and editors and believed that the press did not show enough concern for how ordinary people could be hurt by news coverage. A majority questioned whether newspapers could give fair coverage to other political candidates after one candidate had been endorsed on the editorial page. And almost a fourth said the front page contained more opinion than the rest of the newspaper did.

Today, as we are about to enter a new century, media ethics must be discussed within the context of these increasingly negative perceptions of journalists. We must undertake a fundamental reassessment of the basic mission of the press. A robust and earnest discussion of ethical decisions facing student journalists is one way to begin.

Editing and Ethics

How to decide questions of ethics

What is ethics?

Codes of ethics

Editing with good taste and sensitivity

Situational ethics

Ethics in the 21st century

On lying: Sissela Bok

How to decide questions of ethics

Here are three newsroom scenarios that editors might face:

- Your newspaper's summer intern discovers that the death of a prominent member of the community occurred because of complications associated with AIDS (acquired immune deficiency syndrome). You're the senior editor on duty, and your final edition goes to press in 30 minutes. Should you publish the cause of death?
- As your newspaper's sports editor, you believe your audience wants to read stories about all the games, both home and away, of the professional football franchise in your area. Your newspaper cannot afford to send you to the away games, but the owners of the football team will allow you to travel with the team, free of charge, and will grant you exclusive interviews with the star players as well. Should you accept the team's offer?
- Your newspaper's photographer returns from an assignment with a dramatic photo of an accident scene. In the foreground, a child's covered body, turned away from the camera, lies in the street; in the background, traffic stands still and passersby look on. As the editor who is laying out tomorrow's Page One, you must decide whether to use the photograph.

Most journalists are acutely aware of the need for ethical performance.

Those who are in the business of editing and judging the news face such ethical questions as a matter of routine. Often journalists must find answers within hours—or even minutes—because of the harsh deadlines of publication or broadcast.

What are the benefits of publishing the story about the prominent citizen dying of AIDS? Does the newspaper have a policy calling for inclusion of the cause of death in obituaries? Would a great public good be served by publication? Should respect for the privacy of the relatives and friends of the deceased be considered? What personal values do you bring to bear on your decision?

In the case of the sports editor, the question is whether traveling with the football team legitimately adds value to the newspaper's reporting or to readers' understanding of the sport. Or might the editor simply be submitting to a form of bribery and risking conflict of interest?

What news values in the accident photograph warrant its use? Is the photo a sensational exploitation of the senseless death of a child, or is it a legitimate portrayal of a newsworthy event?

Few ethical decisions are clear-cut, and many are quite complicated. Most of the time, journalists have no detailed ground rules to guide them in making such decisions.

Some groups of professionals are able to turn to rules and principles for help in solving ethical problems. Law students, for example, study the ethics of their profession along with court procedure. Medical students study the ethics of medicine along with anatomy. Both know that the ethical code of their profession is universal and that individual practitioners will be policed by their own colleagues, who have the power to take away their licenses to practice.

Journalists, on the other hand, have no such procedures or universal rules of conduct. For them, the signs are at best blurred and at worst nonexistent. Restraints are few, and a licensing and policing agency like the American Bar Association or the American Medical Association doesn't exist. Most journalists are acutely aware of the need for ethical performance, and most attempt to respect standards for responsible journalism codified by national press organizations. Still, ethics remains a trial-and-error proposition.

What is ethics?

In popular usage, one of the meanings of *ethics* is "a set of principles of conduct governing an individual or group." One writer said that *ethics* refers not only to statements about our conduct and the conduct of others but also to statements of what that conduct ought to be.

People embrace certain ethical standards of conduct because of the moral education provided by their culture—their family, school, church, friends and peers—and because of an inner commitment to culturally defined moral standards. Ethics, therefore, is personal. It is determined and enforced by each of us individually, and it can provide us with certain basic principles by which we can judge actions to be right or wrong, good or bad, responsible or irresponsible.

Because of this background, we make many moral judgments without much thought or deliberation. Most of us, for example, would not hesitate to say that we value telling the truth.

Once in a while, an ethical decision involves more than one moral rule. For example, most of us have been taught that stealing is wrong; we also have been taught that life is highly valued. What if a loved one required medication to live and we had no money to buy that medication? Would we hesitate to steal the medicine from the pharmacy? Would we be morally justified in doing so? Does the value of a life outweigh the harm done by stealing the medicine? Or is stealing always wrong, regardless of the motivation?

When we are looking for a way to balance conflicting ethical rules, we are seeking moral standards, philosophical principles we can invoke to help us justify our decision. One philosopher we might call on to help justify our decision about stealing the medicine is Immanuel Kant. Kant's *categorical imperative* is based on a conviction that human beings have certain moral rights and duties and that we should treat all other people as free and equal to ourselves. Our actions are morally right, then, only if we can apply our reasoning universally—that is, only if we would be willing to have everyone act as we do, using the same reasoning in any similar situation. Kant's view is an absolutist view: Right is right and must be done under even the most extreme conditions. Thus we cannot justify stealing the medicine unless we are willing to let anyone steal medicine under similar circumstances

The argument that a greater good would be served by saving the life of our loved one than by not stealing the medicine might be justified by John Stuart Mill's *principle of utility.* His utilitarian theory is one of the most influential in journalism today. It is based on the notion that our actions have consequences, and those consequences count. The best decisions, the best actions have good consequences for the largest number of people possible. The utilitarian principle prescribes "the greatest happiness for the greatest number." In media situations, this maxim often translates into "the public's right to know." In the example, utilitarians might argue that more good consequences would flow from stealing the medicine and thus saving the life than from any other act we could perform in that situation. Therefore, we would be morally justified in stealing the medicine.

A third philosophical principle, Aristotle's *golden mean,* also could be invoked. This principle holds that moral behavior is the mean between two extremes, at one end excess and at the other deficiency. Find a moderate position, a compromise, between these two extremes, and you will be acting with virtue. In this case, the moderate and ethical position between the two extremes—stealing the medicine or allowing the loved one to die—might be to offer to work for the pharmacist in return for the medicine.

The philosophical principles of Kant, Mill and Aristotle are just three

We make many moral judgments without much thought or deliberation.

Exhibit 5-1

The Potter box can be used to analyze the dimensions of an ethical problem. The first step is definition of the situation. It is followed by outlining the possible values at work and determining the relevant principles to apply. The next step is choosing loyalties. After the four-stage analysis, the final step is to make an ethical decision about whether or not to publish.

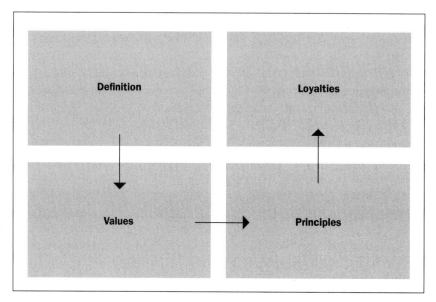

among many that can be used to help justify ethical decisions. At first these three approaches may seem inapplicable to today's fast-paced newsrooms. But on closer examination we can sense how they might hold value for today's editing processes. At the very least, the use of philosophic principles allows us to step back for a moment and ponder the situation more than we might ordinarily do in the rush to publish. In addition, invoking a theory or philosophic principle helps us frame our approach toward solution of the ethical issue; in other words, it helps us see the problem in a broader light rather than isolate it from any historical, social or economic context. Unfortunately, in the day-to-day scramble to publish and broadcast, journalists rarely take time to reason carefully through a thorny ethical problem.

In their book *Media Ethics: Cases and Moral Reasoning,* Clifford G. Christians, Kim B. Rotzoll and Mark Fackler describe a model of moral reasoning called the "Potter box" (see Exhibit 5-1). Formulated by Dr. Ralph Potter of the Harvard Divinity School, the Potter box helps dissect a situation requiring an ethical response by introducing four dimensions of analysis: definition, values, principles and loyalties. To make a decision, we move through each dimension—from defining the situation to considering values to appealing to an ethical principle to choosing loyalties—eventually reasoning our way toward a solution.

To see how this method of moral reasoning works, let's return to one of the scenarios mentioned at the beginning of this chapter. You are editor of the Daily Bugle, a mid-sized newspaper in Hampshiretown. At the 4 p.m. meeting to discuss the next day's paper, you are handed a photograph showing the mangled body of a child hit by a car. The body is partially covered by a sheet, and a small pool of blood is visible in the background. Passersby look on in horror, and a soccer ball is evident in the foreground.

According to the caption information on the back of the photo and an attached story, the girl in the foreground of the photo is 7-year-old Tammy Davis, daughter of William Davis, owner of the town's biggest furniture store and president of the country club.

Tammy was playing soccer in a park after school when the ball rolled into the street. As Tammy chased the soccer ball, she was hit by a car and killed.

Daily Bugle photographer Clara Lenz came across the accident on her way to another assignment, and she took the picture. She strongly believes that the photo should be published and that it should be displayed prominently on Page One.

You know you must get some questions answered before you make a decision. You linger to talk to Mike Modular, the news editor, after the meeting.

Modular tells you that the newspaper's police reporter learned the driver of the car scored 0.25 on his Breathalyzer test—over the legal limit for driving a car—and is sobering up in the city jail. Modular recommends against publishing the photo, especially on Page One.

The Potter box can help you decide whether to publish the photograph, as the photographer wishes, or to not publish it, as the news editor wishes.

Step 1 is to define the situation. Photographer Lenz might define the situation as this: The daughter of a prominent citizen of the community was run down and killed by a drunken driver, and the newspaper has a photograph of the scene. News editor Modular might define the situation as this: The newspaper has a photograph that depicts, in gruesome detail, the scene of an automobile fatality on a city street.

Step 2 is to identify the values underlying the choices. This part of the exercise asks you to define the costs and benefits of publication. What are the positive and negative values that reflect your own personal ethics?

In this case, photographer Lenz might identify these positive values as benefits of publishing the photograph:

- The photo is an accurate depiction of a very newsworthy event, an event that occurred locally, publicly and recently.
- In addition, the victim was the daughter of a prominent local citizen, adding to the newsworthiness of the photo.
- The photo also is well-composed and technically good; it has impact, one of the elements essential in high-quality photojournalism.

News editor Modular, on the other hand, might identify these negative values as the costs of publishing the photograph:

- The photo is in extremely poor taste and is too gruesome; it depicts in graphic detail the senseless death of a child.
- The newspaper's unwritten policy is not to publish photos showing dead bodies.

Step 3 is to appeal to a moral principle to help justify your decision. If you were to agree with Lenz and decide to publish the photograph, you might call on Mill to help justify your decision. The utilitarian principle would argue that the public has a right to know about this newsworthy event and that the more the newspaper can educate the public about this problem, the more likely it is that a solution will be found. "The greatest good for the greatest number" would require publication.

Conversely, if you were to agree with Modular and decide not to publish the photograph, you might call on Kant to help justify your decision. The absolutist view would argue that you should follow the newspaper's policy not to publish photos of dead bodies, no matter what. Right is right, and wrong is wrong. And publishing a tasteless, gruesome photo like this one is wrong.

Step 4 is to choose loyalties. This last step is very significant and often the most agonizing one, because direct conflicts arise among competing rights. To whom is the highest moral duty owed? Is the first loyalty to yourself, to the newspaper, to the family of the victim, to the readers, to your colleagues or to society?

Lenz might argue that the ultimate loyalty is to society and to readers. The

To whom is the highest moral duty owed?

newspaper has a social obligation to inform and educate the public about the problem of drunken driving, and the photograph is part of that campaign. Lenz also might argue that a secondary loyalty would be to herself; publication of the photo might win the praise of her colleagues and could even win a journalistic award.

Modular, on the other hand, might argue that the ultimate loyalty should be to the newspaper and its policies regarding publication of tasteless material. Or he might argue that the highest moral duty is owed the surviving family and that the photo should not be published because it would hurt them even more than they already are hurt by their child's tragic death.

After reasoning your way through the four dimensions of the Potter box, you should be able to reach a responsible and ethical decision. The questions become more and more focused as the discussion proceeds through each of the quadrants. In the end, bringing your own personally defined ethics to bear, what would you decide? Would you publish the photograph or wouldn't you?

Unfortunately, reporters and editors do not often use such methods to make moral judgments. They either react instinctively, hoping that they will make the right decision and that the negative consequences will not be too overpowering, or they try to find answers in a professional code of ethics.

Codes of ethics

The American Society of Newspaper Editors, the Associated Press Managing Editors and the Society of Professional Journalists have compiled generalized statements about well-known unethical behaviors. These codes of ethics provide little substantive guidance to help journalists balance conflicting moral rules. But they do provide a starting point for defining an ethical problem that needs to be resolved.

The principal codes of ethics to which most journalists subscribe appear in Exhibits 5-2, 5-3 and 5-4.

In addition to these general codes of ethics, individual newspapers have developed their own codes or policy statements, most of which address such issues as acceptance of gifts and junkets or conflicts of interest. Here is a sampling, culled from a report by the Associated Press Managing Editors Professional Standards Committee:

Gifts: Editorial employees will accept no gifts or favors of significant value offered in connection with their jobs. (Fort Worth, Texas, Star-Telegram)

We accept no business-connected gifts or gratuities. We do not accept free rooms, sample merchandise, special reduced rates for members of the press, funds provided by gaming establishments and racetracks for members of the media to use, or any other low- or no-pay arrangement. Gifts of insignificant value—a calendar, pencil, key chain or similar item sent out routinely by a corporation, for instance—may be accepted if it would be awkward to send them back. All other gifts will, however, be returned to the donor with the explanation that it is in violation of Inquirer policy to accept any gifts. Bottles of liquor or wine shall be considered gifts of more than token value and may not be retained. Where it is impractical to return a gift, it will be given to charity and the donor will be advised of the reason. (The Philadelphia Inquirer)

Junkets: The News pays all costs connected with travel by staff members on News business. This includes transportation, meals and lodging. Junkets, free trips and reduced fares are not accepted. An exception may be made when the free or subsidized transportation is the only means available to cover an event, such as a police or military flight to or over a disaster area. (Ann Arbor, Mich., News)

Any travel for either a story or story-research is company travel. Even on chartered trips (such as accompanying a sports team) or hitchhiking on a State Police plane, we

Exhibit 5-2
The American Society of Newspaper Editors has published this "Statement of Principles." (Reprinted courtesy of the American Society of Newspaper Editors)

PREAMBLE

The First Amendment, protecting freedom of expression from abridgment by any law, guarantees to the people through their press a constitutional right, and thereby places on newspaper people a particular responsibility.

Thus journalism demands of its practitioners not only industry and knowledge but also the pursuit of a standard of integrity proportionate to the journalist's singular obligation.

To this end the American Society of Newspaper Editors sets forth this Statement of Principles as a standard encouraging the highest ethical and professional performance.

ARTICLE I: RESPONSIBILITY

The primary purpose of gathering and distributing news and opinion is to serve the general welfare by informing the people and enabling them to make judgments on the issues of the time. Newspapermen and women who abuse the power of their professional role for selfish motives or unworthy purposes are faithless to that public trust.

The American press was made free not just to inform or just to serve as a forum for debate but also to bring an independent scrutiny to bear on the forces of power in the society, including the conduct of official power at all levels of government.

ARTICLE II: FREEDOM OF THE PRESS

Freedom of the press belongs to the people. It must be defended against encroachment or assault from any quarter, public or private.

Journalists must be constantly alert to see that the public's business is conducted in public. They must be vigilant against all who would exploit the press for selfish purposes.

ARTICLE III: INDEPENDENCE

Journalists must avoid impropriety and the appearance of impropriety as well as any conflict of interest or the appearance of conflict. They should neither accept anything nor pursue any activity that might compromise or seem to compromise their integrity.

ARTICLE IV: TRUTH AND ACCURACY

Good faith with the reader is the foundation of good journalism. Every effort must be made to assure that the news content is accurate, free from bias and in context, and that all sides are presented fairly. Editorials, analytical articles and commentary should be held to the same standards of accuracy with respect to facts as news reports.

Significant errors of fact, as well as errors of omission, should be corrected promptly and prominently.

ARTICLE V: IMPARTIALITY

To be impartial does not require the press to be unquestioning or to refrain from editorial expression. Sound practice, however, demands a clear distinction for the reader between news reports and opinion. Articles that contain opinion or personal interpretation should be clearly identified.

ARTICLE VI: FAIR PLAY

Journalists should respect the rights of people involved in the news, observe the common standards of decency and stand accountable to the public for the fairness and accuracy of their news reports.

Persons publicly accused should be given the earliest opportunity to respond.

Pledges of confidentiality to news sources must be honored at all costs, and therefore should not be given lightly. Unless there is clear and pressing need to maintain confidences, sources of information should be identified.

• • •

These principles are intended to preserve, protect and strengthen the bond of trust and respect between American journalists and the American people, a bond that is essential to sustain the grant of freedom entrusted to both by the nation's founders.

This Statement of Principles was adopted by the ASNE Board of Directors, Oct. 23, 1975; it supplants the 1922 Code of Ethics ("Canons of Journalism").

This code is a model against which newspaper men and women can measure their performance. It is meant to apply to news and editorial staff members, and others who are involved in, or who influence news coverage and editorial policy. It has been formulated in the belief that newspapers and the people who produce them should adhere to the highest standards of ethical and professional conduct.

RESPONSIBILITY

A good newspaper is fair, accurate, honest, responsible, independent and decent. Truth is its guiding principle.

It avoids practices that would conflict with the ability to report and present news in a fair and unbiased manner.

The newspaper should serve as a constructive critic of all segments of society. Editorially, it should advocate needed reform or innovations in the public interest. It should vigorously expose wrongdoing or misuse of power, public or private.

News sources should be disclosed unless there is clear reason not to do so. When it is necessary to protect the confidentiality of a source, the reason should be explained.

The newspaper should background, with the facts, public statements that it knows to be inaccurate or misleading. It should uphold the right of free speech and freedom of the press and should respect the individual's right to privacy.

The public's right to know about matters of importance is paramount, and the newspaper should fight vigorously for public access to news of government through open meetings and open records.

ACCURACY

The newspaper should guard against inaccuracies, carelessness, bias or distortion through either emphasis or omission.

It should admit all substantive errors and correct them promptly and prominently.

INTEGRITY

The newspaper should strive for impartial treatment of issues and dispassionate handling of controversial subjects. It should provide a forum for the exchange of comment and criticism, especially when such comment is opposed to its editorial positions. Editorials and other expressions of opinion by reporters and editors should be clearly labeled.

The newspaper should report the news without regard for its own interests. It should not give favored news treatment to advertisers or special interest groups. It should report matters regarding itself or its personnel with the same vigor and candor as it would other institutions or individuals.

Concern for community, business or personal interests should not cause a newspaper to distort or misrepresent the facts.

CONFLICTS OF INTEREST

The newspaper and its staff should be free of obligations to news sources and special interests. Even the appearance of obligation or conflict of interest should be avoided.

Newspapers should accept nothing of value from news sources or others outside the profession. Gifts and free or reduced-rate travel, entertainment, products and lodging should not be accepted. Expenses in connection with news reporting should be paid by the newspaper. Special favors and special treatment for members of the press should be avoided.

Involvement in such things as politics, community affairs, demonstrations and social causes that could cause a conflict of interest, or the appearance of such conflict, should be avoided.

Outside employment by news sources is an obvious conflict of interest, and employment by potential news sources also should be avoided.

Financial investments by staff members or other outside business interests that could conflict with the newspaper's ability to report the news or that would create the impression of such conflict should be avoided.

Stories should not be written or edited primarily for the purpose of winning awards and prizes. Blatantly commercial journalism contests, or others that reflect unfavorably on the newspaper or the profession, should be avoided.

No code of ethics can prejudge every situation. Common sense and good judgment are required in applying ethical principles to newspaper realities. Individual newspapers are encouraged to augment these guidelines with locally produced codes that apply more specifically to their own situations.

(Adopted 1975)

Exhibit 5-4
The Society of
Professional
Journalists published
this "Code of Ethics."
(Reprinted courtesy of
The Society of
Professional
Journalists, Sigma
Delta Chi)

The Society of Professional Journalists, Sigma Delta Chi, believes the duty of journalists is to serve the truth.

We believe the agencies of mass communication are carriers of public discussion and information, acting on their Constitutional mandate and freedom to learn and report the facts.

We believe in public enlightenment as the forerunner of justice, and in our Constitutional role to seek the truth as part of the public's right to know the truth.

We believe those responsibilities carry obligations that require journalists to perform with intelligence, objectivity, accuracy and fairness.

To these ends, we declare acceptance of the standards of practice here set forth:

RESPONSIBILITY:

The public's right to know of events of public importance and interest is the overriding mission of the mass media. The purpose of distributing news and enlightened opinion is to serve the general welfare. Journalists who use their professional status as representatives of the public for selfish or other unworthy motives violate a high trust.

FREEDOM OF THE PRESS:

Freedom of the press is to be guarded as an inalienable right of people in a free society. It carries with it the freedom and the responsibility to discuss, question and challenge actions and utterances of our government and of our public and private institutions. Journalists uphold the right to speak unpopular opinions and the privilege to agree with the majority.

ETHICS:

Journalists must be free of obligation to any interest other than the public's right to know the truth.

1. Gifts, favors, free travel, special treatment or privileges can compromise the integrity of journalists and their employers. Nothing of value should be accepted.

2. Secondary employment, political involvement, holding public office and service in community organizations should be avoided if it compromises the integrity of journalists and their employers. Journalists and their employers should conduct their personal lives in a manner which protects them from conflicts of interest, real or apparent. Their responsibilities to the public are paramount. This is the nature of their profession.

3. So-called news communications from private sources should not be published or broadcast without substantiation of their claims to news value.

4. Journalists will seek news that serves the public interest, despite the obstacles. They will make constant efforts to assure that the public's business is conducted in public and that public records are open to public inspection.

5. Journalists acknowledge the newsman's ethic of protecting confidential sources of information.

6. Plagiarism is dishonest and is unacceptable.

ACCURACY AND OBJECTIVITY:

Good faith with the public is the foundation of all worthy journalism.

1. Truth is our ultimate goal.

2. Objectivity in reporting the news is another goal which serves as the mark of an experienced professional. It is a standard of performance toward which we strive. We honor those who achieve it.

3. There is no excuse for inaccuracies or lack of thoroughness.

4. Newspaper headlines should be fully warranted by the contents of the articles they accompany. Photographs and telecasts should give an accurate picture of an event and not highlight a minor incident out of context.

5. Sound practice makes clear distinction between news reports and expressions of opinion. News reports should be free of opinion or bias and represent all sides of an issue.

6. Partisanship in editorial comment which knowingly departs from the truth violates the spirit of American journalism.

7. Journalists recognize their responsibility for offering informed analysis, comment and editorial opinion on public events and issues. They accept the obligation to present such material by individuals whose competence, experience and judgment qualify them for it.

8. Special articles or presentations devoted to advocacy or the writer's own conclusions and interpretations should be labeled as such.

FAIR PLAY:

Journalists at all times will show respect for the dignity, privacy, rights and well-being of people encountered in the course of gathering and presenting the news.

1. The news media should not communicate unofficial charges affecting reputation or moral character without giving the accused a chance to reply.

2. The news media must guard against invading a person's right of privacy.

3. The media should not pander to morbid curiosity about details of vice and crime.

4. It is the duty of news media to make prompt and complete correction of their errors.

5. Journalists should be accountable to the public for their reports and the public should be encouraged to voice its grievances against the media. Open dialogue with our readers, viewers and listeners should be fostered.

Adherence to this code is intended to preserve and strengthen the bond of mutual trust and respect between American journalists and the American people.

The Society shall — by programs of education and other means — encourage individual journalists to adhere to these tenets and shall encourage journalistic publications and broadcasters to recognize their responsibility to frame codes of ethics in concert with their employees to serve as guidelines in furthering these goals.

Adopted 1926; revised 1973, 1984, 1987.

insist on being billed for our pro-rata share of the expense. (Louisville, Ky., Courier Journal and Times)

Meals: Meals and/or drinks shared with news sources should be paid for, wherever possible, by the staff member. When the cost of a meal includes an additional sum (for example, a $500-a-plate political fund-raiser) the staff member will pay the price of the meal. (Detroit Free Press)

The Star prefers to pay for meals that staff members share with news sources. (In instances where insistence on paying would be awkward or otherwise inappropriate, staff members should make it clear that the newspaper will reciprocate in the future.) (Minneapolis Star)

Connections: Employees must not use their position on the paper to their advantage in commercial transactions or for other personal gain. This specifically prohibits such practices as the use of Journal stationery for private business matters, letters of protest or similar dealings. (Milwaukee Journal)

Merchandise: Samples of any products, including but not limited to books, records and tapes, generally should be regarded as gifts, in that those not used for news purposes should be donated to charity, with a letter to the giver explaining the action. Those samples, books, records, tapes, etc. that are desired for news purposes will be purchased from the sender by The Star at the standard retail price and will remain the property of The Star. (Minneapolis Star)

Free books and record albums will not be solicited. Those unsolicited books and albums received will either be given to a reviewer as compensation for the review or be sold at an employee's sale with the proceeds going for charitable purposes. (Des Moines Register and Des Moines Tribune)

Tickets: Free tickets or passes to sports events, movies, theatrical productions, circuses, ice shows or other entertainment shall not be accepted or solicited by staff members.

Staff members covering events which involve an admission charge shall pay for a ticket. The money for the ticket should either be obtained from The Statesman in advance or a voucher submitted for reimbursement after the event. The exception to this will be those events where separate press facilities (press box or table) are provided. In these instances where the public is not being deprived of a seat, no ticket shall be required unless deemed so by the sponsoring group.

Press box and sideline passes are to be used only by reporters or photographers assigned to cover the event.

A staff member who attends an event for background purposes shall buy a ticket and submit an expense voucher.

Season passes to movies will not be accepted.

Any expenses for nightclub admissions, cover charges, meals, refreshments and other expenses for reviewers or critics will be reimbursed. (Idaho Statesman, Boise, Idaho)

Conflicts of interest: It is the policy of this company that no employee shall invest his time or money in any business competitive to this corporation. Investments of this kind usually result in divided loyalty.

Financial investments or other outside business activities by Journal staff members that could conflict with the Journal's ability to report the news, or that would create the impression of such a conflict, must be avoided. (Milwaukee Journal)

Work for a politician or a political organization, either paid or voluntary, is forbidden. Also forbidden is (1) holding public office or (2) accepting political appointment to any position for which there is remuneration other than expenses. There is no quicker source of misunderstanding and suspicion in our profession than the area of politics. We must not give any person reason to suspect that our handling of a story, editorial or picture is related in any way to political activity by a member of the staff. (The Manhattan, Kan., Mercury)

It is crucial to be alert to issues of sensitivity.

Staff members must avoid involvement in public affairs that have the potential for a conflict of interest or could create the impression with the public of a conflict of interest. Non-conflicting community involvement is encouraged. Common sense prevails.

Participation in politics is not permitted.

This section does not preclude voting or registration in a political party for voting purposes.

Work in public relations for pay is prohibited.

Volunteer work in charitable causes is commendable, if limited to non-controversial activities.

The common sense clause requires that all parties maintain communication and understanding so that professional standards may be maintained without undue restraint on personal activities.

Staff members must not act as sports officials, scorers, judges, umpires or referees for pay or as a volunteer at professional, collegiate or high school competitions.

Any outside employment must be cleared in advance with the executive editor. Common sense prevails. (Elmira , N.Y., Star-Gazette and Sunday Telegram)

Editing with good taste and sensitivity

Of all the copy editor's duties, eliminating passages that are in poor taste or that harbor stereotypes can be among the most challenging. Just as it is important to edit stories for accuracy, style, consistency, conciseness and libel, it is likewise crucial to be alert to issues of sensitivity.

Twenty years ago, most newspaper stylebooks would not have dealt with issues of sensitivity. But today, many contain guidelines for handling references to age, dialect, disabilities, race, nationality, religion, gender and sexual orientation, and they outline when it is and is not acceptable to use profanity or graphic detail in a story. Here are some of the commonly adopted rules at many newspapers for these issues:

- *Age.* Ages of individuals should be mentioned in stories and headlines only when relevant or useful in describing them. Avoid terms such as *old, senior, senior citizen, retiree, middle-aged* and *teenager* unless they are specifically relevant to the story. The legal age for adulthood is 18. Persons who are 18 and older are men and women, not boys and girls. Do not refer to young children with obvious or implied adjectives, such as *tiny* or *little.*

- *Sexism.* The basic rule is that people of different gender should be treated the same unless their gender is relevant to the news. Physical descriptions of women or men are permissible only if relevant to the story. Generally, avoid terms that specify gender. For example, use *journalist* instead of *newsman* or *newswoman, firefighter* instead of *fireman* or *firewoman.* Avoid phrases, such as *male nurse* or *woman doctor,* that suggest we think there is something unusual about the gender of the person holding those jobs. When in doubt about sexist word usage, consult Casey Miller and Kate Swift's *The Handbook of Nonsexist Writing* or Rosalie Maggio's *The Nonsexist Word Finder: A Dictionary of Gender-Free Usage.*

- *Race and ethnicity.* Do not mention race, ethnicity or national origin unless it is clearly relevant to the story. In stories involving politics, social action or social conditions, race is not automatically relevant. Avoid terms such as *ghetto, barrio, inner city, suburbs.* They are inaccurate and stereotypical. Do not use a person's race when reporting a crime story unless the incident is racial or ethnic in nature. State the country

Twenty years ago, most newspaper stylebooks would not have dealt with issues of sensitivity.

the person is from if race or ethnic origin is relevant, rather than lumping all Africans, Asians or Central and South Americans into continental categories. Be aware of questionable connotations. *Culturally deprived* or *culturally disadvantaged* implies superiority of one culture over another. In fact, people so labeled often are bicultural and bilingual.

- *Disabilities.* Avoid degrading and inaccurate references to disabilities. Disabilities should not be mentioned in stories or headlines unless they are pertinent. People who are permanently disabled generally do not like to be described as handicapped. Use *disabled* or specify the nature of the disability. When a disability requires use of a wheelchair, say *uses a wheelchair,* not *confined to a wheelchair.* The word *handicapped* is acceptable in describing a temporary disability: "The baseball player was handicapped by a sprained wrist."

- *Sexual orientation.* Sexual orientation—or identifying places and products as being favored by those of a particular sexual preference—should be mentioned only if demonstrably pertinent. When sexual orientation is mentioned, exercise caution in word usage. *Gay* may be used as an adjective but not as a noun: *gay man, gay woman. Lesbian* is generally preferred in reference to homosexual women, *gay* in reference to homosexual men. But do not say *gays and lesbians,* because the first term includes the second. Use *gay-rights activist,* not *gay activist.* Avoid such terms as *admitted* or *avowed.*

- *Profanity, obscenity and violence.* Profanities and obscenities should not be used unless something significant would otherwise be lost. The test should be "Why use it?" rather than "Why not use it?" The simple fact that a person used profanity or obscenity is not in itself justification for printing it. However, it may be used if the term was used in public—especially by a public official or celebrity—and it reflects a mood or frame of mind that can be conveyed in no other way or if the words themselves play a role in the story (as in reports about Supreme Court obscenity rulings). Detailed descriptions of a pornographic film or an episode of violence or mayhem should not be used unless they provide significant information or understanding that would otherwise be lacking in the story.

Newspaper stylebooks cannot suggest guidelines for handling every issue of sensitivity. As both our society and our language change, the ways by which we communicate will necessarily change as well. Newspaper editors recognize that both writing styles and technical styles must adapt to those changes.

In the late 1980s, a coalition of black leaders, including two-time presidential candidate the Rev. Jesse Jackson, called for use of the term *African American* in place of any other name for a member of the black community. Jackson argued that "*black* tells you about skin color. . . . *African American* evokes a discussion of the world." Many newspapers and magazines adopted the new appellation, but linguists, historians, anthropologists and politicians continued to debate its propriety. William O. Beeman, a teacher of linguistic anthropology at Brown University, wrote in the Baltimore Sun:

In linguistic matters, time is the only arbiter. If enough people begin to use the new label, nothing can stop its introduction into general American parlance. When the style sheets of major publications and news syndicates shift, it is clear that American usage has also shifted. The term Negro was dropped in favor of black in the early 1970s. When the media begin to refer to black Americans as African Americans on a routine basis, we will know that this important linguistic change has taken roots.

We will also know that in a subtle and important sense the way the African American community is viewed in the United States has changed forever.

Sometimes, campus publications are at the forefront of style changes. Former student editor-in-chief Nora Wallace and her team of editors at the Golden Gater, a twice-weekly newspaper at San Francisco State University, added this entry about AIDS to their stylebook in spring 1989:

Human Immunodeficiency Virus (HIV) is a disease encompassing three levels: a stage with no symptoms, AIDS Related Complex (ARC) and AIDS. HIV-disease is an increasingly common way of referring to people with AIDS. In all cases, be precise and ask the source.

People with HIV don't necessarily have AIDS.

Use "people with AIDS" or "persons with AIDS" on first reference.

AIDS is not a gay person's disease, and it never should be implied that gay people are the only population affected by AIDS.

People with AIDS should not be referred to as "victims," unless the term is used as "victims of the AIDS epidemic."

Careful editors should have precision as their goal. Remaining alert to issues of sensitivity—whether handling issues of race and gender, referring to the opposing sides on the abortion debate (pro-choice? anti-abortion? pro-life?) or developing precise terminology in stories about AIDS—is a key responsibility of copy editors and one to be taken seriously.

Situational ethics

Editors face many day-to-day ethical decisions beyond remaining alert to issues of good taste and sensitivity. The kinds of ethical dilemmas that reporters face are different from those copy editors face, and copy editors face different dilemmas than managing editors or publishers do.

Reporters are likely to be concerned with questions involving the news-gathering process:

- Should confidential sources be used? Under what circumstances?
- Should classified information be used? Under what circumstances?
- Is going undercover to get the story ever justified? When?
- Is invasion of someone's privacy ever justified? When?

Copy editors are likely to be concerned with decisions involving the writing, editing and production processes:

- Is the use of profane language or obscene photographs ever justified? When?
- Are the implicit biases of the editor or the newspaper as a cultural institution evident in the selection of stories and photos? Should they be? Do certain people, groups or institutions receive more play than others? Conversely, are some people, groups or institutions ignored?
- Are headlines and captions fair and accurate?
- Are stories edited to eliminate bias and opinion? Are subjective words or words suggesting a viewpoint given thoughtful consideration?

Managing editors and other senior editors are likely to be concerned with questions of policy:

- Should victims of crimes be identified? If so, when? In stories about rape? About incest? About battering? In stories involving juveniles?

Careful editors should have precision as their goal.

- Should suspects in crimes be identified? If so, when? At their arrest? When they are charged? At the time of trial?
- Should the cause of death be listed in obituaries involving victims of suicide or AIDS?
- Who in the newsroom should know the identity of confidential sources? Just the reporter? The supervising editor? The managing editor? The publisher? If a reporter pledges confidentiality to a source, are editors bound by the same promise?
- How involved should newsroom employees be in writing and editing special sections that promote consumer products?
- How should corrections and clarifications be handled?

Journalists face these kinds of moral and ethical decisions daily and often have little more to guide them than their own sense of justice and fair play.

In recent years, however, journalists also have begun to heed the messages being delivered by readers and viewers that indicate negative attitudes about the mass media. For example, many newspapers have begun to admit they make mistakes in the reporting and editing process, and some have even encouraged readers to bring errors to the attention of the editors.

The Philadelphia Inquirer stylebook includes this policy about corrections:

> We promptly and forthrightly correct our published errors. An allegation of factual error in our news columns should be treated with the utmost seriousness and should be referred to the appropriate assigning editor immediately. . . . A "Clearing the record" notice may also be used to clarify published facts that, while technically not in error, may have been confusing or misleading.

Many newspapers "anchor" their corrections in the same place every day so readers will know where to find them. The Oakland Tribune's "Corrections & Clarifications," for example, are found on Page 2 of the sections in which the original errors appeared. Exceptions are corrections of TV listings, which appear with the TV logs, and corrections for non-daily sections, such as Food and Travel. Those corrections are published twice, the day after the error was made and the next time the section in which the original error appeared is published.

In addition, editors have begun to listen to others within the newspaper organization, such as those in advertising, circulation and marketing. The relationship between the news staff and the revenue-generating departments historically has been strained because of the perceived need for separation between "objective" news and the subjectivity of advertising.

In recent years, however, because of the need to market the newspaper to remain competitive with other media, the newsroom and the other departments have become less distant from one another. News departments often are involved in writing and editing special advertising sections, such as back-to-school and home-improvement sections, and news executives sometimes participate in marketing promotions and surveys.

Ethics in the 21st century

In *A Life in Letters*, John Steinbeck wrote:

> What can I say about journalism? It has the greatest virtue and the greatest evil. It is the first thing the dictator controls. It is the mother of literature and the perpetrator of crap. In many cases it is the only history we have, and yet it is the tool of the worst men. But over a long period of time and because it is the product of so many men, it is perhaps the purest thing we have. Honesty has a way of creeping in even when it was not intended.

Journalists have begun to heed the messages being delivered by readers and viewers that indicate negative attitudes about the mass media.

Steinbeck's words ring true.

It is not surprising that a 1989 survey by the American Society of Newspaper Editors Ethics Committee indicated that newspaper interns were ambivalent and somewhat skeptical about journalism ethics. One intern had this response:

Ethics is something that cannot be effectively taught to individuals: that's like teaching morality. Literally, there are no right or wrong answers. Each individual finds a balance between his principles and the established code of the paper, which is, as often as not, an amorphous and ill-defined thing. Also, situations present varying challenges for different individuals. Frankly, being a plumber is a lot less burdensome.

Some students may lament the need to balance conflicting values when making ethical decisions and may yearn, as this intern does, for a less burdensome way to react to journalistic situations requiring an ethical response. Yet changing professions—becoming a plumber, for example—is not the solution.

Former public television correspondent Hodding Carter suggested that an "ethical vacuum" exists in the journalism practiced at the close of the 20th century. It is time for the media to fill that vacuum with a process that encourages careful consideration of today's increasingly sophisticated ethical concerns: terrorism and the media, the right to privacy, gruesome photographs, manipulated photographs, conceptual photographs, use of composites and anonymous sources, off-the-record information, political or advertiser pressure not to publish, AIDS obituaries, deception and going undercover, use of quotations out of context and disclosure of the juvenile crimes of adults in the public eye.

Copy editors must be alert to all these potential ethical problems. They must question reporters about their conduct and call perceived ethical problems to the attention of the supervising editors. Copy editors need to be especially diligent in editing for accuracy, fairness and completeness and in making news judgments about what stories and photographs will be published.

The industry's codes of ethics and the policy statements drafted by individual newspapers can be used to help define the ethical situations faced by journalists every day. But only through development, teaching and use of ethical reasoning—based, of course, on subjective cultural values and coupled with an emotional component that often comes into play at the decisive moment—will tomorrow's journalists be prepared to grapple with modern ethical concerns.

Copy editors must be alert to potential ethical problems.

Should physicians lie to dying patients so as to delay the fear and anxiety which the truth might bring them? Should professors exaggerate the excellence of their students on recommendations in order to give them a better chance in a tight job market? Should parents conceal from children the fact that they were adopted? Should social scientists send investigators masquerading as patients to physicians in order to learn about racial and sexual biases in diagnosis and treatment? Should government lawyers lie to Congressmen who might otherwise oppose a much-needed welfare bill? And should journalists lie to those from whom they seek information in order to expose corruption?

We sense differences among such choices; but whether to lie, equivocate, be silent, or tell the truth in any given situation is often a hard decision. Hard because duplicity can take so many forms, be present to such different degrees, and have such different purposes and results. Hard also because we know how questions of truth and lying inevitably pervade all that is said or left unspoken within our families, our communities, our working relationships. Lines seem most difficult to draw, and a consistent policy out of reach.

I have grappled with these problems in my personal life as everyone must. But I have also seen them at close hand in my professional experience in teaching applied ethics. I have had the chance to explore particular moral quandaries encountered at work, with nurses, doctors, lawyers, civil servants, and many others. I first came to look closely at problems of professional truth-telling and deception in preparing to write about the giving of placebos. And I grew more and more puzzled by a discrepancy in perspectives: many physicians talk about such deception in a cavalier, often condescending and joking way, whereas patients often have an acute sense of injury and of loss of trust at learning that they have been duped.

I learned that this discrepancy is reflected in an odd state of affairs in medicine more generally. Honesty from health professionals matters more to patients than almost everything else that they experience when ill. Yet the requirement to be honest with patients has been left out altogether from medical oaths and codes of ethics, and is often ignored, if not actually disparaged, in the teaching of medicine.

As I widened my search, I came to realize that the same discrepancy was present in many other professional contexts as well. In law and in journalism, in government and in the social sciences, deception is taken for granted when it is felt to be excusable by those who tell lies and who tend also to make the rules. Government officials and those who run for

SISSELA BOK

She was born in Sweden and grew up in Switzerland, France and the United States. She received bachelor's and master's degrees in psychology from George Washington University and a doctorate in philosophy from Harvard University. Sissela Bok, now a professor of philosophy at Brandeis University, is the author of two books: *Lying: Moral Choice in Public and Private Life* and *Secrets.*

In 1978, when Bok published *Lying,* Walter Clemons of Newsweek called the book "provocative, highly intelligent." This is what economist John Kenneth Galbraith said: "Everyone will say that Sissela Bok's book is wonderfully timed. All should know that it is also wonderfully incisive and informative. One's mind is turned to all sorts of habits and derelictions of which he was previously unaware."

Anthony Lewis of The New York Times commented: "*Lying* is a fascinating and exceptionally important Book. By reflection and illuminating example it made me understand . . . the causes of lying and its consequences, social and personal."

"In law and journalism," Bok has said, "in government and the social sciences, deception is taken for granted when it is felt to be excusable by those who tell the lies and who tend also to make the rules."

elections often deceive when they can get away with it and when they assume that the true state of affairs is beyond the comprehension of citizens. Social scientists condone deceptive experimentation on the ground that the knowledge gained will be worth having. Lawyers manipulate the truth in court on behalf of their clients. Those in selling, advertising, or any form of advocacy may mislead the public and their competitors in order to achieve their goals. Psychiatrists may distort information about their former patients to preserve confidentiality or to keep them out of military service. And journalists, police investigators, and so-called intelligence operators often have little compunction in using falsehoods to gain the knowledge they seek.

Yet the casual approach of professionals is wholly out of joint with the view taken by those who have to cope with the consequences of deception. For them, to be given false information about important choices in their lives is to be rendered powerless. For them, their very autonomy may be at stake.

There is little help to be found in the codes and writings on professional ethics. A number of professions and fields, such as economics, have no code of ethics in the first place. And the existing codes say little about when deception is and is not justified.*

The fact is that reasons to lie occur to most people quite often. Not many stop to examine the choices confronting them; existing deceptive practices and competitive stresses can make it difficult not to conform. Guidance is hard to come by, and few are encouraged to consider such choices in schools and colleges or in their working life.

As I thought about the many opportunities for deception and about the absence of a real debate on the subject, I came to associate these with the striking recent decline in public confidence not only in the American government, but in lawyers, bankers, businessmen, and doctors. . . .

Suspicions of widespread professional duplicity cannot alone account for the loss of trust. But surely they aggravate it. We have a great deal at stake, I believe, in becoming more clear about matters of truth-telling, both for our personal choices and for the social decisions which foster or discourage deceptive practices. And when we think about these matters, it is the reasons given for deceiving which must be examined. Sometimes there *may* be sufficient reason to lie—but when? Most often there is not—and why? Describing how things are is not enough. Choice requires the formulation of criteria. To lie to the dying, for example, or to tell them the truth—which is the best policy? Under what circumstances? And for what reasons? What kinds of arguments support these reasons or defeat them?

Since I was trained in philosophy, it is natural for me to look to moral philosophers for guidance in answering such questions and providing the needed analysis; for the choices of standards, of action, of goals, and ways of life, as well as of social systems, are the essential concerns of moral philosophy.†

* Scholars in many fields have had no reason in the past to adopt a code of ethics. But some are now exerting so much influence on social choice and human welfare that they should be required to work out codes similar to those that have long existed in professions like medicine or law.

† One of the simplest and, in my opinion, best definitions of ethics is that of Epicurus, quoted by Diogenes Laertius, *Lives of Eminent Philosophers* (Cambridge, Mass.: Harvard University Press, 1925), Book 10, Ch. 30: "Ethics deals with things to be sought and things to be avoided, with ways of life and with the *telos*." ("*Telos*" is the chief good, the aim, or the end of life.)

Suggestions for additional reading

Bagdikian, Ben H. *The Media Monopoly,* 2nd ed. Boston: Beacon Press, 1987.

Bok, Sissela. *Lying: Moral Choices in Public and Private Life.* New York: Pantheon Books, 1978.

Bok, Sissela. *Secrets: On the Ethics of Concealment and Revelation.* New York: Pantheon Books, 1982.

Christians, Clifford G., Kim B. Rozoll and Mark Fackler. *Media Ethics: Cases and Moral Reasoning.* New York: Longman, 1983.

Day, Louis A. *Ethics in Media Communications: Cases and Controversies.* Belmont, Calif.: Wadsworth, 1991.

Fink, Conrad. *Media Ethics: In the Newsroom and Beyond.* New York: McGraw-Hill, 1988.

Goldstein, Thomas (ed.). *Killing the Messenger: 100 Years of Media Criticism.* New York: Columbia University Press, 1989.

Goldstein, Thomas. *The News at Any Cost: How Journalists Compromise Their Ethics to Shape the News.* New York: Simon and Schuster, 1985.

Hulteng, John L. *The Messenger's Motives: Ethical Problems of the News Media,* 2nd ed. Englewood Cliffs, N.J.: Prentice-Hall, 1985.

Journalists and Readers: Bridging the Credibility Gap. Associated Press Managing Editors Credibility Committee Report. New York: Associated Press Managing Editors, 1985.

McCulloch, Frank. *Drawing the Line: How 31 Editors Solved Their Toughest Ethical Dilemmas.* Washington, D.C.: American Society of Newspaper Editors, 1984.

McKenna, George. *Media Voices: Debating Critical Issues in Mass Media.* Guilford, Conn.: Dushkin Publishing Group, 1982.

Meyer, Philip. *Ethical Journalism: A Guide for Students, Practitioners, and Consumers.* New York: Longman, 1987.

Newspaper Credibility: Building Reader Trust. Research Report. Washington, D.C.: American Society of Newspaper Editors, April 1985.

Rubin, Bernard (ed.). *When Information Comes: Grading the Media.* Lexington, Mass.: Lexington Books, 1985.

Schmuhl, Robert (ed.). *The Responsibilities of Journalism.* Notre Dame, Ind.: University of Notre Dame Press, 1984.

1. When the American Society of Newspaper Editors adopted its first code of ethics in the 1920s, William Allen White, editor of the Emporia, Kan., Gazette, said the guidelines would not work. Read the following synopses of two real cases, then re-read the ASNE Code of Ethics in Exhibit 5-2.

Case A

In 1981, Washington Post reporter Janet Cooke became known to all American journalists—not because she had just won the Pulitzer Prize but because she had fabricated her prize-winning story, as well as much of her own background.

Early in April, the Pulitzer jury had awarded Cooke the prestigious prize for her feature story about "Jimmy," an 8-year-old boy who supposedly had been injected with heroin in Cooke's presence. Two days after Cooke received the award, the editors of The Washington Post returned it to Columbia University and the Pulitzer board.

What had happened? Only hours after the Pulitzer Prizes were awarded, Vassar College and the Associated Press called The Washington Post about some discrepancies in Cooke's biography. Her biography said that she had been graduated magna cum laude from Vassar, studied at the Sorbonne in Paris and earned a master's degree from the University of Toledo. Vassar and the University of Toledo claimed that Cooke had attended Vassar for one year, graduated without honors from the University of Toledo and had no master's degree. Moreover, the editors of the Post confirmed that Cooke was not fluent in French.

Finally, the Post editors questioned Cooke about "Jimmy." Although she had written the story without using any last names, claiming they were confidential, and although editors allowed the story to be published, Cooke finally admitted that "Jimmy" did not truly exist. She said he was a composite of sources she had met while investigating heroin use in Washington, D.C. Cooke then resigned.

Case B

One day during the summer of 1980, a professional reporter attended an expenses-paid meeting sponsored by Westinghouse Electric Corp. In addition to food and transportation, Westinghouse provided guests with lodging and a $150 honorarium for listening to a speech advocating nuclear power.

The reporter accepted the food, the travel, the lodging and the honorarium and returned to write a story for his newspaper.

Does the ASNE Code of Ethics cover either or both of these cases? Explain your answer.

2. Read exercise 1 at the end of Chapter 4. What ethical concerns are involved in this case? Write a brief statement either defending or criticizing the news-gathering tactics used by the reporter.

3. Use the three newsroom scenarios outlined on p.128 of this chapter as the starting point for a discussion about editors and ethics. Reason through each example, using the Potter box and your own values and moral standards. Then attempt to invoke one of the philosophical principles mentioned in the chapter (Kant, Mill or Aristotle) or name one of your own to help justify your ethical decision. Discuss your views in class.

4. Name five things you would do to help your hometown newspaper become more credible than it is. Share your ideas in class.

5. Re-read the section in this chapter on situational ethics. Then try to find examples of stories in the newspaper for which the senior editors probably would have drafted a policy, such as listing the cause of death in obituaries or identifying juvenile crime suspects. Share your findings in class.

6. A magazine reveals that 25 years ago Stephen Goodman was released from prison after serving a 10-year term on a conviction of molesting children. During the past 25 years, Goodman has been an outstanding citizen in town and has been honored for his volunteer work with children. Goodman's family, friends and business associates were unaware of his past criminal conviction. What are the ethical implications of publishing this information?

7. Re-read the section in this chapter on sensitivity and good taste. Then edit the following story, paying particular attention to stereotypical images:

Relatives of a Gypsy family with strong ties to Kansas City allegedly have stolen about one million dollars in at least 7 states over the last several years by defrauding dozens of fortune telling customers according to police, prosecuters, and lawyers.

At least 16 relatives of the Marks family, a klan of Gypsy fortunetellers that has for decades had roots in the Metropolitan area, have been found guilty or face charges in connextion with the alleged scams.

Officials are quick to add, however that not all people named Marks are gypsies, nor are all of the estimated 2 dozen Marks gypsies in the metropolitan area involved in fortunetelling fraud. Furthermore, only a small per centage of gypsies in the country are engaged in criminal activities officials said. Only 5 family members in this area have faced such criminal charges in recent years.

Police and prosecutors in several of the seven states where Marks family members have been charged have traded information, only to learn that the same persons allegedly had conducted similar skams in other locations.

Repeated attempts to contract Marks family members

alleged to have been involved in criminal activities were unsucessful.

This year two Marks have been found guilty in Jackson County Circuit court of felony stealing charges, and another relative pleaded guilty in Jan. to a theft charge in Wyandote county.

Three family members, including one already serving a prison term, were indicted Friday by the Jackson County grande jury on charges of stealing over $150.00 by deceit. Det. William Cosgrove, of the Kansas City police department fraud unit, says that case involved alleged promises by fortunetellers to restore a local womans eyesite and to cure her of cancer.

Honest fortunetellers do exist, according to Terry Getsay, a national authority on gypsies who works as a intelligence analyst for the Illinois Dept. of Law Enforcement. "Most just provide a service, he said.

But fortunetelling also is the common denominator among those Marks relatives accused by prosecuters of playing the bujo, a centuries old confidence game that usually victimizes the elderly or those with emotional problems.

And even when the perpetrators are caught, the victims do not necesarily win.

"We've got two convictions (of fortunetellers in Jackson County), and those victims haven't got a dime back said Det. David Parker of the police fraud unit.

Mr. Getsay said the conviction and imprisonment of a gypsy fortuneteller is a rare occurrence. "The likelihood of restitution, probation or dismissal or reduction of the charges are much greater than imprisonment he said.

In the bujo, the fortunteller, after reading palms or Tarot cards, tells the client that the future

holds evil. Slight of hand tricks, such as removing
a clump of hair from a newly-broken egg, are used as
"evidence" that a client is possessed by an evil
spirit.

The fortuneteller then says she must have all the
victim's money — the root of all evil — so it can be
cleansed and the evil removed.

Some fortunetellers say the money will be used to
buy special candles. Others say it will be burned or
buried in a grave yard. Nearly always, however, the
fortune teller promises to return the money, or even
to double or triple the amount, once the evil has
been exorcised.

Instead officials say, the victim frequently sees
neither the money nor the fortune teller again.
"This," Detective Cosgrove said, "is more than just
palm reading.

8. Edit this story for the Centerville daily newspaper:

appointment
Mayor Dwight Smyth held a press conference yesterday
afternoon at 3:30 P.M. at the City-county building in
downtown Centerville. At the press conference the
mayor made known the the assembled press, various
city officials and interested public the identity of
the newly-appointed Director of the Office of Economic Development, whom he selected from a list of
three possibilities submitted to him by a search committee. The person selected by the mayor is Mrs. Mary
Berryman, who has served in a similar capacity in the
city of Riverside.

During the press conference the mayor said "Mrs.
Berry, is a first rate organizer and planner and will
do a first rate job for Centerville citizens in her
new post. Her appointment culmenates a six month
nation-wide search and the search committee couldn't

be happier with it's choice the major said. "We are indeed fortunete to have a person of Mrs. Berrys statute join our city staff Mayor Smyth told onlookers.

Mrs. Berryman is married to Reverend John Berryman, who is a minister of a Baptist church in Riverside. Reverend John Berryman said that his plans are uncertain now but that he hoped to relocate to Centerville now that his wife has gotten this new job. Reverend John Berryman has been pastor of the Second Baptist Church in Riverside for the past 5 years. Before that time he was pastor of a church in Lawrence. He graduate from Southwest Baptist Semenary in Ft. Worth, Tex. in 1975.

Mrs. Berryman was one of 15 applicants for the job in a nation wide search. She was one of three finalists whom was recommended by a search committee appointed by the City Council last July 1991. The search committee screened applicants, conducted interviews and forwarded 3 names to Mayor Smyth, who made the final selection.

As economic development director, Mrs. Mary Berryman will over see a staff composing two assistant directors and three clerical workers. The office is charged with bringing new businesses and industry to Centerville to help increase job opportunities and to broaden the cities' tax base. Mary, a youngish looking grandmother, wore a black dress and long gold earrings for today's ceremony. She used crutches during her introduction because she is recovering from a broken leg which she received last month.

She will move to Centerville from Riverside where she held the position of assistant economic development director for the past 2 years. She has over ten years of experience in municiple financial planning and economic development. She earned a masters degree in public administration in 1980. Mrs. John Berryman replaces Sam Spade in her new post. Spade left the office 6-months ago after ten years on the job. He now has a similiar position in Podunk.

"Frankly, the office is in a financial mess and has been for the past ten years or so" Mayor Smyth said this morning during the announcement ceremony. "The city has spent a bundle on auditers but we still are unable to account for all the money that went through that office during Sam's tgenure, the mayor said. "Mary will be a careful and honest administrater" the mayor said.

Due to financial accounting problems in Centerville and several other cities in the state in recent years, legislation has been introduced in the state legislature which will require anual audits of all city funds in cities throughout the state.

Mrs. Berryman, an articulate black woman, answered questions from newsmen after she was introduced at the press conference. She inferred that she has all ready began efforts to attract a major manufacturer to Centerville. She said that farther meetings with the firm, that she declined to name, were scheduled for later this month. "I know that my predecessor was involved in some questionable financial dealings with city funds, but let me assure the citizens of Centerville that every penny will be accounted for while I'm in charge" Mrs. Berryman told newsmen. Berry said that as one of her first changes in the office, she planned to institute new computer soft-ware to facilitate bookeeping in the office.

Mrs. Berryman is a member of the National City Planners Association, the Women's Christian Temperence Union, and the National Organization of Women. City workers were disappointed that they did not get a free lunch yesterday. Original plans called for Mrs. Berryman to meet with city workers at a noon picnic in the park next to the City-County Bldg. but colder temperatures forced cancellation of the picnic. It will be rescheduled in the Spring.

n today's busy world, newspaper readers are, to a large extent, headline skimmers. A joint project of the Poynter Institute for Media Studies and Gallup Eye-Trac research, published in 1990, found that 56 percent of all headlines were processed by readers participating in the study. In comparison, the average participant in the study looked at only 25 percent of the stories.

Patience, diligence, painstaking attention to detail—these are the requirements.
—Mark Twain

Purposes of news headlines

Readers want information quickly, so the primary purpose of a news headline is to communicate quickly by accurately telling the most important idea in the story. For a story written in the inverted-pyramid style, the headline should be based on the lead. If the most important idea of an inverted-pyramid story is not in the lead, then the copy editor needs to rewrite the lead before turning attention to the headline.

If a headline is inviting and signals a story of interest, readers may pause to read the story. Thus, a second important role of headlines is to attract attention. While communicating the main idea of the news story and doing it in a way to attract readers' attention, the headline writer must be careful to maintain the tone of the story. Just as you wouldn't wear a clown hat to a funeral, don't use an attention-grabbing headline that is inappropriate to the overall tone or mood of the story. Headlines are important indicators of a newspaper's general tone and overall approach to the news. Headlines written for a supermarket tabloid would be out of character in The New York Times or in most hometown newspapers.

Headlines are a key element in the design and layout of a newspaper. The skillful layout editor decides the size and placement of headlines to help indicate the importance of the story and to make the page attractive. At many newspapers it is not uncommon for one person to edit copy, lay out pages and write headlines for one or more pages of the daily paper.

Perhaps no task involved in producing the daily newspaper is both as simple and demanding as good headline writing. Anyone who can use the English language competently can learn, with practice, to write headlines. But headline writing is as much an art as a skill, and not everyone can compose news headlines that crackle or feature headlines that lure readers immediately into the mood of the story. Yet these talents are essential, for modern headlines are designed to

- Summarize the story
- Capture readers' attention
- Maintain the mood of the story
- Help set the overall tone of the publication
- Indicate the relative importance of the story
- Add to the attractiveness of the page

Characteristics of good headlines

When Benjamin Harris published the first newspaper in the colonies, Publick Occurrences Both Foreign and Domestic, in 1690, it contained no headlines. Nobody had thought of them yet. Besides, colonists who were literate were starved for news and needed no headlines as inducements to read every story in the newspaper.

Today the public is flooded with news from many sources: books, magazines, radio, television and newspapers. Most of us hear radio news and see

153

at least one television news report each day. Because the newspaper must compete for a share of the public's time, headlines have become increasingly important.

A headline is, of course, written in skeletonized language. It uses present tense to describe past action and is adjusted to fit a certain space. Each letter, punctuation mark and space that makes up a headline is a unit or a portion of a unit. (Counting individual units of headlines is explained later in this chapter.)

Let's say you are writing a headline with a maximum count of 22.5 units to top a story saying that the New York Yankees won the pennant last night in the Eastern Division of the American League. You might frame the most important facts of the story in this skeleton sentence:

The Yankees won American League Eastern Division pennant

At 53.5 units, this effort is too long to fit the maximum count. It also violates the basic rule that headlines should not be written in the past tense. Present-tense headlines give the news immediacy, and present-tense verbs are often shorter than past-tense verbs. Non-essential words, especially articles (*a, an, the*), usually are omitted to give the headline a sense of telegraphic speed and to enable more ideas to be included in a limited space.

Let's try again:

Yankees win American League East Division pennant

The new headline is better because it eliminates the unnecessary article and uses present tense. But with 46 units, length is still a problem.

How about abbreviating American League? Headline writers in search of a shorter count must resist the urge to use unfamiliar abbreviations, but baseball fans won't have any problem understanding this abbreviation:

Yankees win AL East pennant

At 26 units, the new version is still a bit too long. *Yankees* could become *Yanks,* but we would save only two units on the count. How about *title* in place of *pennant?* That gives us

Yanks win AL East title

Because most papers allow headlines to be slightly shorter than the maximum, this 20.5-unit effort should suffice. But the headline writer willing to work a little longer could come up with a stronger verb and an exact count, 22.5 units:

Yanks clinch AL East title

Ten desk chiefs attending an American Press Institute editing seminar gave these descriptions of a good headline:

- It is accurate in fact, tone, scope and focus, and it emphasizes the main themes of the story. It is balanced and fair and in good taste.
- It is clear, succinct, grammatical, easy to read and easy to understand.
- It has vitality and is strong, active, bright.
- It catches readers' attention and entices them into the story.

- It has freshness and immediacy.
- By its size and shape, it accurately grades the news.

How to write headlines

A headline is written after the story has been carefully edited, a process that generally requires three readings of the story. During each of these readings, the copy editor makes mental notes about headline ideas.

Remember that, unlike the copy editor, the newspaper audience will read the headline before reading the story. A perfectly crafted headline that lacks meaning until after the story is read is unacceptable.

News heads

Well-edited newspapers try to conform to a number of guidelines. Absolutely the most important rule of headline writing is to *be accurate*. This rule has no exceptions. No matter how interesting a headline may be, it is worth nothing unless it is accurate. In the rush to work against deadline pressure, even the best copy editor sometimes has to disregard one or more of the rules of headline writing—but never the rule regarding accuracy.

To be accurate, you must *understand the story thoroughly before writing the headline*. The copy editor who doesn't have a clear view of what the story says isn't likely to write a headline that communicates clearly and accurately.

You can *write the headline from information in the lead, but do not "stutter" by repeating the wording of the lead* so that readers read the same words twice. (Nor should you steal the writer's punch line on feature stories written in suspended-interest form.)

The headline, like the lead, should focus on the most up-to-date information in a continuing story. *Don't put a first-day headline or lead on a second-day story.* First-day headline:

20 injured in tornado

Second-day headline:

'Sounded like a train,' tornado survivor says

Headlines should be as specific as possible within space limitations. "Killer storm hits" is not so good as

Storm kills four

Be sure to *use attribution in headlines that convey opinion and for direct quotations*. Otherwise, the news headline will read like an editorial-page headline. For example, "Budget unfair" is an opinion, which could be taken as the newspaper's unless attributed:

Budget 'unfair,' senator says

Another important guideline for writing headlines is to *avoid libelous statements*. (How to avoid libel is discussed in Chapter 4.) In many states, a libelous headline is grounds for a successful lawsuit, even if the story contains no libelous statements. The headline writer's problem is particularly acute because the headline does not afford space to include qualifying terms from a potentially libelous story.

A related rule is to *respect the rights of defendants*. Don't convict an accused person in a headline. In our system of law, a suspect is considered innocent unless proved guilty. The burden of proof is on the prosecution, not the defendant. The headline "City manager steals from public treasury" could cause problems; a better alternative is

DA charges city manager with stealing public funds

On acquittal, the legal term is *not guilty* rather than *innocent*. However, many publications follow Associated Press style and use *innocent* to guard against the word *not* being dropped inadvertently from *not guilty*.

In more general terms, it is important to *be sure that the headline has only one meaning and that meaning is clear*. Avoid headlines with double meanings: "2 teen-agers indicted for drowning in lake," "FBI ordered to assist Atlanta in child slayings," "Church retains homosexual bar," "5 bullets hit bus on way to Louisville."

Also *avoid repeating words in a headline*, such as "Prosecutor charges city manager with embezzlement of city funds." Occasionally, repetition leads to a good headline. This example from the Lexington, Ky., Herald-Leader is about an actor who turned his back on Hollywood to become a Benedictine monk:

Hollywood actor trades the footlights for the divine light

Write headlines that tell what happened rather than what did not happen:

Storm topples television tower

Storm rips roofs from homes

The headline "No one dies in storm" is less informative.

Every news story headline should have a verb, preferably a strong action verb and preferably in the top line of a multiline headline. Avoid *dead heads,* which merely label stories. For example, "Council session" tells readers very little; a better alternative is

Council fires city manager

This rule applies to news headlines but not necessarily to feature or news-feature headlines, which often use magazine-style titles. Many newspaper editors are flexible about requiring every news headline to have a verb if the final result is an exceptionally good headline.

Do not use forms of the verb to be *when a strong verb will fit the meaning and the space.* They detract from the vigor of a headline. When used, *to be* verbs—*is* and *are*—are often implied rather than stated. But not always, as in this feature headline from The New York Times on a story about quantum physics:

Where Uncertainty Is King and Paradox Shares Throne

Or this news headline, also from the Times:

Under Press Curb, Bad News Is No News

The *to be* verb must not be omitted if it is the principal verb in a clause, unless the clause begins the headline. Generally, a *to be* verb is needed after the verbs *say, deny, assert, warn, allege, maintain, affirm* and *contend*, which would normally be followed by an object. The headline "Mayor says policy fair" sounds awkward, and it is grammatically incorrect. *Policy fair* is a separate clause here, not a direct object of *says*. The word *policy* is used as a subject of the clause *policy is fair*. Assuming that the story isn't about the mayor's ability to enunciate words, the subject of the second clause needs an expressed verb:

Mayor says policy is fair

If the order of the clauses is reversed, then the *to be* verb can be implied without confusing readers:

Policy unfair, mayor says

A related rule is that *the verb in a headline should have a subject.* Otherwise, the publication becomes sprinkled with commands, like this gem: "Throw child in river." Where attribution is essential to avoid editorializing in a headline, copy editors sometimes yield to the temptation to begin a headline with a verb of attribution without any subject: "Says taxes must increase." Resist such temptation.

Use the present tense to indicate both present and past action, future tense for future action. Instead of writing "Jones defeated Smith," write

Jones defeats Smith

Use the active voice, rather than the passive voice, because the active voice gives the headline greater impact. Instead of "Walkout staged by nurses," for example, write

Nurses stage walkout

In multiline headlines, *keep thought units together on the same line.* That is, don't separate parts of a verb, proper nouns that go together, a preposition from its object, or a modifier from the word it modifies. Observe where the lines break in the following examples:

Teachers seek
pay increase

Teachers call
for pay hike

New tax revenue
to improve streets

As a general rule, *omit the articles* a, an, *and* the, both to save space and to speed the pace of a headline. Sometimes, however, an article is essential to understanding. The meaning of "King takes little liquor" is different from the meaning of "King takes a little liquor." Sometimes articles are needed for flow and phrasing of a headline, as in this example from The New York Times:

Game Trophies: What's Good for a Goose Is Bad for a Moose

Use only common abbreviations and acronyms in headlines. Except for abbreviations commonly used in writing for a public audience, abbreviations should not appear in headlines. For example, this headline uses abbreviation correctly:

Navratilova gets win No. 100

This headline misuses abbreviation in three different places: "Floods close Calif., Nev. mtn. passes." *California, Nevada* and *mountain* should all be spelled out, as they are in ordinary writing.

Some acronyms—words formed from the initial letters of a name, like CORE for Congress of Racial Equality—and combinations of initials have become readily understood vocabulary in the United States. *NATO, SWAT* and *AIDS* are acronyms that most American readers immediately recognize and understand, as are the abbreviations *U.S., GM, IBM, CIA* and *FBI.* These familiar terms should be used to condense headlines. Many more acronyms and combinations of initials are not familiar to readers, however, and should not be used in headlines.

A practical method for deciding whether to use a particular abbreviation or acronym in a headline is to make a short list of those that are familiar to readers and common in ordinary public writing. Then, when you question whether you should use an abbreviation or acronym, check your list. If the term is not on it, you may be wise to spell it out or rephrase the headline rather than abbreviate it or reduce it to initials.

It is just as important to *punctuate headlines correctly* as it is to punctuate stories correctly. In most instances, headlines are punctuated like sentences but without a period at the end. Here are a few exceptions:

- *Commas* may be used to replace the word *and*, as in these examples:

Wind topples tower, rips roofs from homes

President selects Smith, Jones as envoys

- *Semicolons* are used in headlines, as in sentences, to separate independent clauses:

Wind topples tower; rain floods city streets

A semicolon is needed in this example because the headline contains two separate clauses, each with its own subject and predicate verb.
- *Periods* are used in headlines for some abbreviations. They are not used to designate the end of a headline.
- *Ampersands* should not be used in headlines except when they are a customary part of a title or phrase, such as *AT&T.*
- *Hyphens* should not be used at the end of a line in a headline, because they interfere with the line-by-line approach that readers use for reading headlines. If you end up with an end-of-line hyphen—

Post goes to write-in candidate, Jones

—rewrite it:

Write-in candidate wins mayor's race

- *Exclamation marks* are almost never needed in a headline. However, in its zeal to emphasize the unusualness of two major league no-hitters in a single day, an Ohio newspaper used seven exclamation marks:

O my! 2 no-hitters!!!!!!

It was a rare feat. One exclamation mark in a headline is normally one too many.

- *Question marks* are rarely effective, because a news headline should answer questions rather than ask them. Exceptions are those few stories that pose questions without answering them or the occasional headline that not only asks a question but immediately answers it, as in this example from The New York Times:

Fake Cheese? No Whey!

- *Quotation marks* in headlines should be single quotation marks, rather than double quotation marks, to save space:

Senate leader calls tax plan 'a windfall for big business'

- *Colons* and *dashes* may be used in headlines to indicate attribution. A verb of attribution, such as *says,* is preferred. But where space does not allow a word, a colon or dash may take its place:

Sen. Jones: budget 'unfair'

Budget 'unfair'— Sen. Jones

Use a colon after the name of the person and *before* the opinion. If the opinion comes first, use a dash.

Depending on the publication's style, *write the headline with upstyle or downstyle capitalization.* In an earlier era, newspapers and magazines commonly set headlines all in capital letters. But legibility research has demonstrated that type set all in capitals is more difficult to read than type set in capitals and lowercase letters, so most publications have abandoned the all-caps style of headline.

Try reading this paragraph:

DOWNSTYLE AND UPSTYLE HEADLINE CAPITALI-
ZATION HAVE SEVERAL ADVANTAGES OVER USING
ONLY CAPITAL LETTERS. MORE CHARACTERS FIT

LEGIBLY IN EACH LINE OF A HEADLINE IN DOWN-STYLE OR UPSTYLE, AND DOWNSTYLE REQUIRES FEWER KEYBOARD FUNCTIONS FOR TYPISTS. MOST IMPORTENT, RESEARCHERS DISCOVERED DURING THE '50S THAT USING ALL CAPITAL LETTERS SLOWS READING.

All-capital type is just as hard to read in headlines as it is in body type. In the paragraph you just read, for example, you may have put so much effort into making out words that you didn't spot the typographical error (*important*) purposefully included in the paragraph.

Some newspapers, such as The New York Times, capitalize the first word of each line and all other principal words. This practice is called "false capitalization" or *upstyle*. Researchers have discovered that upstyle also slows reading. Try reading this paragraph in upstyle:

> Downstyle Headline Capitalization Has Several Advantages Over Upstyle. More Characters Fit Legibly in Each Line of a Headline in Downstyle, and Downstyle Requires Fewer Keyboard Functions for Typesetters. Most Important, Researchers Discovered During the '50s That Starting Each Word With a Capital Letter Slows Reading.

The same reading difficulty you experienced as you read this paragraph affects readers of headlines as well.

Most U.S. newspapers now use *downstyle* headlines, meaning that sentence-style capitalization is used: the first word of the headline and proper nouns. All other words are set in lowercase letters:

Stocks finish ahead after weak start

Another guideline for headline writers is to *use the available headline space to communicate specific facts rather than pad the headline merely to fill space*. For example, in the preceding headline, the phrase *after weak start* provides additional information, whereas *in trading today* would have filled the space with the obvious instead of adding a thought. Headline padding is distracting, is usually obvious and weakens an otherwise good headline.

Always check the headline before returning it to the copy desk chief for approval. Check the facts against the story, recount the lines, and ensure that clarity of meaning and appropriateness of tone have been maintained. One good method to use in checking for ambiguity or obscurity is to put the headline back into skeletonized sentence form to see if it is easily understandable.

Feature heads

Many feature headlines, like feature stories, are considered "dessert." A copy editor has the same license in composing feature headlines that a reporter has in writing feature stories. In fact, a headline should strike the same tone as the story. A Lexington, Ky., Herald-Leader copy editor properly topped a feature story about a convention for match cover collectors in this way:

It's probably not a good idea to smoke around these people

Literary devices are often used in feature headlines:

- *Rhyme.* Copy editors who have a flair for rhyme should restrain themselves when writing headlines for straight news stories. The editor who wrote this headline on a straight news story should have been asked to write another: "Convention parley called by Farley." These rhyming headlines work, however:

Never saw a purple cow, never even hoped; sees purple, sees cow, Bossy had been doped

Big chills of December bring big bills in January

- *Alliteration.* Like rhyme, alliteration sounds cheap and tinny when pursued self-consciously, as in this case: "Yamboree, Yambassadors, Yambitious." But this bit of alliteration caught the spirit of the story:

Plumber's pause for poodle's paws proves profitable

- *Puns.* The pun, too, has a false sound when pursued self-consciously, but these examples are not offensive:

Texas golfer gets a birdie on the wing

To know Italians: knead their bread

Local dinosaur show headed for extinction

- *Twisted cliches.* A trite expression is as objectionable in a headline as it is in a story. But a cliche given a sprightly twist has the advantage of both the familiar and the novel, as here:

Science to take drunk apart to find out what makes him hic

- *Allusion.* There was a time when many newspapers used literary allusions much too freely. "Borgia poisons husband to wed Adonis of beach" was fairly typical. In time, the far-fetched literary allusion became trite. The trend seems to be toward allusions to popular songs and sayings, as in this headline over the story of a music festival celebrated in defiance of a court ban:

The banned played on

When dealing with a feature story, the most important goal is for the headline to reflect the story's tone and epitomize the story's spirit. In feature stories where the surprise twist at the end is the only real point of the story, it is foolish to reveal this point in the headline.

Headline counting
Earlier in this chapter we referred to the difficulty of writing a good headline within limited space. Now it's time to face the problem squarely by learning

Exhibit 6-1

Each character has a unit value corresponding to the amount of horizontal space it occupies, relative to other characters.

Capital letters	=	1 1/2 units
Except: M, W	=	2 units
I	=	1 unit
Lowercase letters	=	1 unit
Except: m, w	=	1 1/2 units
l, i, f, t	=	1/2 unit
Punctuation	=	1/2 unit
Except: dash, question mark	=	1 unit
Symbols (%, #, &, $)	=	1 unit
Numbers	=	1 unit
Except: 1	=	1/2 unit
Space between words	=	1/2 unit

how to count the units—letters, punctuation marks and spaces—that make up a headline.

Until recent years, copy editors wrote their headlines on paper, often on half-size sheets of typing paper, and counted each of the units themselves. A single headline might be counted many times as words were changed over and over in an effort to compose a well-written headline that fit the allotted space.

Today computers programmed to "head fit" have relieved most newspaper copy editors of the drudgery of headline counting. Students should know how to count headlines without the aid of a computer, however, because not all newspapers, magazines and public relations firms have computers with headline-fitting programs. A young journalist shouldn't be rejected for a job for not knowing how to count headlines manually.

Although various styles of type have slightly different widths, Exhibit 6-1 is a useful method of estimating the unit value of each letter, punctuation mark and space.

At a typical newspaper, the process of headline writing begins when the copy editor is given a story to edit. Usually a headline size and style already have been assigned to the story to conform to the page layout. But sometimes the copy is marked *HTK*, meaning "headline to come," so the copy editor can work on the story while the layout is being finalized.

Headline size and style are usually specified in code. For example, the headline designation 1-30-3 BB means that the editor wants a headline one column wide, in 30-point type, with three lines. *BB* refers to the family of type, in this case Bodoni Bold. (Type styles and sizes are discussed in Chapter 9.) Because 72-point type is an inch tall, each line of a 30-point headline is slightly less than half an inch tall.

After receiving the headline assignment, the copy editor consults a head-line schedule like the one in Exhibit 6-2 to determine the maximum number of units in a 1-30-3 headline. The schedule shows that a maximum of 11 units of 30-point Bodoni Bold type will fit on each line when it is set one column wide. The same size of type set two columns wide will accommodate 21 units.

After a few weeks on the copy desk, editors have most of the headline schedule for their publication memorized. The unit counts listed in the headline schedule are the maximum number that will fit for each type size and column width; most publications allow headlines that are as much as two units short of the maximum count.

Typeface: Bodoni Bold (BB) Bodoni Bold Italic (BBI)						
Number of columns wide						
Type size in points	1	2	3	4	5	6
14	22	45				
18	18	35	52			
24	13	26.5	40	53		
30	11	21	33	47	55	
36	9	18	27	35	44	53
48	7	13.5	20	27	34	41
60	5	11	17	21.5	27	33
72	4.5	9	13	18	22	26

Exhibit 6-2
A headline schedule is used to determine how many units can fit in the space allotted for a headline. The entries in the body of the table are the maximum numbers of units for a given type size and column width. The absence of exact multiples in some columns is due to a rounding error.

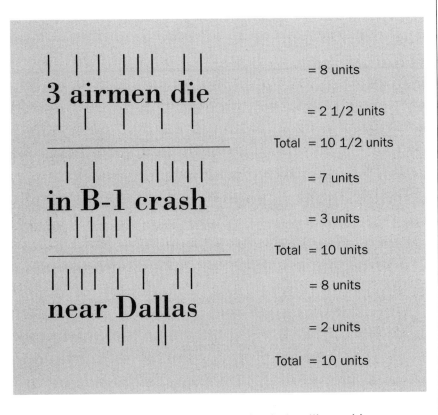

Exhibit 6-3
To estimate the length of a headline, some editors use pencil marks: Marks above the line of type count as one unit, those below as half a unit.

After editing the story, the copy editor begins the headline-writing process, starting with a skeleton sentence and polishing to fit the desired number of units. Copy editors who count headlines manually work out their own techniques for adding up units. One system uses pencil marks above the line for each whole unit and marks below the line for each half unit. Exhibit 6-3 shows how to count a headline that will fit the 1-30-3 BB assignment. With practice, you should be able to count quickly without using little marks above and below the line.

Computers have simplified immensely the job of headline counting. Now the copy editor working at a VDT can strike one or more keys to instruct the computer to count the headline that has been written. The commands that the editor uses vary slightly according to the computer system, but all are relatively easy to learn, and all speed the headline-writing process.

With one widely used computer system, the copy editor hits one key to instruct the computer to enter the "head fit" mode. Then the editor inserts a code for the typeface and size, hits the Execute key, moves the VDT cursor to the top of the story and begins composing the headline. A line at the top of the VDT screen provides a running count of the width as each unit is typed. All guesswork is removed from the process, because the computer has been programmed with the precise width of each letter, number and punctuation mark for all available typefaces and sizes.

With another popular computer system, a highlighted bar at the top of the story shows exactly how much space the editor has for the headline. Any letter typed beyond that highlighted space exceeds the maximum.

Headline writers in the computer era receive another break in fitting headlines, because computers are not bound by the standard point sizes of display type: 14, 18, 24, 30, 36, 42, 48, 60, 72, 84. Let's say that the copy editor has written an excellent headline for a 2-36-2 BB assignment, but one line of the headline counts 18.5 units. As you can see from Exhibit 6-2, 18 is the maximum number of units for each line of a 2-36-2 headline. The editor might achieve the desired width by instructing the computer to set the type at 35 points or even 34 points, just a little smaller than 36 points. Although purists object to deviating from standard point sizes in headlines, this slight variation usually goes unnoticed.

Until recently, copy editors were instructed that the maximum headline count was absolute, because "you can't squeeze type." Today, however, type can be "squeezed" slightly through a technique known as *kerning*. Computers can be programmed for *positive kerning*, which means fitting letters together more closely, or *negative kerning*, moving letters farther apart. But many editors frown on kerning because squeezed and stretched type has an unnatural look.

Limitation of space is one of the greatest difficulties facing the headline writer. The restrictive unit counts indicated by the headline schedule can so intimidate new copy editors that they feel defeated before they begin. The real difficulty may be a reluctance to discard old ideas and try new ones.

Hanging on to a headline idea that is not working is not symptomatic of new copy editors alone. Many experienced editors become so attached to the first line of a headline that they are reluctant to give it up even when they are unable to find a second line to go with it. Editors should see the headline as a whole rather than as a group of separate lines.

Able headline writers keep a good thesaurus close at hand and have many synonyms filed away in their brain. Their headline vocabulary includes many short words, as in Exhibit 6-4.

Placement of headlines

Typically a headline is placed above the story, as in this example:

Japanese company to build auto plant in Tennessee

A headline should never appear below the story, but it may be placed to the side. A *side head* is almost always placed to the left of the story, although in

accident: crash, wreck, collide

accuse, charge: cite

acknowledge: admit, confess

acquire: get

advocate: urge, push, spur

agreement: accord, pledge, pact, harmony, compact

allocate: give, allot, issue, award

alteration: revise, fix, change

answer: reply

appointment: post, job

apprehend: catch, arrest, seize, trap, capture

approve: accept, back, confirm, laud

argument: debate

arrange: set, plan, shape, slate

arrest: seize, hold, net

assemble: meet, gather, rally, unite

attempt: try

beginning: start, opening, initial

bewilderment: puzzle, confusion, mystery

celebrate: mark, stage, perform, fete

celebration: fete, event, party

choose: name, elect, pick

climax: peak

command: lead, rule, direct, reign, sway

commander: leader, guide, chief, ruler

committee, commission: body, panel, board

compete: vie

confess: admit

conspiracy: plan, plot, scheme

construct: build, erect, rise

contract: pact

convene: meet

criticize: score

criticize strongly: blast, flay

damage: hurt, impair, raze, scar, wreck, harm

danger: risk, peril, threat

decision: rule, order, writ, decree

decline, decrease: dip, fall

defeat: loss, fall

defraud: steal, dupe, fleece, rob, swindle, trick, raid

demonstrate: show, display, exhibit, test, try, melee, rebellion, revolt, riot, tumult, turmoil, uprising, uproar, discord, din

destroy: raze

diminish: trim, reduce, lop, cut

discrimination: bias, prejudice

earthquake: quake, jolt, shock, temblor, tremor

encourage: spark, help, aid

examine: scan, study

expose, reveal: bare

former: ex

impede, halt: balk

increase: hike, rise, add, gain, up, add

inform: tell

investigate: probe, study

leader: guide, chief, head, expert, ruler

limit, restrain: curb, relax, save, soften, temper

meeting: session, parlay, assembly

murder: kill, slay

nominate: slate, pick, choose, name

nullify: void

opposition: battle, clash, challenge, combat, differ, divide, lash, quarrel, rap, rebuff, upbraid

organization: board, body, band, club, firm, group, unit

organize: join, form, unite, tie, link, merge

overcome: win, beat

perceive: see, understand, envision, foretell

pledge: vow, agree, oath

position: job, post

postpone: delay, defer, put off, shelve

prevent: bar, ban, curb, stop

promise: vow, pledge, agree

pursuit: chase, hunt, seek, track, follow, trail

puzzle: awe, confuse, stun, mystery, surprise, nonplus, perplex

quarrel: tiff, clash, argue

question: quiz, ask, inquire

realignment: revise, alter, change, shake up

reconcile: settle, peace, patch, pacify, heal

relieve: allay, cure, ease, end, free, help

request: ask, beg, bid, exhort, implore, plead, urge, seek, plea

resign: quit

restrain: stop, avert, check, curb, curtail, deter, foil, halt, hinder, impede, limit, quell, repress, slacken, slow, stall, stem, tie up, pause

reveal: tell

revise: alter, change, shift, vary, switch, transfer, modify

ridicule: chide, deride, insult, jeer, mock, taunt, tease, twit

salute: greet, hail

schedule: slate, set, plan, arrange

separation: rift, break, split

settlement: accord, deal, pact, truce, bargain

silent: mum, mute

steal: rob, loot, take

suggestion: plan, idea, offer, design

suspend: stop, end

thwart: foil, stop, limit

transfer: shift, alter, adjust

violence: battle, struggle, fray, fracas, furor, brawl, chaos, clamor, clash, combat

wrangle: argue, debate

wreck: raze

zealous: ardent, fervent, avid

extremely rare circumstances a side head to the right can be effective. A side head is particularly useful for filling a wide, shallow space at the top of an inside page, like this:

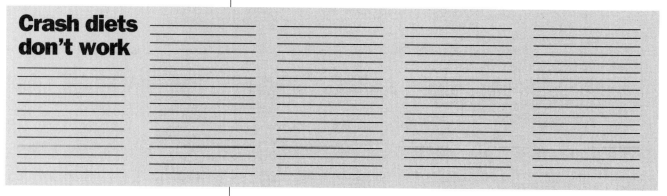

Japanese company to build auto plant in Tennessee

Generally, a headline should cover all columns of a story. That is, if the layout calls for the story to be wrapped across more than one column, then the headline should extend across the top of all the columns. *Raw wraps*, also called *Dutch turns*, are columns of type without a headline above them. Raw wraps should not be used routinely, but they can help give good display to a graphic or other artwork. They also prevent the problem of side-by-side headlines, which are called *tombstones*. The following example shows raw wraps at the tops of columns 2, 3, 4 and 5.

Crash diets don't work

The placement of headlines within a page layout is explained in greater detail in Chapter 10.

Styles of headlines

The main element of a newspaper headline is known as the *top*. A secondary heading under the top is known as a *deck* or *bank*. The top of a headline should contain the main highlights of the story. The decks, if used, should give more information about the story rather than repeat in different words what was already said in the top. Although both the top and the decks should follow the usual headline-writing rules and should be able to stand alone, the decks usually depend on the top for full meaning.

When newspapers were printed on flat-bed presses, mechanical restrictions limited headlines to one column wide. Lead strips, placed between each column to help hold the metal type in place as the page was put together, prevented headline type from extending beyond a single column. In addition, although newspaper pages historically were somewhat wider than today's page, they were divided into eight or nine columns, meaning that headline writers had even less space per column to work with than today's copy editors. These restrictions led to multiple-deck headlines that, for a major story, might run most of the length of a page. This 16-deck headline, with each line centered and each deck ended by a period, was typical of newspaper headlines during the Civil War:

THE WAR.

Highly Important News from Baltimore.

The Massachusetts Volunteers Opposed in Their Passage Through the City.

Bloody Fight Between the Soldiers and the Mob.

Two Soldiers and Seven Citizens Killed.

The Volunteers Succeed in Forcing Their Way Through.

Total Destruction of the Arsenal at Harper's Ferry by the Federal Troops.

Seizure of Northern Vessels in Virginia.

Delaware Assumes the Position of Armed Neutrality.

IMPORTANT FROM WASHINGTON.

PROCLAMATION OF THE PRESIDENT.

BLOCKADE OF THE SOUTHERN PORTS.

Departure of the Rhode Island, Massachusetts and New York Troops for Washington.

The Seventh Regiment, Nearly One Thousand Strong, En Route for the Capital.

Immense Turnout of Ladies and Citizens to See Them Off.

Pathetic Leave Takings at the Railroad Depot.

Flush left: XXXXXXXXX
                       XXXXXXX
                       XXXXXXXX
                       XXXXXXXXXX

Hanging indent: XXXXXXXXXX
                       XXXXXXX
                       XXXXXXX
                       XXXXXXX
                       XXXXXXX

Step line: XXXXXXXXX
                          XXXXXXXXX
                             XXXXXXXXX
                                XXXXXXXXX

Inverted pyramid: XXXXXXXXXXXXXX
                        XXXXXXXXX
                          XXXXX
                           XXXX

Pyramid: XXXX
                         XXXXXX
                       XXXXXXXXXXX
                      XXXXXXXXXXXXXXX

By the time the reader got through all those decks, there was little new information in the body of the story. The New York Times topped its story about the assassination of President Abraham Lincoln with the words "AWFUL EVENT," followed by seven decks.

Newspapers today favor flush-left headlines, but other styles are sometimes used (see Exhibit 6-5).

Modern typesetting and printing technology accommodate a wide variety of headline sizes, typefaces and widths. *Banner* headlines, sometimes called *screamers* or *streamers*, can run the entire width of the page. A *skyline banner* is a headline that runs the width of the front page and is placed above the nameplate. The skyline banner, also referred to as a *promo* or a *teaser,* is used to promote or call attention to an important story on an inside page of the paper.

Research shows that newspaper readers of the 1990s want more information quickly in easily digested chunks. Editors have responded with shorter stories, more graphics and more headlines—especially headlines in styles that allow readers to grab more information at a glance.

A *readout* headline, also called a *dropout*, often is used in combination with a banner headline to draw the reader into the body of the story (see Exhibit 6-6). The readout headline should be written to stand independently of the main headline and should add to information given in the main headline. The example in Exhibit 6-6 shows the readout beneath the end of the main headline, but the readout can also be placed in the first column, under the first words of the banner.

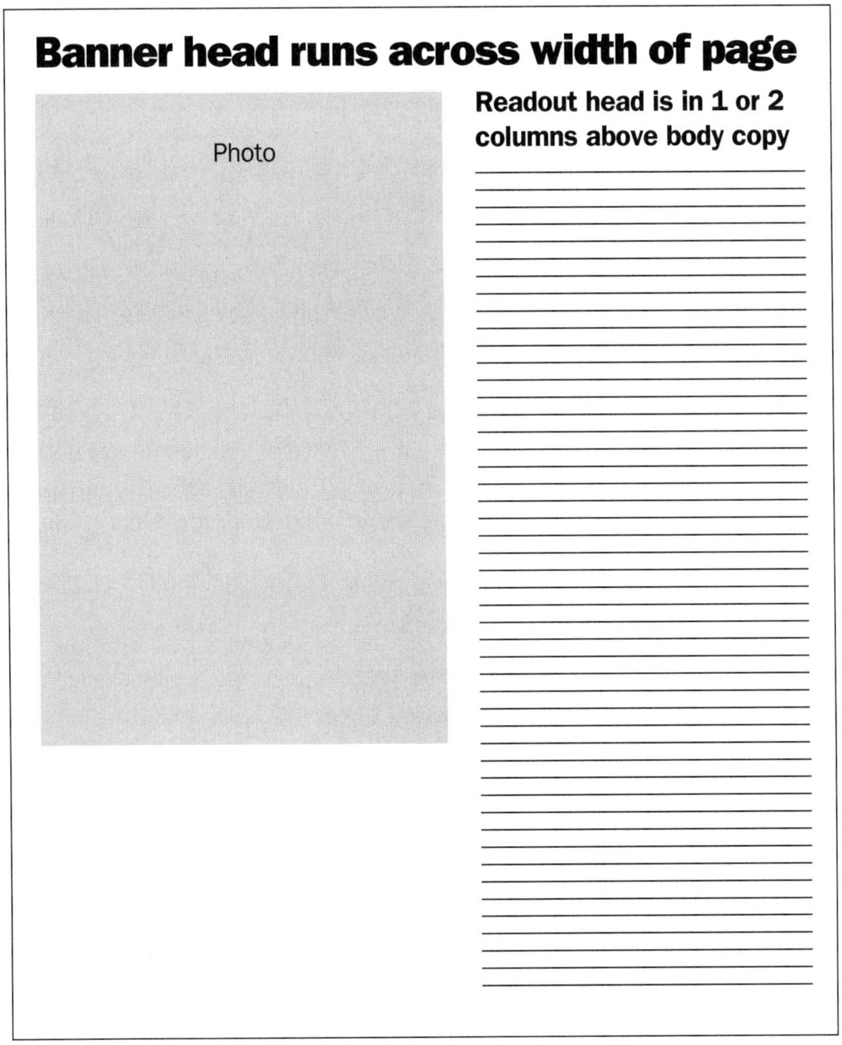

Banner head runs across width of page

Photo

Readout head is in 1 or 2 columns above body copy

Exhibit 6-6
A readout headline is one device used to create greater reader interest in a story and more variety in the look of a page.

Underlines and *overlines* are sometimes used in combination with a multicolumn main headline and are set in type about half the size of the main headline. An underline would look like this:

Main head is flush left, larger type
Underline is in smaller type, usually centered

An overline would reverse the positions of the two lines, with the smaller type above the larger type. Each headline should be a complete thought unit, with the underline or overline amplifying the main headline.

A *kicker*, also called an *eyebrow*, is another headline style. The kicker is sometimes just a label or phrase rather than a clause, with a subject and verb. The main headline should not depend on the kicker for its meaning; that is, the kicker should not read into the main headline. Instead, the kicker should depend for its meaning on the main headline. In addition, the kicker should be set in type no larger than half the size of the main headline and in a different type weight. Because one purpose of the kicker is to introduce white space into the layout, the kicker should extend no more than two-thirds the width of the main headline, usually less, and the main headline should be indented by the same number of points as the size in which it is set. Many publications underline kickers. Here is an example of a headline with a kicker from the Los Angeles Times:

Patchwork Laws

Government
Financing:
Call It Chaos

A *hammer*, also called a *reverse kicker* or *barker*, reverses the ratio of the kicker to the headline's main element, using type twice as large as the main element of the headline. The hammer is set either flush left or centered above the main headline. The main element of a hammer headline should be two lines long and indented the same number of points as the type size of the hammer. Two lines of main headline are needed to create enough optical weight to draw the reader's eye. The indentation forms an area of white space beneath the hammer to balance the space to the right of the main headline. Here is an example:

Plane crash

43 people drown
in Gulf of Mexico

Used less often than the kicker or hammer are three other styles of headlines that add variety to newspaper or magazine layouts. The *tripod* headline has a single line of large type at the left and two lines of smaller type at the right. This headline from the St. Petersburg Times is a typical tripod:

Ticket Wars: Now you can see first-run films for less—at some theaters

Here is an example of a *wicket* headline:

The *slash* headline is like the wicket and tripod headline in type sizes and arrangement, but a six- to nine-point rule is set at a 45-degree angle between the two parts of the headline. The top edge of the left module should be as high as the top of the slash and the bottom edge of the right module as low as the bottom end of the slash. Here is an example:

The large type in a tripod, wicket or slash headline should be twice the size of the smaller type. The break between the two modules composing such a headline should occur in the middle of a column of body type. If the break is at the space between columns, readers might mistake the bimodular headline for two separate headlines. The easiest way to make sure that the break between modules will come midcolumn—and it is easy indeed with computerized "head fitting"—is to keep the subsidiary element in the headline as short as one-and-a-half columns or even half a column wide.

Two other types of headlines—the *subhead* and the *jump headline*—are named for their purpose rather than for their appearance. Many newspapers and magazines use subheads to break up large gray areas of copy and make pages look more inviting for readers. Although subheads run in the body of the story rather than above it, they are usually written by copy editors.

Subheads may be centered or flush left, in the same size as the body type or slightly larger, in boldface or italic. Subheads function as little headlines for the paragraphs immediately underneath them. Except for being only one line long, subheads are written just like headlines, but they are often without verbs. This example of a subhead comes from a long story in The New York Times on environmental damage caused by an oil spill off the coast of Alaska:

The enormous toll on wildlife in the Sound, catalogued in an 18-page summary of 58 scientific studies, also includes losses of killer whales, extensive reproductive defects in salmon and herring fry, and widespread and lingering damage to sea grasses and other plants in tidal zones along 1,200 miles of the western boundary of the Sound and down the coast in the Gulf of Alaska, which were coated by oil for months.

Better Left Alone

Government scientists also said today that efforts to clean hundreds of miles of the Sound's shorelines with pressurized and heated sea water caused more damage to shellfish, sea grasses and other organisms in the tidal zones than if the shorelines had been left alone.

Newspaper feature pages use other spacing and typographical devices to relieve the tedium of reading paragraph after paragraph of body type. Sometimes large capital letters begin occasional paragraphs, allowing extra white space between the end of the previous paragraph and the one with the *initial letter.* For example:

The enormous toll on wildlife in the Sound, catalogued in an 18-page summary of 58 scientific studies, also includes losses of killer whales, extensive reproductive defects in salmon and herring fry, and widespread and lingering damage to sea grasses and other plants in tidal zones along 1,200 miles of the western boundary of the Sound and down the coast in the Gulf of Alaska, which were coated by oil for months.

Many newspapers and magazines use subheads to break up large gray areas of copy.

> **G**overnment scientists also said today that efforts to clean hundreds of miles of the Sound's shorelines with pressurized and heated sea water caused more damage to shellfish, sea grasses and other organisms in the tidal zones than if the shorelines had been left alone.

Some publications simply insert 12 or 18 points of white space between occasional paragraphs or insert *dingbats*, such as dots or small symbols related to the story's content or the nature of the publication. Some publications use boldface *lead-ins*, meaning that the first two or three words of occasional paragraphs—every fifth or sixth paragraph, for example—are set in boldface, either capitals and lowercase or all caps. Here is an example of the use of boldface lead-ins:

> The enormous toll on wildlife in the Sound, catalogued in an 18-page summary of 58 scientific studies, also includes losses of killer whales, extensive reproductive defects in salmon and herring fry, and widespread and lingering damage to sea grasses and other plants in tidal zones along 1,200 miles of the western boundary of the Sound and down the coast in the Gulf of Alaska, which were coated by oil for months.
>
> **GOVERNMENT SCIENTISTS** also said today that efforts to clean hundreds of miles of the Sound's shorelines with pressurized and heated sea water caused more damage to shellfish, sea grasses and other organisms in the tidal zones than if the shorelines had been left alone.

Another popular method of breaking long passages of type is to use a *breakout quotation,* or *pullout quotation,* within a story. This is an interesting or important passage in the story, often a direct quotation, that is repeated in larger type and set in a box or sideless box within the story. A very long story, particularly one that jumps to another page, may have more than one breakout quotation. This treatment relieves the grayness of the page and provides another point of entry to lure readers into the story. Exhibit 6-7 is an example of a breakout quotation in a 1991 story about plans to check for toxic chemicals in the water at the vice presidential mansion and the White House after President and Mrs. Bush were diagnosed with similar medical problems.

Jump heads are used to identify a story that is being continued from a previous page. Readers often complain about having to turn to another page to read the rest of the story, and they find it particularly irritating to have to search for the continuation of the story on the jump page. How a newspaper or magazine treats its "continued" lines and its jump headlines is part of the publication's overall design and should be consistent from page to page and issue to issue so readers become familiar with the style.

Some newspapers write a separate display headline, often multicolumn,

Another popular method of breaking long passages of type is to use a breakout quotation.

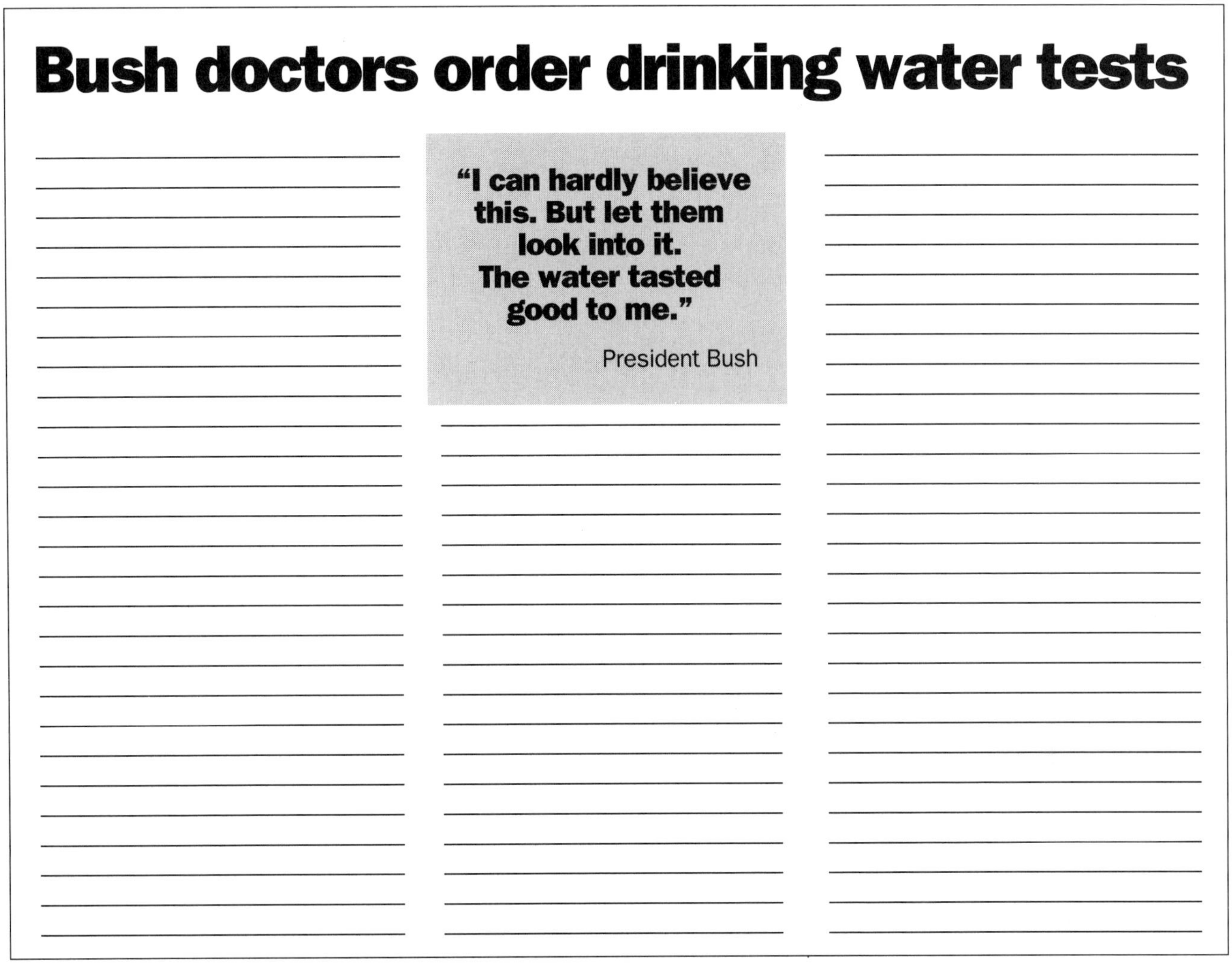

Bush doctors order drinking water tests

_____
_____
_____
_____
_____
_____
_____
_____
_____
_____
_____
_____
_____
_____
_____
_____
_____
_____
_____
_____
_____
_____

"I can hardly believe this. But let them look into it. The water tasted good to me."

President Bush

_____
_____
_____
_____
_____
_____
_____
_____
_____
_____
_____
_____
_____
_____
_____
_____
_____
_____

for the part of the story that is jumped. A line placed at the top of the first column of body type under the headline informs the reader that the story is "continued from Page 1." Other editors dislike this style because they think it confuses the reader and needlessly uses valuable space. These editors prefer to use a one-word headline, often set in 24-, 30-, 36- or 42-point type, that repeats the main word of the top headline or is the key word of the story. That word is followed by the "continued from Page 1" line. For example:

JONES
(continued from Page 1)

Exhibit 6-7
A breakout quotation, also called a pullout quotation, relieves the grayness of the page and provides another point of entry to lure readers into the story.

THE UNAPPRECIATED ART OF WRITING HEADLINES

By Lynn Ludlow

On a day of summer news, editors at the San Francisco Examiner chose to fill the upper left corner of the front page with a report on ants. It called for an appropriate headline, one of 153 that would appear in the afternoon edition of July 22, 1988. The slot editor, Courtenay Peddle, electronically dispatched the headline order to the video display terminal of George K. "Tommy" Thompson, an old-timer in the demanding but unappreciated art of headline writing.

For newspaper readers who skim, which includes just about everybody, headlines are more than ephemeral signposts in the information swamp. The reader pauses, reads "Ant incursions bother housewives" and moves on to other headlines about the news of the day.

Good copy editors are multitalented masters of news journalism. They edit stories for grammar, spelling, punctuation and conformity to style rules. In the computer era they also serve as proofreaders, looking for typographical errors and problems with typesetting. They must encode the text in the computer so that it will be set in the correct size, width and type style. As for content, the copy editors check facts, fill holes, look for balance, guard against libel, clarify ambiguities, trim superfluities and, sometimes, reorganize the text of a reporter's golden prose. Then they must compose a headline that will summarize or highlight the salient point, a creative process that relies on a critical analysis of the story as a whole.

Reporters are expected to be assertive, confident, action-oriented and eloquent. Copy editors are perceived instead as shy, semireclusive, analytical and self-deprecatory. When complimented on a particularly apt headline, for example, Tommy Thompson will mumble that even a blind pig can sometimes snuffle up an acorn.

But this was a routine day when he was handling a routine headline order on a routine story. He scrolled through the ant text, which had been written the night before by veteran reporter John Todd. He began like this:

When Anita Lowry goes to the cupboard to pack a lunch for her kids, it's no picnic.

Every time she opens the door, the shelves are crawling with ants.

"I've never seen anything like it," the San Rafael housewife said. "There are millions of them. I've almost cried."

Driven from their nests by the drought and extraordinarily hot weather, armies of ants are marching on the Bay area. . . .

The headline order came from the news desk, where the front page is designed. The editor had requested a 1-36-3 with a 1-15-2 deck. This is a standard one-column headline for the top of a page. It consists of three flush-left lines of boldface letters in a basic headline font, a plain typeface known as Helvetica. The size category is 36 points, or half an inch. It seems bigger because it sits on a cushion of white space. Underneath is a bank (in some shops called a deck, occasionally a readout). It consists of two lines of 15-point medium Helvetica, which is lighter than the boldface type above.

Thompson couldn't just write whatever words that might come to

Reprinted from *Et Cetera*, Vol. 45, No. 3, with permission of the International Society for General Semantics.

mind, such as "Marching myrmidons molest Marin manors." Aside from informal bans these days on alliteration and obscure terms of classical origin, headlines are all the news that's print to fit. They can't exceed their assigned space. On most newspapers, they must also fill out at least three-fourths of the line.

The width of each standard news column at the Examiner, as in most six-column formats nowadays, is 12 picas plus three points. Each pica is a sixth of an inch. The column width is therefore about as wide as 2 inches and a toothpick. Thompson could barely fit about 10 medium-sized characters into each line, a task made more complicated by variations in the width of each letter. A capital *M*, for example, takes up two spaces; a lowercase *i* is less than a half space. *Wham* is more than twice as wide as *fill*. This helps explain why headline writers are fond of the Illini sports teams at the University of Illinois. It's why Eisenhower became Ike.

Thompson's job became somewhat more difficult because the 1-36 headline, a common form in newspapers of the world, normally appears in a prominent position. Copy editors thus feel a professional obligation to produce a headline of quality, something concise, bright, accurate, clear, fresh, catchy and memorable.

Hmmmm. Give it a try. Three lines of 10 counts each followed by two lines of 22 counts each. I came up with this one. Pick up a pencil and see if you can improve on it.

Ants invade households in Bay Area

Drought and heat drive pests from their nests

Such a headline would probably satisfy the average copy editor. Thompson is not average. Although 72 years old in a line of work now dominated by intense editors half his age, he is frequently handed the toughest headline orders of the day.

It's been his job for more than 30 years. Thompson began his career on small newspapers in the Midwest and arrived as a reporter in 1941 on the old San Francisco Call-Bulletin, which merged with the News in 1956. He then switched to the copy desk, surviving the newspaper's merger with the Examiner in 1965.

Computers were figments of science fiction when Thompson began writing headlines around the rim of the traditional newspaper copy desk, which was shaped something like a horseshoe. Inside the slot was the chief copy editor, known in the East as a slotman; in the West, as the dealer.

Copy would arrive at the old copy desk in takes, a term coined when copy boys would take stories sheet by sheet from the smoking Underwood of a reporter on deadline. The news editor, who would decide how to play each story, would mark the layout dummy with the story's name, or slug, and choose an appropriate headline. He would scribble the headline size and style on the first take. Then the story would go to the dealer, who would pass it to one of the deskmen. The copy editor would inscribe corrections on the copy and mark it with directions for the Linotype operators. Headlines were usually written with pencils on half-sheets of newsprint and sent to the backshop, there to be cast in type.

The headline itself is considered an American invention. It came after centuries when newspapers were festooned instead with captions, the term used for static labels or headings. Present-tense verbs burst into headlines near the end of the 19th century, when the new-fangled rotary press brought mass circulation dailies into urgent competition for readers.

Editors began to talk of banners, screamers, skylines, ribbons, wrap-arounds, snappers, kickers and eyebrows. Headlines were staggered, hung, stepped, indented, centered, boxed or shaped like a V. The language of headlines was shorn of auxiliary verbs, conjunctions, prepositions and articles. Verbs, ignored in caption days, became queens. As nouveau royalty, predicates began in the 1950s to kill off their subjects. Consider the Chicago Tribune's screamer of April 11, 1951: "FIRES GEN. M'ARTHUR."

The copy editor's language favored staccato yelps: *rap, pit, foe, rid, tie, cap, pry, ebb, cut, nip, nab, vow, rip, set, din, bid, aid, jar, try, act, rid, aim, fix, due, ban, jam, row,* etc. Perhaps a student of general semantics will someday attempt to analyze the subconscious effects on generations of newspaper readers assaulted each day with a headline vocabulary of Anglo-Saxon terms chosen for brevity and violent impact: *fray, whip, rout, stun, raid, curb, howl, lash, spur, rout, slap, slash.*

Strangely, considering that copy editors live by the printed word, the lore of headline writing is passed down from one generation to the next by way of oral guidelines, mostly negative, mostly barked.

No, says the dealer, I *never* want to see *set* used again in this paper; it makes it too easy.

No, don't write heads with acronyms unless the story is about acronyms (in the Seattle Times: "You CETA Words but They Have NOAA Meaning").

No, don't use overworked pun ploys ("Jane is Fonda exercise").

No, *may* is unacceptable; someday, pigs "may" fly.

LYNN LUDLOW

After his first byline on the Tam News at Mill Valley, Calif., Tamalpais High School, Lynn Ludlow never seriously considered any other line of work. He later edited the Golden Gater at San Francisco State University, where eventually he received a degree in English. After Army service, he began his professional journalistic career as a sports writer and city-side summer replacement at the San Rafael, Calif., Independent Journal.

His next job was in the Midwest as the entire editorial staff of the Paxtin, Ill., Daily Record. He worked three years at the Champaign-Urbana, Ill., Courier, spent two more years at the San Jose, Calif., Mercury News and arrived at the San Francisco Examiner during the final two years of its circulation wars with the San Francisco Chronicle.

During the 1960s, Ludlow reported the Selma-to-Montgomery march of Dr. Martin Luther King Jr.; the free-speech movement at the University of California, Berkeley; the Oakland draft riots; the Republican convention in 1964; and years of violent antiwar protests at UC Berkeley and San Francisco State University. He produced a series of reports from Vietnam after the first Tet offensive of 1968.

In the 1970s, he specialized for a time in writing on consumer issues and white-collar crime. In the 1980s, in addition to reporting on public affairs in San Francisco, he went to Mexico to examine its collapsed economy and to Belfast to analyze the conflicts there.

Thrice nominated for the Pulitzer Prize, Ludlow has won the Scripps Foundation's Roy M. Howard Service Award and several awards from, among others, the Associated Press, San Francisco Press Club, San Francisco Consumer Action, American Association of Political Scientists and National Wildlife Federation.

For 20 years Ludlow was a lecturer in journalism and a campus newspaper adviser at San Francisco State University, where in 1987 he was honored for distinguished teaching. From 1968 to 1973, he supervised the Examiner's in-house intern program for minority reporters. He was also a faculty member with the Summer Program for Minority Journalists when it was taught at Columbia University.

Active in his unit of the Newspaper Guild, Ludlow was co-editor of its monthly newspaper. Later he co-founded Feed/back, the California Journalism Review, which was published for 11 years. He is associate editor of Et cetera, quarterly journal of the International Society for General Semantics. In this connection, he conceived and founded the Wuxtry Awards, named for the cry of newsboys at the turn of the century. The awards honor excellence in headline writing.

CREATIVE EDITING FOR PRINT MEDIA

No, avoid abbreviations. No, avoid officialese. No, avoid jargon. No, avoid cliches.

William P. G. Chapin, former chief copy editor at the San Francisco Chronicle, adds more oral tradition:

It helps to have a dirty mind if you're a headline writer. If you don't, you may in haste write headlines that are inadvertently smutty and sometimes downright obscene. I once let this headline slip past me:

Sex Crimes Laid to Soft Penal Policy

And then, minutes later, I rushed out to the composing room to retrieve it before it got into the newspaper.

Another worry is the prohibition against the crime known as a bad split, particularly if it appears to cast a verb as a noun.

Ants jam into homes of Bay Area wives

Headline writers on many newspapers aren't allowed to break closely associated words from one line to another or end the top line with a preposition, conjunction or article. They won't break up two-word titles or names. Nouns and associated adjectives must stick together on the same line; same with verbs and their parts, prepositions and their phrases, etc.

Most editors also agree with these rules:

- Use the active voice.
- Don't repeat key words.
- Avoid abbreviations (*Gov't, Int'l*).
- Avoid familiarity in serious news ("Ronnie Rips Gorby"), although it's usually okay in sports or entertainment ("Liz Awed by Doctor J").

These are far from trivial issues to mild-mannered copy editors, who tend to become crazed with argument over such questions as the "label headline." Some veterans of competition wars insist that headlines without verbs don't supply enough speed or action to lure readers into the story. Others, like Chapin, dislike inflexibility.

"Sometimes the verb does this, and sometimes it just eats up space that could be used to good advantage in another way," he said. "If you have a headline that says 'TOTAL WAR IN EUROPE,' it has no verb but sounds pretty damned active to me."

We tend to forget the honest, exciting and accurate headlines of the day. Instead, we remember the goofs, catastrophes and double entendres.

These stand out as:

- *Amazingly two-faced:* "DEAD BABY NAMES RACKET" (San Francisco Examiner, 1974)
- *Famously wrong:* "DEWEY DEFEATS TRUMAN" (Chicago Tribune, 1948)

- *Appallingly ignorant:* "More of us will live to be centurions" (Dover–New Philadelphia Times-Reporter, 1987).
- *Apocryphally possible:* "Illini Face Northwestern with Peters Out" (Champaign-Urbana News Gazette, 1929).

So many flubs are produced these days that editors of the Columbia Journalism Review get about 300 contributions from readers for every dozen examples that appear in each edition's amusing collection, "The Lower Case." The best have been collected in a coffee table gift booklet, "Red Tape Holds Up New Bridge."

Among them:

Jerk Injures Neck, Wins Award

FORMER PRESIDENT ENTERS DINAH SHORE

Newspaper to recieve seven awards

Gates asks Reagan to recall name

Belfast man charged for Harrods bomb

Copy editors just shrug. Instead, they tend to recall favorite examples of word play: Willis Peck in the San Jose Mercury, "Nature sends her egrets"; Fred Faour in the Houston Chronicle, "OOOOOOOOOOO-rioles do it!"; John Woolard in the Los Angeles Herald Examiner, "Odds Man Out as CBS Analyst."

Although wire stories have brought a kind of uniformity to the nation's press, headlines are individually written at each newspaper. Perhaps, ahem, a well-traveled copy editor will snag an idea from one paper and offer anew at the next stop. That may explain why newspapers coast to coast have headlined diet stories with "A waist is a terrible thing to mind."

Same-day duplication is a bit more rare. DeWitt Scott, a copy editor and consultant at the San Francisco Examiner, recalls that in 1956, as Princess Grace waited to give birth, he wrote this headline in the Los Angeles Times: "Monaco Forecast: A Little Rainier." On the same day in New York, a copy editor on the old Mirror had a longer head count but came up with "Monaco Forecast: A Little Rainier in February."

Headlines are remembered also for flamboyance, as on the San Francisco Chronicle's story on the front page about the quality of restaurant coffee: "A Great City Forced To Drink Swill."

And for sarcasm, as in an Examiner sports headline when the baseball team was performing poorly: "Giants get runner to 2nd."

And for screwups, as seen in an Examiner real estate page: "3-line hed goes here."

And for impact, as with the famous New York Daily News headline that probably helped President Gerald Ford lose the 1976 election. When he refused to approve bailout funds for New York, the front page screamed: "Ford to City: DROP DEAD!"

And for semantic confusion, as in two headlines collected by Russell Joyner, executive director of the International Society for General Semantics. Both are based on a United Press International dispatch from Nashville: "Eight maximum-security inmates of Metropolitan Jail became intoxicated with 'Jailhouse Julep' Friday night and broke into the women's section, where six of them had sexual relations with women prisoners, the inmates told a magistrate yesterday. . . ."

The San Francisco Chronicle: "Sex Orgy Fueled by Jail Julep."

The San Francisco Examiner: "Jailbreak ends when male cons reach women's prison."

In general semantics, Joyner said, analysts expect to find differing patterns of abstraction and different mixes of description and inference. Amused nonetheless, he looked at the contrasting perspectives and said, "How different can we expect the mixes to be?"

Michael Parenti, commenting in "The Politics of the Mass Media" (St. Martin's, New York, 1986), wrote:

Not only can headlines mislead anyone who skims a page without reading the story. They can create the dominant slant on a story, establishing a mind-set that influences how we do read the story's text.

Same story, different emphasis: In the San Jose Mercury News, "Shultz unhurt by bomb"; in the Oakland Tribune, "Bomb just misses Shultz in Bolivia."

"Jordan yields to PLO," says the Mercury News. "Jordan to Cut Key Ties to West Bank," says the Los Angeles Times.

Different mind-set or different head count?

Dominant slants were far from Tommy Thompson's mind as he contemplated the ant story, a nice diversion from the usual workload of politics, crime and catastrophe.

Much else has changed in his line of work. The rim and the slot no longer exist except as job descriptions. They junked the horseshoe-shaped copy desks with the advent of computer terminals. Eyeshades, Underwoods and teletype machines have gone the way of the Linotype machine. The VDT now includes an automatic check on spellings. The computers handle most work formerly assigned to typesetters, proof-readers, clerks and attendants.

Thompson sat at one of the VDT tables arranged in no particular form within a windowless room crowded with other tubes. He pecked at his keyboard and snuffled up an acorn:

Ants, ants, ants, ants, ants, ants

Their tiny armies march into Bay Area households

Suggestions for additional reading

Bernstein, Theodore M. *Watch Your Language*. New York: Atheneum, 1976.

Garst, Robert F., and Theodore M. Bernstein. *Headlines and Deadlines,* 3rd ed. New York: Columbia University Press, 1961.

"The Lower Case," a regular department in *Columbia Journalism Review*, published bimonthly.

1. Read at least one issue of the Columbia Journalism Review, especially the inside back cover, which features "The Lower Case," a collection of awkward headlines cited by the editors. Then skim the headlines in several newspapers and bring to class the best candidates for a place in "The Lower Case."

2. For each of the following words, list at least three synonyms that would take less space:

   a. falsehood _____

   b. organization _____

   c. contributor _____

3. Shorten each of the following phrases:

   a. during the time _____

   b. on the order of _____

   c. at that time _____

   d. due to the fact _____

   e. a softly blowing wind _____

   f. attain victory _____

4. The two headlines below have "bad breaks," or awkward line splits. Rewrite each one to keep verb phrases together on one line and to keep modifiers and the words they modify on the same line. Don't worry about the count, but try to keep all lines about the same length.

   a. **Provost will resign today**

   b. **Russia may ratify new treaty today**

5. Rewrite these headlines to remove unproven accusations:

   a. **Child murderer goes on trial**

   b. **Cops nab 40 hoods in gambling raid**

6. Rewrite this headline to correct unattributed opinion:

   Regents hit students with stiff tuition

   The Board of Regents today set tuition for next year at $2,000, an increase of 12 percent more than the current level.

7. Correct the punctuation in these headlines:

a. **Mayor opposes tax cut; prepares new budget.**

b. **"President is doing a good job", head of veterans group says.**

c. **"President doing good job": Vets chairman**

d. **Tennessee beats Kentucky; claims SEC championship**

e. **State assembly votes no on death penalty bill, and ends session**

8. Show correct capitalization for downstyle headlines:

a. **President Signs Trade Treaty With Japan**

b. **Educators Consider Ways to Combat Illiteracy**

9. Refer to the headline-writing rules discussed in this chapter. Then, without considering the count, explain why each of the following headlines is poor:

a. **School board plans to study admission policy**

b. **Fair manager tells plans for fair**

c. **Beat grandmother, three children**

d. Kidnap victim trys to identify captors

e. Ashdown, Smith spar in second campaign debate

f. Inmate escaped from prison farm

g. Council passes sales tax despite protest

10. Use the standard headline-counting method explained in this chapter to give the count for this headline:

Amityville horror real, psychic detectives say

11. Refer to the headline schedule in Exhibit 6-2 to give the maximum number of units for each line of these headline assignments. Remember, the first number refers to the number of columns; the second number is the point size of the type; the third number is the number of lines in the headline.

    a. 2-48-2 _____

    b. 1-24-3 _____

    c. 5-60-1 _____

    d. 4-36-2 _____

12. Use the standard headline-counting method explained in this chapter to give the count for this headline:

Governor summons special session

Does the headline above fit properly for a 2-48-2 headline assignment? If not, change it so each line will be within the maximum count and no shorter than two units less than the maximum count.

13. Here are five news stories that need headlines. Although none of the stories is complete, you will find more than enough material to write a downstyle headline. In almost all news stories, you need not go beyond the first few paragraphs to find material on which to base the headline. (This rule does not apply, of course, to feature stories.)

    You will find a headline assignment at the top of each story. Refer to the headline schedule in Exhibit 6-2. Practice writing your heads on scrap paper; then transcribe the completed version to the appropriate place at the top of each story.

    a. 1-30-3:

A 62-year-old man, blinded in a traumatic accident nine years ago, regained his sight after he was struck by lightning near his home, his wife and doctor said yesterday.

Doctors confirmed that Edwin E. Robinson, a former truck driver, could see for the first time since he became blind as the result of a spectacular highway accident nine years ago.

"It (his sight) isn't completely restored," Robinson's wife, Doris, said. "But he can see straight in front of him, which he hasn't been able to do in nine years.

"You read about things like this, but you can't really believe then," she said.

Robinson was knocked to the ground by lightning Wednesday when he took shelter under a tree during an afternoon thunderstorm. After 20 minutes, he managed to climb to his feet, said Mrs. Robinson, who found him in his bedroom later that afternoon.

"I can see you! I can see you! I can see the house! I can read!" she quoted him as saying. She also said he was able to hear perfectly well without his hearing aid.

Dr. William F. Taylor examined Robinson yesterday and confirmed that he had regained both sight and hearing. Calling it "one for the books," Dr. Taylor said the rubber-soled shoes Robinson was wearing when he was struck by the lightning may have saved his life.

Robinson's ophthalmologist, Dr. Albert Moulton, of Portland, Ore., attributed the dramatic event to trauma.

"It was traumatic when he lost his sight, so maybe his sight was restored by this trauma. Anything is possible," Dr. Moulton said.

Mrs. Robinson said she was being deluged with calls from friends and well-wishers who heard about her husband's recovery.

b. 4-30-1:

Former Secretary of State Henry Kissinger was treated at New York Hospital several hours after he suffered head injuries in a fall during a St. Louis speaking engagement, it was revealed yesterday.

Kissinger was X-rayed and examined about 8 p.m. Saturday. He was released following treatment of head trauma.

The accident occurred at a St. Louis hotel where Kissinger was waiting to address the Illinois Bankers Association. As he sat down, his chair slipped off the back of the stage, and he fell about 2 feet to the floor.

Audience members rushed to his aid. He returned to the stage, seemingly unhurt, and later gave his speech.

Afterward, he flew to New York and went to the hospital.

c. 2-24-3:

Jacques Bailly, a 14-year-old eighth-grade student from Denver, yesterday won the National Spelling Bee by correctly spelling "elucubrate."

Jacques got his chance when Paige Pipkin, a 12-year-old seventh grader from El Paso, Texas, missed on "glitch." She spelled it "glitsch."

After Jacques properly spelled "glitch," he breezed through "elucubrate" before pronouncer Richard Baker could provide the definition.

Jacques is no stranger to elucubration—laborious work, especially at night or by candlelight.

"Well, you read a lot and you work a lot," he said, explaining his secret of success.

Jacques and Paige were the top of 112 finalists who came to Washington for the 53rd annual competition sponsored by Scripps Howard Newspapers.

Jacques spelled "auburn," "finesse," "maladroit," "nimiety," "juratory," "davit," "abecedarian," "frijoles," "blatherskite," "wassail" and "halcyon" to reach the final face-off.

Jacques won $1,000 and a loving cup. Paige won $500.

d. 2-36-3:

The Western industrialized world faces "an extended period of painfully slow growth" because of rising oil prices and the need of Draconian measures to combat inflation.

This scenario implies high unemployment and other "social and human costs" and recognizes, as well, the inevitability of sizable and growing international payments deficits for poor and rich countries alike.

These are among the main conclusions of the 50th annual report today of the Bank of International Settlements. Based in Basel, Switzerland, the BIS is the clearinghouse of the major Western nations. Influential in fostering international monetary cooperation, it is sometimes called "the central bankers' central banker."

The report, signed by the bank's general manager, Rene Larre, has two main themes. First, it says that while last year's doubling of oil prices is of the same magnitude in real terms as that of 1973–74, prospects for 1980 are not entirely gloomy.

But second, while a certain amount of "equanimity" can be sustained for this year, "clouds seem to be gathering on the horizon to darken the outlook for next year onwards."

Concerns about a sharp turn for the worse beginning in 1981, pushing the world into what BIS suggests will be "an outright recession," have been expressed as well in recent weeks by another key agency, the International Monetary Fund.

The underlying problem cited by the BIS is that the oil cartel, apparently, has the power to force real petroleum prices up even higher. Meanwhile, the oil cartel nations are piling up surpluses that will be difficult to spend, invest or even "recycle"—that is, lend through the commercial banking system to those who need money.

15. The following headlines appeared in various newspapers in the United States. Can you find fault with any of them? Identify any problems in conceptual terms.

a. **Gorillas vow to kill Khomeini**

b. **School chief hears offer in men's room**

c. **Volcano killed by suffocation**

d. **Police brutality postponed**

e. **Court orders church to produce woman**

f. **British aide says all inmates to gain now that fast over**

g. **State provides motorists with winter conditions**

h. **Excess of vitamins harmful, expensive specialist warns**

i. **Airport commission to consider holding hearing on runway**

j. **Shuttle passes test; a worker is killed**

k. **Museums utilizing TV to attack visitors**

l. **Defendant's speech ends in long sentence**

m. **Jury is still out on composting toilets**

n. **White House kills fund-raiser after complaints about tactics**

Editing Copy from News Services

Primary news services
Supplemental services
Editing news-service copy
Wire editing on a metro daily

In this age of mass-media marketing, editors of newspapers continually try to determine "what sells." That is to say, editors base their judgments about what kinds of stories to publish on many factors, including results of reader surveys in the area in which the newspaper is circulated.

There are only two forces that can carry light to all corners of the globe—the sun in the heavens and the Associated Press.

—Mark Twain

Although the percentages vary from city to city, most research indicates that readers of daily newspapers want a variety of news topics from a variety of geographic locations. Some readers may be highly interested in news about transportation, science and education; others may be highly interested in news about politics, sports and business. Some read local news with vigor. Others prefer national and international news.

Selecting and publishing news that appeals to the diverse interests of readers is imperative if a newspaper is to survive. But only the most widely circulated newspapers can afford to situate reporters in offices outside their primary market area. Most U.S. newspapers, as well as broadcast stations, therefore rely on the news services to provide wide-ranging, non-local coverage.

The U.S. mass media employ thousands of workers, but even more are employed by institutions that serve the media: news services, such as the Associated Press and United Press International; supplemental news services, such as the New York Times News Service; syndicated services, such as Universal Press Syndicate; advertising agencies; and public-relations firms.

Four primary news services offer broad coverage of world events, without direct governmental support. They are the Associated Press and United Press International in the United States, Reuters of Great Britain, and Agence France Presse of France. Agence France Presse is not directly subsidized, but French government ministries pay handsomely to subscribe to its news services, an arrangement one AFP official admitted "could be called a disguised subsidy."

Although AP and UPI are the only news services in the United States that attempt to provide a full range of coverage in the nation and around the world, many supplemental news services offer specialized coverage, focusing on the important stories of the day, analysis pieces, feature reports and opinion columns. Most metropolitan newspapers subscribe to several supplemental services, as well as AP and UPI, Reuters and AFP. Most small and mid-sized dailies receive news from only one of the major news services and perhaps one or two of the supplemental services.

Primary news services

In the early 1920s, Marlin Pew, longtime editor of Editor & Publisher magazine, remarked after returning from a trip across the country, "Hundreds of newspapers, though published in cities scattered from coast to coast, were as alike as so many peas in a pod."

Some would argue that Pew's remarks were exaggerated then, that the New York Daily News only vaguely resembled the Kansas City Star and that the San Francisco Chronicle and the Los Angeles Times seemed to have their state of publication as their only similarity.

Nonetheless, Pew's observation offers an appropriate, important and— many would argue—disturbing insight into U.S. newspapers of the last 100 years: In the aggregate, U.S. newspapers are distinctly similar, especially in content and increasingly in design. One observer called this phenomenon the "blanding" of American journalism.

The quality of sameness that impresses so many who travel across the United States can be traced primarily to the fact that many of the nation's newspapers use the same reports from the Associated Press and United Press International, the two largest suppliers of breaking news stories.

Associated Press

The Associated Press, the oldest and largest news agency in the world, began in 1848. Representatives from six New York newspapers met and decided to pool their resources to save money and widen their news coverage through the use of a new invention called the telegraph.

Previously the newspapers had been involved in all-out competition, committing themselves to cover the news through extraordinary expense and means, including privately hired boats, railroads, ponies, pigeons and runners. Because use of the telegraph to transmit copy would be too expensive for any one newspaper, the editors decided to form a cooperative venture to serve all six newspapers.

Today, almost 150 years later, more than a billion people a day hear or read news transmitted by the Associated Press. AP stories appear in 97 percent of the daily newspapers in the United States, representing 97 percent of newspaper circulation. More than 15,000 newspaper and broadcast outlets around the world receive AP services. The annual AP budget, which in 1848 was less than $20,000, exceeded $350 million in 1992 (see Exhibit 7-1).

The cooperative, not-for-profit structure of the Associated Press is unique. AP members share the costs of its services—including news, features, photos, graphics, stock market listings and sports statistics—and make their reports available to the entire membership. AP directors are elected from newspaper membership ranks and appointed from broadcast membership. Each member, therefore, can take from the AP system what it needs, and each is responsible for feeding into the system. Members share news through "electronic carbons," copies of member-generated stories sent via computer to AP bureau offices. AP editors then edit and transmit the stories to other members.

AP also cooperates with other news agencies in Asia, Latin America, South America, Africa, Europe and Australia by entering into reciprocal agreements or by paying for the right to use the news and photo services of a national agency outside the country of origin.

Technological progress. The Associated Press has been a leader in applying new technology to increase the speed of disseminating its material. In 1899, for example, the news service tested Marconi's wireless to disseminate news of international yacht races. In 1916, AP directly transmitted the first play-by-play report of a sports event: the World Series games between the Brooklyn Nationals and the Boston Red Sox.

AP began transmitting pictures daily in 1935 with the birth of Wirephoto (now called LaserPhoto). It began to use computers regularly in 1962 to automate stock market listings. The service started using computer terminals in 1970 to write and edit copy for transmission.

In 1974 AP introduced LaserPhoto, the first laser-scanned pictures for transmission, and at the same time began transmitting copy at 1,200 words a minute. (Previously, wires transmitted stories at 66 words per minute.)

Since 1984, AP has continued to introduce new technology. It has over-

ach member can take from the AP system what it needs, and each is responsible for feeding into the system.

2,374	News/photo employees in the United States
749	News/photo employees in other countries
3,123	**Total news/photo employees worldwide**
143	Domestic news bureaus
86	Foreign news bureaus (in 67 countries)
229	**Total news bureaus worldwide**
	$363.5 million projected revenue for 1992
1,558	Members—daily, English-language, U.S. newspapers (97% of total, serving 99% of readers)
230	Members—non-daily, non-English-language and college newspapers
1,788	**Total domestic newspapers**
6,000	**Total broadcast/TV outlets taking AP**
1,000	**Total outlets taking AP Network News**
1 billion	Estimated number of people worldwide who hear or read AP news each day
8,500	**Total foreign subscribers**
112	**Total countries served by AP**

Exhibit 7-1
The Associated Press is a worldwide organization with considerable assets for gathering and disseminating the news. (Source: 1991 fact sheet)

seen the installation of 4,000 satellite dishes, the news industry's largest network of receivers. It has introduced AP NewsPower 1200, the first high-speed service for broadcasters. It has introduced computer-to-computer graphics, moving high-quality artwork and illustrations from AP to member newspapers and broadcast stations. And it has introduced a 9,500-words-per-minute DataStream service.

Two AP photo systems have been on the cutting edge of the technological revolution. AP PhotoStream is an electronic picture network that delivers by satellite, in one to three minutes, digitalized signals for high-quality pictures in both black and white and in color. AP Leafax is a portable machine that quickly transmits pictures directly from the news scene, using negatives or transparencies rather than prints. Using either system, a photographer can edit a negative, write a caption and then send them directly to the wire service or to an electronic darkroom on site in a matter of minutes. AP used this digital camera technology in 1989 to transmit photos of the inauguration of President George Bush to AP members.

The job of an AP editor. A few years ago, Richard Spratling, Boston news editor of the Associated Press, wrote the following about a typical day at work:

You can spot me on the subway. Look for the guy reading two newspapers at once, stuffing notes in his pockets and mumbling at his wristwatch.

News editors are creatures of time. The clock doesn't merely mark the hours; it gives my day subtitles.

There's the 8 o'clock rush: that's a half hour to start the day by reading through the Massachusetts–Rhode Island overnight state report. I check signals quickly with Boston photo editor Walter Green and day supervisor Dick Braude.

We have no single deadline to meet—newspapering in Massachusetts ranges from the afternoon dailies with less than 6,000 circulation to the all-day Boston Globe with more than 500,000. But for a few hours each morning we take the time to add stories, refocus or update to meet the deadline for almost every paper.

The 8:30 a.m. telephone ritual: the calls come in bunches. Chief statehouse correspondent Steve Cohen checks in from Beacon Hill, regional reporter Jane Anderson from Washington, correspondent Trudy Tynan from Springfield. I call counterparts at Concord, N.H., and Hartford, Conn. We share a common interest—the Boston hub computer supplies lines serving newspaper and broadcast members throughout New England.

The 9:30 a.m. moment of truth: I know it is at hand because a half dozen wire editors call with questions. At many newspapers, this is deadline time for pages.

Around 10:30 a.m., it's big picture time. In New York, the general desk is narrowing the list of offerings for the AMs wire budget to be sent at noon. So by mid-morning, I make one last check around the bureau to make sure we haven't overlooked any possibilities.

One recent morning a tip from our photo desk turned up a zoo psychologist giving parenting lessons to a pregnant, 221-pound gorilla. The photo and story combo won great play across the country.

Shortly before noon, for reasons of their own, the justices of Massachusetts' Supreme Court are prone to disclose rulings of mighty import. Naturally, they hit right at page one deadline for most of our members. I call it the hour of the big ruling.

That's how a typical day gets going in Boston. But there's really no typical day as AP news editors shepherd local, regional and national coverage. In Washington, John McClain starts at 7 a.m., parceling out his reporters to beats, news conferences, and as many as 70 simultaneous congressional hearings. In Honolulu a full-time staff of four, including News Editor Ron Staton, must cope with some awesome geography: One member newspaper is located on Guam, more than 3,000 miles away.

Whatever the bureau makeup, there's one vital part of every news editor's day. It's usually known as planning time. Each afternoon I tune out the phones and take time to consider what we'll be doing the next day, the next week and the next few months.

Each afternoon I tune out the phones and take time to consider what we'll be doing the next day, the next week and the next few months.

United Press International

In 1907, under the restrictive rules of the Associated Press as they existed then, AP members could deny service to those seeking membership. E. W. Scripps, publisher of the Scripps-McRae newspapers, founded a competing news service, which he called United Press Association. He believed those who wanted to buy news from a news service should not be prohibited from doing so:

I regard my life's greatest service to the people of this country to be the creation of the UP. I have made it impossible to suppress the truth or successfully disseminate falsehood. The mere fact that the UP can be depended upon to disseminate news that is of value to the public makes it not only worthwhile to put out such information but positively dangerous to withhold it.

In 1957, United Press merged with International News Service, an agency founded by William Randolph Hearst in 1909, and became United Press International. The merger intensified the battle between AP and UPI, and the two services competed against each other throughout the 1960s and 1970s.

An intriguing decade. As the 1980s began, however, UPI had increasing difficulty coping with sharp inflation costs at home and a worldwide recession. The Scripps Howard organization, which held a majority of UPI shares, reported losses running into the millions. In 1982, UPI's 75th anniversary year, Scripps sold the service to Media News Corp., a group of owners of American newspapers, cable companies and television stations.

Throughout the 1980s, UPI continued to experience financial trouble, dwindling newspaper subscribers and ownership changes. In 1989 Infotechnology Inc., the parent company of Financial News Network, announced that it had purchased UPI for about $16 million. By the end of the decade, only about 400 newspapers were receiving UPI.

UPI's early vitality and fresh thinking were illustrated by its development of a distinctive broadcast news style. In 1935, UPI was the first news service to supply news to radio, which helped revolutionize the distressingly inadequate radio reporting of the time. Recognizing that news reports easily understood in print sometimes are difficult to follow when read aloud, UPI developed techniques for *telling* the news instead of *reading* the news.

Technological progress. UPI, like AP, has been a leader in applying new technology. In 1951, UPI introduced a teletypesetter service that enabled U.S. newspapers to set type automatically from news transmissions. In 1952, UPI established the first international newsfilm service for television. The following year, the news service developed a fully automatic facsimile receiver to supplement the traditional manually operated telephoto service.

Like its competitor, the Associated Press, UPI began transmitting news at 1,200 words a minute in 1974. In 1978, UPI began operating a 24-hour cable news service, and in 1981, it began transmitting news via satellite.

Because UPI was established as a for-profit business rather than a cooperative like AP, clients do not share news. UPI generally pays stringers, often reporters from the local newspaper or broadcast station, to send news to the nearest UPI bureau.

Supplemental services

Almost every daily newspaper in the country is either a member of the Associated Press or a client of United Press International or both. Thus, almost every daily newspaper receives basically the same national and international news reports as everyone else. But the burgeoning of supplemental news services and syndicated services during the last 20 years has given newspapers a much larger choice of story content and style.

Dozens of supplemental news services and hundreds of syndicated feature services are available. They offer—for a fee, of course—a startling variety of material.

One of the best, the New York Times News Service, has for many years focused on in-depth stories and analysis of news from around the world. More than 550 newspapers throughout the world subscribe to the New York Times News Service. They get a daily report from the news pages of The New York Times, as well as background pieces, opinion columns, sports columns, feature stories and computer graphics.

The New York Times News Service also offers reports from the Financial Times of London; the International Herald Tribune, published in Paris; Le Monde of France; Corriere Della Sera of Italy; and news services in Spain and Japan. In addition, the news service transmits stories from the San Francisco Chronicle and the Los Angeles Daily News and from smaller news services such as Cox (which includes stories from the Atlanta Journal & Constitution), Newhouse (which includes stories from the Portland Oregonian) and McClatchy (which includes stories from the Sacramento Bee and the Tacoma News Tribune).

Another supplemental news service, the Los Angeles Times Syndicate, offers articles from such magazines as Rolling Stone, Harper's and Time and from the Christian Science Monitor and the Gallup Poll news services. Some

UPI developed techniques for telling the news instead of reading the news.

media corporations, such as the Gannett Co., Inc., offer supplemental news services to their individual newspapers. Others offer services to the newspapers they own as well as to other media clients. Knight-Ridder News Service, distributed through Tribune Media Services, and Scripps Howard News Service, distributed through United Media, are examples.

In addition, more than 350 syndicated feature services offer to media clients thousands of political cartoons, comic strips, astrology columns, crossword puzzles, games and quizzes, advice and humor columns, commentary pieces, television listings, business features, entertainment and sports features, maps and charts, and computer graphics packages.

Among the best-known syndicated services are United Media, which sells the comics Peanuts, Garfield and Marmaduke, as well as the columns Miss Manners, James Jacoby on Bridge and Jack Anderson; King Features, which sells Beetle Bailey, Blondie and Andy Capp, as well as the columns Ask Dr. Ruth, Hints From Heloise and Calvin Trillin; the Los Angeles Times Syndicate, which sells columns by Art Buchwald, Jesse Jackson and Sylvia Porter, as well as comics such as Pogo; the Washington Post Writers Group, which sells commentaries by Ellen Goodman, David Broder and George Will, as well as columns by Tom Shales on television and Jane Bryant Quinn on personal finance and the Sunday-only comic strip Outland.

For a fee, AP and UPI electronically deliver copy from the supplemental news services and syndicated feature services to subscribing newspapers. Supplemental and syndicated services still send photos and illustrations by mail, although technological advances may result in electronic delivery of artwork in the future.

Editing news-service copy

In the mid-1980s, a committee of the Associated Press Managing Editors asked editors of small and medium-sized newspapers how the news service could improve foreign news coverage. The committee said it wanted useful ideas that could be adopted without great expense. The response included this advice for editors who handle foreign news:

- Know your readers, and target coverage to meet their needs.
- Use news-service reports the way a reporter uses sources, asking questions and not just funneling stories.
- Strive to tell the right story at the right time, creating impact with readers.
- Look ahead and help readers anticipate news.
- Do the little extra things, such as using maps and graphics, that make foreign news seem less foreign.
- Develop your own expertise in international affairs, instead of expecting readers to be experts.

These ideas might just as well apply to the handling of any news-service copy. The key is to pay consistent attention to these points. Most newspapers throw away far more news copy than they use, generally because of space limitations. In addition, a focus on local news generally requires that national and international news stories be condensed or digested. To help busy editors keep pace with the vast quantity of news, the news services have developed coding systems that enable editors to route stories easily and efficiently.

Priority and category codes

Priority codes, which appear at the top of all news-service stories, help assure that stories move over the news-service wires according to their urgency. At

Most newspapers throw away far more news copy than they use, generally because of space limitations.

f: *Flash, highest priority.* Seldom used, except for stories of the utmost importance, such as presidential assassination.

b: *Bulletins, first adds to bulletins, kill notes.*

u: *Urgent, high-priority copy, including all corrections.* Must be used on all stories determined to be urgent; may be used on stories that are not urgent but require urgent transmission.

r: *Regular priority.* Used for advisories, digest stories, other late-breaking stories and special fixtures, such as People in the News.

d: *Deferred priority.* Used for spot-news items that can be delayed if more urgent material is available.

a: *Weekday advances.* Intended to be used more than 12 hours after transmission. (Hold-for-release stories transmitted for use in less than 12 hours carry priority code **d**.)

s: *Sunday advances.* Designed for use more than 12 hours after transmission.

w: *Release-at-will items.* Used for stories that have publishing value during and after current transmission cycle.

x, y, z: *Internal routing among AP bureaus.*

Exhibit 7-2
The AP uses these priority codes to indicate a story's urgency.

---

a: *Domestic general news items.* Excludes news from Washington.

b: *Special events.*

d: *Stories about food and diet.* Primarily advance features.

e: *Selected entertainment stories.* Movie reviews, television reviews and columns, etc.

f: *Stories for use on business and financial pages.* (Editors are advised, however, that an important story of financial interest is routed to both the financial and news desks.)

i: *International news items.* Includes stories from all foreign datelines, the United Nations, U.S. possessions and undated roundups keyed to foreign events.

l: *Selected lifestyle stories.*

n: *State and regional items with domestic datelines.* (If the dateline is foreign, the **i** category code is used. If the dateline is Washington, the **w** category code is used. If the story is written primarily for the business pages, the **f** category code is used.)

p: *National political copy.* Used only in election years.

q: *Results or period scores of a single sporting event.*

s: *Sports stories, standings and results of more than one event.*

v: *Advisories about any stories or photos transmitted on the news-service wires.* Designed for news digests, news advisories, lists of advance stories and indexes.

w: *Stories datelined Washington, D.C.* (If a subsequent lead shifts the dateline to another city, the category code changes to **a** or **b**.)

Exhibit 7-3
Category codes are used to indicate the type of story coming across AP wires.

newspapers, editors often use the codes to help decide order of importance. See Exhibit 7-2 for the principal priority codes used by AP.

Category codes, which also appear at the top of all news-service stories, are designed to help editors sort copy into the equivalent of electronic stacks—for example, one stack for Washington news, another for sports stories, another for entertainment and so on. Before computer editing, copy editors performed the same function by hand, separating the news stories into paper stacks to make the editorial selection process as efficient as possible. Computer systems have streamlined the process. The AP's principal category codes appear in Exhibit 7-3.

In addition to using category codes and priority codes, the news services supply other information helpful to busy news editors. News *budgets,* for example, digest the stories considered most important by the news service. A budget is transmitted at the beginning of each cycle of publication; the one for morning newspapers usually is transmitted about noon Eastern time, and the one for afternoon newspapers usually is transmitted about midnight. Subscribers to the New York Times News Service also receive a list of the stories The New York Times plans to use on its Page One the following morning. Exhibit 7-4 is an example of part of an Associated Press budget for morning newspapers; the sample came over the wires at a newspaper in the West.

As you read through the news digest, you will notice that the news service uses other key words to tell editors more about the stories. For example, note that AP will send LaserPhotos (news photographs) with some stories, such as the one about the shuttle launch. Some stories are "developing" (still being reported and written); others "may stand" or "should stand" (the information probably won't change very much, and the news service probably won't do much updating or rewriting). Here is other information supplied by the news services to help editors find and sort the copy:

- *Key word or slug.* Names the story and is repeated on all subsequent versions. Editors use this slug throughout the editing process, including on page layouts (see Chapter 10).
- *Cycle designator.* Indicates that morning newspapers have first use of the story (*AM*), afternoon newspapers have first use of the story (*PM*), or the item is available to both cycles (*BC*).
- *Word count.* Estimates the length of the story.
- *Story version vocabulary.* Reveals whether the story is on the news schedules (budget) for that day (*Bjt*); whether the story is the first version—first lead (*1st Ld*)—or a later version (*2nd Ld, 3rd Ld*, etc.); whether the transmission is simply advising or alerting editors (*Advisory*); whether the transmission is an advance story (*Adv 01*); how many takes (a take, or a page, usually does not exceed 450 words) the story is (*2 takes*); whether the transmission is an addition to the first take (*1st Add, 2nd Add,* etc.), an insert to the story (*Insert*), a substitution for part of the story (*Sub*), a correction (*Correction*), or a complete rewrite of the story, including all inserts, substitutions and corrections (*Writethru*).

Before computer technology, news editors had to collect all these bits of information as they were transmitted—at a very slow 66 words per minute—and literally paste them all together into a cohesive story to send to the composing room for typesetting. Today, computers perform the cut-and-paste function, and editors now have more time to devote to editing, writing headlines and planning the layout.

Anatomy of a news story

Exhibit 7-5 is a series of news-service transmissions on a single breaking news story: the launch of the space shuttle Columbia on Aug. 8, 1989. Seeing the entire series will help you understand the process of editing news-service stories.

Wire editing on a metro daily

The person who oversees copy from the news services is commonly known as the wire editor, because in the years before satellite transmission, news services sent their stories by telegraph and later telephone wires. The wire

Exhibit 7-4
An AP news budget is an overview of the day's events.

1. *In the first line are the date of transmission (Aug. 8); the time of transmission (9:09 a.m. Pacific time, which is 12:09 p.m. Eastern time, just after the start of the new transmission cycle); and the word ADVISO, which means the transmission is an Advisory. In the second line is the story number (A9990). In the third line are the cycle designator (AM for morning newspapers); the key word or slug (News Digest); and the word count (0960).*

2. *The space shuttle story is labeled "developing" because, although the space shuttle had already been launched by the time this news digest moved on the wires, AP reporters were still monitoring Columbia's progress and revising their stories. This item also tells editors that three photographs accompany the space shuttle story. With AM-Astronaut Thumbnails indicates that brief biographical sketches of each astronaut have been transmitted earlier in the cycle. Editors may choose to publish these sketches as a sidebar to the main story.*

3. *"Lynn Fire" is another story that an AP reporter is developing for morning newspapers. Notice that this digest item does not indicate the number of words that the story will contain, because the story is still being compiled.*

4. *"AM-Hostages" has already been written, so its length (900 words) is included in the digest. This story includes new information from a story transmitted earlier about the hostage situation. Because new developments could necessitate yet another story, the notation may stand is included in the news digest. Accompanying this story is a new, related story slugged "Iran from Nicosia."*

5. *The news digest for newspapers published on the AM cycle includes two more related stories: "Japan" and*

1 08/08 09:09 ADVISO
A: 9990
AM-News Digest, 0960
AMs AP News Digest
For Wednesday AMs

Here are the top stories at this hour from The Associated Press. The General Desk supervisor is Marty Sutphin (212-621-1602). The LaserPhoto Desk supervisor is Rich Kareckas (212-621-1900).

For repeats of AP copy, the Service Desk can be reached at 212-621-1595 or 1596.

SHUTTLE: Columbia Sets Out to Put Spy Satellite in Business.
    CAPE CANAVERAL, Fla.--Columbia rejoined NASA's fleet of active space shuttles Tuesday, setting out with five astronauts to put a 10-ton spy satellite on a path over the Soviet Union, China and the Middle East.
2 Slug AM-Space Shuttle. Developing.
By Harry F. Rosenthal. LaserPhotos CSB2, shuttle rises behind US flag; CSB 3, launch clock with shuttle in background; CSB 4, color of CSB 2.
With AM-Astronaut Thumbnails.
NO ESCAPE: Fire Guts Rundown Rooming House; 3 Die, Dozen Missing.
    LYNN, Mass.--Fire gutted a dilapidated rooming house where some rooms were equipped with pieces of rope because there were no fire escapes or operating alarms, tenants said. Three people died and a dozen more were missing.
3 Slug AM-Lynn Fire. Developing.
HOSTAGES: Captors Refuse Talks; Report Syria May Intervene.
    BEIRUT, Lebanon--Shiite leaders again reject talks Tuesday on trading three Israeli servicemen and the Western hostages for a kidnapped Moslem cleric amid reports Syria may negotiate on Iran's behalf in the hostage crisis.
4 Slug AM-Hostages. New material, may stand. 900 words.
By Farouk Nassar.
With AM-Hostages--Iran from NICOSIA: Further splits surface in Iranian government policy on the hostages, with a newspaper saying Tehran is willing to help, while the interior minister urges Shiite Moslems to continue fighting the United States. New.
ISRAEL: Arab Gunman Wounds American, Is Slain in Shootout.
    JERUSALEM--A lone gunman who infiltrated from Jordan shot and wounded an American and held an off-duty soldier hostage for four hours Tuesday before being killed by Israeli troops, the army said.
Slug AM-Israel-Attack. Developing.
By G. G. LaBelle.
5 JAPAN: New Prime Minister Pledges to Regain Public Trust.
    TOKYO--Toshiki Kaifu, due to be named prime minister Wednesday, pledges to rebuild his beleaguered governing party and regain the public's trust after two administrations already have fallen this year.
Slug AM-Japan.
By Terril Jones. Developing from parliament meeting, due to start midnight EDT. LaserPhoto TOK9, Kaifu celebrates victory; LaserPhoto staffing meeting.
With AM-Japan--Analysis from TOKYO: After a two-month false start, Japan's governing party is on another "clean start" to reform itself. New.
BUSH: President Speaks to National Urban League

Exhibit 7-4
(continued)

"Analysis from Tokyo." Exact word counts are not given because they are developing stories.

6. *"Bush-Urban League" is yet another developing story for a speech scheduled to begin at 1 p.m. EDT. An AP photographer plans to attend the speech. During a single cycle, a wire service may transmit several stories about the president; thus, it is essential that editors not shorten the slug to "Bush."*

7. *The digest item for the story slugged "Older Drivers" notes that the story contains new material and is 550 words long.*

8. *This story and the two immediately following on the news digest include exact word counts and the notation* should stand, *meaning that no new additions are planned.*

WASHINGTON--President Bush addresses the National Urban League, following Cabinet members who have tried to assure the group that his administration stands for fairness and for opportunities for blacks.
6 Slug AM-Bush-Urban League. Developing.
By White House Correspondent Terence Hunt. Speech at 1 p.m. EDT. LaserPhoto staffing.
OLDER DRIVERS: Old Folks Benefit from 'Driver Ed,' Too.
   WASHINGTON--"Driver ed" works for old folks, too, says the American Association of Retired Persons. A California study shows that older drivers who took a refresher driver-training course had fewer traffic convictions and accidents involving death or injury than other people their age.
7 Slug AM-Older Drivers. New material. 550 words.
By Nancy Benac.
WRIGHT REPLACEMENT: Race for Ex-Speaker's Seat May Be Toss-Up.
   FORT WORTH, Texas--For more than three decades, Democrats have had a lock on the District 12 congressional seat. But with this month's contest to replace deposed House Speaker Jim Wright, they face the prospect of a Republican representative. "It's a race that we shouldn't lose, but we could lose," said the Texas Democratic Party Chairman.
8 Slug AM-Wright Replacement. New, should stand. 650 words.
By Patrice Gravino.
CHILD MOLESTATION: Five Family Members Accused of Molesting Girl.
   OCILLA, Ga.--In the quiet Pleasure Lake community, where houses and mobile homes cluster around a fish pond crowded with cypress, some neighbors had a feeling something was wrong at one rundown trailer. Last month, a girl who lived there walked across the street and told her story. A few hours later investigators arrested the child's stepfather and her four brothers.
Slug AM-Child Molestation. New, should stand. 750 words.
MARKET REVIVAL: Second Chance at Bull Market on Wall Street.
   NEW YORK--As the stock market challenges the record highs it reached two summers ago, the suspense builds on Wall Street--is this deja vu or something new? Although the current rally's true believers say there are a lot of differences from the runup that preceded the Crash of 1987, comparisons inevitably are being drawn.
Slug AM-Market Revival. New, should stand.
By Business Writer Chet Currier. Moving on FFF-level news wires. LaserGraphic planned.
With AM-Wall Street.
PIE FIGHT: Restaurant Owners Fight for Slice of Business.
   HOT SPRINGS, Ark.--The pies lining the two shelves behind the counter at the Club Cafe have always been in demand. Now, they're in court. When Robert McNanna bought 51 percent of the cafe in May, he thought he was buying the restaurant's award-winning recipes, too. But when the baker left, she took her recipes, and McNanna has sued to get them back.
Slug AM-Pie Fight. New, should stand. 750 words.
By Mary Freeman.

Exhibit 7-5

As a breaking story develops, the AP transmits a series of coded updates to keep its members current.

1. Note that the date of transmission is Aug. 7 at 23:31, which is 11:31 p.m. Pacific time—or 2:31 a.m. Eastern time on Aug. 8. The timing explains the use of the word today in the lead. Howard Benedict wrote this version of the story for afternoon newspapers in the East, some of which have very early morning deadlines.

2. The story number is a0445. The PM designation in the third line denotes use in afternoon newspapers. The story slug is "Space Shuttle." The Bjt code means the news service thinks the story is significant and will appear on the day's news digests, or budgets. The story has 625 words. The fourth line suggests a possible headline for the story. The fifth line advises editors of the expected time of launch and of the certainty of a new lead. The sixth line advises editors that a photograph will be taken.

3. The third and fourth paragraphs of the story attempt to explain the tricky timing for media coverage of the launch. Also, the fifth paragraph becomes important as the countdown continues (see the lead in the next transmission).

1 08/07 23:31 NATWIR

2 A:0445

PM-Space Shuttle, Bjt, 0625

Space Shuttle Columbia Ready for Launch on Secret Military Mission

Eds: Launch expected about 8 a.m. EDT. Will be led.

LaserPhoto staffing.

By HOWARD BENEDICT

AP Aerospace Writer

  CAPE CANAVERAL, Fla. (AP)--Space shuttle Columbia was fueling up and ready to fly today on a secret military mission with five astronauts who intend to deploy a high-tech satellite to spy on the Soviet Union.

  With the weather looking good, shuttle managers gave the go-ahead Monday to pump 528,000 gallons of liquid hydrogen and liquid oxygen into the spaceship's huge external fuel tank.

3 Because most details about the flight are classified, the Pentagon would allow NASA to announce only that liftoff would occur between 7:30 a.m. and 11:30 a.m.

  The likely time was just before 8 a.m., but the countdown was being made public just nine minutes before the planned liftoff.

  The five astronauts, all military officers, were scheduled to board the craft about two hours before launch.

  The commander is Air Force Col. Brewster Shaw, a veteran of two earlier missions. The others are Navy Cmdr. Richard Richards, Air Force Lt. Col. James Adamson, Air Force Maj. Mark Brown and Navy Cmdr. David Leestma, who flew once previously on a shuttle.

  Although mission details are classified, sources close to the program said the astronauts will deploy a sophisticated 10-ton reconnaissance satellite to gather intelligence information over a wide area of the globe, including much of the Soviet Union, China and the Middle East.

  The satellite is designed to take highly detailed photographs of troop movements, military installations and other targets of interest.

  The sources said that in the shuttle's cargo bay was a package of scientific instruments for military research, possibly for the "Star Wars" missile defense project.

  What the astronauts do will not be reported by the National Aeronautics and Space Administration or the Pentagon.

  A blackout was to be imposed throughout the flight, and only three brief announcements were planned to report on the health of the shuttle and to reveal when it will land at Edwards Air Force Base, Calif.

  The mission is expected to last five days.

  The flight is the eighth for Columbia, the oldest of the shuttles, but its first since it flew the last mission before the Jan. 28, 1986, Challenger explosion.

  After the accident, NASA concentrated on modifying the newer orbiters, Discovery and Atlantis, and Columbia spent much of the past few years as a "hangar queen," stripped to provide spare parts for its sister ships.

  Discovery and Atlantis each have made two trips into space since post-Challenger flights resumed last September.

  During the flight, the astronauts were to check out 258 modifications made to Columbia to improve safety and reliability as a result of the accident.

  The flight is the 30th for the shuttle program and the fourth dedicated solely to a Defense Department mission.

  The Defense Department had planned at least 13 more military launches from the shuttle through the 1990s, but, in the wake of the Challenger accident, cut that number to seven, shifting several payloads to unmanned rockets to get away from reliance on a single launch vehicle.

Exhibit 7-5
(continued)

The Pentagon contends the secrecy of the shuttle military flight is necessary to make it more difficult for Soviet satellites and spy ships off the Florida coast to monitor the flight and know its purpose.

Critics argue that the secrecy is unnecessary because the Soviets, with their intelligence capabilities, undoubtedly already know a great deal about Columbia's mission, and that once the satellite is in orbit, the Russians will be able to track them precisely and know what they are doing.

08/08 02:45 NATWIR
4 A:0485
5 PM-Space Shuttle, 2nd Ld-Writethru, a0465, 0684
Space Shuttle Columbia Ready For Launch on Secret Military Mission
Eds: LEADS with 6 grafs to UPDATE with astronauts boarding shuttle; picks up 6th graf, "The commander . . . ;" launch expected about 8 a.m. EDT.
LaserPhoto staffing.
By HOWARD BENEDICT
AP Aerospace Writer
6 CAPE CANAVERAL, Fla. (AP)--Five military astronauts boarded the space shuttle Columbia today and prepared to fly on a secret mission to deploy a high-tech satellite to spy on the Soviet Union.

The weather was perfect and there were no technical problems as a blacked-out countdown advanced toward a liftoff expected about 8 a.m.

Because most details about the flight are classified, the Pentagon would allow NASA to announce only that liftoff would occur between 7:30 a.m. and 11:30 a.m. The countdown was to be made public just nine minutes before the planned liftoff.

A van carrying the astronauts, accompanied by security cars and a hovering helicopter, arrived at the launch pad shortly after 5 a.m.

The flight will be the first for Columbia in 3[1/2] years. During the hiatus, the craft has received 258 safety modifications dictated by the 1986 Challenger explosion.

The ship's return to space will give the space agency a fleet of three orbiters to handle an increasing flight schedule. Three more flights are planned this year and nine in 1990.

The commander is Air Force Col. Brewster Shaw, a veteran of two earlier missions. The others are Navy Cmdr. Richard Richards, Air Force Lt. Col. James Adamson, Air Force Maj. Mark Brown and Navy Cmdr. David Leestma, who flew once previously on a shuttle.

Although mission details are classified, sources close to the program said the astronauts will deploy a sophisticated 10-ton reconnaissance satellite to gather intelligence information over a wide area of the globe, including much of the Soviet Union, China and the Middle East.

The satellite is designed to take highly detailed photographs of troop movements, military installations and other targets of interest.

The sources said that in the shuttle's cargo bay was a package of scientific instruments for military research, possibly for the "Star Wars" missile defense project.

What the astronauts do will not be reported by the National Aeronautics and Space Administration or the Pentagon.

A blackout was to be imposed throughout the flight, and only three brief announcements were planned to report on the health of the shuttle and to reveal when it will land at Edwards Air Force Base, Calif.

4. The story number is a0485; 40 other items have been transmitted between the budgeted version of the space shuttle story (a0445) and this version, which is called the second lead write-through (2nd Ld-Writethru), meaning this story includes updated information and incorporates earlier versions.

5. The number of the first lead write-through, a0465, is listed here so editors can pick up information from it if they only have time to edit and typeset the first six paragraphs of a0485 (note the instruction to editors on line 5). The first lead write-through was substantially the same as a0445, the budgeted version of the story. On line 3, the number following a0465 (0684) is the word count.

6. The time of this transmission is 5:45 a.m. Eastern time (2:45 a.m. Pacific time), a little more than two hours before scheduled launch. Story a0445 told us the astronauts would board about two hours before launch. This version, a0485, leads with that fact.

Exhibit 7-5
(continued)

The mission is expected to last five days.

The flight is the eighth for Columbia, the oldest of the shuttles, but its first since it flew the last mission before the Jan. 28, 1986, Challenger explosion.

After the accident, NASA concentrated on modifying the newer orbiters, Discovery and Atlantis, and Columbia spent much of the past few years as a "hangar queen," stripped to provide spare parts for its sister ships.

Discovery and Atlantis each have made two trips into space since post-Challenger flights resumed last September.

During the flight, the astronauts were to check out 258 modifications made to Columbia to improve safety and reliability as a result of the accident.

The flight is the 30th for the shuttle program and the fourth dedicated solely to a Defense Department mission.

The Defense Department had planned at least 13 more military launches from the shuttle through the 1990s but, in the wake of the Challenger accident, cut that number to seven, shifting several payloads to unmanned rockets to get away from reliance on a single launch vehicle.

The Pentagon contends the secrecy of the shuttle military flight is necessary to make it more difficult for Soviet satellites and spy ships off the Florida coast to monitor the flight and know its purpose.

Critics argue that the secrecy is unnecessary because the Soviets, with their intelligence capabilities, undoubtedly already know a great deal about Columbia's mission, and that once the satellite is in orbit, the Russians will be able to track them precisely and know what they are doing.

---

7. *For many East Coast newspapers, this advisory was crucial. It was transmitted at 7:53 a.m. Eastern time, just minutes before the scheduled launch. Because of the delay, editors holding their presses for actual launch may have decided that in order to meet delivery times, the presses had to roll without news of the launch. Earlier versions of the space shuttle story, therefore, became important and usable. Note that 24 other items moved on the news-service wire between the last space shuttle story and this advisory.*

7 08/08 04:53 ADVISO
A:0509
PM-Space Shuttle, Advisory, 0034
EDITORS:
  NASA is holding up the countdown, waiting for fog to burn off. Launch is expected around 8:30 a.m. EDT. We will advise on all developments.
The AP

Exhibit 7-5
(continued)

8. *This advisory is interesting for a couple of reasons: First, it seems apparent that the news editors have not communicated the latest information about the launch delay to the photo staff. Just 19 minutes before, AP transmitted an advisory with an expected launch time of 8:30 a.m.; this advisory lists launch time in much more general terms. Second, this photo advisory is available to editors on both the AM and the PM cycles; the designation BC (both cycles) is printed on the third line. The advisory does attest to AP's speed; transmitting a wirephoto 40 minutes after the event allows many newspapers to use the photo in that day's editions. Note that only one item was transmitted between the last shuttle item and this advisory.*

8 08/08 05:12 ADVISO
A:0511
BC-LaserPhoto Advisory-Columbia, 0110
EDITORS:
   LaserPhoto will be staffing the military launch of the Space Shuttle Columbia this morning. At this time the only information on the launch time is it will be in the window between 7:30 a.m. and 11:30 a.m. EST. We will not be informed of the precise launch time until nine minutes before liftoff.
   We will transmit black-and-white photos within 40 minutes of launch with color about one half hour later. Because of government restrictions we will not have any remote cameras. NASA is expected to release photos about 5 hours after the launch.
The AP

9. *At 8:31 a.m. Eastern time (5:31 a.m. Pacific time), the news service alerts editors that the space shuttle Columbia will be launched in six minutes, allowing editors on tight deadlines to react. Two items moved between the last shuttle item (a0511) and this advisory (a0514). There are 22 words in this advisory.*

9 08/08 05:31 ADVISO
A:0514
PM-Space Shuttle, Advisory, 0022
EDITORS:
   NASA has resumed the countdown. Liftoff is expected at 8:37 a.m. EDT.
The AP

10. *Less than one minute after the scheduled launch, at 8:38 a.m. Eastern time (5:38 a.m. Pacific time), AP sends its Bulletin, used to designate top-priority stories. Note third-line coding: PM is for afternoon newspapers; "Space Shuttle" is the slug; 3rd Ld is third lead of the cycle; a0485 is the most recent complete version; and 0043 is the number of words in the bulletin. Also notice that the word* More *appears as the last line of the story, indicating to editors that more information will follow. Two items intervened between the last shuttle item (0514) and this bulletin. This lead is timely, informative and interesting.*

10 08/08 05:38 NATWIR
A:0517
PM-Space Shuttle, 3rd Ld, a0485, 0043
BULLETIN
   CAPE CANAVERAL, Fla. (AP)--Columbia, NASA's oldest shuttle, rocketed away from Earth today on its first flight in 3[1/2] years, carrying five military astronauts on a se-cret mission to send a spy satellite into orbit.
MORE

Exhibit 7-5
(continued)

11. The news-service editors are building a new story now, using the bulletin (a0517) as the first paragraph. This story, transmitted two minutes after launch, is the first addition (3rd Ld-1st Add) to the bulletin; the bulletin was the third lead. The line CAPE CANAVERAL, Fla.: into orbit tells editors the first and last words of the story that has moved so far.

12. One minute later, the second addition to the third lead (3rd Ld-2nd Add) moved. Again, the line CAPE CANAVERAL, Fla.: Middle East tells editors the first and last words of the story that has moved so far.

13. The story picks up into the sixth paragraph of the full third lead (a0485) version. Note that in a0485 the sixth paragraph does begin with the words "The ship's . . . ." Editors will delete the first five paragraphs of a0485 (2nd Ld-Writethru), replacing them with a0517 (3rd Ld), a0518 (3rd Ld-1st Add) and a0519 (3rd Ld-2nd Add).

14. The news wires stood idle for seven minutes as writers and editors worked to update the story. This version (a0520) moved as an Urgent at 8:47 a.m. Eastern time (5:47 a.m. Pacific time), just 10 minutes after the shuttle launch. An Urgent is a high-priority story but not as important as a Bulletin or a Flash. This version, then, becomes the fourth lead (4th Ld) and incorporates material from a0517, a0518 and a0519. It contains 315 words. Editors are advised that this story updates previous stories, leading with the shuttle reaching orbit. Howard Benedict's byline reappears.

11 08/08 05:39 NATWIR
A:0518
PM-Space Shuttle, 3rd Ld-1st Add, a0517, 0092
CAPE CANAVERAL, Fla.: into orbit.
The 125-ton winged spaceship blazed away from its seaside launch pad at 8:37 a.m. after a blacked-out countdown and darted northeastward.
Two minutes after liftoff, the two solid fuel booster rockets burned out and jettisoned as planned toward the Atlantic. A failed booster rocket joint led to the destruction of Challenger and loss of its seven crew members in 1986.
The satellite reportedly can focus its instruments on the Soviet Union and world hotspots such as the Middle East.
MORE

---

12 08/08 05:40 NATWIR
A:0519
PM-Space Shuttle, 3rd Ld-2nd Add, a0518, 0126
CAPE CANAVERAL, Fla.: Middle East
The exact launch time was not made public until nine minutes before liftoff, when the Pentagon lifted the blackout. Earlier, officials had said only that the launch would take place between 7:30 a.m. and 11:30 a.m.
Liftoff was delayed about 40 minutes to allow fog to burn off.
Columbia, which flew the first shuttle mission in 1981, spent the past few years as a "hangar queen," stripped of parts to keep the two other remaining shuttles flying. It underwent 258 safety modifications after the Challenger explosion.
The five-day mission is the fifth shuttle flight since launches resumed last September.
13 The ship's, 6th graf, a0485

---

14 08/08 05:47 NATWIR
A:0520
PM-Space Shuttle, 4th Ld, a0517-a0518-a0519, 0315
URGENT
Columbia Rockets Into Orbit With Spy Satellite
Eds: UPDATES with shuttle reaching orbit.
By HOWARD BENEDICT
AP Aerospace Writer
CAPE CANAVERAL, Fla. (AP)--Columbia, NASA's oldest shuttle, returned to space for the first time in 3[1/2] years today, rocketing into orbit with five military astronauts on a secret mission to send a spy satellite aloft.
The 125-ton winged spaceship blazed away from its seaside launch pad at 8:37 a.m. after a blacked-out countdown and darted northeastward.
"We're tracking it right down the middle of the pike," the flight guidance officer said about four minutes into the flight.
Nearly nine minutes after liftoff NASA announced that Columbia was in orbit more than 100 miles above the Earth, streaking along at more than 17,400 mph.
After that report, the space agency imposed a news blackout. Apart from three brief status announcements during the five-day mission, silence will be broken only if there is a major problem, NASA said.

Exhibit 7-5
(continued)

The satellite reportedly can focus on the Soviet Union and world hotspots such as the Middle East.

The exact launch time was not made public until nine minutes after liftoff, when the Pentagon lifted the blackout. Earlier, officials had said only that the launch would take place between 7:30 a.m. and 11:30 a.m.

Liftoff was delayed about 40 minutes to allow fog to burn off.

The mission is the fifth shuttle flight since launches resumed last September after a 2[1/2]-year hiatus prompted by the Challenger disaster.

Columbia, which flew the first shuttle mission in 1981, spent the past few years as a "hangar queen," stripped of parts to keep the two other remaining shuttles flying. It underwent 258 safety modifications after a failed rocket joint caused the Challenger explosion in 1986 that killed all seven crew members.

15 The ship's, 6th graf, a0485

---

15. *The story again picks up with the sixth paragraph of a0485, beginning with the words "The ship's . . . ."*

16. *Only one story, a0521, moved before AP returned to the shuttle story, nine minutes after the last version. Again, this version has high priority (*Urgent*). Editors are advised that a quotation from the launch commentator about the smooth ascent has been added (fifth paragraph). This version is the fifth lead (*5th Ld*), and it includes information from a0520.*

16 08/08 05:56 NATWIR
A:0522
PM-Space Shuttle, 5th Ld, a0520, 0199
URGENT
Columbia Rockets Into Orbit With Spy Satellite
Eds: UPDATES with launch commentator reporting smooth ascent.
By HOWARD BENEDICT
AP Aerospace Writer
    CAPE CANAVERAL, Fla. (AP)--Columbia, NASA's oldest shuttle, returned to space for the first time in 3[1/2] years today, rocketing into orbit with five military astronauts on a secret mission to send a spy satellite aloft.

The 125-ton winged spaceship blazed away from its seaside launch pad at 8:37 a.m. after a blacked-out countdown and darted northeastward.

"We're tracking it right down the middle of the pike," the flight guidance officer said about four minutes into the flight.

Nearly nine minutes after liftoff NASA announced that Columbia was in orbit more than 100 miles above the Earth, streaking along at more than 17,400 mph.

"We had a completely clean and smooth ascent. There are no problems whatsoever to report," said launch commentator Brian Welch.

The space agency then imposed a news blackout. Apart from brief periodic status reports during the five-day mission, silence will be broken only if there is a major problem, NASA said. Crew conversation will not be broadcast.

17 The satellite, 7th graf a0520

17. *AP erred in its pickup instructions, telling editors to pick up the seventh paragraph of a0520 with the words "The satellite." The pickup actually is the sixth paragraph of a0520.*

Exhibit 7-5

(continued)

18. *Fourteen minutes later, 33 minutes after launch, the news service moved a write-through of the story. One story got on the wire between the last version of the story and this sixth lead (6th Ld-Writethru). This version, editors are told, incorporates all previous material, including the urgent series, and has minor editing. The story continues to move as an Urgent, alerting editors on deadline that the story has high priority. The write-through story has 713 words.*

18 08/08 06:10 NATWIR
A:0524
PM-Space Shuttle, 6th Ld-Writethru, a0522, 0713
URGENT
Columbia Rockets Into Orbit With Spy Satellite
Eds: COMBINES pvs urgent series. Minor editing throughout.
By HOWARD BENEDICT
AP Aerospace Writer
   CAPE CANAVERAL, Fla. (AP)--Columbia, NASA's oldest shuttle, returned to space for the first time in 3[1/2] years today, rocketing into orbit with five military astronauts on a secret mission to send a spy satellite aloft.
   The 125-ton winged spaceship blazed away from its seaside launch pad at 8:37 a.m. after a blacked-out countdown and darted northeastward.
   "We're tracking it right down the middle of the pike," the flight guidance officer said about four minutes into the flight.
   Nearly nine minutes after liftoff NASA announced that Columbia was in orbit more than 100 miles above the Earth, streaking along at more than 17,400 mph.
   "We had a completely clean and smooth ascent. There are no problems whatsoever to report," said launch commentator Brian Welch.
   The space agency then imposed a news blackout. Apart from brief periodic status reports during the five-day mission, silence will be broken only if there is a major problem, NASA said. Crew conversation will not be broadcast.
   The satellite reportedly can focus on the Soviet Union and world hotspots such as the Middle East.
   The exact launch time was not made public until nine minutes before liftoff, when the Pentagon lifted the blackout. Earlier, officials had said only that the launch would take place between 7:30 a.m. and 11:30 a.m.
   Liftoff was delayed about 40 minutes to allow fog to burn off.
   The mission is the fifth shuttle flight since launches resumed last September after a 2[1/2]-year hiatus prompted by the Challenger disaster.
   Columbia, which flew the first shuttle mission in 1981, spent the past few years as a "hangar queen," stripped of parts to keep the two other remaining shuttles flying. It underwent 258 safety modifications after a failed rocket joint caused the Challenger explosion in 1986 that killed all seven crew members.
   The ship's return to space will give NASA a fleet of three orbiters to handle a heavier flight schedule. Three more flights are planned this year and nine in 1990.
   The commander is Air Force Col. Brewster Shaw, a veteran of two previous missions. The other crew members are Navy Cmdr. Richard Richards, Army Lt. Col. James Adamson, Air Force Maj. Mark Brown and Navy Cmdr. David Leestma, who flew once previously on a shuttle.
   Although details are classified, sources close to the program said the astronauts will deploy a 10-ton satellite to gather intelligence over a wide area of the globe, including much of the Soviet Union, China and the Mideast.
   The satellite is designed to take highly detailed photographs of troop movements, military installations and other targets of interest.
   The sources said that in the shuttle's cargo bay was a package of scientific instruments for military research, possibly for the "Star Wars" missile defense project.
   The flight is the eighth for Columbia, the oldest of the

Exhibit 7-5
(continued)

shuttles, but its first since it flew the last mission before the Jan. 28, 1986, Challenger explosion.

After the accident, NASA concentrated on modifying the newer orbiters, Discovery and Atlantis, using parts from Columbia. Discovery and Atlantis each have made two trips into space since post-Challenger flights resumed.

During the flight, the astronauts were to check out the safety modifications made to Columbia. The shuttle is to land at Edwards Air Force Base, Calif. The exact day and time will be disclosed during the mission.

The flight is the 30th for the shuttle program and the fourth dedicated solely to a Defense Department mission.

The Pentagon had planned at least 13 more military shuttle launches through the 1990s, but after Challenger cut that to seven, shifting several payloads to unmanned rockets to get away from reliance on a single launch vehicle.

The Pentagon contends secrecy is necessary to make it more difficult for Soviet satellites and spy ships off Florida to monitor the flight and know its purpose.

But critics argue that the Soviets with their intelligence capabilities undoubtedly already know a great deal about Columbia's mission and can track the crew precisely and know what it is doing.

---

19. *The final version of the story for afternoon newspapers moved as the seventh lead write-through (*7th Ld-Writethru*) at 10:34 a.m. Eastern time (7:34 a.m. Pacific time). This story incorporates material from the previous version and adds comments from the launch director and NASA officials. Remember that the news cycle for afternoon newspapers (*PM*) began about midnight. Aerospace writer Howard Benedict and the editors and photographers involved in AP's coverage have been at it for more than 10 hours. Now it is time for the AM-cycle staff to take over. Both the shuttle launch and AP's coverage were successful.*

19 08/08 07:34 NATWIR
A:0535
PM-Space Shuttle, 7th Ld-Writethru, a0524, 0767
URGENT
Columbia Rockets Into Orbit With Spy Satellite
Eds: LEADS with 14 grafs to ADD comment from launch director on shuttle and space center director on NASA returning all three shuttles to space; PICKS UP 14th graf pvs, "Although details . . ."
By HOWARD BENEDICT
AP Aerospace Writer

CAPE CANAVERAL, Fla., (AP)--Columbia, NASA's oldest shuttle, returned to space for the first time in 3[1/2] years today, rocketing into orbit with five military astronauts on a secret mission to send a spy satellite aloft.

The 125-ton winged spaceship--for years a "hangar queen" that was stripped of parts to keep newer shuttles flying--blazed away from its seaside launch pad at 8:37 a.m. after a blacked-out countdown and darted northeastward.

Nearly nine minutes after liftoff NASA announced that Columbia was in orbit more than 100 miles above the Earth, streaking along at more than 17,400 mph.

"We had a completely clean and smooth ascent. There are no problems whatsoever to report," said launch commentator Brian Welch.

"It's going to be a gem of a bird," said launch director Bob Sieck.

Soon after the shuttle reached orbit, NASA imposed a news blackout. Apart from brief status reports during the five-day mission, silence will be broken in case of a major problem only, NASA said. Crew conversation will not be broadcast.

The satellite to be released by the astronauts reportedly can focus its super-sharp cameras on the Soviet Union and world hotspots such as the Middle East.

Because the mission is classified, the exact launch time was not made public until nine minutes before liftoff. Earlier,

Exhibit 7-5
(continued)

officials had said only that the launch would take place between 7:30 a.m. and 11:30 a.m.

Liftoff was delayed about 40 minutes to allow fog to burn off.

The mission is the fifth shuttle flight since launches resumed last September after a 2[1/2]-year hiatus prompted by the Challenger disaster.

Columbia, which flew the first shuttle mission in 1981, underwent 258 safety modifications after a failed rocket joint caused the Challenger explosion in 1986 that killed all seven crew members.

The ship's return to space gives NASA a fleet of three orbiters to handle a heavier flight schedule. Three more flights are planned this year and nine in 1990.

"I think the recovery process is over," said Forrest McCartney, director of the Kennedy Space Center. "We've modified all three birds; we've flown all three birds now, and that's something we can be proud of."

Columbia's commander is Air Force Col. Brewster Shaw, a veteran of two previous missions. The other crew members are Navy Cmdr. Richard Richards, Army Lt. Col. James Adamson, Air Force Maj. Mark Brown and Navy Cmdr. David Leestma, who flew once previously on a shuttle.

Although details are classified, sources close to the program said the astronauts will deploy a 10-ton satellite to gather intelligence over a wide area of the globe, including much of the Soviet Union, China and the Mideast.

The satellite is designed to take highly detailed photographs of troop movements, military installations and other targets of interest.

The sources said that in the shuttle's cargo bay was a package of scientific instruments for military research, possibly for the "Star Wars" missile defense project.

The flight is the eighth for Columbia, the oldest of the shuttles, but its first since it flew the last mission before the Jan. 28, 1986, Challenger explosion.

After the accident, NASA concentrated on modifying the newer orbiters, Discovery and Atlantis, using parts from Columbia. Discovery and Atlantis each have made two trips into space since post-Challenger flights resumed.

During the flight, the astronauts were to check out the safety modifications made to Columbia. The shuttle is to land at Edwards Air Force Base, Calif. The exact day and time will be disclosed during the mission.

The flight is the 30th for the shuttle program and the fourth dedicated solely to a Defense Department mission.

The Pentagon had planned at least 13 more military shuttle launches through the 1990s, but after Challenger cut that to seven, shifting several payloads to unmanned rockets to get away from reliance on a single launch vehicle.

The Pentagon contends secrecy is necessary to make it more difficult for Soviet satellites and spy ships off Florida to monitor the flight and know its purpose.

But critics argue that the Soviets with their intelligence capabilities undoubtedly already know a great deal about Columbia's mission and can track the crew precisely and know what it is doing.

editor is the news editor's link to events of the day. The wire editor is responsible for providing the news editor with complete budgets, updated news stories and advisories on breaking news. The news editor prepares advance copy and edits stories.

Communication is the key to the wire editor's job. Working closely with the news editor results in a well-packaged and informative newspaper.

The wire editor's job

At an afternoon newspaper with several editions, published in a city with a competing morning paper, the job of the wire editor begins at 2 a.m. He or she reads the morning newspaper, paying close attention to the AP stories that its editors chose to use. The editor for the afternoon newspaper does not want to duplicate a wire story that has appeared in the morning paper.

An afternoon copy aide has been told to leave the final afternoon edition from the previous day on the wire editor's desk. Doing so helps the night news editor, who may not have seen the last edition, and also helps the wire editor refresh his or her memory about the previous day.

The news editor will mark a copy of the budget, the news service's list of stories that will be transmitted during the cycle. The stories selected should be processed first.

To make certain of what is in the computer system for the day, the wire editor begins to scan the *queues*, computer files of news-service stories sorted according to broad categories. The news editor also scrolls through the queues periodically. These are the broad categories used to organize the queues:

NA: National stories
FO: Foreign stories
FL: Florida stories (varying, of course, with the state)
NX: New York Times and other supplemental news services
AV: Advance stories for supplemental news services
AD: Advance stories for the AP

The wire editor scans the queues for stories that can be killed—multiple write-throughs of the same story or versions for morning papers. The wire editor checks the morning version before killing any story in case the morning version is better than the afternoon version. The editor may decide to use a morning version if the competition hasn't already used it.

Moving through the queues, the wire editor keeps in mind the news editor's plan for the day, suggests stories that can be packaged and makes sure the news editor knows whether a story is expected to change.

The wire editor is on the lookout for stories that are important. The news editor needs to know about developing stories that will be transmitted later in the morning and about fresher versions of a story that appeared in the morning paper in another form. One way to keep the news editor informed is to use the *slug field* space at the top of the computer screen. A "good" or "wow" message there will tip off the news editor.

The news editor must have clean copy that can be sent to the copy desk with minimal effort; speed is essential. The wire editor can help reduce the time that the news editor spends with each story by doing these things:

- *Removing all news-service labels and numbers at the top of each story.* Anything that should not appear in print should be deleted. Only the news-service credit line, byline and dateline should remain. Many newspapers omit news-service bylines unless the story is a particularly important news story, a feature, an analysis or an op-ed piece. A story in which the writer exhibits personal flair usually warrants a byline.

Communication is the key to the wire editor's job.

- *Making certain the credit line is correct.* For example, a story transmitted by AP should not be published with the credit line for another news service.
- *Removing the news-service instructions at the bottom of the story.* Unless removed, these extra lines will be reflected in the total length of the story, which will cause problems when page layouts are drawn.

The wire editor sometimes rewrites news-service stories to get a better angle or, where possible, to give the story a local angle. With important international and national stories, it is often useful to combine stories to save space and avoid duplication. For example, often stories on the Consumer Price Index and on other governmental economic or employment statistics can be combined. The newspaper may add local figures. Stories about U.S. Supreme Court decisions, several of which may be handed down on the same day, also can be combined into one story.

The first edition

The bulk of the stories should move to the news editor of the afternoon newspaper by 5 a.m. Late-breaking stories and Page One stories should be completed by 5:30 a.m. The afternoon weather story usually moves about this time. The AP story slugged "Nation's Weather" gives this information. If weather is particularly newsworthy—like an earthquake, blizzard or ice storm—AP usually moves a separate story. The wire editor will alert the news editor if this happens.

The first edition may be wrapped up by 8:30 a.m. Before the story conference, where chief editors and section editors discuss the day's stories and how the paper should handle them, the wire editor checks the paper to see which stories made the first edition and which ones the news editor held back.

The wire editor pays close attention to the news briefs, because many of them were prepared early the previous evening. Several items that moved across the wires too late to make the first edition are good substitutes for stale news briefs. These are shortened and passed on to the news editor.

The story conference

Wire editors usually prepare for the morning story conference, or budget meeting, while they process news-service copy for the first edition. They do this by jotting down the sluglines of stories that are expected to develop during the day. AP is good about keeping member papers advised of developing stories, and many such stories are obvious. For example, a two-sentence story at 6 a.m. about a plane crash can grow into a lead story as information about the crash becomes available. Another key as to what is developing is the morning advisory that AP moves about 8 a.m., which lists stories the AP expects to "top"—send new leads for—during the day.

The story conference usually is attended by the managing editor, metro editor, wire editor, section editors, photo chief and perhaps others in the newsroom. At this time the editors discuss stories that are ready or will be ready shortly for the day's editions and decide which stories will get Page One treatment. The news editor or wire editor may suggest local angles that staff reporters could develop as sidebars or additions to news-service stories. Decisions about the use of photographs or other art or graphics are made during this brief meeting.

During and after the crunch

The times between the multiple editions of an afternoon newspaper are critical. Often the deadlines come no more than an hour apart. The wire editor

It is often useful to combine stories to save space and avoid duplication.

must work quickly and work closely with the news editor to put out a successful follow-up to the first edition.

After the budget meeting, any stories requested by other editors are sent to the news editor. The wire editor will check frequently with the news editor to make sure needed copy is in the queue. The wire editor will notify the news editor when stories are updated to see whether they should be re-edited. Minor changes may not be worth the trouble.

The wire editor tries to supply most of the second-edition copy to the news editor by 9:15 a.m. and the latest-breaking stories by 9:45 a.m. The wire editor will add 40 minutes to these deadlines for the third edition but will send copy earlier for inside pages.

By 11 a.m., the bulk of the wire editor's work for the day's afternoon editions is usually completed. During lulls, feature and advance copy moves to the proper departments. By noon, the wire editor should have all queues clean, taking out advisories that are intended for editors and printing copies for the managing editor, the assistant managing editor and the news editor.

Features and advance copy

Wire editors are responsible for distributing a large amount of copy. Here is a list of specific queues at one metropolitan newspaper and copy that is routed to them:

BZ/BA: *Business.* These are the business incoming wires. When a business-type story breaks that may not be on the business wire, the wire editor moves the story to the business desk, and the editor is notified.

CS: *Consumer.* These are consumer-related stories and columns. "News to Use" from AP is a regular consumer feature.

ED: *Editorial.* The editorial page at this paper uses Jack Germond, Jules Witcover, Mike Royko, Mary McGrory, William Buckley, George Will, Art Buchwald, Jim Fain, Carl Rowan, Richard Reeves, and New York Times writers Tom Wicker, James Reston, William Safire, Russell Baker and Anthony Lewis.

FD: *Food.* Most of these stories move on Fridays and Mondays. The food editor may appreciate news stories about additives, food legislation and market prices, but the wire editor should make sure the news editor has the first opportunity to use these stories.

IG: *Etcetera column items.* Look here for the weird and woolly in the world of news.

LW: *General lifestyle.* Features, fashion, entertainment, and columns such as Erma Bombeck, Dear Abby, Joyce Brothers and the like are sent to LW. Also in this queue are book reviews, the New York Times bestseller list and entertainment reviews.

PP: *People.* The AP and New York Times news services both supply columns highlighting the activities of celebrities.

SB/SF: *Sports.* Sports scores that are transmitted on the national and state wires can be deleted because they duplicate transmissions fed directly to the sports department. The wire editor contacts the sports editor if a story breaks that relates to sports, such as the death of an athlete.

SC: *Scanner desk.* Horoscopes, word games and bridge columns are moved here.

TR: *Travel.* Several of the supplemental news services send regular columns and features concerning travel.

Wire editors are responsible for distributing a large amount of copy.

TV: *Television and radio stories.* FCC-related stories and other media stories are moved to this queue for the radio-television writer.

WA: *Politics.* AP stories about politics are routed to this queue automatically.

Copy editors who handle news-service material are responsible not only for sorting and then distributing stories to various newspaper sections. They are responsible also for avoiding the publication of duplicated stories, for choosing the best version of a story from among the several news services and for merging several different versions into one story. They also help the news editor decide the top national and international stories of the day.

The wire editor also must work closely with those responsible for the newspaper's computer system to determine the most efficient way to retrieve, sort and store the vast volume and variety of news-service material transmitted each day.

Suggestions for additional reading

Desmond, Robert W. *Windows on the World: World News Reporting 1900–1920.* Iowa City: University of Iowa Press, 1980.

Emery, Edwin, and Michael Emery. *The Press and America: An Interpretive History of the Mass Media,* 6th ed. Englewood Cliffs, N.J.: Prentice-Hall, 1988.

Rosewater, Victor. *History of Cooperative News-Gathering in the United States, 1865–1935.* New York: Appleton-Century-Crofts, 1930.

Schwarzlose, Richard A. *The Nation's Newsbrokers—Volume 1: The Formative Years, From Pretelegraph to 1865.* Evanston, Ill.: Northwestern University Press, 1989.

Schwarzlose, Richard A. *The Nation's Newsbrokers—Volume 2: The Rush to Institution, From 1865 to 1920.* Evanston, Ill.: Northwestern University Press, 1989.

Tuchman, Gaye. *Making News: A Study of the Construction of Reality.* New York: Free Press, 1978.

1. Define the following news priority codes:

   a. **f** _____

   b. **b** _____

   c. **u** _____

   d. **r** _____

   e. **s** _____

2. Define the following news category codes:

   a. **w** _____

   b. **i** _____

   c. **a** _____

   d. **n** _____

   e. **f** _____

3. Explain the differences among primary news services, supplemental news services and syndicated feature services. Describe the offerings of one of each.

4. Describe in a short essay the chief differences between the Associated Press and United Press International.

5. Almost 90 percent of American newspapers receive their national and international news from one news service. Discuss in a short essay either the pros or the cons of this fact.

6. Read an AP or UPI report in a newspaper, then listen to a broadcast radio report on the same subject. Describe in a short essay the differences in reporting styles.

7. Choose an important local news story from a daily newspaper. Discuss in class why it should or should not have been picked up by either wire service.

8. The following four stories are about the same event. Edit each story as though it is complete, because your newspaper has four editions. The headline for the story will grow larger as the event becomes more striking. Unless your instructor provides a different headline schedule, use the one in Exhibit 6-2 (p. 163).

   a. Edit these paragraphs, and write a 2-36-2 headline:

   ```
   10:43

   A0117

   PM - Boys, 1st Ld, a0052, 0099

     SAN MATEO (AP)--A circling C-130 cargo plane spotted sev-

   eral survivors of a group of four teenage boys who were

   lost in San Francisco Bay on a small raft today, The Coast

   Guard reported.
   ```

The airplane dropped a 21-foot skiff to the boys who, the flyers reported, were swimming in the water. A Coast Guard cutter sped to their aid.

The four had been swept out into the bay at dusk last night.

An extensive air-sea rescue force of 12 planes had converged on the spot as the bay was blown by gusts up to 50 miles an hour.

The four, boy scouts, 4th graf a0052

b. Edit these paragraphs, and write a 4-48-1 headline:

10:48

A0120

PM - Boys, 2nd Ld, a0117, 0033

SAN MATEO (AP)--A Coast Guard cutter picked up "three or possibly four" boys today who had been adrift 16 hours in a rubber raft on the San Francisco Bay, the Coast Guard announced.

MORE

10:56

A0121

PM - Boys, 2nd Ld - 1st Add,   a0120, 0062

BULLETIN MATTER

SAN MATEO: announced.

Commander Russel Waszche, the Guard's public relations officer, said he had learned this by radio from the USCGC Resolute. The cutter took the boys to San Mateo.

The commander said he did not know what condition the survivors were in. He said they probably would be hospitalized.

The boys were cast adrift on a rubber life raft just before dark last night.

MORE

11:00

A0122

AM - Boys, 2nd Ld - 2nd Add,   a0121, 0039

BULLETIN MATTER

SAN MATEO: night.

Of the four, only three could swim. The boys were spotted still on the raft by a C-130, one of twelve planes in the air-sea rescue.

The twin-engine cargo plane dropped a 21-foot skiff equipped with two outboard motors.

The four, 5th graf, a0117

c. Edit these paragraphs, and write a 5-48-1 headline:

11:11

A0132

AM - Boys, 3rd Ld, a0122, 0032

BULLETIN

SAN MATEO (AP)--The bodies of four boys who had drifted overnight on a little rubber raft were taken today from the wind-chopped waters of San Francisco Bay. All four were pronounced dead.

MORE

11:12

A0133

PM - Boys, 3rd Ld - 1st Add,   a0132, 0030

BULLETIN MATTER

SAN MATEO: dead.

A Coast Guard cutter pulled their bodies off the raft. Crewmen applied artificial respiration.

Later, Coroner W. R. Carl pronounced the boys dead. He said they had died of exposure.

MORE

11:14

A0136

PM - Boys, 3rd Ld - 2nd Add,   a0133, 0029

BULLETIN MATTER

SAN MATEO: exposure.

The boys had been swept into the bay at dusk last night as they went after a drifting canoe. An air-sea rescue force had searched all night for them.

Of the four, 5th graf, a0120

d. Edit these paragraphs, and write a 6-60-1 headline:

```
11:20

A0140

AM - Boys, 4th Ld, a0136, 0195

URGENT
```

SAN MATEO (AP)--Four teenage boy scouts whose little rubber raft drifted on wind-whipped San Francisco Bay for nearly 17 hours were found dead today.

Coroner W. R. Carl officially pronounced them dead. He said exposure was the cause. They had been battered by high waves and chill winds since dusk Thursday night.

Their raft was sighted this morning by a Coast Guard C-130 cargo plane, one of a dozen planes and helicopters searching the bay. The C-130 guided the helicopter-equipped USCGC Resolute, a 210-foot Coast Guard cutter, to the raft.

The boys were members of a Boy Scout troop in San Mateo. They were David L. Hahn, Rolan Reimer and Richard Bauer, each 13, and William Von Hof, 14.

They had set out from Coyote Point Thursday night to retrieve a drifting canoe. Winds swept their yellow raft into the bay.

The Coast Guard, on the basis of reports from the twin-engine cargo plane, had reported survivors aboard the raft. The plane's radio report had indicated that signs of life were seen.

But when the cutter reached the raft, no signs of life could be found. Crewmen applied artificial respiration but it was too late.

9. Edit the following story from the Associated Press, and write a 2-36-2 headline:

High medical bills--a burden shared by most Americans--are due in part to a relatively few ill people. And, people who generate much of the nation's medical expenses are often suffering from the effects of smoking, alcoholism, and obesity.

Few are burdening the many, in terms of medical bills. And researchers in Boston suggest that perhaps it's time for those few to pay a cost more like their share. The researchers' work, published last week in the "New England Journal of Medicine," turned up the finding that less than one and a-half percent of the nation's population may use half the hospital resources in a year.

The scientists suggest that these people should have to pay higher insurance premiums, or higher taxes, if national health insurance ever becomes a reality, after all, the doctors say, these people are ill because of harmful personal habits. Food, drink and cigarettes--carried to excess--have landed them in the hospital.

Naturally, many people with big medical bills may not have been able to prevent their illnesses. They may develop some kind of illness that could not have been predicted and that's tough to cure.

Some insurance companies already offer lower premiums for those who don't smoke--but the problem remains, proving that you don't smoke when you ask for that lower rate.

Blue Cross-Blue Shield is also encouraging subscribers to cut costs. It's promoting same-day surgery, procedures done on an outpatient basis instead of those requiring an overnight or longer stay. Among those procedures are biopsies some methods of sterilization, removal of the tonsils, and maybe some oral surgery.

Blue Cross says this not only saves money--it also shortens the nerve-wracking waiting period, and gets you back to work quicker.

And, you can seek a second opinion, which may save not only money but also the pain and trauma of surgery. At least one citizens Watchdog group feels there are too many unnecessary operations done, many of them paid for by taxes. The group, the Better Government Association (of Chicago), says that perhaps a third of all operations may not be medically necessary.

The association, which took many of its figures from House Subcommittee Hearings, also says major elective surgery in the U-S is increasing at four times the rate of the population.

Editing Pictures and Infographics

The term *visual journalist* has assumed greater importance for the newspaper industry during the 1990s. The concept of repackaging the news to attract new readers and to regain former subscribers has sparked a flurry of newspaper redesign projects. Generally they call for shorter stories and increased use of visual elements to help produce a "reader-friendly" newspaper. Journalists skillful at communicating information quickly and clearly have gained enhanced status in the newsroom.

Marty Petty, vice president/deputy executive editor of the Hartford Courant, speaking at an American Press Institute seminar on newspaper design, said the visual journalist of the future will be a hybrid reporter-editor-artist:

Readers depend on their newspapers to not only provide interesting pictures, but to tell them what is happening, to explain all parts of a picture that might puzzle them and to make certain they have a clear understanding of what the photo is portraying.
—*Jenk Jones Jr.*, Tulsa, Okla., Tribune

The artists producing news graphics must also strengthen their journalistic skills. Newspapers will shift responsibility for the basic one-column and two-column chart, graph or map to the layout desks, copy editors and maybe reporters and origination editors. We will rely on them to have advanced computer skills, solid reporting and research skills and analytical skills as well as possibly a specialization in illustration. . . .

The graphics editor, art director and photo editor will play much more active roles in planning the news sections, news packages and special sections. Technology will make the execution of their traditional tasks simple and fast, and increase the number of graphics on our pages. Again, solid journalistic skills will be a first priority for them as well as a complete understanding of the production process. They will need to know how to build data for expanded news packages and graphics.

At the modern newspaper, copy editors play a role in processing photographs and informational graphics.

Editor-photographer relationships

As Petty observed, the realities of the modern newspaper industry demand teamwork among reporters, editors, photographers and graphic artists. The first requisite of photographers and graphic artists is to see creatively, and although few writers are visually oriented, they can learn to adapt their own talent to complement visual ideas. Whether the outcome of a graphic idea is tired and trite or new and vigorous depends largely on the shared ideas of both verbal and visual members of the team.

Photographers for a daily newspaper or news magazine do more than simply take pictures. They are expected to generate ideas for photos and photo spreads, to process their own film and do their own printing, to gather information for all cutlines (or captions), and to handle model releases when required.

As explained in Chapter 4, photographers do not need permission to take pictures of people engaged in newsworthy events. However, photographers who take pictures intended for advertising rather than news purposes must secure model releases from people they photograph. Model releases are signed consent forms in which photographic subjects give permission to use their pictures and names in advertisements.

Almost all newspaper photographers work in miniature format, 35 millimeter as opposed to 2.25 inches by 2.25 inches. Single-lens reflex cameras are preferred over viewfinder or twin-lens reflex cameras. Modern printing technology allows newspapers to use color photography to a far greater extent than in the past.

Many conscientious journalists carry cameras in their cars and are trained in basic principles of photography. But on a metropolitan daily, professional photographers are on hand to assist writers who see a photo angle to a story. The usual procedure is for a reporter or editor to fill out a photo request form, which is then processed by the city desk or by the photo editor.

Although reporters and editors suggest possibilities for illustrating stories, photographers are expected and encouraged to contribute their own ideas as well. On a typical day, the photographer will work with two or three writers and be expected to shoot some "stand-alone" photos along the way—shots that are unconnected with any news story but entertaining and informative.

At larger newspapers, the photo editor is the photographer's immediate supervisor. Experienced photographers are often promoted to the position of photo editor, but that job might be filled by a person without a photography background. In addition to processing requests for photographers, the photo editor is expected to work with writers and photographers to flesh out ideas for illustrating a story. When out of the office, photographers are in constant touch with the desk via a two-way radio or a telephone paging device. Once the photographer's work is out of the darkroom, in the form of contact prints or black and white glossy prints, the photo editor sorts through the material to select the best illustrations. The photo editor then works with the news editor to decide which photos will be published. Graphic designers and layout editors often are involved in these decisions, especially at larger publications.

Large publications employ photo lab supervisors, who handle such tasks as mixing darkroom chemicals, maintaining equipment, stocking darkroom supplies, scheduling equipment and loading film cassettes. When a photographer is in a hurry, the supervisor may fill in by processing the photographer's film. Newspapers too small to have a full-time supervisor may have a lab technician who mixes chemicals, processes some of the film and cleans up at the end of the day. At some small papers, a single photographer does everything.

Rob Heller, a newspaper design consultant and photography teacher at the University of Tennessee–Knoxville, suggests that photographers give special attention to these elements:

- *Point of view.* Always look for a more interesting angle from which to take the photograph. High or low angles can present the world in a unique way.
- *Subject contrast.* Make sure that the subject stands out from the background. Dark against light or light against dark allows the viewer to distinguish the important parts of the photograph.
- *Framing.* Examine all parts of the frame very carefully as you look through the viewfinder. This is the time to look for distracting elements such as a telephone pole coming out of a subject's head.
- *Lighting.* The lighting should enhance the photograph, not detract from it. Stay away from flat, frontal lighting. Look for more interesting light from the side or back of the subject.
- *Camera-to-subject distance.* An overall or long shot establishes the location of an event. A medium shot describes the action. A close-up examines the details of a situation. Shoot all three to give coverage as complete as possible.
- *Decisive moments.* Make sure to always tell the story of an event or

Experienced photographers are often promoted to the position of photo editor.

news situation. Try to capture the decisive moment, the instant when all the above elements come together to form a powerful photograph.

Finally, Heller says photographers should observe the photojournalistic axiom "*f*8 and be there," meaning that photographers should always carry a camera loaded with film and ready to shoot.

Selecting pictures

The procedures for showing photographs to editors vary from publication to publication. Some photographers make *contact prints*, proofs of the negatives that are the same size as the negatives themselves. Although small, they are easily inspected with a *linen tester*, a small 8- or 10-power magnifying glass. Editors work from contact prints to select the photographs to be printed. The prints are usually to 8 inches by 10 inches, although some economy-minded newspapers use 5-inch-by-7-inch prints. At other publications, the photographer may skip the contact prints and make 8 × 10 or 5 × 7 prints of the best photographs.

In making picture selections, editors and photographers will choose photos that best accomplish the primary goals of photojournalism:

- To communicate effectively, as either stand-alone art or accompaniment to a story
- To attract readers' attention and provide a point of entry to the page
- To enhance the overall appearance of the page

Space is a valuable newspaper commodity, so editors must choose wisely in allocating that space. Will a photograph best accomplish the goals within limited space, or should an informational graphic be used? Or perhaps a sidebar to accompany the main story?

Criteria that make a story newsworthy apply also to picture selection:

- *Impact.* Pictures that illustrate events and situations with an impact on many people are more likely to be published than pictures with limited scope.
- *Unusualness.* Shots of an unusual happening or pictures taken from unusual angles or that use different approaches to routine events win favor with editors.
- *Prominence.* Readers like to see photographs of famous and infamous people.
- *Action.* Modern cameras, with fast shutter speeds and high-speed film, allow photographers to freeze action. Editors may be compelled to use an occasional "grip and grin" or lineup photo, especially in small-town papers, but such trite pictures are largely a relic.
- *Proximity.* People want to see pictures of their friends and neighbors, of people in their own community. Other factors being equal, editors give the nod to local photographs over wire photos.
- *Conflict.* Just as conflict makes an event or situation worth writing about, it also adds to the value of photographs. But editors must guard against selecting a conflict-filled photo that distorts an event. It would be poor news judgment, for example, to publish a photo of a minor fight that was an isolated incident at an otherwise peaceful event.
- *Timeliness.* In judging the timeliness of photographic coverage, editors must consider whether readers still are interested in something that hap-

Criteria that make a story newsworthy apply also to picture selection.

pened last week or even just this morning. Television also influences newspaper photo selection, because editors seek to publish pictures different from those seen on television.

- *Technical quality.* A blurry, out-of-focus print rarely attracts a second look from photo editors—unless its news value vastly outweighs its poor quality. Pictures of the first moon landing and the assassination of President John F. Kennedy are among the rare examples of news value overcoming poor technical quality.

Preparing photographs for publication

Once the responsible editor has selected photos and other illustrations to be used, the art must be prepared for the production department. The art must be cropped, sized and scaled. In addition, photographs sometimes need to be retouched.

In performing these tasks, everyone who handles photographs and other artwork should do so with care. Fingerprints and smudge marks may show up when the art is published, so keep it clean. Never cut a picture to eliminate unwanted parts. Instead, use a wax or soft-lead pencil to mark, with both horizontal and vertical lines, the part of the photograph that should be reproduced. These *crop marks*, as they are called, can be erased and changed if necessary.

Never write on the face of a photograph. Place crop marks in the margins of the photo, and write instructions to the production department on the back of the picture or on an instruction tag attached to the picture. To write on the back of a picture, use a grease pencil or soft-lead pencil. A ball point pen or hard-lead pencil may crack the glossy face of the photograph or show through.

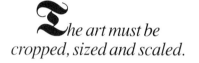

The art must be cropped, sized and scaled.

Cropping

To crop a picture is to decide how much or what part of a print should be published. Editors crop to eliminate busy backgrounds, people who are superfluous to the photo's theme and other elements that distract from the picture's center of interest.

Begin cropping by covering up parts of the photo that contain no information or irrelevant information. What remains will have greater impact if reproduced at an adequate size.

To help decide how the picture should be cropped, editors often frame the picture with a rectangle formed between extended thumbs and forefingers, with strips of paper or with "cropping angles" designed for this purpose.

Keep in mind the following guidelines when cropping photographs:

- Avoid cropping pictures in fancy or irregular shapes unless there is an unusual and compelling reason for doing so.
- For head shots, most editors prefer to leave some space on the side that the subject faces. At a few newspapers, however, all head shots—also called mug shots—are cropped extremely tightly, so that ears and sometimes the top of the subject's head are trimmed.
- For an action picture—for example, a racing boat or a runner—leave space in front of the thrust of the action.
- When in doubt, crop it out.

Exhibit 8-1 shows how to place crop marks and how cropping affects the image's impact.

Scaling

Other terms for scaling are *proportioning* and *sizing*. Few publications print photographs or draw artwork "to size," meaning the exact size that they will appear in the finished publication. Deadline considerations preclude a return to the darkroom to print photographs to size after page layouts are completed; in fact, layouts for the latest news and sports pages often are finished only minutes before press time. Thus, most publications work with 8 × 10 or 5 × 7 glossy prints and scale them for enlargement or reduction (called the *reproduction* size).

Proportion is the key concept in enlarging or reducing photographs. A vertical picture cannot fit a horizontal space on the layout, unless, of course, the picture can be cropped to make it horizontal. In an ideal world, the person who does the page layout has a variety of excellent photographs to select from and, knowing that the desired shape is available, can design an attractive page.

But this isn't an ideal world. Often the layout editor has no choice about the shape of the photograph and must plan the layout accordingly. The layout editor can choose, however, to enlarge or reduce the photo.

Figuring the enlargement or reduction size while maintaining proportionality can be done by one of three methods:

• By using a formula to compute the unknown dimension

Exhibit 8-1
Crop marks are placed in the margins of the photograph, along both the horizontal and the vertical dimensions. Cropping a photograph gives it greater impact.

- By using a mechanical scaling device, such as a proportioning wheel or slide ruler
- By applying the diagonal-line method

A ruler, preferably one calibrated in picas, is needed for all three scaling methods.

Regardless of the method used, remember to work with the dimensions of the photograph or other artwork *as cropped*. If part of an 8 × 10 photo has been cropped, then the part of the picture that has been eliminated is not used in figuring the new size. After cropping, when we speak of the *original* or *present* size, we mean the cropped size, the size within the crop marks.

Formula method. The formula method is simple and requires no special tools other than a ruler. The three known dimensions (the width and depth of the original photo and one of the dimensions of the reproduction size) are plugged into this formula:

$$\frac{\text{Original width}}{\text{Original depth}} = \frac{\text{Reproduction width}}{\text{Reproduction depth}}$$

Because proportion is being figured, the result would be the same if the formula were set up this way:

$$\frac{\text{Reproduction width}}{\text{Original width}} = \frac{\text{Reproduction depth}}{\text{Original depth}}$$

This formula can be applied to any unit of measurement: inches, picas, feet, and so on.

Let's say you have a horizontally shaped picture that measures 10 inches by 8 inches. (It is customary to give photo dimensions with the width stated first.) You crop two inches from the vertical (depth) dimension, making the original dimensions within the crop marks 10 inches by 6 inches. The layout has been planned for a picture 5 inches wide. You need to know how deep this 10 × 6 picture will be when it is reduced to fit a space 5 inches wide. Plug these measurements into the formula, letting X represent the unknown dimension:

$$\frac{\text{Reproduction width (5)}}{\text{Original width (10)}} = \frac{\text{Reproduction depth (X)}}{\text{Original depth (6)}}$$

$$10 X = 30$$

$$X = 3 \text{ inches}$$

An original photo cropped at 10 inches by 6 inches will be in proportion when it is reduced to 5 inches by 3 inches. The reproduction size drawn on the layout should be 5 × 3.

Your scaling work is not complete, however, because the person in the production department who screens the photograph and reduces it must know the percentage of reduction. This figure should be written on the back of the picture or on an instruction tag attached to the photo. To determine the percentage of reduction or enlargement use this formula:

The formula method is simple and requires no special tools.

$$\frac{\text{Reproduction width or depth}}{\text{Original width (or depth)}}$$

$$\frac{5}{10} = 50\%$$

$$\frac{3}{6} = 50\%$$

When computing the percentage, mentally check to be sure that the percentage is "going in the right direction." If the published art is to be smaller than the original art, the percentage should be less than 100 percent. If the original is to be enlarged in the published version, the percentage should be more than 100 percent. Percentage errors occur if the formula is turned upside down. Comparing depth and width instead of the same dimensions (depth with depth or width with width) will also produce an incorrect percentage of reproduction.

Because most newspapers use a six-column layout, with each column measuring slightly more than 2 inches wide (typically $2^1/_{16}$ inches), the formula method requires working with fractional inches. To avoid dealing with quarters, eighths and sixteenths, use a pica ruler. It is permissible to round off dimensions to the nearest one-half pica.

Although the figures for dimensions in picas will be larger than when calculating in inches, multiplying and dividing whole numbers is easier than working with fractions with different denominators, especially if a pocket calculator is used.

Six picas equal one inch, so the previous calculation can be rewritten as

$$\frac{\text{Reproduction width (30)}}{\text{Original width (60)}} = \frac{\text{Reproduction depth (X)}}{\text{Original depth (36)}}$$

$$60\ X = 1{,}080 \text{ picas}$$
$$X = 18 \text{ picas (same as 3 inches)}$$

To figure the percentage:

$$\frac{\text{Reproduction width}}{\text{Original width}} = \frac{30 \text{ picas}}{60 \text{ picas}} = 50\%$$

$$\frac{\text{Reproduction depth}}{\text{Original depth}} = \frac{18 \text{ picas}}{36 \text{ picas}} = 50\%$$

Proportioning wheel. A scaling device like a proportioning wheel uses the same principle as the formula method. But the proportioning wheel is more commonly used, because it eliminates the need to multiply and divide. Several companies produce proportioning wheels, some with directions for their use printed on the wheel itself.

The wheel consists of two circular pieces of cardboard or plastic, one slightly smaller than the other. The pieces are attached in the center so they

When computing the percentage, mentally check to be sure that the percentage is "going in the right direction."

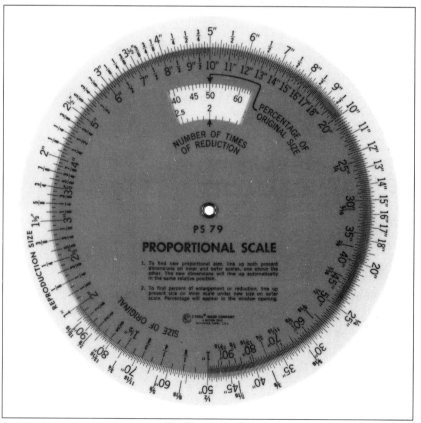

Exhibit 8-2
A proportioning wheel simplifies calculation of the amount by which a photo should be reduced to fit in the allotted space. In this example, the wheel is aligned to show the reproduction depth of a photograph 60 picas wide by 36 picas deep that is to be published at 30 picas wide, or 50% of its original size. Editors, such as this copy editor at the Seattle Times, often perform these calculations. (Photograph above by Kerric Harvey/courtesy of the Seattle Times)

can revolve (see Exhibit 8-2). Calibrations, which can represent any unit of measurement, are printed on the rim of each circle. In addition, a cutout area near the center of the wheel indicates the percentage of original size.

To operate the wheel, an editor first crops the artwork and measures the dimensions within the crop marks. Then the known reproduction dimension, usually the width, is located on the outer circle of the wheel and lined up with its counterpart dimension of the original photo, as cropped, on the inner circle. In that alignment, the two measurements of the other dimension, usually the depth, align—original dimension on the inner circle, reproduction dimension on the outer circle. An arrow in the window of the wheel points to the percentage of reduction or enlargement.

For example, note in Exhibit 8-2 that the present width (60 picas), found on the inner rim, is aligned with the reproduction width (30 picas), on the outer rim. Now look on the inner rim for the present depth (36 picas). On the outer circle is the reproduction depth (18 picas). The arrow in the center window points to 50, the percentage by which the original image must be reduced to fit in a 30-pica-by-18-pica space.

Diagonal-line method. The diagonal-line method is yet another way to scale photographs. A sheet of clear plastic or a sheet of onion-skin paper is placed over the photograph. The overlay is placed with its edge aligned with the vertical crop marks on the left side of the photograph. A diagonal line is drawn from the top left of the cropped photo to the bottom right, again at the crop mark. The vertical and horizontal dimensions of any right angle intersecting on the diagonal will be in proportion to the original photograph.

Some editors prefer this method because it allows them to keep the art in view throughout the process. However, the other two methods are more popular and less cumbersome. If you decide to use the diagonal-line method, it is worth investing in a commercial plastic overlay instead of using onion-skin paper. The commercial overlays have inches or picas marked along both the vertical and horizontal axes and come with a diagonal piece or a string attached at the upper left corner that can be rotated to the proper position (see Exhibit 8-3). For newspaper use, some of the commercial overlays are ruled in column widths.

Exhibit 8-3
This editor uses the diagonal-line method of scaling a photograph. (Photograph by Kerric Harvey/ courtesy of the Seattle Times)

Cropping and scaling when reproduction dimensions are known

People who are inexperienced at scaling photographs sometimes become confused when their task is reversed so that the reproduction size is known. This reversal occurs when the layout is completed before the art is scaled. Assuming that the layout editor did not lay out a horizontal space for a vertical picture that can't be suitably cropped, this assignment should pose no difficulty.

The first step is to determine one of the artwork's original dimensions. Measure the dimension that is least flexible (the dimension that cannot be cropped or that can be cropped the least). Now you have three of the dimensions: reproduction width, reproduction depth, and either original depth or original width.

Plug these known dimensions into the formula, align them on the proportioning wheel or draw the right angles on the plastic overlay. The fourth dimension can be figured readily. Once you have the fourth dimension, do not forget to crop the original photograph accordingly.

Retouching

The increasing use of computer-assisted graphics has eliminated much of the need for retouching photographs. Graphics can communicate more effectively some of the things that retouching once was used to illustrate—for example, circles or arrows drawn on photos to draw attention to a critical element that might otherwise be overlooked or dotted lines drawn to show a route.

The role of artists and designers at newspapers and magazines has expanded in recent years. Today's readers are unwilling to read dull, gray-looking publications and want information quickly. The traditional position of photo retoucher has been replaced by new positions in the editorial art department.

Editing pictures electronically

Proportioning wheels and diagonal-line scaling devices will soon be as obsolete at most newspapers as Linotype machines are today. Cameras that use film, darkroom chemicals and light-sensitive paper also may be relegated to newspaper museums, replaced by digital cameras and electronic darkrooms and picture desks.

More than a dozen companies displayed such newfangled photography equipment at the American Newspaper Publishers Association's 1991 Technical Exposition and Conference. They all promised enhanced reproduction quality, lower materials costs, potentially lower labor costs and the ability to introduce photographs into full electronic pagination.

Editors say that changes in the ways they select and prepare photographs for publication will be as significant as the changes they went through when newspapers shifted from typewriters to VDTs. Instead of manually sorting through photographs, editors will sit at terminals with as many as 16 small pictures displayed on the screen at one time. Editors can select the pictures they want to publish, crop them electronically, enlarge or reduce them to fit the layout and sharpen the images to enhance reproduction quality—all without producing paper copies of the photographs.

By 1992 the Associated Press's new Leaf electronic picture desks became available to all AP member newspapers. The equipment allows photographs to be transmitted electronically by satellite and to be outputted electronically. Some papers use similar picture desks manufactured by other companies, and more than one system is in place at a few newspapers.

The role of artists and designers at newspapers and magazines has expanded in recent years.

News-service photographers transmit by satellite, of course, and many local staff photographers can use electronic equipment and standard telephone lines to transmit photographs directly from the field to their newspaper's computer system.

For example, the Union-News in Springfield, Mass., has used electronic darkroom systems since 1987 and by 1992 was electronically processing 98 percent of its wire photos and about 75 percent of all local photos. Norman C. Roy, photo editor, said in 1992 that the newspaper was saving as much as $25,000 each year on photo-processing materials alone. In addition, electronic darkroom systems allow the Union-News to rescue marginal pictures, sharpening images that would have been too "soft" without the electronic manipulation.

Informational graphics

According to John Bodette, a newspaper designer, "The gray slabs of beef that make a page uninviting are avoided by adding more 'points of entry' for readers." Those "points of entry" include not only photographs but also informational graphics—diagrams and charts—that add color and variety to the printed page.

A graphics explosion took place at U.S. newspapers during the late 1980s. Photographs continue to predominate, but even small papers without an artist in the newsroom are now using simple graphics produced by computer-literate reporters and editors or are receiving material from a graphics network. The trend is more pronounced at large papers. A special report on newspaper art published by the American Newspaper Publishers Association in February 1989 said that two-thirds of the daily papers employing artists had an average of four staff artists. The editorial art departments at several papers had more than 40 staff members.

Several factors account for the growth of newspaper graphics:

- *Need to attract more readers.* Market research in the late 1970s and early 1980s showed that the growth of newspaper circulation in the United States was not keeping pace with population growth. Studies indicated that newspapers faced increasingly tough competition from other media. Other activities competed for leisure time, leading people to drop the newspaper-reading habit or to spend less time with a newspaper each day.
- *Changes in newspaper reading habits.* Spending less time with their daily papers, many readers became "scanners," moving through an issue rather quickly, glancing at headlines and pictures but infrequently stopping to read an article. Layout editors and designers began to use the term *points of entry* to describe eye-catching elements that would get readers to stop scanning, to "enter" a page and spend some time there. Headlines, photographs and graphics make good points of entry.
- *New technology.* What high-speed cameras and film and offset printing were to photojournalism in the 1960s, developments in color reproduction, computers and laser printers were to newspaper graphics in the 1980s. Although an artist could produce more sophisticated material with the new technology than could a non-artist, papers that could not afford a staff artist could buy a Macintosh personal computer, graphics software and laser printer, which even in the hands of a non-artist could yield simple graphics. Satellite technology permitted fast transmission of computer graphics from networks, the first of which was begun by Knight-Ridder in 1982.

Headlines, photographs and graphics make good points of entry.

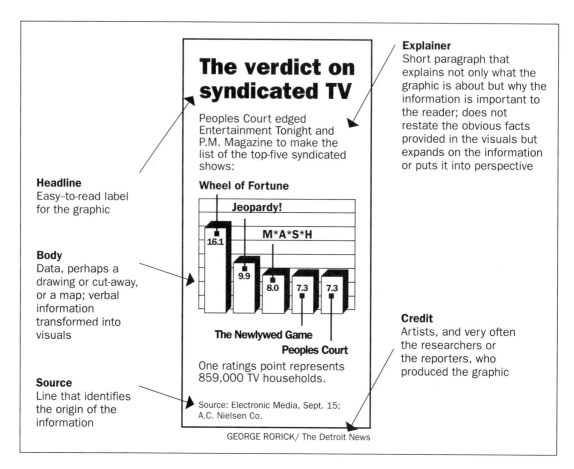

The verdict on syndicated TV

Peoples Court edged Entertainment Tonight and P.M. Magazine to make the list of the top-five syndicated shows:

Wheel of Fortune

Jeopardy!

M*A*S*H

16.1

9.9

8.0   7.3   7.3

The Newlywed Game

Peoples Court

One ratings point represents 859,000 TV households.

Source: Electronic Media, Sept. 15; A.C. Nielsen Co.

GEORGE RORICK/ The Detroit News

Headline
Easy–to-read label for the graphic

Body
Data, perhaps a drawing or cut-away, or a map; verbal information transformed into visuals

Source
Line that identifies the origin of the information

Explainer
Short paragraph that explains not only what the graphic is about but why the information is important to the reader; does not restate the obvious facts provided in the visuals but expands on the information or puts it into perspective

Credit
Artists, and very often the researchers or the reporters, who produced the graphic

Exhibit 8-4
An infographic has five elements: headline, body, source, explainer and credit.

- *Competition and example of USA Today.* USA Today entered the market in 1982 with extensive color and graphics, a formula layout and uncommonly short news stories. It did not win universal critical acclaim, but it did attract attention. Other newspapers copied its graphic techniques, especially the color weather map.

Essential elements of an infographic

The function of an informational graphic (infographic) is simply to convey a message in a visual form that is easy to understand. Like a story, a graphic should have a beginning, a middle and an end. The five essentials of informational graphics are shown in Exhibit 8-4.

If any of these essential elements is missing or is poorly executed, the graphic will not achieve its goal. Exhibit 8-5 analyzes a graphic with problems and suggests alternatives. Exhibit 8-6 is a set of informational graphics produced by the graphics staff at Gannett News Service and USA Today.

Creation of an infographic

The process of creating an infographic varies, of course, from publication to publication and from artist to artist. Martin Gehring, an artist for the Knoxville, Tenn., News-Sentinel, emphasizes the importance of early and ongoing communication among reporters, editors and artists on each assignment that has graphic potential. If the artist is involved at the time the reporter begins working on the story, graphic possibilities are less likely to be overlooked, and the artist will have more time to produce high-quality graphic art.

Speaking to students in an editing class at the University of Tennessee, Gehring explained a 12-step process artists can use to help themselves think visually and produce infographics:

Weak Graphic

Tourism brings sales tax dollars

Grant County collects 45 percent of its annual sales tax revenue during May, June, July and August, when tourism is at its peak.

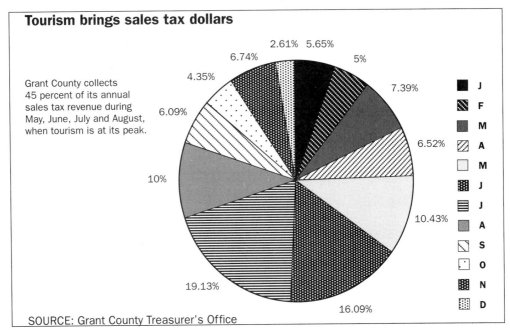

SOURCE: Grant County Treasurer's Office

Headline type is too small. Body copy is too small, especially in comparison with type size for source line. Figure in body copy is inconsistent with figures shown on pie chart. White space between box and text is insufficient; graphic appears crowded. Because pie chart is divided into 12 slices, it is difficult to understand quickly. Legend is too complicated. Variations in shading are hard to distinguish from one another.

Improved Graphic

Tourism brings sales tax dollars

Grant County collects about 50 per cent of its annual sales tax revenue during May, June July and August when tourism is at its peak.

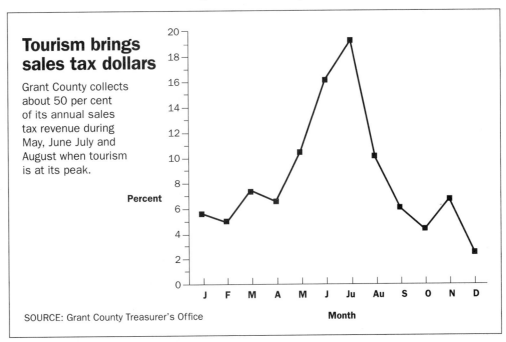

SOURCE: Grant County Treasurer's Office

Enlarge headline type to 18-point Franklin Gothic, and position headline to lead into body copy. Set body copy in 11-point Franklin Gothic, 2 points larger than type for source line. Allows 1-pica gutter around graphic so elements do not appear crowded in box. Use line graph instead of pie chart to show changes over time; readers can see immediately which months have greatest amounts.

Exhibit 8-5
Copy editors should check informational graphics with the same care they give to copy. Do the figures add correctly? Is the graphic appropriate for the type of information being communicated? Are the design elements executed for maximum effectiveness? Shown here are techniques for improving a poorly designed graphic.

Computer filing soars

Electronic filing – first tested in 1986 – saves taxpayers and the Internal Revenue Service money. It is also more accurate and results in quicker refunds. Here's how it's growing:

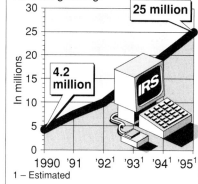

25 million

4.2 million

In millions

30
25
20
15
10
5
0

1990 '91 '92¹ '93¹ '94¹ '95¹
1 – Estimated

STEPHEN CONLEY, GNS   Source: IRS

Mound builders' puzzling legacy

A thousand years before the arrival of Christopher Columbus, the Hopewell – a nation of mound builders – developed a sophisticated culture centered in Ohio but extending west into Iowa, north to Wisconsin and south to St. Louis.

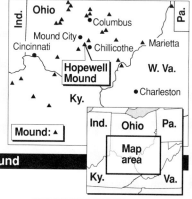

Ind. Ohio | Pa.
Columbus
Mound City
Cincinnati • Chillicothe • Marietta
Hopewell Mound
W. Va.
Ky.
• Charleston

Mound: ▲

Ind. | Ohio | Pa.
Map area
Ky. | Va.

Anatomy of a typical Hopewell mound

Capped with gravel and pebbles

Five alternating layers of sand and earth

A low earth mound

Ashes, cremated human remains and fragments of artifacts: pottery, copper tools and spearpoints

Clay platform lined with an inch-deep layer of sand or fine gravel

Size comparison

The largest of the mounds, the Hopewell Mound, was 33 feet tall, 500 feet long and 180 feet wide.

The Hopewell Mound

Football field (330 feet long and 159 feet wide)

STEPHEN CONLEY, GNS   Source: National Park Service, U.S. Department of Interior

Sun spots

Fifty percent of men and women say they use sunscreen 'all over.' The areas most important to those who target specific areas:

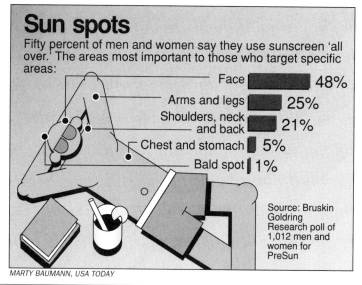

Face — 48%
Arms and legs — 25%
Shoulders, neck and back — 21%
Chest and stomach — 5%
Bald spot — 1%

Source: Bruskin Goldring Research poll of 1,012 men and women for PreSun

MARTY BAUMANN, USA TODAY

Exhibit 8-6
Using a Macintosh II computer and Aldus Freehand software, staff artists at the USA Today produced these infographics. (Reproduced by permission)

1. *Listen.* Talk with the reporter and editors working on the story. Listen carefully and take notes. Try to understand as much as possible about the story at the time the reporter begins working on it.

2. *Question.* Ask the reporter and editors for their ideas about the kind of art that might accompany the story. Brainstorm with them. What tone should the graphic use? How many pieces of art are needed? What is the deadline? What is the working title for the infographic?

3. *Believe.* Believe that you can produce work to accompany this particular story better than anyone else can.

4. *Gather information.* Reporters and editors should supply you with information as well as printed material available from interview sources. Reporters should remember to ask their sources for such materials, including maps, diagrams, reports and statistics. Even though the reporter may not plan to use these materials in the story, they can be immensely valuable to you. Also get a copy of the reporter's early drafts of the story. In addition to getting information from the reporter, you will often have to conduct research at a library. Reference librarians at the newspaper library or at a public or university library can be among the artist's best friends.

5. *Think.* After you have the necessary information, you must mull it over and decide how much of the information to present and the most effective way of presenting it to readers. What will communicate best—a bar chart, pie chart, fever chart, table, diagram, map, illustration, photograph or photo illustration?

6. *Write.* Using the working title and ideas gathered during earlier stages in this process, create two lists: a concept list and an emotion list.

7. *Draw.* Create many thumbnail sketches from your concept list. Don't hold back at this stage. Be daring.

8. *Judge.* Sit back, look at your sketches, and decide which one is most appropriate to illustrate the story. Draw a rough sketch of that particular thumbnail to the approximate size that it will be published.

9. *Justify.* Think of all the reasons you can to justify why you used the concept that you chose. Be prepared to present these arguments to your colleagues and your boss.

10. *Show.* Show all of your thumbnail sketches to your colleagues in the art department. Get feedback from these experts. Then select no more than three of the sketches to show the art editor and other editors involved in producing the story. More than three sketches tend to confuse the issue.

11. *Get approval.* Get feedback and make improvements. Finally, get your boss's approval.

12. *Finalize.* Create the final camera-ready art. Then take a break.

What will communicate best?

Role of the copy editor

The artist may be ready for a break, but the art doesn't go to the production department until the copy editor checks it. Ideally, copy editors are involved in the early stages of creating a graphic, to check the accuracy of information that the artist uses. After the artist delivers the camera-ready art, the copy editor again is called into service to check the accuracy of information, style, spelling and grammar.

Just as the copy desk is the last line of defense against errors in stories, copy editors perform a similar function in dealing with graphics. The copy editor should study the graphic carefully to ensure that it tells a complete story. Like a story, it should have a beginning, a middle and an end.

It should be able to stand alone, understandable to people who do not read the accompanying story. Check to see that the graphic contains the essentials: headline, body, explainer, source and credit line. Guard against graphics that are so complex they may confuse readers.

Consult with the artist about items that could be improved. A major overhaul near deadline time is usually impossible, but many changes—changes that could make the difference between an excellent graphic and one that fails to communicate—can be made in a matter of minutes on the computer.

Copy editors should edit informational graphics with the same care they give to stories: make sure the numbers add up; check the labeling on maps to be sure that cities, states, or entire countries haven't been misplaced; look at the typefaces used in the graphic to ensure consistent size and style for parallel items. Finally, if the drawing is not made to size, it will have to be scaled.

Copy editors who learn to produce computer graphics as well as to edit them have acquired yet another valuable skill. According to the February 1989 ANPA report, about one-third of the daily papers do not have a graphics or art department. Many of those have trained a reporter or copy editor to use a personal computer and off-the-shelf software to produce infographics. The graphics revolution has had an impact on the duties of copy editors, whether they produce the graphics or edit those created by someone else.

Captions

The key to fusing words and pictures is to write to, not merely about, a picture or series of pictures. Many editors write most successfully to a picture by imagining that it is the lead of the story and that the caption, or cutline, is a continuation that explains and amplifies the lead. It is essential, however, that the editor first distinguish the obvious from the obscure.

Responding to an Associated Press Managing Editors survey, one editor wrote

Photo captions are some of the most important text we write every day. Standards of clarity, good writing, accuracy and completeness are—if anything—higher than for body text. Desk chiefs should give the highest priority to writing photo captions.

Another editor made this observation about the importance of captions: "The picture captures a moment, but few pictures stand alone and almost all pictures are enhanced by basic information that will help the viewer/reader audience understand the particular moment caught by the image."

In the APME report, compiled by Jenk Jones Jr. of the Tulsa, Okla., Tribune, editors said that these are the goals in producing well-written captions:

- *Explain fully.* Few individual pictures exist without the framework of an event. Freezing a particular moment in time freezes only that moment. It tells nothing of the moments and events that preceded that image—or what followed. Only the photographer can place that picture in perspective by providing the necessary background information. In doing so, the photographer becomes more than a photographer; he or she becomes a photojournalist. A good caption includes the outcomes of events like sporting contests and elections.
- *Avoid ambiguity.* Explain unusual objects; don't leave the reader wondering. Explain any ambiguities. For example, is the pope laughing or crying? Usually captions should identify anyone whose face is clearly recognizable and who appears to be part of the main action.
- *Avoid duplication.* One of the most frequent sins of captions is stressing something the picture already has made obvious to the reader; even worse is to state something in the caption that the picture shows is obviously not true. When a picture accompanies a story, it is also foolish to spend much space in the caption duplicating information in the story. Avoid duplicating the headline on the accompanying story.
- *Be accurate.* Have the photograph in front of you when writing the caption; don't guess or write from memory. You cannot make sure you have everyone identified if you are not looking at the picture. Count the number of names in the caption and make sure that number corresponds with the number of people; look at the crop marks to ensure that those

P̶hoto captions are some of the most important text we write every day.

identified in the caption have not been cropped out of the photo.

- *Make it interesting.* Tell it with punch, with sound descriptive words. The same standards used for writing stories should be used in writing captions. Don't ramble, and use the active voice. The key details should come near the beginning of the caption. Make captions short, but do not write them like telegrams. Eliminate such references as *is shown, is pictured* and *pictured above.*

- *Pay attention to verb tense.* Generally, a caption for an action picture starts with a sentence in the present tense. This practice is in keeping with the idea of fusing word and picture: The photographer has captured a moment in time, and the words that enhance the moment should be in the present tense to heighten the effect. However, sentences that are more indirectly related to the picture—references, for example, to the subject's actions at another time—are usually written in the past tense. A cardinal rule is that verb tense should never be changed within a sentence. Editors and reporters should distinguish between action pictures and posed pictures: Action is in the present; posed is from the past.

- *Avoid editorializing.* "Club-swinging police officer" may cast shadow on the officer, but "eyes blazing defiance, the protester" may shift prejudice in the opposite direction. Let the reader make value judgments from the look of the clubs and the eyes. Don't describe a picture as *beautiful, dramatic* or *grisly* or use any of the other colorful adjectives. Let the viewer decide. Don't use facial expression to try to interpret what the photographic subject was feeling or thinking,

- *Avoid libel.* People can be libeled in a photo caption just as in text and headline copy.

- *Achieve a compatible tone between photo and caption.* It is just as jarring to read a tragic story and see a smiling face in an accompanying photo as it is to read a caption that is out of tone with the photo. Don't try to be light and bright in the caption unless the photo warrants. Again, look at the photo while writing the caption.

- *Be honest with readers.* Point out anything unusual about the way the picture was made, particularly if perspective has been altered, magnification is extreme, a wide-angle lens was used, or the photo was taken under unusual lighting conditions. If file pictures are used and the time lag is relevant, let readers know.

Don't ramble, and use the active voice.

Picture stories

Good picture stories are like picture essays: Both must be planned. Great picture stories require a theme or central idea before the photographer starts work. Certainly happy accidents can result from haphazard shooting, but experience teaches that a good picture story is developed rather than stumbled upon.

A good picture story is usually created by

- Choosing a dominant picture
- Avoiding the cluttered look that results from crowding too many pictures into the available space
- Facing pictures toward the related text
- Avoiding "rivers of gray" caused by captions meeting irregularly near the same level
- Using a caption with each picture and a headline overall
- Arranging similar captions to have the same width, type and number of lines

• Focusing simultaneously on a subject or personality as well as a theme or mood

Writing to a picture story differs from writing to a single picture. The writer must focus on both individual pictures and continuity from photograph to photograph. Continuity can be achieved with a central block of copy that relates to all the pictures and echoes the spirit of the pictures as a group.

Ruthlessly hold captions to a maximum length. Readers like to leap from picture to picture, so each caption should be short. Captions can be related to pictures by proximity, keyed letters or numbers, or arrows—preferably by proximity and contiguity. Don't put a caption too far from the photo. The reader's eye moves from photo to caption and back to photo, perhaps several times.

It is advisable to include a headline for a photo layout of two or more pictures on the same subject to tie the package together.

Caption styles

In addition to giving careful attention to the content of photo captions, editors are concerned about the style of presentation. Captions are an important element of the publication's overall design, and editors should maintain graphic consistency. (This idea is discussed further in Chapter 10.) The photo caption style for any publication—newspaper, magazine or brochure—should include the following components.

Type size and style. Publications generally set captions in a typeface that contrasts with the typeface in the body so that captions stand out. For example, captions may be set in a sans serif typeface (like Helvetica or Gothic), in boldface or in a slightly larger type size, like 10- or 11-point type alongside nine-point body type. (Type is discussed in greater detail in Chapter 9.)

Some publications introduce captions with a brief *lead-in,* also called a "tagline" or "legend." The lead-in typically is set in boldface or in capital letters (see Exhibit 8-7). The first several words of the caption can become the lead-in.

Width of type block. The captions that go under one- and two-column photos usually are set the width of the photo. Some publications set captions one or two picas less than the width of the picture on each side so that the resulting white space helps captions stand out.

For photos wider than two columns, captions with only one or two lines of type can run the full width of the photo without hindering readability. When two lines are used, the second line of type should fill most of the space, avoiding a *widow,* a line of type containing only a word or two so that the line is mostly white space (see Exhibit 8-8). If the second line cannot be filled without obvious padding, the caption should be edited to one line.

Under photos wider than three columns, captions longer than one or two lines should be set in two columns (see Exhibit 8-9).

Placement in relation to photo. Standard placement for a caption is directly under the photograph, but captions may be placed to the side of photo. Captions rarely are set above photographs except where one caption accompanies two or more related photos. Exhibit 8-10 shows variations on the standard placement.

Overlines. An *overline* is a word, phrase or clause set in headline type, placed above a photo or between a photo and its caption (see Exhibit 8-11). Some publications consistently use overlines, also referred to as "catch lines"

Captions are an important element of the publication's overall design.

Photo credit

Linked Sausages: Don Maile reacts to the smoke as he prepares Italian sausages for hungry customers at his food booth at the Festa Italiana at Seattle Center. Maile and his wife, Marcella, operate the Chicago Red Hots restaurant at 12504 Lake City Way. The festival included Italian music and dancing, an Italian car show, wine tasting and a grape stomp.

Photo credit

NEW ARRIVALS: More families arrive Sunday at the West Germany Embassy in Warsaw, Poland, as another 1,000 East Germans entered West Germany over the weekend. The exodus gained steam in September when Hungary opened its borders.

Photo credit

COTTON PICKING TIME – A cotton harvester works slowly down the rows as picking time arrives. Workers on this farm near Alexandria, La., began harvesting this year's cotton crop recently.

Photo credit

Bowman and her 'puppy,' 'BJ,' enjoy a moment at her Spencer Street home.

Photo credit

The University of Pittsburgh's 42-story Cathedral of Learning is home for 23 popular ethnically inspired Nationality Rooms.

Photo credit

There was heavy trading on the stock exchange in Frankfurt, West Germany, where the index fell 12.8%.

Exhibit 8-9

*Multiple lines under a
photo three columns
or wider should be set
in two columns rather
than running the
width of the photo.
Note in this example
the unequal number
of lines in each
column. An even
number of lines is
preferable.*

Photo credit

WHY'D THE FISH CROSS THE ROAD? — Two fishermen stand in the middle of the road into McFarland Park in Florence, Ala., trying for those fish that might have been brought into the flooded park by recent high waters. The park is closed every now and then when rains are heavy and the dam upstream opens its flood gates and swamps the park, which lies on a bank of the Tennessee River.

Exhibit 8-10

*Captions are not
always placed below
the photo. In the
example to the right,
the caption is placed
along the left edge of
the photo and is set
flush right, ragged left.
In the other examples,
the caption is placed
to provide a visual link
for more than one
photo.*

**Jessie Gronek
talks things over
with a horse owned
by Ray Gill. Each of
the eight players
uses six horses
during a polo
match.**

Yosemite Beckons Clicking Cameras for a Fall Show

The cameras come out in Yosemite National Park when the road reaches a point offering the park's classic views, like the one above featuring El Capitan, in left of photo. Another picturesque spot is Vernal Falls, at left. And in October as the leaves change, the foliage becomes a point of special interest to shutterbugs.

Photo credit

Photo credit

Angry demonstrator, above, screams at driver outside Beverly Hills High School, where substitutes had to cross striking teachers' picket line. All but 15 of the district's 300 teachers, nurses, counselors and librarians struck the 4,700-student system. Tensions ran high but there was no violence.

234

Exhibit 8-11
Overlines to captions can be treated in various ways. Note the type styles and sizes and the placement of these examples.

Photo credit

An eye for art

Chicago students look over a sculpture called "Song of Spring," which is part of the East Side Sculpture Walk on the banks of the Chicago River east of Michigan Avenue.

Radiant City

TURN ON THE LIGHTS — Many downtown Chattanooga buildings, such as American National, had all their lights on Thursday night to allow local photographers a chance to participate in the "Chattanooga at Twilight" photography contest. A booklet of entries in the contest will be compiled by Creative Yard Concepts and the Chattanooga Area Convention and Visitors Bureau. Also participating in the project is Downtown Alliance. (Photo credit)

Photo credit

CUBS' JEROME WALTON LEAPS INTO IVY
Spearing Long Drive By Giants' Robby Thompson

Photo credit

A gathering of legends

London was the site of a gathering of three of boxing's greats Tuesday when Joe Frazier, left, George Foreman, center, and Mohammad Ali appeared in a ring at the London Arena. The three former champions were promoting the release of "Champions Forever," a videotaped tribute to their careers.

Airport protest in Japan

Leftist students and workers on Sunday protest the expansion of the Tokyo International Airport.

or "taglines," for stand-alone photos that do not accompany a story. Overlines are effective devices to attract readers' attention, add information about the photo and allow white space into the layout.

Credit lines. The source of the photo, usually the name of a photographer or news service, should always be indicated. The photo credit line may come at the end of the caption, set off by parentheses. More commonly, it is set in type smaller than the caption type and placed under the lower right corner of the photograph.

HOW ARTISTS AND REPORTERS WORK TOGETHER

By Charlotte Tongier

I grew up surrounded by art. Both my parents were artists, so drawing always seemed a perfectly natural thing to be doing.

By the time I was in junior high school, I was getting enough positive feedback from teachers and others outside my family to start considering art as a way of life. As I headed off to college, I had dreams of becoming another Georgia O'Keeffe or Mary Cassatt, but circumstances and real life forced me into a more practical direction, and here I am making a living at a newspaper.

I believe the newsroom operates like the human brain, having two spheres: a left and a right. The graphics department is like the right sphere of the brain, and the reporters are like the left sphere. When both halves are working together harmoniously and in cooperation with each other, the end result should be a complete package of interesting, provocative, concise information for the readers.

Creating a piece of artwork is a very "right-brained" activity. It involves the "creative process," whatever that is—visualizing, feeling, it's intuitive. Reporting also takes a type of creativity, but I consider it more of a "left-brained" activity, in that it involves mostly fact gathering and processing. A reporter deals with facts, figures and information that he or she must organize and put together in a logical form so the uninformed reader can understand what is going on.

CHARLOTTE TONGIER

Winner of the Scripps Howard prize for graphics (see Exhibit 8-12), Charlotte Tongier says she keeps herself physically, mentally and spiritually alive and well by rock climbing in the Sandia Mountains outside Albuquerque. It prepares her mind for prolific creation of illustrations, charts and graphics at The Albuquerque, N.M., Tribune.

Tongier was born near Philadelphia and was a scholarship student at Moore College in Philadelphia. Later she majored in fine arts at the University of New Mexico. After marriage and three children, she studied art history, drafting, pasteup, layout and illustration. In 1978 she joined The Albuquerque Tribune as an illustrator. Since then, she has seen her work reproduced in every section of the newspaper.

Tongier says, "The last 10 years here at The Albuquerque Tribune have been a continual growing and learning process. With the progress in reproduction capabilities, I have moved from doing nothing but black and white line drawings, with occasional use of color flaps, to full-color illustrations.

"My goal for the next year is to become skilled at creating graphics on a Macintosh computer. Wow, what a challenge for my left brain!"

To make an effective illustration or graphic, an artist should be able to take the information provided by the reporter and then interpret and synthesize it into a visual image that clarifies or exemplifies what is being written. An illustration should immediately draw your attention and interest into the story. And finally, it should be designed together with the body of type and the headline into a complete package on a page so that it works as a whole, solid piece—not two separate parts.

Reprinted courtesy of Scripps Howard News.

Exhibit 8-12
Charlotte Tongier produced these graphics for the Albuquerque Tribune. Judges for the Scripps Howard award commented: "Charlotte Tongier's contribution to The Albuquerque Tribune is outstanding. Her illustrations, charts and graphs add impact throughout the paper, from the front page to special sections. Her work is not only artistic, but full of meaning." (Reprinted courtesy of Scripps Howard News)

Suggestions for additional reading

Design: The Journal of the Society of Newspaper Design, a publication of the Society of Newspaper Design, PO Box 17290, Dulles International Airport, Washington, D.C. 20041.

Edom, Clifton C. *Photojournalism: Principles and Practices*. 2nd ed. Dubuque, Iowa: Wm. C. Brown, 1980.

Finberg, Howard I., and Bruce D. Itule. *Visual Editing: A Graphic Guide for Journalists*. Belmont, Calif.: Wadsworth, 1990.

Garcia, Mario, and Don Fry. *Color in American Newspapers*. St. Petersburg, Fla.: Poynter Institute for Media Studies.

Gassan, Arnold. *Exploring Black and White Photography*. Dubuque, Iowa: Wm. C. Brown, 1989.

Holmes, Nigel. *Designer's Guide to Creating Charts and Diagrams*. New York: Watson-Guptill Publications, 1984.

Pocket Pal: A Graphic Arts Production Handbook. 14th ed. New York: International Paper, 1989.

Tufte, Edward R. *The Visual Display of Quantitative Information*. Cheshire, Conn.: Graphics Press, 1983.

1. Refer to the photo below:

a. Size this picture to be reproduced three columns wide for a newspaper that uses columns 12 picas (2 inches) wide with 1 pica (¹/₆ inch) of white space between columns. Show crop marks, even if you decide not to crop anything out of the photo. Indicate the size of the original as cropped, the size of the photo as it will be published and the percentage of reduction from the original.

b. Write a caption with an overline to accompany this stand-alone photo. Here is information for the caption:

What: parade by pro-choice group, anti-abortion adherents watching from along parade route

Where: around state Capitol building in your state

When: yesterday at noon

Who: estimated 300 marchers, sponsored by Pro-Choice of your state

Why: pro-choice and anti-abortion proponents seeking to persuade state legislators to pass legislation supporting their respective points of view; state legislature expected to vote this session on legislation concerning abortion

Photo credit: Miles Carey, Knoxville, Tenn., News-Sentinel

2. Refer to the photo below:

a. Crop this photo to run one column (12 picas or 2 inches) wide. Show your crop marks, the size of the original as cropped, the reproduction size and the percentage of reduction from the original.

b. Write a caption that can be used in a layout combining this photo and the photo in exercise 1 (see the information in exercise 1).

Who: Molly Yard, former president of the National Organization for Women

What: rally of pro-choice supporters

When: yesterday at noon, immediately after pro-choice parade

Where: on steps of state Capitol building in your state capital

Why: (see information in exercise 1)

Other: size of crowd at rally, which included supporters of both pro-choice and anti-abortion positions and curious onlookers, estimated by Capitol security officers at 3,000

Photo credit: Miles Carey, Knoxville, Tenn., News-Sentinel

3. Refer to the photo below:

a. Crop and proportion this photo to fill a space four columns (51 picas or 8¹/₂ inches) wide by 28 picas (4²/₃ inches) deep. You may crop one or more of the young dancers from the photo if necessary. Show crop marks, the size of the original as cropped, the reproduction size and the percentage of reduction from the original.

b. Write a caption for the picture. Unfortunately, the list of names of the children has been misplaced, and it is close to deadline time, so you will have to write the caption without naming the children.

Who: five girls waiting their turn to audition

What: audition for "The Nutcracker"; 28 girls auditioned

Where: at Monroe Auditorium

When: auditions last night; "The Nutcracker" to be presented at the Monroe Auditorium December 1 through December 6

Photo credit: Miles Carey, Knoxville, Tenn., News-Sentinel

4. Refer to the photo below:

a. Without cropping anything, size the photo so it can be reproduced three columns (38 picas or 6½ inches) wide. Specify the depth and the percentage of reduction from the original.

b. Crop and size the photo so the piece of sculpture alone will be published in a space one column wide (12 picas or 2 inches) by 22 picas (3⅔ inches) deep. Don't forget to mark the margins for cropping. Specify the reproduction size of the original, as cropped, and the percentage of reduction from the original.

5. Refer to the photo below:

a. Size this photo to run three columns (38 picas or 6⅓ inches) wide. Specify the reproduction size of the original, as cropped, and the percentage of reduction from the original.

b. Write a caption from the following information. Use an all-capital, boldface lead-in.

Who: John Smith (No. 41 in white uniform) from Central High, Bryan Langford (dark uniform) from Halls High School

What: Smith's touchdown run during fourth quarter; 30 seconds left to play

Where: Central High Stadium

When: last night

Other: Central High had ball on Halls' 45-yard line; Smith took hand-off from quarterback, went around right end and scored; Bryan Langford had hold of Smith jersey as Smith turned corner, but Langford lost his grip; no other Halls defender could catch Smith; this was winning score; Central won 14–7

Photo credit: Miles Carey, Knoxville, Tenn., News-Sentinel

T

The personality of a newspaper usually can be determined from a distance of five feet. It is expressed largely in the kinds of stories that are emphasized and in the quality of the writing. But with relatively few exceptions, story emphasis and writing style have the same flavor as does the newspaper's design. A newspaper whose "black" or splashy design seems to shout at readers is likely to play up highly controversial or sensational stories and to be written saucily, raucously or both. A gray-looking paper is likely to demonstrate restraint in handling news and to feature quiet, sophisticated prose. Look at Exhibit 9-1. The San Francisco Examiner shouts the news with a large banner headline and a large photograph. But it's business as usual for the immutable Wall Street Journal, one of the country's largest dailies. In the Journal's case, large, splashy headlines and graphics are not essential to maintain its dominant market position and million-plus

Simplicity, carried to an extreme, becomes elegance.

—Jon Franklin

Nine

Typography

Type sizes
Type widths
Type styles
Type weights
Type families

Reprinted courtesy of the San Francisco Examiner.

Exhibit 9-1
Typography expresses the character of a newspaper. The San Francisco Examiner sometimes shouts the news, while The Wall Street Journal appears refined and sophisticated.

circulation, whereas the Examiner is fighting for market share in its position as an afternoon newspaper. Most American newspapers fall somewhere between these two extremes.

The earliest known attempts to record thoughts visually—symbols depicting objects, called pictographs—date back 20,000 years. Succeeding pictographs were more abstract ideographs, cuneiforms and hieroglyphics, the latter perfected by the Egyptians around 2500 B.C. Ten centuries later, around 1500 B.C., the Phoenicians used the first formal alphabet, then made up only of consonants. The Greeks acquired the Phoenician alphabet about 1000 B.C. and refined it over the next six centuries into a 24-letter alphabet that included vowel sounds.

Evidence of the first example of printing from movable type dates to around A.D. 1500. But type cast from metal was believed to be widely used in China and Japan in A.D. 1200. In 1440, Johann Gutenberg, probably unaware of the progress being made in the Orient, brought the West up to date with his invention of movable type. Until Gutenberg's system of separate characters for printing on a press with ink and paper, books were laboriously handwritten by scribes. By the end of the 15th century, however, presses were operating in all major European cities, publishing hundreds of thousands of books. Our common typefaces are simply imitations of early handwritten letters.

Today, teams of editors and artists design printed products, often using type created centuries ago. Many believe that design should reflect the elements of a product's personality.

Readers who pay attention to their newspapers find that the design can

- Attract their attention
- Grade the news for them, expressing the relative importance of items by headline size and placement
- Provide an orderly pattern for the currents of news flow

A large part of that design depends on typography, which combines with layout to create an integrated, cohesive and sometimes unusual graphic look.

Typography is the art of designing and arranging type to have desired effects on readers. All of us have ideas about typography, because some things look better to us than others. But it is the designer's job to assure that the typography and design of the newspaper enable readers to read easier and faster. To do so, the designer—and the editors who perform page design and layout—must recognize the subtle ways in which type can be differentiated. Typefaces can differ in at least five ways: size, width, style, weight and family.

Type sizes

Type has its own system of measurement. Feet and inches are the basic units of measurement for most of us, but for printers, the basic units of measurement are picas and points. As you may recall from Chapter 8, a pica is equal to about $1/6$ inch, and a point is equal to about $1/72$ inch. Both 6 picas and 72 points, then, equal an inch. Within the type measurement system itself, the conversions are easy to make: 1 pica is exactly equal to 12 points.

When we measure typefaces, we use points. When we measure larger elements, such as the width of columns or photos, we generally use picas.

Typefaces themselves used to be manufactured in standard sizes. A complete series of type would include at least the sizes shown in Exhibit 9-2. Today, however, phototypesetting and digital computer systems can produce virtually any size of type simply by manipulating the image electronically.

Typefaces can differ in at least five ways: size, width, style, weight and family.

6 point	abcdefghijklmnopqrstuvwxyz
8 point	abcdefghijklmnopqrstuvwxyz
9 point	abcdefghijklmnopqrstuvwxyz
10 point	abcdefghijklmnopqrstuvwxyz
12 point	abcdefghijklmnopqrstuvwxyz
14 point	abcdefghijklmnopqrstuvwxyz
18 point	abcdefghijklmnopqrstuvwxyz
24 point	abcdefghijklmnopqrstuvwxyz
30 point	abcdefghijklmnopqrstuvwxyz
36 point	abcdefghijklmnopqrstuvwxy
42 point	abcdefghijklmnopqrstuv
48 point	abcdefghijklmnopqrst
60point	abcdefghijklmnop
72 point	abcdefghijklmn

Sizes below 14 points are called *text types* or *body types*, and sizes of 14 points or larger are called *display types*. The text of a newspaper is set in body type—in fact, 70 percent of American newspapers use either 8-point or 9-point body type—and the headlines are set in display type. A 72-point headline is usually reserved for the most urgent news. Larger sizes exist but are rarely used.

Although in most modern newsrooms computers can set type in any point size desired, most editors continue to use the traditional type sizes, probably because they are easy to use under deadline pressure. Sometimes, however, copy editors may "squeeze" the type size and generate a 33- or 34- or 35-point headline instead of a 36-point headline in order to get the headline to fit. When type was set in lead, squeezing type was unheard of. In fact, many

Exhibit 9-2
The standard type sizes are still those used most often, although computer typesetting permits the use of non-standard sizes.

Exhibit 9-3

Two measures of
type are commonly
used: type size,
from the tops of
ascenders to the
bottoms of
descenders, and
x-height, which does
not include
ascenders and
descenders.

Sensitivity

x-height — 36 points

editors recall the days when backshop printers would yell out to the news-room: "Type isn't made of rubber, you know!" The headline wouldn't fit unless it had been written with a high degree of exactitude.

On a typical news day, a 48-point or 60-point headline will serve to identify the main story on the front page. On the inside, 42-point headlines generally are large enough to identify the most important story on each page.

Type size can be a difficult concept to understand, but for our purposes, it is sufficient to define the size of type as the distance from the top of the ascender (the long upstroke over such letters as *b, d, h* and *l*) to the bottom of the descender (the long downstroke under such letters as *j, p, q* and *y*). Look at Exhibit 9-3. The type size of the word can be measured by first drawing a horizontal line across the top of the ascenders (*i, t, i, i* and *t*) and then a horizontal line across the bottom of the descender (*y*). Next, measure the distance between the two lines, using the point scale on a ruler or a pica pole. Your measurement should tell you that this word is set in 36-point type.

Another way to talk about type is in terms of the *x-height* of the letters. The x-height is simply the height of the lowercase letters without ascenders and descenders (see Exhibit 9-3). Even though not technically a means of measurement, the x-height is important because it helps determine the visual impact of the type. Typefaces of the same point size may appear unequal because of slight variations in the x-height. Look at the following examples of three different typefaces, all set in 10-point type, which appear to be different sizes because of slight variations in the x-height:

(10-point Bodoni) — To determine the x-height of any typeface, simply use the point scale on your ruler or pica pole to measure the distance between the top and the bottom of any lowercase letter without ascenders or descenders.

(10-point Times) — To determine the x-height of any typeface, simply use the point scale on your ruler or pica pole to measure the distance between the top and the bottom of any lowercase letter without ascenders or descenders.

(10-point Helvetica) — To determine the x-height of any typeface, simply use the point scale on your ruler or pica pole to measure the distance between the top and the bottom of any lowercase letter without ascenders or descenders.

Type widths

Type is two-dimensional. In addition to its vertical size, editors also need to know its width. In the printing business, the width of a typeface, meaning the width of the lowercase alphabet, is referred to as its *set width*.

In most typefaces, the width of a capital *M* is equal to the type size. In fact, typesetters often used to refer to the concept of an *em,* which is the square of the type size. The em, therefore, is a variable measure: An 18-point em is 18 points wide and 18 points high; it is bigger than a 14-point em, which is 14 points wide and 14 points high. In body type, "one em space" is a typical paragraph indention.

The em method of measuring type width gradually is being superseded by the more precise *unit* system. The reference point still is the capital *M,* but instead of being a variable measure, the *M* is divided into 18 units or some multiple of 18. The width of all other characters, and their letter spacing, is then defined as a certain number of these units. Lowercase letters such as *i, j* and *l*, for example, are usually 4 units wide.

If we take each character of the alphabet and squeeze it slightly, we reduce the set width of the alphabet, thereby creating what is called a *condensed* typeface. Alternatively, we could make each character fatter, thereby creating an *extended* or *expanded* typeface. When typographers say, for example, that a given typeface is "12-point, 11½ set," they mean that the face is slightly condensed. Both of the examples below are 24-point Helvetica type, but the bottom one is condensed:

Art is life reflected through vision.
Art is life reflected through vision.

A complete inventory of display types at any newspaper includes some condensed and some extended typefaces, not only for contrast but also for situations in which the perfect word will not fit the available space. Newspapers with a predominantly horizontal design (see Chapter 10) use condensed typefaces sparingly and prefer faces of normal width. In a newspaper with a predominantly vertical design, however, condensed typefaces appear quite normal.

Body types apply the same rules. For example, more news can be packed into the newspaper by using condensed body type. But such use of type can make for a gray paper, which sometimes leads to difficulty in reading and tends to draw complaints from subscribers. To make a newspaper brighter, designers sometimes use the following techniques:

- Use a larger type size—9-point, for example, rather than 8-point.
- Use a normal, rather than a condensed, typeface.
- Use more paragraph indentions.
- Insert more space between paragraphs.
- Insert more space between lines.

This last technique, inserting more space between lines, is called *leading* (pronounced "ledding") or *leading out*. The term comes from the practice of inserting strips of lead between lines of type in the days when type was cast from a molten lead alloy. Type that has no space between the lines is said to be *set solid*—and sometimes the descenders of one line touch the ascenders of the line below it.

An 8-point type that has 1 point of leading is said to be set 8 on 9; an 8-point type that has 2 points of leading is said to be set 8 on 10, and so on. Here is an example of 8-point type set solid:

> The quantity and quality of informational graphics in newspapers increased dramatically in the late 1980s, largely because of the use of Macintosh computers and electronic graphics networks.

Here is an example of 8-point type set 8 on 9:

> The quantity and quality of informational graphics in newspapers increased dramatically in the late 1980s, largely because of the use of Macintosh computers and electronic graphics networks.

In a newspaper with a predominantly vertical design, however, condensed typefaces appear quite normal.

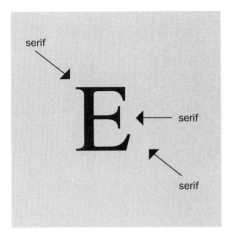

And here is an example of 8-point type set 8 on 10:

> The quantity and quality of informational graphics in newspapers increased dramatically in the late 1980s, largely because of the use of Macintosh computers and electronic graphics networks.

Leading—spacing between lines—usually makes type easier to read. On the other hand, studies have indicated that too much leading may hinder readability, because the eye "gets lost" in switching from the end of one line to the beginning of the next line.

For the same reason, type that is set either too wide or too narrow is difficult to read. Research studies differ on the best line length. But a common approach is to use this formula: $O = lca \times 1.5$. Translated, this formula means that the optimum line length (O) is equal to one and one-half times the width of the lowercase alphabet (lca). So, for example, if the width of the lowercase alphabet set in 10-point type is 112 points, the optimum line length would be 168 points (112×1.5), which equals 14 picas.

Type styles

Typefaces can be classified in many different ways, none of them precise. The classification system used most frequently in the field of graphic arts puts typefaces in seven main categories, also referred to as *races* of type: roman, italic, sans serif, square serif, text, script and decorative.

Roman typefaces are familiar to us because most of what we read is set in roman type. The chief characteristic is the *serif*, a small cross stroke at the end of each main stroke of the letter, as shown in Exhibit 9-4.

Roman type gets its name from the similarity of its capital letters to the alphabetic characters chiseled by stonemasons on the public buildings of the Roman empire. In 1490, an imaginative Frenchman, Nicholas Jenson, combined these characters with a more ornate set of characters to create the complete uppercase and lowercase English alphabet we know today. (The terms *uppercase* and *lowercase* stem from the early typographers' habit of storing small letters in a case below that of the capital letters.) Jenson's typeface, known today as Cloister Old Style, is a classic example of old-style roman type, known for its blunt serifs. Other examples of old-style roman type are Garamond and Caslon.

Bodoni, a roman typeface, has been one of the most popular headline typefaces in American newspapers. It was introduced in 1789 by Giambattista Bodoni, an Italian printer:

Art is life. (36-point Bodoni)

Times Roman and Century are roman styles commonly used for body type. Times Roman was designed in 1931 by Stanley Morison for The Times of London:

Art is life. (36-point Times Roman)

Century was designed in 1894 by L. B. Benton and T. L. DeVine for Century magazine, a leading publication of its day:

Art is life. (36-point Century Book)

Sans serif type, from the French *sans,* meaning "without," literally means "without serifs." In addition to the absence of serifs, sans serif typefaces—or *gothic* typefaces, as they sometimes are called—are recognizable by their uniformity of stroke. The following example reveals little or no variation in the widths of strokes used to create the characters:

Art is life. (36-point Futura)

In newspapers, sans serif typefaces play a significant role in headlines, captions and some "informational" material, such as stock market listings, sports scoreboards and television listings. Futura, Avant Garde and Univers are just a few of the many sans serif typefaces commonly used for newspaper headlines.

Art is life. (36-point Avant Garde)

Art is life. (36-point Univers)

Readers often have greater difficulty reading a sans serif typeface than a serif one, however, unless the sans serif typeface is either set large or leaded out. Most newspapers, therefore, have rejected sans serif type as their body type. The gothics do play important roles, however, in brochures, road signs, billboards, magazine advertisements and consumer product labels.

Square serif typefaces live up to their name. Their serifs are like small, rectangular slabs. Some typographers categorize these typefaces as roman because they have serifs on them; others categorize them as decoratives. When treated as an independent group, they have been referred to as the *Egyptians.*

Examples of square serif, or Egyptian, typefaces include Glypha, Memphis and Lubalin Graph.

Art is life. (36-point Glypha)

Art is life. (36-point Memphis)

Art is life. (36 point Lubalin Graph)

Readers often have greater difficulty reading a sans serif typeface than a roman face.

Italic typefaces, characterized by slanted letters, were designed to save space:

Art is life. (36-point Italic Goudy Old Style)

Because italic type is difficult to read in large quantities, it is used sparingly in newspaper body type—and then only to emphasize words, such as the first word of this paragraph. Italic type is used in headlines, however, and sometimes as a special design element. Roman and sans serif typefaces all have italic variations.

Text typefaces, which sometimes are called *Old English* or *blackletter* typefaces, play only a nominal—albeit curious—role in newspapers. Many of this country's large newspapers—The New York Times, the Los Angeles Times, The Washington Post, the Portland Oregonian, and the San Francisco Chronicle, among others—use text typefaces in their nameplates, or flags, the name of the newspaper displayed on Page One. Despite this apparent allegiance to tradition, the use of text typefaces in this fashion is atypical, according to noted editor Harold Evans:

The most hideous blackletter titles survive around the world from Victorian days because they are "traditional," but in fact the earliest titles, such as those of the first daily paper, The Daily Courant (1702), and the first evening paper, The Evening Post, and America's New England Courant (1721), were all in good bold Roman lower case.

With all the breezy, modern sans serif typefaces available today, it is a wonder that the blackletters (the tight, bold types that originated in Germany) have managed to survive. A few famous ones are still in circulation, including Fette Fraktur and Linotext:

Art is life. (36-point Fette Fraktur)
Art is life. (36-point Linotext)

Script typefaces look like handwriting:

Art is life. (36-point Mistral)

Most of the time they should not be used either in headlines or in the body of the paper. Occasionally, however, layout editors may use script typefaces on feature stories where such use is appropriate to the subject matter. Script typefaces are worth mentioning here only as an adjunct to a discussion of typography.

Decorative typefaces likewise play very little role in newspaper typography but are developed to reflect trends in fashion and advertising. Parisian,

> *Because italic type is difficult to read in large quantities, it is used sparingly.*

for example, usually is associated with art deco and is currently enjoying a revival:

ART IS LIFE. (18-point Parisian)

Type weights

Most typefaces are designed and manufactured in lightface and boldface versions. A few also have medium, demibold and extrabold versions. Below are examples of the different weights of type:

Futura Light

Futura Medium

New Baskerville Bold

Palatino Demi Bold

Cooper Black

COPPERPLATE GOTHIC

Helvetica Black

Futura Extrabold

Research studies on type legibility have indicated that, although boldfaces are more readable than lightfaces, because they contrast more with the background of the page, regular weights (medium) are preferred. The extrabolds are the least legible.

Type families

The individual members of type families share similar characteristics, yet they also vary in width, style and weight. Some families have only a few members; others have quite a few. Here are some of the 30 members of the Helvetica family:

Helvetica Light

Helvetica Medium

Helvetica Medium Italic

Helvetica Medium Condensed

Helvetica Bold

Helvetica Bold Italic

Helvetica Bold Condensed

Helvetica Black

The extrabolds are the least legible.

Newspaper designers generally try to limit the number of typefaces used in order to maintain a consistent appearance. For example, the body type might be Times Roman and the news headline font another serif typeface, such as Century Schoolbook. For captions, section labels and page headers, complementary fonts of a sans serif typeface like Univers might be preferred.

Suggestions for additional reading

Baird, Russell N., Arthur T. Turnbull and Duncan McDonald. *The Graphics of Communication*, 5th ed. New York: Holt, Rinehart and Winston, 1987.

Carter, Rob, Ben Day and Phillip B. Meggs, *Typographic Design: Form and Communication*. New York: Van Nostrand Reinhold.

Craig, James. *Designing With Type*. New York: Watson-Guptill, 1981.

Design: The Journal of the Society of Newspaper Design, a publication of the Society of Newspaper Design, PO Box 17290, Dulles International Airport, Washington, D.C. 20041.

Rehe, Rolf. *Typography and Design for Newspapers*. Carmel, Ind.: Design Research International, 1985.

Solomon, Martin. *The Art of Typography*. New York: Watson-Guptill, 1986.

1. Identify each of the following samples of type according to its classification (race): roman, sans serif, square serif, italic, text, script, or decorative.

Bookman

Futura

Lubalin Graph

Times

Zapf Chancery

Palatino

Helvetica

2. Look at your campus or local newspaper, and tell which classification of type is used for each of the following:

Largest headline on Page One _____

Other headlines on Page One _____

Nameplate _____

Body copy on Page One _____

Captions _____

Section labels (logos) _____

Bylines _____

Agate type in the sports section _____

Does the paper use the same weight of type for all headlines on Page One? Does the paper use the same typeface and size for body copy throughout the paper (except for ads)?

3. Measure the following type samples. Express the measurements in points.

The flag hangs high above the Capitol.

The flag hangs high

The flag hangs

The flag hangs

4. Measure the x-height (in points) for each of these samples:

18-point Bookman

18-point Helvetica

18-point New Century Schoolbook

18-point Times

5. How much space (depth) is needed for each of the following headlines?

   a. 2-36-2: _____ inches or _____ picas

   b. 4-48-1: _____ inches or _____ picas

   c. 4-48-1 with a 24-point underline: _____ inches or _____ picas

   d. 1-30-3: _____ inches or _____ picas

   e. 1-18-3: _____ inches or _____ picas

6. In each of the following pairs, which type would be easier to read for body copy in a newspaper?

   a. Black type on white or reverse type (white type on black)?

   b. Serif or sans serif type?

   c. Nine-point type leaded 1 point or 9-point type leaded 10 points?

   d. Caps and lowercase type or type in all caps?

   e. Roman type or text type?

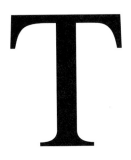

The main purpose of newspaper design is to communicate, to help move readers easily and efficiently through the page. Editors who design and lay out pages are responsible for telling readers which stories are most important and for helping readers find the stories they want to read.

In addition to having a knowledge of news values, copy editing and typography, the layout editor must understand some of the principles of design, the basic structures or forms of newspaper layout, and the language of newspaper design.

Good order is the foundation of all good things.

—Edmund Burke

Design principles

All designers call on the basic principles of design to help them create. Beginning layout editors should follow these principles until they become experienced. The standard design principles most applicable to newspapers are balance, contrast, proportion and unity.

Balance

Many early designers believed that page balance was achieved by matching identical elements (copy, headlines, photos, borders, colors) on the page. This *formal* balance had only one requirement: The right half of the page (at the time, four columns on an eight-column page) had to be matched on the left side with the same elements (see Exhibit 10-1). Not only did editors have to

Newspaper Design and Layout

Design principles
Design elements
Forms of layout
Page layout
Layout advice from a veteran editor:
Bill Chapin

Exhibit 10-1
The Los Angeles Times of 1980 used formal balance, so that elements on the right side of the page were balanced by similar elements on the left. (Reprinted by permission)

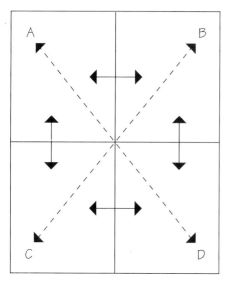

match the lower right corner with the lower left corner exactly, they also had to match headline weights across the page. For example, a two-column, 24-point, two-line headline in columns seven and eight called for exactly the same quantity of headline in columns one and two. A one-column, 36-point, three-line headline in column six called for the same quantity of headline in column three. Even the headlines and photographs at the bottom of the page were balanced symmetrically.

Formal balance, however, tended to sweep the news into a form with no consideration for its importance. In other words, the news of the day didn't seem to matter as much as design; form dictated content. Because formal balance required that the page be divided down the middle, the resulting balance was from side to side. And because headline schedules universally required that important stories be billed with large headlines and placed high on the page, top-to-bottom balance was not feasible. Big, bold headlines and large photos dominated the top of the page, and the bottom trailed off into grayness, like a news story written in inverted-pyramid style.

Balance is not achieved by merely matching identical elements on the page. Other factors, such as the apparent weights of the elements on the page, come into play. *Informal*, or asymmetrical, balance can be achieved with little specialized knowledge.

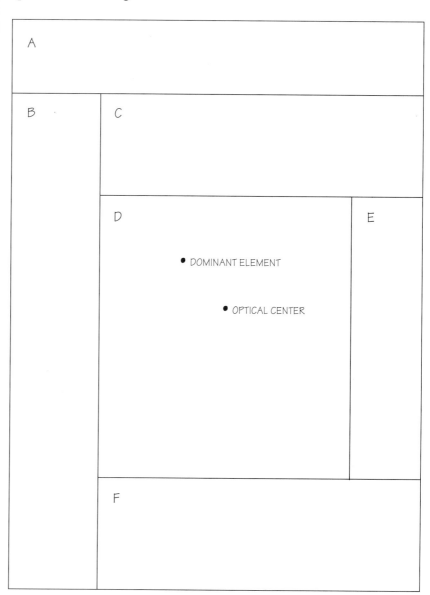

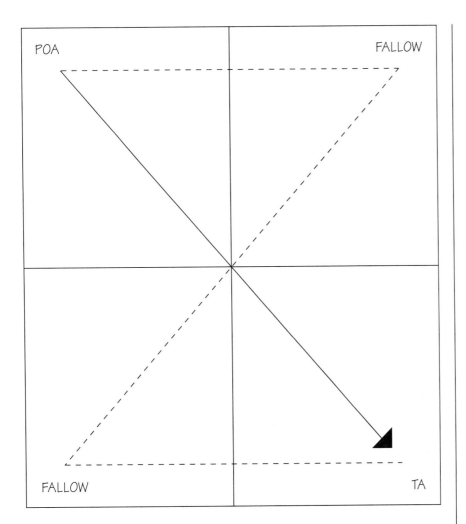

POA

FALLOW

FALLOW

TA

Exhibit 10-4
The reader's eye progresses diagonally through the page from the primary optical area (POA) in the upper left corner to the terminal area (TA) in the lower right corner. The remaining two quadrants on the page are fallow corners. A strong design will attract the reader's eye to the fallow corners, so that it follows a Z pattern across the page.

To balance the right against the left and the top against the bottom (remember that formal balance only matched the right against the left), beginning layout editors should section the page into four *modules* or quadrants, splitting the page down the middle vertically and then horizontally across the fold (see Exhibit 10-2). Each of the modules should contain some graphic mass or weight—a headline, a photograph, a piece of artwork, white space—to help balance the page, but the weighted elements can extend beyond the boundaries of the modules.

Experienced layout editors make little effort to attain line-by-line balance. Neither must the page remain in quadrants; an arrangement of several rectangular modules may flow from the basic page division.

The sequence of the design also becomes important in achieving balance. The layout editor should attempt to place the major display element—whether it is a photograph, a story or both—just to the left of the *optical center* of the page (a point just above the measured center). Such placement serves as a focal point for balancing the rest of the page (see Exhibit 10-3).

Edmund Arnold, author of several books on newspaper design, refers to the "Gutenberg diagram," a visualization of the way readers approach and use a piece of printed information. He notes that the first place a reader looks—called the *primary optical area,* or POA—is the upper left corner of the page (see Exhibit 10-4). The lower right corner—called the *terminal area,* or TA—also has strong visual attraction, because readers know they have finished when they reach that area. The two remaining corners of the page, upper right and lower left, are called *fallow corners.* They require special design attention, because the reader's eye doesn't travel there automatically.

Arnold suggests that the basic movement of the eye follows a diagonal line from upper left to lower right, in a pattern that resembles a Z. The reader stops along the way, lured by "optical magnets," such as photographs and headlines. The designers of USA Today, for example, determined that the lower left fallow corner would be anchored by an infographic (see Chapter 8) and that the terminal, which USA Today editors call the "hot box," always would contain a bright, interesting story placed inside a colored box (see Exhibit 10-5).

Noted newspaper designer Mario Garcia makes a case for a somewhat different concept, one he calls the *center of visual impact* (CVI). He suggests that the two points on the page traditionally associated with the point of entry (the primary optical area) and the point of exit (the terminal area) need not be located in the corners of the page. He suggests that the CVI, which should attract the reader's visual attention at a glance, may be located anywhere on

Exhibit 10-6
The center of visual impact on Page One of the Seattle Times is the package (photo and story) on desegregation. (Reprinted courtesy of the Seattle Times)

the page. The CVI then becomes the reader's point of entry into the page (see Exhibit 10-6).

Garcia recommends using only one CVI on a page, because including other strong elements weakens the total effect. Photographs, typography and packaging all could be used as dominant elements on the page, leading the reader's eye to the point of greatest visual interest.

Contrast

A broadsheet or tabloid newspaper page, a magazine page, a newsletter page, or even a part of a page, such as an advertisement, should have a focal point or center of visual interest surrounded by smaller, contrasting elements. The point of focus reveals the publication's priorities and shows readers what the editor believes is important. The layout editor may emphasize a particular element—a story or a photograph—simply by making it larger than any other element. This concept of contrast, similar to Garcia's center of visual impact, is called the *dominant element*. On a standard, open (no ads) newspaper page, a dominant horizontal element should extend across more than half the page.

In addition, newspapers increasingly rely on color to bring contrast to a page. The use of a color border around a photograph or a color screen behind a story can spotlight the element for the reader.

The layout editor also may use contrasting typefaces and shapes to focus and balance a page. Many modern newspapers use lightface dropheads, also called underlines, and breakout quotations to contrast with boldface main headlines. Designers often choose sans serif type for captions, standing headlines and drop-in logos to accent the serif type used in body type and headlines.

Layout editors also use contrasting shapes to lend visual interest to a page. Items placed horizontally contrast with those placed vertically—for example, a thin, horizontal story contrasts with a strong vertical photograph. The use of differing shapes of elements adds visual impact to the layout. The key is simply to remember to work in modules.

Proportion

The ratio between elements on a page is called proportion. Artists have discovered that the most aesthetically pleasing ratio is 3-to-5. Whenever possible, the shapes of elements should be rectangular, similar to a 3×5 notecard. In design, rectangles are more pleasing to the eye than squares.

Not all elements on the page have to follow this proportion rule, of course. But if many elements do, the one unusual shape will become the focal point.

Unity

To achieve unity, a publication carries its design themes throughout all pages as well as within individual layouts. In a unified publication, all elements of the design are related. The section headings, headlines, captions and column logos are stylistically consistent, and the sections and columns appear in the same place in each issue.

Unity also refers to the idea that individual stories or related elements packaged together can have greater visual impact if they are designed in a modular fashion. That is, laying out stories or packages of related elements as if they were bounded by an imaginary rectangle helps create a sense of unity and cohesion for the reader. Most contemporary newspapers use a modular format, and layout editors who imagine each element of the page as a module—whether it is a long, vertical photograph or a rectangular, horizontal copy block—are able to create simple, uncluttered designs that aid in readability.

Most newspapers have very detailed stylebooks that attempt to ensure such consistency in design. Without these stylebooks, clutter and chaos result, and the reader can be left confused. Most modern design, beautiful in its simplicity, puts a premium on unity because a unified approach communicates the message more effectively to readers.

Several years ago, noted newspaper designer Roger Fidler published the checklist for unified design shown in Exhibit 10-7. It is a good tool to help assess layout.

The ratio between elements on a page is called proportion.

A checklist for functionally integrated design

Functionally integrated layouts are not created with magic words or rigid rules. They require organized and creative thinking developed through experience. And even with experience, not everyone has the visual sensitivity and judgment to become a good layout editor.

The following checklist is by no means all-inclusive. It is merely a tool for assessing layouts and should not be regarded as a newspaper design dogma.

If you can answer yes to all questions designated with an open ballot box and no to all those designated with a solid box, the page layout is probably well-designed.

Organization

☐ Are readers guided smoothly and naturally through the page?

☐ Do all elements have a reason for being?

☐ Are all intended relationships between elements readily apparent?

☐ Are packages clearly defined?

■ Does the design call attention to itself instead of the content?

■ Does the page appear cluttered?

■ Do any type or art elements appear to be floating on the page?

■ Do any elements appear lost?

■ Are any editorial elements easily confused with advertising?

Readability

■ Do any elements interrupt reading or cause confusion?

■ Are any legs of type perceptually truncated by art or sell lines (i.e., quotes, liftouts, etc.)?

■ Is the line width of any text too narrow or too wide for easy reading?

■ If text is set to follow the shape of adjacent art, is the story difficult to read?

■ Do any headlines or sell lines compete with headlines or sell lines in adjacent columns?

☐ Are the starting points for all stories easily determined?

Accuracy and clarity

☐ Does the layout accurately communicate the relative importance of the stories contained on the page?

☐ Do the art elements accurately convey the tone and message of the stories?

☐ Are logos consistent and differentiated from headlines?

☐ Are the devices used in a layout appropriate for the content of the page?

Proportioning and sizing

☐ Are all elements sized relative to their importance?

☐ Are the shapes and sizes of elements appropriate for the content of the elements?

☐ Do the shapes of elements add contrast and interest?

☐ Does the page have a dominant element or package of elements?

■ Does the shape of an element appear contrived or forced?

■ Do any logos or headlines seem out of proportion with the size of the story or column?

■ Are several elements similar in proportion and size?

Efficiency and consistency

☐ Do all areas of white space appear as if they were planned? (When it appears as if something fell off the page, the white space is not functional.)

☐ Is spacing between elements controlled and consistent?

☐ Are areas of white space balanced on the page?

☐ Is all type, especially agate material, set at the most efficient measure for the information contained?

☐ Is the size of column gutters constant?

■ Does the number of elements and/or devices used in a package seem excessive.

Design elements

Modern editors combine at least six basic elements to lay out pages: type for body copy and display (headlines); borders or rules; white space; art, which includes photographs, illustrations and informational graphics, such as maps, graphs and charts; and color, a design element used more frequently in newspapers today than ever before.

Body type

Most body copy is set in 8- or 9-point type with 1 point of leading, or space, between lines. Most newspaper pages today are set in a six-column format, forced by the standardization of advertising units in the 1980s. Most columns are set on a 12- to 14-pica measure, allowing optimum readability.

Most newspapers continue to *justify* their body type, meaning that the copy is set both flush left and flush right. A few newspapers, however, set their body copy *ragged right*, meaning that the copy lines up evenly on the left but has irregular space at the end of the lines on the right. Some newspapers use the ragged-right format when setting editorials.

Exhibit 10-7
Roger Fidler's checklist can help layout editors evaluate their own work. (Reprinted from Newspaper Design Notebook, Vol. 2, No. 1, by permission of Roger Fidler)

Exhibit 10-8
The San Francisco Chronicle published an extra edition after the Oct. 17, 1989, earthquake. Notice the extra-large (more than 200-point) headline. (The headline and story later proved inaccurate; fewer than 70 people died as a result of the 7.1 magnitude quake.) (Reprinted courtesy of the San Francisco Chronicle)

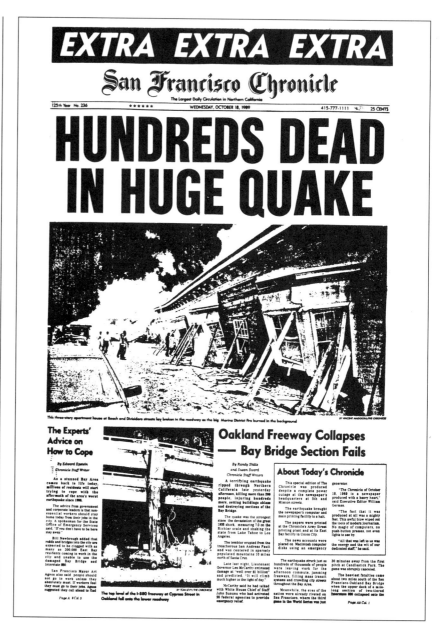

When laying out a page, particularly in a horizontal format, editors often place body copy in several adjacent columns. Such columns of type are called *legs*. A story that is laid out over four columns, for example, has four legs of type.

Display type

Some of newspapering's most colorful jargon is related to headlines. As noted in Chapter 6, headlines serve two major functions: They summarize the news for busy readers, and they grade the relative newsworthiness of each story. As a typographic device, headlines introduce large areas of black and white to give the page visual interest.

Headlines usually range from 14-point type to 72-point type, although some newspapers magnify headline type even larger when an extraordinary story occurs (see Exhibit 10-8).

Layout editors designate headlines in terms of size and space. A 2-36-3 headline, for example, is a two-column, 36-point, three-line headline.

Typically, the most noticeable display type on Page One is the *nameplate*, or *flag*, which tells the name of the publication and usually the date, the price and the city of publication. Some nameplates also include *ears*, information set on either side of the name itself, such as the weather, a daily quotation or a small index.

A *banner* is a headline that extends horizontally across all the columns of the page. Usually the banner is the lead headline, and it is set larger than all the other headlines on the page. Many newspapers reserve the use of banners for highly significant stories and use smaller lead headlines, extending perhaps across only three columns, on a day-to-day basis. Other forms of banners are known as *streamers* or *ribbons*. These headlines usually are smaller than Page One banners and are frequently used on inside pages.

A *deck* is a smaller headline just under the main headline that gives the reader more information about the story. Early American newspapers often used one-column decks that numbered scores of lines and extended halfway down the page.

A *kicker* is a small headline above the main headline, used most often by layout editors when white space is desired. The kicker is set half the point size of the main headline (an 18-point kicker above a 36-point headline, for example). Often it is flush left over an indented main headline, and it may be underlined. Kickers generally extend no more than a third of the width of the main headline.

A *jumphead* appears above a story as it continues from one page to another. The jumphead usually is smaller than the main headline and may contain typographic devices known as *dingbats*, ornamentation like dashes, stars, *ballot boxes* (small squares) or *bullets* (circles or dots). Jumpheads usually repeat a key word or phrase from the main headline to help guide readers to the continuing story. Careful copy editors also make sure that the story's *jumpline* (last line of type before the jump, referring readers to the correct page number) contains the same key word or phrase as the jumphead.

Upstyle headlines are those in which all the words are capitalized, except prepositions; *downstyle* headlines are those in which only the first word and proper nouns are capitalized. Most modern newspapers use a downstyle format. Some traditional newspapers, however, such as The New York Times, retain upstyle headlines.

Examples of these headlines and many others are displayed in Chapter 6.

Borders

Publications use a variety of borders to separate one element from another. Most advertisements are boxed, some with quite ornamental borders; some stories are also boxed, but usually with simple, plain lines called *rules*. Because the rules are placed along the edge of the column, elements within the box—body type and art—must be narrower.

Rules and borders are often produced by applying tape manufactured with lines in varying widths and styles; they can also be produced on a computer. Most commonly used in editorial pasteup are 1-point and 2-point rules, but many publications are designed to use heavy 6-point or even 12-point rules.

Rules are used not only to box stories but also to border photographs and other artwork; to underline kickers; as design elements in standing headlines, page headers (such as Sports) and column logos; and as cutoffs to separate unrelated elements.

White space

The use of *white space,* sometimes called negative space, helps achieve unity of design. Well-designed publications use consistent amounts of white space between columns of type, between photographs and their captions, above and

Kickers generally extend no more than a third of the width of the main headline.

below headlines, between the flag and the rest of the page, between the headline and the byline, and between the byline and the first paragraph of the story.

White space also can be used to relieve massive quantities of gray type. The use of liberal amounts of white space on pages that tend to be type-heavy, such as editorial pages, is a good design technique.

White space should be thought of as a frame around the page. Layout editors should try to push it to the perimeter of the page, never letting white space become trapped on the interior of the page. Trapped white space is particularly unattractive on photo-page layouts.

Some newspapers use more white space between elements in certain sections than in others. Liberal use of white space in the arts and entertainment sections, for example, provides them with a personality distinct from that of the news sections.

Art

For most layout editors, art is the starting point for laying out a page. In some cases, the shape of the art actually determines the layout.

Most art requires reduction or enlargement before it is published (see Chapter 8), and the layout editor determines the size.

Simple black and white illustrations (sometimes called line art) need only be the correct reproduction size before they can be pasted onto the page. Black and white photographs, however, require one additional step before they can be printed on a press; they need to be *screened*, or converted into halftones by breaking the continuous image into dots. Other names for a halftone are *PMT* (photomechanical transfer), *velox* or *screened print*. They all mean a photo print whose image is in a dot pattern rather than in continuous tones.

Color illustrations or photographs require several other, more complex, production steps before they are ready for printing.

The art of layout is to know not only how to size and crop but also how to judge the value of photos and illustrations on a page. In most circumstances, the art is the dominant element on a page; as a result, its quality and use require special attention.

Color

Editors are increasingly using color in photographs and in artwork to add meaning to the content of the newspaper. A 1988 survey of American Society of Newspaper Editors members indicated that 64 percent were using more color than a year earlier; 84 percent said they would be using more color within the next five years; and 89 percent said color would be more important by the year 2000.

Color is quickly and easily processed by the brain, and a person's response to color is both learned and inherited. The response depends on such factors as age, gender, intelligence, education, temperature, climate, socioeconomic background and regional attitudes.

Basically, color is different wavelengths of light. A ray of sunlight reflected through a prism is diverted into visible bands of color. Red is the least diverted, violet the most diverted. Red has the longest waves, violet the shortest. This phenomenon, known as the color spectrum, was first recorded by Sir Isaac Newton in the early 18th century.

The main purpose of color as a design element is to draw attention to the content. Most studies indicate that color is better than black and white to grab

For most layout editors, art is the starting point for laying out a page.

readers' attention for the quick appeal. However, black and white images are better for a response requiring more thought.

Most of the time, color is available either as *spot color* (an extra shade of ink used along with black) or as full color, which is a combination of four color inks: cyan (blue), magenta (red), yellow and black. Full color also is called *process color.*

Full-color halftones are being used increasingly, as the technology for quickly processing color film has become available. High-speed *scanners*—machines that make high-quality color separations—have revolutionized the way color photos are handled, and they have become affordable for most newspapers.

For new designers and layout editors, the best rule to follow when adding color to a page is not to use too much. Resist the temptation to splash color everywhere. Instead, color should be used as an accent that connects related elements and enhances the meaning of the content.

Robert Bohle, in his book *Publication Design for Editors,* suggests that spot color be used sparingly. He recommends a few of the ways to do so:

- Use color as a content connector, or as a "people mover." To do so, use color as a background for an entire spread, thus tying everything into a neat package, or use it to link similar items, such as small boxes in an informational graphic, so that the reader can see the layout as a whole and not just as a bunch of parts.
- Use color to color "things," not background. Color the elements on the page, such as certain type, illustrations and graphics. Screening the background of a box of type is a weak use of color.
- Use color as a background for color photographs. Sometimes a complementary color can be used to help a photograph pop out from the page. The key is contrast. Selecting a dominant color from the photograph is a weak choice because of the lack of contrast. A light gray is a good choice; the colors look brighter compared to the gray.

As in all good design, the key to using color is to keep it simple. More is not necessarily better.

Forms of layout

Two broad categories describe most newspaper layouts: vertical and horizontal.

Vertical layout, most notably displayed in The New York Times and The Wall Street Journal, is characterized by columns of type that run vertically down the page. Vertical newspapers tend to publish few headlines or photographs more than two columns wide. Most headlines are a single column wide, and stories often run the full length of the column. A striking vertical effect was achieved by early newspapers using eight- or nine-column formats. Today's standard six-column formats mean wider columns, but a vertical look is still possible (see Exhibit 10-9).

Newspapers that use a vertical layout generally have a high story count on the front page. They are relatively easy to produce, both in the newsroom and in the composing room.

Horizontal layout is characterized by columns of type that flow across the page. Wide photographs—sometimes spread across the full six columns—contribute to this effect, and the many multicolumn headlines form wide blocks that give the pages their horizontal appearance. These large photos and

Exhibit 10-9
The New York Times maintains a vertical look. (Copyright © 1989 by The New York Times Company. Reprinted by permisssion.)

Exhibit 10-10
The Orlando Sentinel is laid out on a horizontal format. (Reprinted by permission of The Orlando Sentinel)

Exhibit 10-11
The Oakland, Calif., Tribune combines vertical and horizontal elements. (Reprinted by permission of The Oakland Tribune)

headlines attract the reader's attention and add contrast to the page (see Exhibit 10-10).

Today's modern layouts often are not readily identifiable as either vertical or horizontal. However, almost all are modular. Many layout editors use both vertical and horizontal forms to create balance, focus and contrast on the page (see Exhibit 10-11).

Page layout

Laying out a page is known as *dummying*. The dummy, as a mock-up of a page is called, is used as a map by pasteup personnel for placement of stories, headlines, photographs and captions. The dummy is completed by layout editors in the newsroom and sent to the composing room, where compositors view the map as an exact guide for the placement of page elements. Exhibit 10-12 is a list of terms used in layout and printing.

As more newspapers and magazines invest in pagination technology, dummies will become relics. Pagination is a system of electronic dummying, which allows the editor to lay out the page on the computer and print it in its final version, bypassing the pasteup functions of the composing room altogether.

A good dummy is proportional in size to the actual printed page. If the printed page is 13 inches wide by 21 inches deep, for example, a proportionate dummy page could be 6.5 inches wide by 10.5 inches deep (50 percent of the actual size) or about 8.5 inches wide by about 13.5 inches deep (65 percent of the actual size).

The first and most important rule of dummying the page is to keep the dummy neat and legible. The more precise and detailed the dummy, the better the chances of precise and accurate pasteup.

Basic guidelines

Sometimes, beginning editors peer at the blank dummy sheet resting on the desk in front of them—the dummy sheet that eventually will become their first page layout—and freeze, wondering how to begin. Here are some steps that may help:

1. Before dummying begins, the layout editor must have an assessment of the day's news. At small newspapers, news judgments may be made by the editor who also does the layout. At mid-sized and large newspapers, however, the judgments about what stories are placed on which pages are made by news editors in consultation with other department editors at meetings called story conferences.

Judgments about which stories are significant vary, of course, depending both on the newspaper's philosophy and mission and on the individual editor's interests or biases. Some newspapers emphasize local news, others emphasize national and international news. Some (especially morning papers) might put a premium on timeliness and consider last night's city council meeting important enough for Page One. Others (especially evening papers) might emphasize another news value, such as unusualness, and play a story about a bizarre occurrence. Many newspapers rely on traditional news values when judging the significance of stories: timeliness, proximity, prominence, unusualness, conflict and human interest.

The news services help local editors make news judgments by providing summaries of the major stories of the day, called news budgets. Often the budgets lead with the stories considered most important by the news-service editors. (The New York Times News Service even moves a list of stories that

Agate line: Standard of measurement for the depth of advertisements; roughly, 14 to the inch.

Bleed: When the printed image extends to the trim edge of the page; used more often in magazines than in newspapers.

Crop marks: Indication to eliminate unwanted areas in a photograph or other piece of art.

Double truck: Two pages at the center of a section pasted up as a single unit.

Dummy: Diagram outlining the layout of a page, as it will appear in its printed form; blueprint for pasteup.

Flat: Layout sheets, also called grid sheets, onto which the publication's copy and artwork are pasted. For offset printing, a photograph is taken of the finished flat, and the negative is used to make a printing plate, which is then placed on the press for printing.

Folio: Page number, date and name of publication on each page.

Galley: Shallow tray used to hold metal type; almost non-existent in today's modern production facilities.

Gutter: Margin between facing pages or between columns on the page.

Legs: Columns of type placed adjacent to each other.

Logo: Specially designed signature in an advertisement or design element used consistently with certain features, such as editorial columns.

Moire (pronounced *muare-ay*): Undesirable pattern caused by incorrect screen angles when overprinting halftones.

Register: To fit two or more printing images on the same paper in exact alignment. A color photograph is said to be in registration if all the color images are aligned and the resulting picture has clarity.

Tombstone: Bumping headlines of the same size, so that one headline reads into the other; to be avoided.

Widow: A line of type with only one or two words appearing at the end of a paragraph, usually at the top of a column of type; to be avoided.

Exhibit 10-12
Layout editors and pasteup artists use these terms as they lay out a newspaper's pages. A page dummy, drawn here in the traditional paper-and-pencil method, serves as a map for production personnel. Type, headlines and other page elements are pasted into place by "backshop" staff. The page will be photographed, and the resulting negative will be used to make a plate, which is then mounted on an offset printing press. (Photographs by Kerric Harvey/courtesy of the Seattle Times)

the next day's Times will use on its Page One.) Such lists and budgets are used to determine the content and play of stories and are among the reasons newspapers often publish the same stories in the same relative positions on any given day.

2. After decisions have been made about what stories to use on the page, the layout editor is ready to begin dummying. The first step is to dummy all the standing items, those elements that appear every day. For Page One, standing items include the nameplate (or flag), the index, promotional boxes (sometimes called refer boxes), the weather and so on. Usually, the nameplate appears at the top of the page, just under promotional boxes, if they are used. The index and weather often appear at the bottom of the page.

3. Next the layout editor selects and dummies the dominant visual element for the page. Often the dominant element is a piece of art—a photograph, illustration or infographic, such as a map. Sometimes the dominant element is a combination of several related elements, such as a story, a sidebar and a photograph all packaged in one modular unit. The page's dominant element is not necessarily the most significant or important story of the day; it simply is the most visually attractive and represents a point of entry for the reader's eye.

4. Placement of the dominant visual element automatically creates positions for the other elements on the page. The lead story, if it is not the dominant element, can be dummied above or adjacent to the dominant element. Secondary stories and packages can be placed below the dominant element. Special care should be taken, however, to make certain that the bottom of the page also contains interesting visual elements.

5. Actual markings on the dummy include these:

- The areas allocated for all pieces of art—photographs, illustrations and infographics—are marked with a large *X* to distinguish them from stories.
- Stories that will be boxed are drawn as boxes on the dummy and are labeled with the story slug and the word *box*. Usually the size of the border rule to be used is noted as well.
- Stories that will jump to an inside page are indicated by writing on the dummy the word *jump* and the page number to which the story will be continued.
- A small *x* usually signals the start of the story; a number sign (*#*) signals the end. Both symbols usually are circled on the dummy.

6. One of the most difficult problems facing layout editors is choosing headline sizes. Traditionally, headlines at the top of the page are larger than those at the bottom. Horizontal formats have changed that tradition, however, and today the length of the headline often is more of a determinant of size than placement on the page is. Another factor is the design philosophy of the publication. Some newspapers are designed to use smaller headlines than other newspapers.

Here are some general rules of thumb for choosing headline sizes, however:

- *One-column headlines.* Usually they range between 18-point and 36-point type. The larger type size generally is used at the top of the page.

Often the dominant element is a piece of art.

A larger headline requires greater writing skill than a smaller one, because of its short count (see Chapter 6). Most one-column headlines run two or three lines, although some contemporary newspapers allow five or six lines.

- *Two-column headlines.* Generally they range between 24-point and 42-point type; larger sizes appear near the top of the page. Most two-column headlines run two lines, although some newspapers allow three lines on larger-sized headlines, such as those used on lead stories.
- *Three-column headlines.* Generally they range between 36-point and 48-point type. Most three-column headlines run two lines, although some newspapers allow one line with a kicker.
- *Four-column headlines.* Generally they range between 36-point and 60-point type, depending on placement on the page. Most four-column headlines are one line.
- *Five- and six-column headlines.* They range between 48-point and 72-point type, depending on placement on the page. Some newspapers allow 36-point headlines on five- and six-column stories at the bottom of the page. Most five- and six-column headlines run one line.

Headline sizes and the number of lines are clearly marked on the dummy, as is the headline slug (first two words).

7. Good layout editors are careful to mark any special instructions on the dummy sheet. Such instructions might designate colors, screens, "refers" to related stories, special typesetting instructions or art sizes, and the like.

8. As a final check, the layout editor makes sure the dummy reflects the following do's and don'ts:

- Think about balance, contrast, proportion and unity as you dummy the page.
- Remember to work in modular units.
- Avoid tombstones (bumping headlines) unless your newspaper's design allows them.
- Avoid raw wraps (when a story wraps into an adjacent column without a covering headline).
- Avoid juxtaposing similar elements; don't dummy unrelated photographs next to each other, for example.
- On inside pages, avoid placing art adjacent to advertising.
- Avoid "paneling," allowing the gutter between columns to run the full length of the page.

Dummying Page One, step by step

Exhibit 10-13 is Page One of the University Daily Kansan, the student newspaper at the University of Kansas in Lawrence.

1. The first order of business when dummying a page is to make proper news judgments about the content; the form of the page will follow. In this case, the layout editor has decided to use these stories: "Vote," lead story about the student government election, 18 inches long, with photo, election results graphic and "refer" graphic; "Tacha," about a snag in the nomination of a vice chancellor to the federal bench, 11 inches long; "Football," about a lawsuit filed by players against the university, 12.5 inches long; and "Gottfried," a profile on the head football coach, 20 inches long, with file photo.

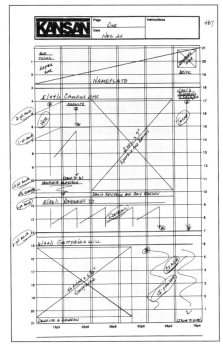

Exhibit 10-13
Page One of the University Daily Kansan is modular in design. Notice that the dummy for Page One is neat and legible and that all elements are marked for easy identification. (Reprinted by permission of The University Daily Kansan)

2. The first horizontal line on the dummy shows how deep the six-column nameplate (or flag) is: about 2.5 inches from the top of the printed page. The size of the nameplate is constant from day to day.

3. Within the nameplate are two ears, one referring to an inside story (on the left) and the other referring to the weather (on the right).

4. Immediately under the nameplate, about 2.75 inches from the top of the printed page, are two headlines. The lead headline is five columns, 54-point type and one line long; it is slugged on the dummy with the first two words of the headline, "Campus has." The off-lead headline, even though placed in what traditionally is the lead position, is one column, 30-point type and three lines long. It is slugged "Judgeship is delayed." Note that lines are designated on the dummy for each line of the headline; one line is drawn and centered above the "Vote" story, and three lines are drawn and centered above the "Tacha" story. Also note that the slugs of the stories, which may be different from the headline slugs, are written on the dummy.

5. Between the "Vote" and "Tacha" stories is a photograph. Photographs and other artwork usually are designated by an *X*. Each piece of art requires the marking of its size. The Epstein and Brown photo is three columns wide by 7 inches deep and is marked 3 col × 7" on the dummy.

6. The vertical lines show where the body copy is to be placed. Some layout editors mark a small *x* (circled) at the beginning of each story to help compositors paste up quickly. If a story extends across several columns, diagonal lines should be marked to connect the legs of type. The vertical lines end in an arrow. An end mark (# circled) also is required if the story ends on the page. If the story jumps to another page, that fact also should be marked on the dummy (*jump to 6* on the "Vote" story, for example).

7. Borders or other unusual typographical treatments are marked in the margins of the dummy. Note the markings for rules above and below the election-results graphics, the designation of a 10-percent screen behind the second election graphic and the rule separating the Gottfried story from the rest of the page.

8. Type or artwork requiring special treatment also should be noted on the dummy. The Gottfried photo, for example, is three-and-a-half columns wide and is marked using pica width (46 picas) rather than column width so it will be easier to paste up. Similarly, the Gottfried copy is set wider than the normal columns, so the dummy is marked with wiggly lines and a note designating a different set width (15 picas, rather than the standard 12 picas).

9. The dummy is now ready to send to the composing room for pasteup. If the dummy is neat and accurate, the page will be pasted up as the layout editor envisioned.

Dummying inside pages

Laying out pages inside the newspaper is at once easier and more difficult than laying out Page One or section covers. Although most of the same rules of thumb apply—such as maintaining modularity in design—inside-page layout differs because inside pages contain advertisements.

Usually, layout editors for daily newspapers receive the inside-page dummies from the "product makeup" person in the advertising department the day before publication. The product makeup person dummies ads on pages based on a variety of factors, including their size (only one five-column-by-17-inch ad will fit on a page, for example), their content (tire

Type or artwork requiring special treatment also should be noted on the dummy.

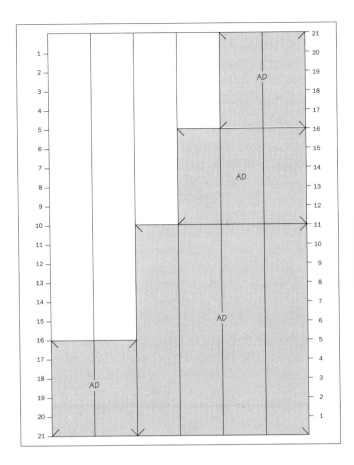

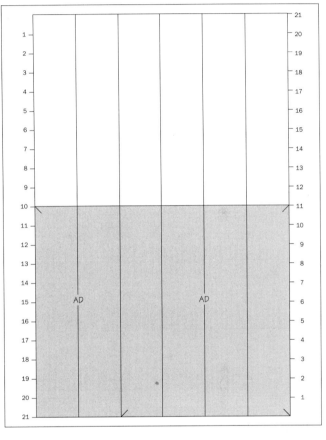

ads usually go in Sports, movie ads usually go in Entertainment), their use of color (only a few color positions are available) and their competition (competitors usually are not placed adjacent to each other).

Most modern newspapers and magazines are laid out using one of two advertising configurations: pyramid construction or modular construction (see Exhibit 10-14). In a pyramid format, ads are stacked either to the left or to the right on the page. News content touches each of the ads, as desired by the advertising department. In a modular format, ads are "squared off" across the bottom of the page. Some ads may be stacked atop others in order to accomplish this modular design.

Most editors like to work with a modular ad format because it is easier to design and because it often improves the look of a newspaper or magazine. But for editors who must lay out stories and art around ads in a pyramid format, attractive design is still possible. Professor Daryl R. Moen, in his book *Newspaper Layout and Design*, suggests that editors can create modular units with the non-advertising space on a page by working off the corners

Exhibit 10-14
In this pyramid ad layout, ads are dummied to the right up the page. In the modular layout, ads are squared off across the bottom of the page, giving editors greater flexibility in dummying stories and pictures.

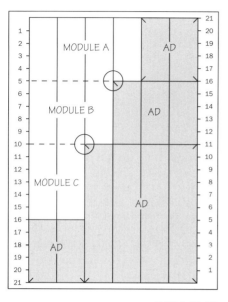

of the ads. By that he means that editors may draw imaginary dotted lines from the corners of the ads to the margins of the page to create modular layout units (see Exhibit 10-15). Such modules then may be used for editorial copy and artwork.

Pagination

Pagination, which is the electronic dummying of pages, was predicted to sweep through the newspaper industry in the 1980s, but it was just beginning to creep into newsrooms by 1990. Only two editors responding to a 1991 survey reported that their papers were fully paginated. The survey, sponsored by the Bakersfield Californian and American Newspaper Publishers Association, included 735 newspapers with 25,000 circulation or larger. Although 60 percent reported that their papers were using electronic page composition to some extent, most often for classified advertising pages, slightly less than 60 percent thought their papers would be fully paginated by the year 2000.

Bob Johnson, director of corporate communications for the Californian, was quoted in the July 1991 issue of Presstime:

I know there are people who say pagination is here now, but this survey shows the majority of us believe it is still five to 10 years down the road. I also believe the survey indicates there is a great deal of confusion out there. There are a lot of newspapers that are hesitant about which direction to take and which equipment they should buy.

Because of the huge initial costs of the equipment and the desire to wait until the "best" system is developed, newspaper executives have used caution in committing to pagination.

Full pagination means that editors can put together entire pages—including copy, ads, photos and graphics—on a computer terminal. Manipulating this vast amount of computer data requires sophisticated technology. The resulting material is then printed as a complete page, bypassing the pasteup function formerly served by compositors. Then the page is photographed, producing a negative from which a printing plate is made. Some systems use laser platemakers or direct-to-film output, eliminating the manual steps of both page pasteup and negative/plate production.

Publications using pagination systems have on-screen layout grids corresponding to the paper dummies formerly used to design pages (see Exhibit 10-16). Editors may electronically position, move or remove from a page stories, captions, headlines, photographs and graphics. Type for stories is electronically wrapped from column to column, and the editor may watch this phenomenon on the video screen.

Pagination involves two quite different processes: page planning, the electronic equivalent of dummying, and page assembling, the electronic equivalent of pasteup. Senior newsroom editors in the future will be required to determine the role of copy editors in these processes. The 1991 Bakersfield Californian/ANPA survey found that 84 percent of editors think pagination will be a newsroom, rather than backshop, function.

The key advantages of pagination are that newsroom personnel gain ultimate control over the newspaper, the overall quality improves and enormous cost savings may be realized. An assistant managing editor of the Windsor, Ontario (Canada) Star said that, after only a few months of using pagination, the newspaper was saving $16,000 a month in production costs. Also, the Star saved so much time in the newsroom that the deadline for Page One was extended 45 minutes, allowing more time to assure quality.

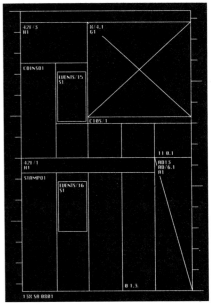

Exhibit 10-16
A designer uses a computer to plan a page layout. The computer coding on the dummy of the Sunday book section of The Philadelphia Inquirer is matched with codes on stories, headlines and photos. Pagination, the process of using a computer to place elements on a page, is expected to become more widespread in newsrooms during the 1990s, eliminating the pasteup stage of newspaper production. (Photograph by Kerric Harvey/courtesy of the Seattle Times)

LAYOUT ADVICE FROM A VETERAN EDITOR

By Bill Chapin

A blank dummy sheet can be daunting if you've never seen one before. It's just a piece of paper with a few parallel lines and a few numbers. You're asked to make a schematic picture out of a bunch of news stories and news photographs. Where to start?

That's why I told my student editors to "keep it simple." The simpler the layout, the easier the execution. But I had an ulterior motive, because I firmly believe that the simplest layout is usually the best layout. I hate "busy" newspaper pages. I hate acrobatic layouts. I hate layouts that call attention to themselves at the expense of what is really important: the news of the day.

Layouts should be vehicles, sturdy but not flashy.

That is Rule No. 1. Rule No. 2 follows logically enough: If you, the news editor, have drawn two layouts of the same page with the same news material, and one layout is "pretty" but distorts the news values while the other layout isn't very pretty but accurately reflects the news values, always choose the latter. To remind students periodically of the wisdom of Rule No. 2, I resorted to a cliche: Don't let the tail wag the dog.

Of course, ideally your page should be accurate and pretty. Occasionally that happens; often it doesn't. Life isn't perfect, and neither are newspaper pages.

The larger, the emptier a page is, the harder it is to lay out. Put another way, the more options you have, the more choices you're compelled to make, the harder the job. Dummying, then, becomes a process of reducing the options. It follows that Page One, because it has no ads, looks like a yawning expanse and is the hardest page to dummy.

Conversely, the smaller the news hole on a page, the easier the task. It doesn't take a Piet Mondrian to figure out that if you're confined to a rectangle six columns wide and 3 inches deep, there's not much you can do with it. Run a six-column "spreader" headline across the top and wrap the story beneath it. So the story is a little too short? Increase the size of the headline by 6 points or use a drop-in box, a quotation from the story. So the story is a little too long? Trim it or choose another story.

Let's consider a hypothetical Page One. It's six columns wide and 21 inches deep, which means 126 column inches of space to fill. As news editor, you have eight stories and three pictures that are Page One possibilities. First, draw in the newspaper's flag at the top of the page. That eats up 12 inches of space.

Next, select your best news story and best photograph—this is where your news judgment comes in— and place them on the page. Use, perhaps, a four-column, two-line headline with the story running down the right-hand column. Run the picture three columns wide in the "jaw" of the headline. That eats up 42 more inches of space (take my word for it).

You've got a lively feature about a man who breeds llamas in Northern California. Wrap it 3 inches deep across the bottom of the page with a 48-point headline. Another 24 inches of "vacuum" has disappeared. Your job is virtually finished. The rest is what I call filling in the chinks. The options are down close to zero, and you only have about 35 inches left in which to exercise them. Stick in two more medium-sized stories and one little story and you're done.

That's about it.

Is there a Rule No. 3? Sure, and it's embodied in another cliche: If at first you don't succeed, try and try again. Do a lot of doodling with dummy sheets and pencil. If a page doesn't feel right, scrap it and draw another one. Dummy pads are cheap.

BILL CHAPIN

In the course of his long career with newspapers, Bill Chapin has been a copy clerk, a reporter, a rewrite person, a sports columnist, a copy editor, a chief copy editor, a layout editor, a telegraph editor, an assistant news editor, an assistant city editor and a journalism teacher. He has often rather ruefully thought of himself as the quintessential swing person: proficient at any job in the newsroom, excelling in none of them.

After graduation from Dartmouth College, where he says he majored in skiing, Chapin began his career in 1940 as a cub reporter on the Rutland, Vt., Herald, a newspaper so solid and conservative in its journalistic philosophy that, competing against such giants as The New York Times, it twice won the Ayer Cup for outstanding design.

During his third week on the Herald, Chapin wrote a wedding story in which he managed to marry the bride to the best man. The next night, after work, the Herald's city editor took his new reporter out into the country, got him drunk and told him that if he didn't start to hack it right away, he would be fired. Chapin says that, thus goaded, he has been hacking it pretty well ever since. In fact, he won an Associated Press award for the best news story in New England, and much later, he was twice nominated for a Pulitzer Prize.

A bomber pilot in World War II, Chapin lost a leg when his plane was shot down over Yugoslavia. That injury persuaded him to switch from reporting to desk work when he returned to the Rutland Herald. He became assistant news editor and got his first experience in layout.

In 1948 he moved to the copy desk of the Worcester, Mass., Gazette. Chapin says the Gazette was a lousy newspaper then, and he learned what not to do as a copy editor.

In 1951 Chapin moved with his wife and their two small children to California. He put in one year on the copy desk at the Oakland Tribune before moving to the San Francisco Chronicle. In 1954 he became chief copy editor, a post that he occupied for the next 10 years. During that decade, he regularly filled in as news editor and dummied the news section of the Chronicle. Also during that decade, he took a year's leave of absence to serve as chief copy editor of the Pacific Stars & Stripes in Tokyo.

During his final four years on the Chronicle, Chapin was a sports columnist and later a reporter/rewrite person. He also dabbled in public television.

In 1970 Chapin began teaching editing and feature writing at San Francisco State University. He frequently served as faculty adviser to the student newspaper. He retired as a full professor in 1983 and now lives with his wife in Sonoma, Calif., where he devotes a lot of his time to losing tennis matches and winning poker games.

Suggestions for additional reading

Bohle, Robert H. *From News to Newsprint: Producing a Student Newspaper*. Englewood Cliffs, N.J.: Prentice-Hall, 1984.

Bohle, Robert H. *Publications Design for Editors*. Englewood Cliffs, N.J.: Prentice-Hall, 1990.

Campbell, Alastair. *The Graphic Designer's Handbook*. Philadelphia: Running Press Book Publishers, 1983.

Editors of the Harvard Post. *How to Produce a Small Newspaper: A Guide for Independent Journalists,* 2nd ed. Harvard and Boston: The Harvard Common Press, 1987.

Garcia, Mario R. *Contemporary Newspaper Design: A Structural Approach,* 2nd ed. Englewood Cliffs, N.J.: Prentice-Hall, 1987.

Guide to Quality Newspaper Reproduction. New York and Washington, D.C.: American Newspaper Publishers Association and National Advertising Bureau, 1986.

Harrower, Tim. *The Newspaper Designer's Handbook,* 2nd ed. Dubuque, Iowa: Wm. C. Brown Publishers, 1991.

Moen, Daryl. *Newspaper Layout and Design,* 2nd ed. Ames, Iowa: The Iowa State University Press, 1989.

Morrison, Sean. *A Guide to Type Design*. Englewood Cliffs, N.J.: Prentice-Hall, 1986.

Newspaper Design: 2000 and Beyond. J. Montgomery Curtis Memorial Seminar. Reston, Va.: American Press Institute, 1988.

The Next Newspapers. Future of Newspapers Report. Washington, D.C.: American Society of Newspaper Editors, 1988.

Pocket Pal: A Graphic Arts Production Handbook, 14th ed. New York: International Paper, 1989.

1. Pin up on the wall three different newspaper front pages. Judging from the display type and layouts, guess from five feet away which of the papers features highly controversial stories. Then read the three front pages and report on your findings at the next class meeting.

2. Compare the layout of Page One of The New York Times to the layout of the first page of the Times' business section. What differences do you notice, and why do you suppose such differences exist?

3. Review Page One of three daily newspapers for one week. Choose the Page One that, in your view, is the best-designed front page. Write a one-page explanation of why you think so, using as criteria what you have learned in this chapter about layout and design and what you have discussed in class. Include with your explanation a tearsheet of the page you have chosen. Then copy the layout of the page on the dummy sheet provided.

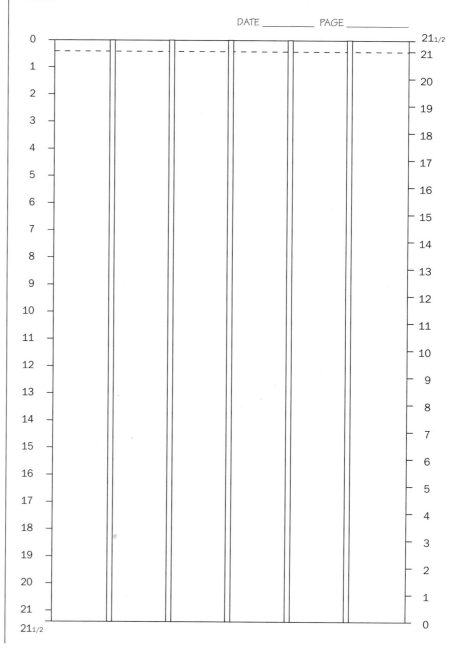

DATE _____ PAGE _____

4. You are the news editor of the Daily News. Your newspaper has a six-column format, and the nameplate is six columns across and 2 inches deep. The headline type runs from 14 points to 72 points.

You have 10 stories and six pictures available for Page One (see table below). You cannot place all of these on Page One, so use your editorial judgment to select the most important stories while providing variety on the page. Keep in mind that you can jump stories. A 30-inch story, for example, need not be finished on Page One. How much of the story will appear on the front page is up to you.

A dummy sheet is provided on the following page.

Story slug	Col. inches	Description
Ahearn	21	Local story. Karen Ahearn, president of the local university, announces her resignation after losing a bitter fight to get a better budget.
Streakers	15	Wire story. Roundup showing a nationwide revival of the streaker craze.
Demos	30	Wire story. Ben McClinton wins the party's nomination for the presidency at the Democratic National Convention.
Demo clash	18	Wire story. Demonstrators and police clash outside the Democratic convention hall in Miami.
Hurricane	12	Local story. The U.S. Weather Bureau warns that Hurricane Adam may come close enough to do damage.
Mayor	10	Local story. Mayor Joyce Durham holds a press conference and says she supports salary increases for firefighters.
China—space	20	Wire story. China announces that it has put its first spaceship into orbit.
Ransome	25	Local story. William Ransome, local author and recent winner of the Pulitzer Prize, is interviewed by the Daily News.
Burglary	8	Wire story. Burglars break into the Museum of Modern Art in New York and steal a valuable Picasso.
Diet	15	Wire story. Physician in Atlanta, Ga., devises a new diet. The dieter eats nothing and drinks a gallon of sarsaparilla every day.

Picture slug	Size	Description
McClinton	2 col. × 5"	Wire photo. Presidential nominee speaking to convention delegates.
Ransome	1 col. × 3"	Local photo. Mug shot of the interviewed author.
Clash	3 col. × 5"	Wire photo. Action shot of the fight at the Democratic convention.
Streakers	4 col. × 4"	Wire photo. Streakers disrupt a viola recital; one of the incidents mentioned in the roundup story.
Ahearn	1 col. × 3"	Local photo. Mug shot of the university president.
Kids	4 col. × 7"	Local photo. Three boys, each 4 years old, try to boost a large dog into a bathtub; good stand-alone feature picture.

DATE _____ PAGE _____

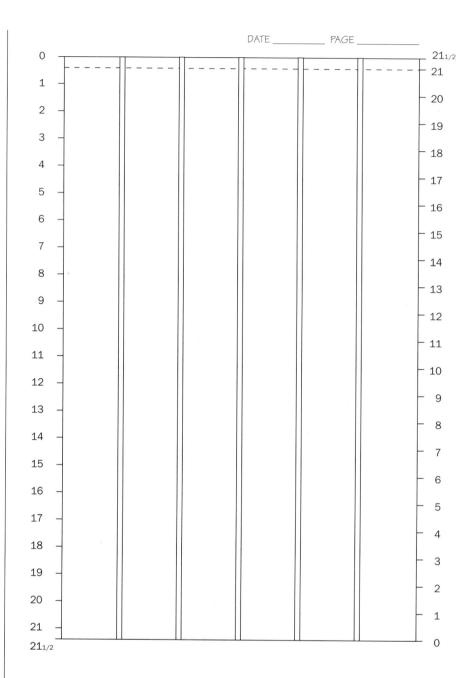

5. Use the copy and pictures left over from your Page One layout in exercise 4 to fill the news holes on the two inside pages below and on the next page. Use a modular format.

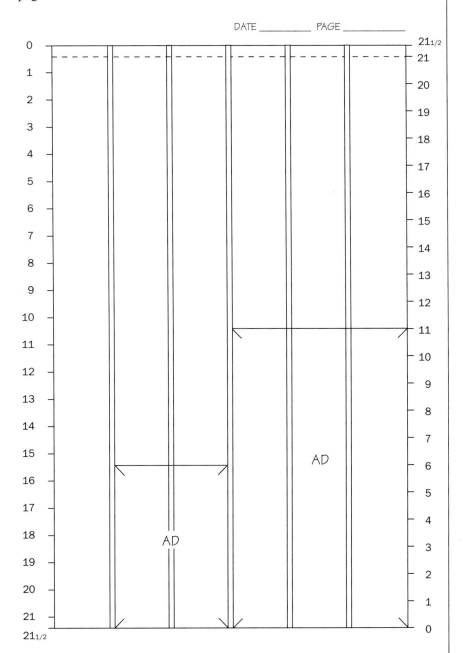

DATE _____ PAGE _____

AD

AD

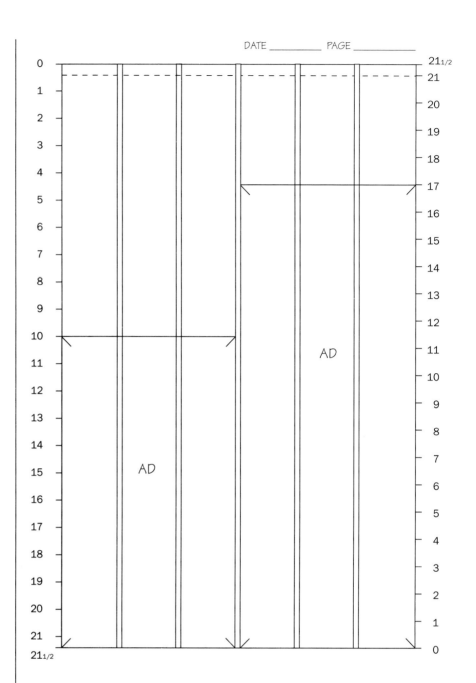

 he following information may be used as a primer for the Associated Press stylebook. Much of the information was gleaned from the Oakland Tribune and other newspaper stylebooks.

Abbreviations

Abbreviations are used to save space, especially in headlines, and to improve readability. They should not be overused or used if they are unfamiliar or confusing.

Most all-capital abbreviations are spelled without periods: *FBI, CIA, ABC, AFL-CIO, NASA*. But all-capital abbreviations of places and of the United Nations take periods: *U.S., U.N.*

Most other abbreviations take periods: *c.o.d., Inc.* An exception: *55 mph*. Abbreviations should not be used at the beginning of a sentence.

Acronyms. Acronyms may be used after the first reference if they are well-known. Some commonly used acronyms may be used on first reference: *NAACP, FBI, AIDS*.

Addresses. Use the abbreviations *Ave., Blvd.* and *St.* only with numbered addresses: *1600 Pennsylvania Ave.* Spell them out and capitalize when they are part of a formal street name without a number: *Pennsylvania Avenue*. Do not abbreviate *Circle, Court, Drive, Highway, Lane, Road, Place* and so on.

Businesses and organizations. Abbreviate *Co., Corp., Ltd.* and *Inc.* when used at the end of a business's name: *The New York Times Co.* Spell out *Association, Bureau, Department* and *Division*.

Dates and times. Abbreviate *Jan., Feb., Aug., Sept., Oct., Nov.* and *Dec.* only when they are used with specific dates: *Jan. 25, 1947*. Spell out *March, April, May, June* and July. *A.D., B.C., a.m.* and *p.m.* take periods; *PDT, MDT, EST* and the like don't.

Military. Abbreviate military ranks before names on first reference (*Gen. Irene Smith*); do not use rank after the first reference (*Smith*). Some common abbreviations are *Gen., Col., Maj., Capt., Lt., Sgt.* and *Pfc*. See the complete listing of military ranks in the AP stylebook.

States. Spell out *United States* when used as a noun; abbreviate *U.S.* as an adjective: "The U.S. plan failed."

Most state names are abbreviated when they follow the name of a town or city. The correct abbreviations are

Ala.	Ind.	N.C.	R.I.
Ariz.	Kan.	Neb.	S.C.
Ark.	Ky.	Nev.	S.D.
Calif.	La.	N.H.	Tenn.
Colo.	Mass.	N.J.	Va.
Conn.	Md.	N.M.	Vt.
D.C.	Mich.	N.Y.	Wash.
Del.	Minn.	Okla.	Wis.
Fla.	Miss.	Ore.	W.Va.
Ga.	Mo.	Pa.	Wyo.
Ill.	Mont.		

Do not abbreviate Alaska, Hawaii, Idaho, Iowa, Maine, Ohio, Texas or Utah.

Titles. Abbreviate *Gov., Lt. Gov., Sen., Rep., Dr.* and *the Rev.* before a name on first reference. Do not use titles after the first reference. Do not abbreviate *Attorney general, Controller, Detective, District attorney, Officer, Professor* or *Superintendent.*

Other abbreviations. *AWOL, GI, POW, SOS* and *TV* are acceptable on first and succeeding references. Academic degrees take periods: *B.A., M.S., Ph.D.* Do not use periods in plane or ship designations: *USS Enterprise, SST.*

Capitalization

In addition to capitalizing the first word of a sentence, you should capitalize the following:

Academic degrees. Capitalize formal names of degrees: *Bachelor of Arts, Master of Science.* Lowercase general references: *bachelor's degree, master's degree.*

Geography. Capitalize regions: *West Coast, East Coast, the South, the West, Pacific Coast, the Northwest.*
Capitalize natural features: *Blue Ridge Mountains, Gulf Stream, Continental Divide.* Capitalize popular names of natural features: *Deep South, Bible Belt, Texas Panhandle.*
But lowercase plurals and general directions: *western, the coasts, boat on the bay.*

Government. Capitalize full names and short forms: *the U.S. Postal Service, Postal Service; the Federal Reserve Board, the Fed.* Lowercase general terms: *delayed at customs, the post office.*
Capitalize *city* as part of a formal name: *Kansas City.* Lowercase *city* elsewhere: *the city of Seattle, a Missouri city.*
Capitalize formal names of committees: *the Senate Appropriations Committee.* Lowercase informal names of legislative committees and names of subcommittees.

Politics. Capitalize political organizations or movements: *the Democratic Party, Republicans, Communists.* Lowercase political philosophies: *socialism, communism, democracy.*

Religion. Capitalize all recognized faiths and their members: *Protestants, Catholics, Jewish faith.*

Titles. Capitalize official titles before names, unless they are simply job descriptions: *Pope John Paul III* (but *the pope*), *Professor Lisa St. Clair, Officer Jay Brown, engineer Mary Jones.*

Trade names. Capitalize trade names when their use is necessary: *Kleenex, Jello, Band-Aid.* Generic references are preferred: *tissue, gelatin, bandage.*

Other capitalization. Capitalize the names of official and historical documents, doctrines, legal codes and laws. Capitalize designating terms before figures and letters: *Room 222, Section 8, Title 9, Channel 60.* Lowercase the seasons: *winter, spring, summer, fall.* Lowercase academic departments unless they are proper nouns or adjectives: *journalism department, department of journalism; English department, department of English.*

Lowercase informal names of legislative committees and names of subcommittees.

Numerals

Generally, spell out the numbers one through nine; use figures for 10 and higher: "The couple has four cats and two dogs"; "She needs 10 more tickets to win."

Use figures for

- Addresses and streets numbered 10 and higher: *15th Avenue, 12th Street*
- Ages of people and things: *the 11-year-old prodigy, in their 60s, the car was 3 years old*
- Dates and time: *June 1, 1992; 7 p.m.*
- Decimals and percentages: *cost of living rose 5 percent, unemployment down 0.5 percent, $2.5 million*
- Decisions, rulings, odds and votes: "The Supreme Court ruled 5–4"
- Dimensions and measurements: *a 4-foot fence*
- Exact dimensions and measurements: "The star player is 6 feet 4," "The puppies each weighed 2 pounds, 5 ounces," "The rug is 9 by 12 feet"
- Fractions contained in numbers greater than one: *5 1/2 inches*
- Geographical and political districts: *5th Congressional District*
- Mathematical designations
- Monetary units: *5 cents, $5, $500, $5 million*
- Numerical ranking: *No. 1 choice*
- Recipe amounts: *2 cups of flour*
- Speeds: *5 mph, 5 miles per gallon*
- Sports scores, standings and odds
- Temperatures

Use words for:

- Addresses and streets below 10: *Fifth Avenue*
- Distances below 10: *five-mile race*
- Fractions smaller than one: *one-half inch*
- Indefinite or approximate figures: "Thanks a million," "We walked five miles," "A thousand times no!"
- Numbers used at the start of a sentence, except for a numeral that identifies a calendar year: "Five hundred people protested," "1990 was a good year"

Punctuation

The most common marks of punctuation are the ampersand, apostrophe, colon, comma, dash, exclamation point, hyphen, parentheses, period, question mark, quotation marks and semicolon.

Ampersand. Do not use the ampersand (&) in place of *and* in body copy or in headlines—except when it is part of a company's formal name.

Apostrophe. Use an apostrophe to form the possessive. Refer to Rules 19 through 28 in Chapter 2 for information on using apostrophes to make nouns possessive.

Use an apostrophe to indicate omitted letters in contractions: *I'm , doesn't, rock 'n' roll, it's* (*it is,* not to be confused with the pronoun *its*). Contractions reflect informal speech and should be used only in that context in journalistic writing.

Use an apostrophe to indicate omitted figures: *the celebration of '90, the '20s* (no apostrophe needed before the *s*). Use an apostrophe also to make the plural of a single letter: "She made 3 *A's* and 2 *B's* on her report card," "The Oakland *A's* won the World Series."

Use an apostrophe to indicate omitted letters in contractions.

Do not use an apostrophe with multiletter plurals or with the plurals of numbers: "The company ordered new *747s*," "This is the section for *VIPs*."

Colon. Use a colon at the end of a sentence to introduce lists, tabulations or texts: "These bills passed during the legislative session:" (the list follows, often in separate paragraphs, each introduced with a dash, bullet or some other typographical device).

Use a colon to introduce a direct quotation of more than one sentence that remains in one paragraph:

The coach said in his resignation letter: "It is with regret that I leave this university. We've had a long, successful run, and I expect that my successor will maintain the winning tradition of this great institution. It's time for me to turn to other opportunities."

When used with quotation marks, a colon goes outside the quotation marks unless it is part of the quotation itself.

Use a colon to introduce a single item for emphasis: "His thoughts were concentrated on one thing: revenge."

Use a colon in time designations, except for the even hour: *1:30 a.m., 2:15 p.m.* (but *7 a.m.*).

Use a colon to separate the main title and subtitle of a book or an article, a chapter and verse in the Bible, and sections of statutes: *The Truth Hurts: A Critique of a Defense to Defamation, John 3:16, Tennessee Code 5:2.*

Use a colon in a headline to replace a verb of attribution if the speaker is at the beginning of the headline:

Jones: 'Taxes are too high'

Comma. The comma is the most misused mark of punctuation, probably because of its frequency.

Use commas to separate the elements in a series. But note that news-service practice, observed on most U.S. newspapers, omits the comma before the conjunction in a simple series: "She ordered a hamburger, fries and orange juice." But use a comma before the conjunction in a series if an integral element of the series requires a conjunction: "She ordered orange juice, toast, and ham and eggs."

Use a comma to separate a series of equal adjectives. If the adjectives can be separated by *and* without changing the sense, they are equal: *an old, bent tree; a slow, deliberate manner.*

Use commas to set off non-essential phrases and clauses (review Chapter 2 if you need more information):

```
His mother, on the other hand, lived in New York
City. (non-essential phrase)

His mother, who is an artist, lives in New York City.
(non-essential clause)
```

Non-essential phrases include items like hometowns, ages and political affiliation. All should be set off with commas.

Use a comma to set off a dependent clause that introduces a sentence:

```
Because of his appeal to elderly voters, he was con-
sidered a sure bet to win re-election to the Senate.
```

Use a comma to set off a long introductory phrase. But no comma is needed after a short introductory phrase unless its omission would slow comprehension:

```
In the morning she will feed her cats.
Across the street, lives my sister. (comma helps com-
prehension)
```

Use a comma before the conjunction in a compound sentence: "The mayor unveiled her plan for redevelopment of a downtown park, but each member of the city council expressed concern about the estimated cost of the project."

Use a comma to set off a direct quotation from its attribution. For quotations that are more than one sentence long within a single paragraph, use a colon to set off the attribution.

```
He said, "Let's go now."
"Let's go now," he said.
He said: "Let's go now. It will be dark soon, and the
headlights on my car are not working properly."
```

A comma setting off attribution after a direct quotation always goes inside the quotation marks.

Commas are not used to set off attribution in paraphrased quotations or partial quotations:

```
He said he wanted to leave immediately.
He said that it was "of upmost importance" that they
leave.
```

Use a comma to set off nouns of direct address and *yes* and *no* at the beginning of a sentence: "James, please pay attention"; "Yes, I will pay the bill."

Set off the name of a state if the state name follows a city; separate the names of the city and the state: "Nashville, Tenn., is a music publishing center." Note that newspaper style is to abbreviate state names when they are used with a specific city but not when they stand alone in a sentence: "Nashville, *Tenn.,* is a book and music publishing center"; "Tourism is a major source of state revenue in *Tennessee.*"

Use commas to set off conjunctive adverbs: "It is essential, *therefore,* that we pay the bill"; "*However,* we could ask the company to extend the time period."

News services and most newspapers use commas for figures of 1,000 or more because the comma speeds comprehension. This rule would not apply for figures of more than 1 million or those that are part of a street address, room number, serial number, telephone number or year.

Dash. Most typewriters do not have a separate key for a dash. Instead, two hyphens are typed to represent a dash. When working at a VDT, be sure to use the dash key rather than striking the hyphen key twice.

Use dashes in a sentence to denote an abrupt change in thought or an emphatic pause: "His selection as chairman—*much to the surprise of the committee*—was based on political favors rather than merit." Also use dashes to set off a list or parenthetical material that contains commas: "The notice listed the qualifications—*80 wpm typing speed, knowledge of computers, good writing skills*—that the successful applicant must have."

Use a dash in a headline to replace a verb of attribution if the quotation comes before the name of the speaker:

'Taxes are too high'—Jones

Use a comma before the conjunction in a compound sentence.

Use a dash before an author's or composer's name at the end of a quotation:

```
"Despite its cost, the children need the school lunch
program."
                                        — Mayor Jane Doe
```

Use a dash after the dateline at the beginning of a story:

```
KNOXVILLE, Tenn. (AP)—A $75 million complex opened . . .
```

Exclamation point. Use an exclamation point after an expression of surprise, incredulity or other strong emotion, but avoid overuse. A comma rather than an exclamation point is used after mild interjections, and mildly exclamatory sentences should end with a period.

When used with quotations, the exclamation point goes inside the quotation marks when it is part of the quoted material:

```
"Stop!" he shouted.
```

The exclamation mark goes outside the quotation marks when it is not part of the quoted material:

```
We loved the movie "Batman"!
```

Hyphen. Hyphens are used to join words that form a single idea. Use a hyphen between two or more words that form a compound modifier placed before the word they modify:

```
She took a photograph of the  moss-covered tree.

Out-of-date merchandise was on sale.

He is a part-time teacher.

He teaches part time. (no hyphen; modifier comes after
the word it modifies, teaches)
```

For the use of hyphens in prefixes, consult a dictionary.

As in the last example, combinations that are hyphenated before a noun are not hyphenated when they come after the noun. However, after a form of the verb *to be,* such combinations are generally hyphenated to avoid ambiguity: "His second novel was *second-rate*"; "They are *top-notch.*" Do not use a hyphen after adverbs that end in *ly* or after the adverb *very.*

Some publications use a hyphen to designate dual heritage: *Japanese-American, Mexican-American.* Not all stylebooks agree on this point, however, so follow the style used at the publication where you work. These terms do not refer to dual heritage and are therefore not hyphenated: *Latin American, French Canadian.*

For the use of hyphens in prefixes, consult a dictionary. The general rule is that a hyphen is used if a prefix ends in a vowel and the word that follows begins with the same vowel: *re-elect, pre-election, anti-intellectual, pre-empt, pre-exist.* Use a hyphen to attach a prefix to a proper noun: *anti-American.*

Use a hyphen, not the word *to,* between numbers that express odds, ratios, scores, some fractions and some vote tabulations:

```
The odds of her winning are 5-4.

The ratio of water to sugar is 2-1.

The Yankees beat Boston 3-2.

Two-thirds of the books were sold.
```

Use a hyphen to spell out two-word numbers when the first word ends in *y: forty-five, twenty-two, fifty-one.* The usual newspaper style is to use figures rather than to spell out numbers greater than nine, but numbers that begin a sentence should be spelled out.

Two prefixes may be linked to one word by using suspensive hyphenation: "She accepted the deal on a *one- to three-month* trial basis"; "Those selected had a *50- to 90-vote* margin."

Parentheses. Parentheses are used to set off an aside, information that explains or qualifies but is not essential to the sentence. Journalists use parentheses sparingly. The AP stylebook indicates that the temptation to use parentheses is a clue that the sentence is becoming contorted; suggested solutions are to rewrite the sentence or, if the sentence must contain incidental material, to use commas or dashes.

If the material enclosed in parentheses comes at the end of a sentence but the enclosed material is not a complete sentence, put the period outside the closing parenthesis. If the enclosed material is a complete sentence, include the period at the end of the sentence within the closing parenthesis:

```
She is an excellent reporter (and a fine writer).
(If you don't know French, you might not like the
movie.)
```

Period. Use a period at the end of a declarative sentence and at the end of a mildly imperative sentence:

```
She is coming to the party. (declarative)
Please come here. (mildly imperative)
```

Use a period in many abbreviations—*B.A. degree; Baton Rouge, La.; U.N. headquarters; U.S. military*—and as a decimal point in figures—*$1.8 million, 4.6 miles, $3.25.*

Periods, like commas, always go inside quotation marks:

```
The speaker told the crowd, "Our government should
help us."
```

Three spaced periods are used to form an ellipsis, which is used to indicate the deletion of one or more words in condensing quotations, texts and documents. If an ellipsis comes at the end of a sentence, put the required mark of punctuation—period, question mark or exclamation point—and then a space before typing the ellipsis: "My administration will uphold the law. ..."

Question mark. Use a question mark at the end of an interrogative: "Who is responsible for this mess?" Do not use a question mark to indicate the end of indirect questions: "He asked who was responsible for the mess."

Question marks go inside or outside quotation marks, depending on the meaning. If the quotation is a question, the question mark is included within the quotation marks. But if the quoted material is not a question, the question mark goes outside the quotation marks:

```
She asked, "Are you ready to go?"
Who wrote "War and Peace"?
```

Do not use a comma before the attribution in a direct quotation if a question mark is needed to end the quoted material:

```
"Are you ready to go?" she asked.
```

Quotation marks. Surround the exact words of a speaker or writer when reporting them:

The AP stylebook indicates that the temptation to use parentheses is a clue that the sentence is becoming contorted.

"I think it is important to finish quickly," Jones
said.

Running quotations—those that continue for more than one paragraph—should not have a close-quote mark at the end of the first paragraph if the quoted material is a complete sentence. However, open-quote marks are needed at the beginning of the second paragraph to indicate that the quotation is continuing:

Jones said, "I think it is important to finish
quickly to make up for unavoidable delays caused by
bad weather.
    "Our credibility is at stake here because we prom-
ised to have the job finished before July 1."

If the first paragraph of a continuing quotation ends with a partial quotation, close-quote marks should be used at the end of the partial quotation and open-quotation marks should be used at the beginning of the next paragraph:

Jones attributed the delays to "bad weather."
    "Our credibility is at stake here because we prom-
ised to have the job finished before July 1."

Do not use quotation marks with a question-and-answer format. Each speaker's words should start a new paragraph:

Q: Who was responsible?

A: John Smith

Use quotation marks around a word or phrase that is used in an ironical sense or that is unfamiliar on first reference:

The "doctor" treated people for two years before being exposed as a fake.

To save space, single quotation marks are used for direct quotations in headlines:

'I will campaign for re-election,' Rep. Jones says

Use single quotation marks around a quotation within a quotation:

She testified, "John never told me specifically, 'I
plan to kill my boss.' "

Note that three quotation marks—a single quote and double-quote marks—are used when, as in the last example, two quoted elements end at the same time.

Follow the style used by your publication regarding the use of quotation marks with titles of books, plays, movies, television shows, poems, songs and works of art. Some publications have switched from quotation marks to italics for such titles. Electronic typesetting equipment allows newspapers and magazines to use italics with relative ease, whereas insertion of italics was time-consuming with previous typesetting technology.

News-service style is to put quotation marks around the titles of all books, movies, operas, plays, poems, songs, television programs, lectures, speeches and works of art—except for the Bible and books that are primarily catalogs of reference material, including almanacs, directories, dictionaries, encyclopedias, gazetteers, handbooks and similar publications.

The period and comma always go within the close-quotation marks. Other marks of punctuation go within the quotation marks when they apply to the

Do not use quotation marks with a question-and-answer format.

quoted matter only. They go outside the quotation marks when they apply to the whole sentence.

Semicolon. In general, use the semicolon to indicate a greater separation of thought and information than a comma can convey but less than the separation that a period implies. In a compound sentence, for example, a comma is insufficient separation between the two independent clauses. A comma and a coordinating conjunction can be used between the two clauses, or a semicolon alone can be used:

```
The city has committed $500,000 to the project, and
private developers also will put money into it.

The city has committed $500,000 to the project; pri-
vate developers also will put money into it.
```

Use semicolons to separate elements of a series when individual segments contain material that must be set off by commas: "Club members elected Jane Smith, president; Robert Blake, vice president; Sam Brown, secretary."

Be sparing with semicolons. To many readers, a semicolon signals a difficult passage and becomes a point at which to exit the story.

Time

A specific time should precede the day, and the day should precede the place: "The production will begin at 8 p.m. Friday at the Opera House."

Use *noon* and *midnight,* not *12 a.m.* and *12 p.m.*

Avoid redundancies: *5 p.m. tomorrow,* not *5 p.m. tomorrow night.*

Use *today, this morning, tomorrow* and the like as appropriate. Use the day of the week elsewhere. Use *Monday, Tuesday* and so on for days of the week within seven days before or after the current date. Use the month and a figure for dates beyond this range. Avoid redundancies, such as *last Thursday* or *next Friday;* the verb tense should denote usage. Always spell out days of the week.

Use an apostrophe for omitted figures in years: *events of '89.*

Use figures for decades, with an apostrophe for omitted figures: *the 1990s, the '90s.*

For centuries, lowercase the word *century* and spell out century numbers below 10: *the third century, the 20th century.*

𝔄*void redundancies.*

Other style issues

- *Long titles.* Avoid their use before a name. Use *John Jones, assistant undersecretary for the interior* rather than *Assistant Undersecretary for the Interior John Jones.*
- *Time zones.* Capitalize the names of time zones in formal usage: *Eastern Standard Time, Pacific Daylight Time, EST, PDT.*
- *Weather terms.* A *blizzard* has winds of 35 mph or more and considerable falling or blowing snow, with visibility near zero. A *cyclone* is a storm with strong winds rotating about a moving center of low atmospheric pressure. A *funnel cloud* is a violent, rotating column of air that does not touch the ground. *Gale winds* are sustained winds within the range of 39 to 54 mph (34 to 47 knots). A *hurricane* is a warm-core tropical cyclone in which the minimum sustained surface wind is 74 mph or more. A *tornado* is a violent rotating column of air forming a pendant and touching the ground. A *knot* is one nautical mile (6,076.10 feet) per hour. To convert knots into approximate statute miles per hour, multiply knots by 1.15. Always use figures to express the result: "Winds were at 7 to 9 knots."

- *Temperatures*. Use figures for all except zero: "The day's low was minus 10." Temperatures get higher or lower; they don't get warmer or cooler. The temperature scale generally used in the United States is Fahrenheit rather than Celsius. In the Fahrenheit scale, the freezing point of water is 32 degrees and the boiling point is 212 degrees. To convert a Fahrenheit temperature to Celsius, subtract 32 from the Fahrenheit figure, multiply by 5, and divide by 9 (77 − 32 = 45; 45 x 5 = 225; 225 ÷ 9 = 25 degrees Celsius).

n the next several pages are words that often are misused in both written and spoken English. A few are homonyms that are unlikely to be confused; others are word substitutions that people commonly but erroneously make. A few of these words have fallen into such common misusage that even the experts debate the merits of maintaining the original distinctions. But to professional writers and editors who want to say exactly and concisely what they mean, the distinctions are important. Exercises 1 through 6 at the end of Chapter 3 test your knowledge of these words.

according to: It is better to avoid *according to* as an attribution unless the intent is to cast doubt on the speaker's credibility: "According to Jones, he was at home in bed at the time of the crime."

adverse, averse: *Adverse* means unfavorable: "Adverse weather delayed our departure." *Averse* means opposed or reluctant and is used with *to:* "She was averse to her daughter's choice of friends."

advice, advise: *Advice* is a noun: "His advice was to study harder." *Advise* is a verb: "He advised the student to study harder."

affect, effect: *Affect* is a verb: "His illness affected company policy." *Effect* is a noun: "The effect of his illness is unclear." *Effect* also may be used as a verb meaning "to bring about": "His illness effected change in the company's insurance costs."

afterward: Preferred usage in the United States. The British use *afterwards.*

aggravate, irritate: The distinction between these two words seems to be lost, and most authorities say they are interchangeable. Traditionally, *aggravate* means to make an existing situation or condition worse, and *irritate* means to annoy or to provoke to anger: "He aggravated his knee injury and was unable to play football. That irritated him."

all right: Not *alright.*

all together, altogether: *All together* means in a group: "Let's go all together in one car." *Altogether* means thoroughly or entirely: "It is an altogether ridiculous idea."

allude, elude, illusion: To refer indirectly to something is to allude to it: "The author alluded to his previous bouts with alcoholism." *Elude* means to escape a pursuer: "The criminal eluded the police." *Illusion* comes from the Latin word meaning "to mock." An illusion is a false idea or conception, as in *illusions of grandeur.*

altar, alter: An altar is a table or platform used for sacred ceremonies at a church; *alter* means to change: "They said their wedding vows at the altar. They altered the traditional wedding vows."

annual: Something that happens every year. It is incorrect to write *first annual.*

appraise, apprise: *Appraise* means to set a value on: "The bank wants to appraise the property before granting a loan." *Apprise* means to notify or inform: "Please apprise me of your progress on the project."

ascent, assent: A climb is an ascent; the verb form is *ascend:* "They will ascend the stairs"; "The trip to the top of the hill was a steep ascent." *Assent* is a noun or verb meaning "an agreement" or "to agree to": "I want their assent before I continue this program."

awhile, a while: *Awhile* is an adverb and *a while* is an article plus a noun: "We fished for a while, but the fish weren't biting, so we swam awhile."

bail, bale: *Bail* refers to dipping water out of something or posting a bond. To bale something is to tie it into bundles, as to bale old newspapers to take them to a recycling plant.

balance, remainder: Do not use these words interchangeably. Use *balance* in fiscal contexts to report the equality of debits and credits or the difference between them. Use *remainder* for what is left when a part is taken away.

baloney, bologna: *Baloney* refers to nonsense; bologna is lunch meat.

bazaar, bizarre: One might buy odd (bizarre) items at a bazaar.

beach, beech: One vacations at the beach. *Beach* may also be used as a noun meaning "to run aground" (as in beaching a ship). Beech trees are not associated with beach areas.

because of, due to: *Due to* is an adjective and should modify a noun: "The accident was due to carelessness." *Because of* explains why something happened: "Because of my good work, I received a salary increase." Roy Copperud, in *American Usage and Style: The Consensus,* discusses the disagreement on this point among usage experts and writes that the distinction is hairsplitting.

believe, feel, think: These words should not be used interchangeably. Use *think* when mental processes and reason, rather than emotion, are used to form an opinion: "The mayor thinks the city council will pass her proposal." Use *feel* to describe emotional or physical sensations: "He feels unhappy"; He feels the texture of the paper." Use *believe* to express ideas that are accepted on faith: "She believes in God." Usage experts are not unanimous on this rule, however. Many accept the use of *feel* as standard in all three senses.

berth, birth: A resting place is a berth: "The captain guided the boat into its berth." Birth is the act of bringing forth offspring or of being born: "She gave birth to a girl."

beside, besides: "The cat lay beside her." *Besides* means in addition to: "Besides the professional musicians, the show will include high school choirs."

better, bettor: One who gambles is a bettor.

biannual, biennial: Something that happens twice a year is biannual; a biennial event occurs once in two years.

bloc, block: A bloc is a coalition of people or a group with a single purpose or goal: "Farmers were a powerful voting bloc in the last election." *Block* is a different word, with about 40 dictionary definitions.

boar, boor, bore: A male hog is a boar. An insensitive person is a boor: "His behavior at the party shows that he is a boor." *Bore* refers to someone who is boring; *bore* as a verb means to drill: "We like our neighbors, but they are such bores that it is difficult to stay awake when visiting with them."

born, borne: A baby is born. *Borne* is the participle of the verb *bear,* meaning "carry": "She has borne great responsibilities during her husband's illness"; "She has borne three children."

bouillon, bullion: *Bouillon* refers to broth; *bullion* is gold or silver that has been cast into bars or some other convenient shape: "After working with the bullion all morning, the workers stopped for a lunch of chicken bouillon and sandwiches."

breadth, breath, breathe: *Breadth* means width: "The river's breadth is nearly a quarter mile." *Breath* is a noun meaning "air taken into the lungs and then let out"; *breathe* is the verb form: "I took a deep breath"; "It is unpleasant to breathe smoke-filled air."

Britain, Briton: The country is Great Britain; an inhabitant of Britain is a Briton. *Britain* is acceptable usage for reference to Great Britain, which is an island comprising England, Scotland and Wales. The United Kingdom is Great Britain plus Northern Ireland. *The British Isles* applies to the United Kingdom and the islands around it: Scilly to the southwest, the Isle of Man to the west, the Channel Islands to the east, and the Orkneys and the Shetlands to the north of Scotland.

broach, brooch: To broach is to start a discussion or to make a hole in so as to let out liquid; as a noun, *broach* can refer to a tapered bit for drilling holes. A brooch is a large ornamental pin with a clasp: "She wore her favorite brooch that night because she planned to broach the subject of their future together."

burglary, robbery, theft: These words should not be used interchangeably. *Bur-*

292

glary, as defined by common law, means forcible entry with intent to commit a crime. *Robbery* means stealing with force or threat of force; *theft* means stealing without force or threat of force. A holdup is a robbery.

burro, burrow: A burro is a donkey. *Burrow* as a noun refers to a hole in the ground, usually dug by an animal; as a verb, *burrow* means to dig a hole in the ground.

callous, callus: Both words come from the same Latin word meaning "hard skin." A callous person is one who is unfeeling, who is hardened. *Callus* refers to a thickened place on the skin: "The guitar player has calluses on his fingers."

Calvary, cavalry: Calvary is the biblical place where Jesus was crucified. *Cavalry* means combat troops mounted originally on horses but now often on motorized armored vehicles.

canvas, canvass: Canvas is a type of cloth. To canvass is to go through places or among people to ask for something like votes, opinions or orders: "We will canvass this neighborhood in support of our political candidate."

capital, capitol: The city is the capital; the building is the capitol. *Capital* means principal or chief and also refers to money. A capital letter should be used when writing about specific state capitols, such as the Tennessee Capitol, or about the Capitol in Washington, D.C.

carat, caret, carrot, karat: The carat is the unit of weight (200 milligrams) for measuring precious stones and metals. *Carat* is also spelled *karat*. A caret is an editing mark used to indicate an insertion. A carrot is a vegetable.

cement, concrete: Cement is a powdered substance made of lime and clay that is mixed with water and sand or gravel to make concrete. Most cement is portland cement, so named by its inventor because it resembled stone quarried on the Isle of Portland. The term is a generic and is not capitalized. *Cement* also may be used as a verb.

cemetery: Not *cemetary*.

censor, censure, censer: *Censor* and *censure* both come from a Latin word meaning "to judge," and both can be used as either nouns or verbs. *Censor* means to prohibit or suppress; *censure* means to disapprove or sharply criticize. A book or film may be censored (suppressed, prohibited) or censured (sharply criticized), but a person is censured, not censored: "The Senate formally censured Sen. John Doe." *Censer,* unrelated to the other two words, is a noun meaning "a container in which incense is burned."

cession, session: A cession is a ceding or giving up to another: "The treaty provided for the cession of individual rights to the territory." A session is a period of activity of some kind. A legislative session, for example, might include many meetings and extend for several weeks or months.

childish, childlike: Childish is a disparaging description of an adult who is silly or foolish: "His childish behavior was inappropriate at the office." *Childlike* means of or like a child in the sense of innocent and trusting: "Her childlike manner made her a delightful companion."

chord, cord: A combination of three or more tones sounded together in harmony is a chord. *Cord* refers to a string or a measure of wood; it is also the word to apply to vocal cords or the spinal cord.

cite, sight, site: One cites (quotes) a source or receives a citation ordering a court appearance. *Sight* refers to seeing: "It was a beautiful sight"; "The man was out of my range of sight"; "He carefully aligned the rifle sights with the target." A site is a place: "This is the site for our new house."

climactic, climatic: *Climactic* refers to the final culminating element in a series, the highest point of interest or the turning point of action: "The climactic scene in the movie was the death of the title character." *Climatic* pertains to weather, as in *climatic conditions*.

collide: Two objects must both be in motion before they can collide. A car might smash into or hit a fence but not collide with it.

commensurate, commiserate: *Commensurate* means equal in measure or size: "She wants a salary commensurate with her value to the company." To commiserate is to feel or show pity for, to condole: "We commiserate with the family during this sad time."

compare with, compare to: *Compare with* means to note both differences and similarities, and this is usually the intended meaning: "Jim compared his report card with John's." *Compare to* means to note similarities alone.

complacent, complaisant: One who is complacent is self-satisfied: "She was complacent with her life." A complaisant person is willing to please or obliging: "He was complaisant regarding his mother's wishes."

complement, compliment: As a verb, *complement* means to complete; as a noun it refers to that which completes or perfects: "The sauce complemented the main dish." *Compliment* means praise, and it too can be used as either a verb or a noun: "He complimented her on her outstanding work"; "He gave her a compliment on her work."

complementary, complimentary: These are the adjective forms of *complement* and *compliment:* "The service department is complementary to the sales department." *Complimentary* can also mean free or given as a courtesy: "He received complimentary tickets."

compose, comprise: The parts compose the whole; the whole comprises its parts: "The U.S. government comprises the executive, legislative and judicial branches." The consensus among usage experts is that the expression *is comprised of* should be avoided. *Comprised* is a transitive verb, so it needs a direct object. These usages are correct: "Nine players compose the team"; "The team is composed of nine players"; "The team comprises nine players."

comprehensible, comprehensive: That which is comprehensible is understandable: "Now that I know the whole story, his actions are comprehensible." *Comprehensive* means inclusive, wide in scope: "The exam at the end of the semester will be comprehensive."

connotation, denotation: A word's connotation is its suggested or implied meaning; the denotation is the actual meaning or dictionary definition of a word: "The denotation of this word is neutral, but it has a negative connotation."

conscience, conscious, consciousness: Conscience is an awareness of right and wrong: "Let your conscience be your guide." *Conscious* is an adjective meaning "awake"; *consciousness* is a noun meaning "awareness": "He was conscious throughout the ordeal"; "She regained consciousness after a few minutes."

contagious, infection: A contagious disease is spread by contact, whereas an infectious disease is transmitted by the presence in the body of certain microorganisms. An infectious disease also may be contagious.

contemptible, contemptuous: A contemptible thing deserves scorn or contempt: "His behavior was contemptible." Something is contemptuous when it expresses contempt, as a contemptuous remark does.

continual, continuous: Something that is repeated often at intervals (intermittent) is continual: "The rain today was continual" (meaning that it rained off and on during the day). *Continuous* means going on without interruption or incessant action: "The rain was continuous today" (meaning that it never stopped raining today). Copperud suggests use of the words *intermittent* for continual and *incessant* or *uninterrupted* for continuous to ensure that the correct meaning is conveyed.

council, counsel, consul: A council is a group called together for discussion, as in *a city council.* A counsel is one who gives advice or is a lawyer. A consul is a diplomat.

councilor, counselor: A councilor is a member of a council. A counselor is an adviser or a lawyer.

couple of: The *of* is necessary: "A couple of dollars should be enough for a hamburger."

credible, creditable, credulous: Something that can be believed is credible, as in *a credible story. Creditable* means deserving credit or praise: "His service to the community was creditable." A credulous person is one who tends to believe too readily, who is gullible.

crochet, crotchet, crotchety: Crochet is a type of needlework; to crochet is to do such needlework. *Crotchet* is a noun meaning "a particular whim or stubborn notion"; thus a crotchety person is one who is stubborn or cranky.

croquet, croquette, coquette: Croquet is an outdoor game. A croquette is a small meat or fish patty. *Coquette* is a French word meaning "a girl or woman flirt."

cue, queue: A cue is a stick used in billiards or pool to strike a ball. A queue is a pigtail or, in Britain, a line, as of persons waiting to be served: "The queue was quite long when we arrived at the restaurant." *Queue* is also used as an intransitive verb with *up,* as in "We queued up to wait for a table at the restaurant."

currant, current: A currant is a small seedless raisin from the Mediterranean area. *Current* means at the present time or circulating (as electricity): "On our current visit to the Mediterranean, we ate some currants."

cymbal, symbol: A musician uses a cymbal, a circular brass plate that makes a ringing sound when hit. A symbol is an object used to represent something abstract; a mark or letter standing for a quality or process, as in music or chemistry; or an editing mark.

cypress, Cyprus: A cypress is an evergreen tree. Cyprus is the name of an island country in the east end of the Mediterranean. A citizen of Cyprus is a Cypriot.

defective, deficient: Something that has imperfections or is faulty is defective: "The car had defective brakes." *Deficient* means lacking in some essential, incomplete or inadequate in amount: "The doctor said her diet was deficient in vitamin C."

demolish, destroy: These words mean that something is done away with completely, so it is redundant to say *completely demolished* or *totally destroyed.*

demur, demure: To demur is to hesitate because of doubts or to have objections; *demur* is also a noun meaning an objection: "The lawyer filed a demur with the court." To be demure is to be affectedly modest or coy: "She wore a demure dress for her appearance in court."

deprecate, depreciate: To deprecate is to express disapproval of, to belittle: "He deprecated her efforts." To depreciate is to lessen in value: "A car depreciates rapidly."

desert, dessert: To desert is to abandon, to forsake, as to leave a military post without permission and with no intent to return. *Desert* also refers to a dry, barren, sandy region, such as the Sahara Desert. A dessert is the final course of a meal.

detract, distract: To detract is to take away: "An unkept lawn detracts from the appearance of a house." To distract is to draw the mind in another direction, to divert, to confuse or bewilder: "The child's crying distracted the man from his work."

different from: Not *different than:* "Mary's political views are different from those of her sister." *Differ with* indicates disagreement: "I differ with her political views."

dilemma: A choice between two alternatives, both bad. *Dilemma* should not be used to mean a choice of more than two or a choice between a good alternative and a bad one: "To leave the car and walk toward town during the blizzard or to wait for help that wasn't likely to come before daybreak: that was his dilemma."

disapprove, disprove: To disapprove is to have or express an unfavorable opinion: "She disapproved of John's work." To disprove is to prove to be false: "He disproved the belief that the earth is flat."

disburse, dispense, disperse: To disburse is to pay out, as in *disbursing wages.* To dispense is to give out or distribute, as with medicine or justice: "The judge will dispense justice; the nurse will dispense pills." *Disperse* means to break up and scatter: "They attempted to disperse the oil that had spilled into the bay."

disinterested, uninterested: One who is disinterested is impartial or unbiased, as in *a disinterested judge.* An uninterested person is indifferent or lacks interest. The distinction between these two words is being lost in common usage, so a writer or speaker might prefer to use *impartial* instead of *disinterested.*

distinctive, distinguished: Something that is distinctive is different or characteristic. It is not necessarily good or bad, just different. *Distinguished* means excellent, outstanding. A teacher who wears unusual clothes, stands on her desk and shouts at students can be said to have a distinctive teaching style, but it may or may not be considered distinguished: "He had a distinctive speaking style. Later he became a distinguished diplomat."

dose, doze: A dose is an amount of medicine to be taken at one time; to doze is to sleep lightly or nap: "He took a dose of medicine and then sat in front of the television set to doze."

drier, dryer: *Drier* is the comparative form of *dry:* "A desert is drier than a river valley." A dryer is a person or thing that dries, such as an appliance for drying clothes.

drown: Should not have an auxiliary or helping verb unless the victim was helped in the drowning. Just say "He drowned," not "He was drowned."

drunk, drunken: Use *drunken* as a modifier before a noun, as in *drunken driver.* Use *drunk* as a predicate adjective, as in "He was drunk."

dual, duel: *Dual* means something composed of two, a double, as in "The car has dual headlights." A duel is a prearranged fight between two persons armed with deadly weapons.

each other, one another: The consensus among grammatical experts is to use these interchangeably instead of applying *each one* when the meaning is limited to two and *one another* when more than two are involved.

eager, anxious: Experts are divided about whether these may be properly interchanged. *Anxious* refers to foreboding; *eager* means to look forward to: "She was anxious about the surgery"; "She was eager for the vacation trip."

ecology, environment: *Ecology* refers to the relationship between organisms and their environment. It is not a synonym for *environment.*

eek, eke out: *Eek* is an exclamatory expression: "Eek! There's a snake." *Eke out* means to get something with great difficulty: "During the Depression, they barely managed to eke out a living." In *American Usage and Style,* Copperud dismisses as pedantic critics who object to the expression *eke out a living,* noting that the dictionaries he consulted cited the expression.

elder, eldest; older, oldest: Some dictionaries make a distinction, applying *elder* and *eldest* to people and *older* and *oldest* to either things or people. At what age these terms should be applied to people is highly subjective. The AP stylebook cautions that they should not be used to describe anyone younger than 65 and should not be used casually in referring to anyone beyond that age. *Elderly* is appropriate in generic phrases that do not refer to specific individuals, as in *concern for the elderly* or *a home for the elderly.* If the intent is to show that an individual's faculties have deteriorated, the AP stylebook says to cite a graphic example: "His memory fades"; "She walks with a cane."

elicit, illicit: *Elicit* is a transitive verb meaning to draw forth or evoke (a response): "The teacher sought to elicit answers from her students." *Illicit* is an adjective describing something that is unlawful, improper or prohibited, as in *an illicit affair.*

emigrant, immigrant: One who leaves a country is an emigrant; one who comes into a country is an immigrant.

eminent, imminent: *Eminent* is an adjective describing something that is high, lofty, prominent or renowned: "An eminent person will be the best candidate for the university presidency." Something that is likely to happen without delay, that is impending, can be said to be imminent: "Judging from the appearance of the sky, I think a storm is imminent."

ensure, insure: The consensus among usage experts is that these terms may be used interchangeably to mean make certain, but AP style is to use *ensure* for that meaning: "Additional testing will ensure quality control." *Insure* is the correct word to mean guarantee against loss, as in *to insure your automobile* (buy insurance).

envisage, envision: Both words mean to form an image in the mind, to visualize, but *envision* has the connotation of less immediacy than *envisage,* which might refer to imagining something not yet in existence.

epithet, epitaph: An epithet is a word or phrase characterizing a person or thing; in common usage it has come to be associated with derogatory descriptions. An epitaph is an inscription, as for a tomb, in memory of a dead person.

erasable, irascible: A pencil mark is erasable, meaning that it can be erased or rubbed out. An irascible person is one who is easily angered or is hot-tempered.

especially, specially: *Especially* means to an outstanding extent or particularly: "I am especially happy about the good news." *Specially* means for a special purpose: "She bought the dress specially for the party."

every day, everyday: *Every day* is an adverb: "She wore a suit every day to work." *Everyday* is an adjective meaning usual, common or suitable for everyday use: "She wore an everyday dress rather than her best suit."

evoke, invoke: To evoke is to call forth, to elicit: "His soothing voice evoked memories of her father." To invoke is to call on a higher authority, like God or the Muses, for blessing or help; to resort to (such as a law or ruling) as pertinent; to conjure, beg for, implore. The noun form is *invocation.*

exalt, exult: *Exalt* is to raise in status or dignity, to praise or glorify, to fill with joy or pride, as in *exalted ruler. Exult,* an intransitive verb, means to rejoice greatly or to glory; the noun form is exultation: "They exulted in the news of their victory."

excite, incite: *Excite* means to make active, to stimulate, to arouse emotionally; *incite* means to urge to action. A speaker might excite a crowd, for example, without inciting the crowd to take action, but generally a crowd will not become incited without first becoming excited: "The sound of a doorbell excites the dog and causes it to bark"; "The dynamic speaker incited the inmates to begin fighting the guards."

execute: To take life by due process of law. Terrorists or gangsters do not execute people, although they may engage in execution-style murders.

exercise, exorcise: *Exercise* pertains to physical activity, as in *an exercise class to promote good health. Exorcise* means to expel (such as evil spirits) by incantations or to free from such spirits; noun forms are *exorcism* and *exorcist.*

expose: To lay open, generally to something undesirable, such as danger or attack: "The worker was exposed to radiation"; "The revelations exposed the candidate to political attacks from his opponents." *Expose* should not be used in the sense of making known, as in "Our travels abroad exposed us to new cultures."

extant, extent: *Extant* means still existing: "This is the oldest extant structure in North America." *Extent* means space, amount, degree to which a thing extends, size, scope, limits: "The child tested the extent of his mother's patience."

facetious, factious, factitious, fictitious: *Facetious* means joking or amusing, as in *a facetious comment. Factious* refers to creating dissent, especially in political matters: "The trade legislation was factious in this congressional session." *Factitious* means forced or artificial. *Fictitious* means of or like fiction, imaginary, false, assumed for disguise not necessarily with the intent to deceive, as in *a fictitious account* or *a fictitious title.*

fact: A reality, a truth. It is redundant to say *true fact, real fact* or *actual fact.*

farther, further: Use *farther* to refer to physical distances: "She can run farther than I can." *Further* means to a greater extent or degree, as in "Investigate the matter further." *Further* also can mean in addition: "Further, I will not do as you ask because your plan is unethical."

feat, fete: *Feat* describes an accomplishment of unusual daring or skill: "Few of Babe Ruth's feats have been matched." A fete is a festival, entertainment or lavish party: "The fete honored her 100th birthday."

ferment, foment: *Ferment* means to undergo fermentation by the addition of some substance, such as yeast: "Grapes ferment to become wine." *Foment* means to stir up (such as trouble), to incite: "He sought to foment trouble among the workers."

fewer, less: Use *fewer* for items that can be separated in the quantities being compared; use *less* for items that cannot be separated easily: "He has less experience as a copy editor than she does"; "He has fewer years of experience than she does."

fiancé, fiancée: Despite efforts toward a gender-neutral language, this distinction remains. General usage and AP style reserves *fiancé* for males and *fiancée* for females.

figuratively, literally: *Figuratively* is an adverb describing an action that is not in its usual or exact sense or is metaphorical, as in *a figure of speech:* "He spoke figuratively." *Literally,* often misused for *figuratively,* means exactly, actually, precisely as stated. As used to mean a display of great emotion or anger, a sentence like "He literally hit the ceiling" is incorrect. What is meant is he figuratively hit the ceiling, not that he actually (literally) made contact with the ceiling.

fiscal, physical: *Fiscal* means financial, as in *the nation's fiscal policy.*

flack, flak: *Flack* is a slang term for a press agent or public relations practitioner. It is often used in a derogatory sense. *Flak* was first used during World War II as an acronym for a German antiaircraft gun and the shells fired by the gun. It has come to mean criticism: "He took a lot of flak for his stand on the issue."

flagrant, fragrant: *Flagrant* means obviously evident and connotes outrageous or shocking conduct: "He was flagrant in his disregard for rules and regulations." Something that is fragrant smells good.

flaunt, flout: To flaunt means to show off proudly or in an ostentatious manner: "She flaunted her wealth." *Flout* means to defy, mock or scorn: "His behavior flouts authority."

flier, flyer: The news-service stylebooks prefer *flier* for both aviators and handbills. Other usage guides prefer *flyer* for handbill. *Flyer* is the proper name for some trains and buses: *the Western Flyer.*

flounder, founder: In addition to denoting a variety of fish, *flounder* means to struggle awkwardly or to speak or act in an awkward, confused manner: "He floundered in the deep snow." *Founder* as a verb means to stumble, fall or go lame, as in "The horse foundered." *Founder* also means to fill with water and sink, as in *to founder a ship.*

forbidding, foreboding: *Forbidding* is an adjective meaning difficult or looking dangerous or disagreeable, as in *a forbidding climb to the top of a mountain. Foreboding* as a noun means a prediction, usually of something evil: "She believed that the dream was a foreboding of doom."

foregoing, forgoing: *Foregoing* is something previously said or written, as in *the foregoing paragraph of the speech. Forgoing* is the present participle form of the verb *forgo,* meaning to do without, to abstain: "He will forgo eating meat."

fortuitous, fortunate: *Fortuitous* means happening by luck or chance: "Our meeting here is fortuitous because I want to talk with you." *Fortunate* means having good luck: "She was fortunate throughout her career."

funeral service: A redundant phrase. A funeral is a service.

gantlet, gauntlet: A gantlet was a punishment in which the offender ran between two rows of men who struck him (running the gantlet). Now *gantlet* is used to mean a series of troubles. Originally, *gauntlet* meant a knight's armored glove. *Throw down the gauntlet* meant to challenge to combat. Opinion is divided on whether modern usage correctly allows these to be used interchangeably. Several dictionaries indicate that they are the same, with *gauntlet* the preferred spelling.

genteel, gentle: *Genteel* means polite or well-bred, with modern usage referring to affectedly refined or polite: "His genteel mannerisms seemed out of place in his current state of homelessness on New York City streets." *Gentle* means refined, courteous, tame, not harsh or rough, as in *a gentle man* or *a gentle animal.*

gorilla, guerrilla: A gorilla is the largest and most powerful of the humanlike apes native to Africa. A guerrilla is a member of a small defensive force of irregular soldiers.

gourmand, gourmet: Both terms refer to someone who likes good food and drink, but *gourmand* is used in the sense of eating or drinking to excess, as a glutton would: "John is a gourmand and weighs 350 pounds." *Gourmet* connotes one who is an excellent judge of fine foods and drinks, a connoisseur: "June is a gourmet cook."

grisly, gristly, grizzly: *Grisly* means horrible or gruesome, as in *grisly crime.* *Gristly* means having gristles, as in *gristly meat. Grizzly* means gray or streaked with gray, having gray hair.

half brother, stepbrother: If they have one parent in common, they are half brothers; if they are related by the remarriage of parents, they are stepbrothers. Because in some cultures it is considered insensitive to identify family members as half brother, half sister, stepmother and so on, some newspapers do not specify such family relationships except when germane to a story or specified by the persons involved.

half-mast, half-staff: Flags on ships or at naval stations are lowered to or flown at (but not raised to) half-mast. Flags in other places are lowered to half-staff.

hangar, hanger: A hangar shelters airplanes. A hanger is used to support clothes or other objects.

hardy, hearty: *Hardy* is an adjective meaning bold and resolute, robust, or vigorous, as in *a hardy species of plants. Hearty* means warm and friendly, jovial, unrestrained, as in *a hearty laugh.*

head up: Incorrect usage. A person heads a committee, perhaps.

healthful, healthy: Something that is conducive to good health is healthful: "Exercise is healthful." Something that has good health is healthy: "The healthy man exercises daily." Today, *healthy* is commonly used in both senses.

historic, historical: *Historic* means important to history, as in *a historic battle. Historical* means of or concerning history: "It is a historical novel."

holey, holy: *Holey* means full of holes: "Throw the holey socks in the trash." Holy refers to sacred things: "He considered his work to be a holy duty." Neither word should be confused with *wholly,* which means entirely.

hopefully: One of the most commonly misused words. It should be used as an adverb to describe the way the subject feels; it should not be used as an adjective. Thus, it is incorrect to write "Hopefully, he will make an A in the course." The correct wording is "He hopes he will make an A." To describe his feelings, write "He looked hopefully at his grade report."

if, whether: Use *if* to introduce a condition: "If it rains, the picnic will be canceled." Use *whether* when an alternative is stated or implied: "He asked whether the picnic had been canceled." *Whether or not* is redundant.

impassable, impassible: *Impassable* means not capable of being passed, as in *an impassable obstacle.* An impassible person is one who is incapable of showing emotion: "He was impassible as the judge sentenced him to prison."

imply, infer: The speaker or writer implies; the listener or reader infers: "In her speech, the company president implied that major policy changes were forthcoming"; "After listening carefully, I inferred that the policy changes would not involve my department."

inapt, inept: *Inapt* (also *unapt*) means inappropriate or not suitable: "To wear a hat at the dining room table is inapt behavior." *Inept* is sometimes used in that sense, but usually it refers to something that is foolish or incompetent: "Mary is a computer expert, but she is inept in diagnosing problems with her car."

incidence, incidents: *Incidence* refers to the rate of occurrence, as in *the incidence of measles in the United States.* An incident is an occurrence. An incident may or may not involve attack or violence: "It was an incident that he would remember fondly for the rest of his life."

incite, insight: To incite is to urge to action, as in *to incite violence* (see entry *excite, incite*). *Insight* is a noun meaning the ability to see and understand clearly the inner nature of things, especially by intuition: "She had a keen insight into the situation."

incredible, incredulous: Something that is unbelievable is incredible; *incredulous* means skeptical: "I was incredulous when I heard about his feats on the basketball court, but when I saw him perform, I realized that he was capable of incredible plays."

ingenious, ingenuous: An ingenious person is inventive; an ingenuous person is honest or open to the point of being naive: "We know that Benjamin Franklin was ingenious, but he probably was not ingenuous."

insoluble, insolvable, insolvent: An insoluble substance cannot be dissolved. An insolvable problem is one that cannot be solved. A person who cannot pay debts is said to be insolvent.

interment, internment: To inter is to put into a grave or tomb, so interment is a burial. *Internment* means detention, as in *internment camp.*

interstate, intrastate: *Interstate* means between states: "The truck was used for interstate commerce along the eastern coast." *Intrastate* means within a single state.

intestate: Not having a will: "He died intestate."

into, in to: The preposition *into* is not interchangeable with the adverb *in* followed by the preposition *to*: "The firefighter ran into the burning building"; "The escaped convict turned himself in to the police."

irrespective: An adjective meaning regardless. Do not use *irregardless.*

judicial, judicious: *Judicial* refers to a judge or court or their functions, as in *a judicial system* or *the judicial branch of government. Judicious* means having or showing sound judgment: "His actions demonstrate that he is judicious."

lam, lamb: *Lam* is a slang expression for a headlong flight, as in fleeing. A person in this situation is said to be "on the lam." A lamb is a baby sheep.

lama, llama: A priest or monk in Tibet or Mongolia is a lama. A llama is an animal found in the South American Andes.

leach, leech: To leach is to wash a solid substance with a filtering liquid or to extract from some material. A leech is a bloodsucker, originally a bloodsucking worm; now the term is also applied to a person who clings to another to get what he or she can.

leak, leek: *Leak* is a verb meaning to let fluid in or out accidentally or, as a noun, meaning a hole: "The boat had a leak"; "Water leaked into the boat." A leek is an onionlike vegetable.

levee, levy: A levee is an embankment to prevent a river from flooding adjacent land: "They stood on the levee to watch the barges float downstream." *Levy,* as a noun, is an imposed tax or fine; as a verb it means to impose a tax or fine: "The state legislature will levy an income tax; the amount of the levy has not been determined."

lie, lay: See Rule 31 in Chapter 2.

lightening, lightning: *Lightening* means making something less heavy or less dark, as in *lightening the color of paint* or *lightening the load.* Lightning is a flash of light in the sky caused by the discharge of atmospheric electricity.

like, as: *As* is a conjunction; *like* is a verb or a preposition: "She looks like her sister"; "The two women look as though they might be sisters." *Though* or *if* is needed with *as* when what follows is a clause; a conjunction, not a preposition, is needed to join the dependent clause and the main clause.

linage, lineage: Linage is the number of written or printed lines on a page. In journalism, *advertising linage* refers to the number of lines of advertising matter in an issue. *Lineage* means descent from an ancestor: "She traced her lineage to the Pilgrims."

loath, loathe: *Loath* is an adjective meaning reluctant; the expression is *loath to:* "She is loath to give a speech before a large audience." *Loathe* means to dislike intensely: "She loathed her boss because of his sexist behavior."

locate: To fix the position of, to situate or become situated, to discover. *Locate* is not a synonym for *find;* "She located her car keys" is incorrect. Correct usage: "The city council decided to locate the new city hall at Fourth and Main streets."

Magna Carta, Magna Charta: In the United States, *Magna Carta* is the preferred spelling.

majority, plurality: More than half is a majority. A plurality is less than half but is the largest number. For example, if the votes of 11 people were 5 for, 4 against, and 2 undecided, you could say that a plurality voted in favor. At least 6 of 11 people would have to vote the same way before there would be a majority. Do not use *majority* in place of *most* or *many* or where numbers are not involved. Do not use *majority* in the comparative sense, as in *greater majority* or *greatest majority.*

marshal, marshall: *Marshal* is the correct word for the verb form (*marshal the forces*) or the noun (*fire marshal, parade marshal*). *Marshall* is the usual spelling for a proper noun (*John Marshall*).

masterful, masterly: *Masterful* means domineering: "She feared her masterful teacher." *Masterly* means skillful or expert: "It was a masterly performance." *Masterful* often is misused in the latter sense, perhaps because there is no adverbial form of *masterly.*

may be, maybe: *May be* is a verb, as in "I may be selected for the job." *Maybe* means perhaps, as in "Maybe I will be selected for the job." *Maybe* should not be used as an adjective: *a maybe fun party.*

mean, median: *Mean* is a synonym for average, referring to the sum of all components divided by the number of components. The median is the middle number, meaning that half the components are larger and half are smaller: "The test scores were 95, 85, 70, for a mean of 83.33, but the median grade was 85." Some authorities object to using *average* to mean common or ordinary, as in *an average person.*

media, medium: *Media* is plural: "The media are business enterprises." *Medium* is singular: "The artist's medium was watercolor."

motor, engine: An engine develops its own power, usually through internal combustion or the pressure of air, steam or water passing over vanes attached to a wheel: *an airplane engine, an automobile engine, a jet engine, a missile engine, a steam engine, a turbine engine.* A motor receives power from an outside source: *an electric motor, a hydraulic motor.*

nauseated, nauseous: A person becomes nauseated because of something that is *nauseous,* which means causing nausea. It is wrong to say a person who is ill is nauseous: "While on the trip, she was nauseated because she suffers from motion sickness."

naval, navel: *Naval* pertains to a navy. The navel is the scar on the abdomen where the umbilical cord was attached to the fetus; a navel orange has a similar-appearing bump on one end.

negligent, negligible: To be negligent is to be careless, inattentive or neglectful: "This place will shelter the children of negligent parents." *Negligible* refers to that which can be disregarded, a trifling: "At the end of the week, the amount of work left to do on the house was negligible."

odious, odorous: *Odious* means hateful, disgusting or offensive, as in *an odious task.* Something fragrant is odorous, as in *odorous flowers.*

oral, verbal: *Oral* refers to human speech, something spoken. *Verbal* means relating to words, so it can refer to either written or spoken communication. Verbal skills are a person's ability to use language, either spoken or written, but oral skills are a person's speaking ability.

over, more than: *Over* refers to spatial relationships: "The boy jumped over the chair." Although *over* can be used with figures, as in "She is over 30," *more than* is the preferred usage with figures: "More than 40,000 attended the game."

palate, palette, pallet: The palate is the roof of the mouth. Although the taste buds are not located there, in common usage the word *palate* applies to taste. An artist uses a palette for mixing paints. A pallet is a small, simple bed or a low platform for moving and stacking materials, as at a warehouse.

parlay, parley: To parlay is to bet an original wager plus its earnings on another race or game: "He parlayed $10 into $1,000." *Parley* comes from the French word for speak and means to confer, especially with an enemy.

partially, partly: Most dictionaries list these words as synonyms in the sense of part of the whole. *Partially* also can mean showing favoritism. If there is room for ambiguity, use *partly:* "The work was partly done."

pedal, petal, peddle: You pedal a bicycle. A flower has petals. When selling something, you peddle it.

pendant, pendent: A pendant is an ornamental hanging object, such as a locket or earring: "She wore a silver pendant." *Pendent* means suspended, overhanging, undecided or pending.

peremptory, pre-emptory: *Peremptory* comes from a Latin word meaning "to destroy." In a legal sense, *peremptory* means barring further action or final, as in *a peremptory challenge. Pre-emptory* means prior: "That television show will pre-empt the one I wanted to see."

perquisite, prerequisite: A perquisite is something in addition to the regular pay for one's work: "A perquisite of the position is the use of a health club." A short form of *perquisite* is *perk.* A prerequisite is something required beforehand as a necessary condition. In education, for example, a student must complete basic courses as prerequisites to more advanced courses.

persecute, prosecute: To persecute is to afflict constantly so as to injure or distress, particularly for reasons of race or religion: "The Jewish people were persecuted by the Nazis." To prosecute is to conduct legal proceedings against one accused of a crime: "The state will prosecute those arrested for selling illegal drugs."

perspective, prospective: *Perspective* refers to the appearance of objects as determined by their relative distance and position; it refers also to a sense of proportion: "The artist's paintings had unusual perspective." It has come to be used as a synonym of *viewpoint:* "What is your perspective on this matter?" *Prospective* is an adjective meaning "expected" or "likely": "Jones is the prospective candidate for the job."

persuade, convince: People are *persuaded to,* meaning they are talked into or induced. *Convince* should not be followed by an infinitive. People are *convinced that* it is so or *convinced of* a fact: "She persuaded her father to allow her to attend the party"; "He was convinced that it was the right thing to do."

podium, lectern: A speaker stands on a podium or dais. The speaker stands behind a lectern.

populous, populace: A thickly populated place is populous: "The cost of living usually is high in such populous places as New York City." *Populace* refers to the common people, the masses: "The politician was admired by the populace."

pore, pour: *Pore* as a transitive verb means to study carefully, to ponder. It is used with *over,* as in *to pore over books.* Its meaning is unrelated to the verb *pour,* which means to cause liquid to move out of a container in a continuous stream: "I will pour the milk from the bottle."

precede, proceed: To precede is to go ahead of something or someone: "The attendants will precede the bride down the aisle." *Proceed* means to continue some action: "He proceeded to read the newspaper." The plural noun *proceeds* refers to the yield derived from a commercial or fund-raising venture.

predominant, predominate: *Predominant* is an adjective; *predominate* is a verb. Both refer to having influence over others or being dominant in frequency: "The New York Yankees were the predominant baseball team during the 1950s"; "The teams predominated the American League."

prescribe, proscribe: Prescribe means to order, as a medicine is prescribed by a doctor. *Proscribe* means to prohibit, outlaw or denounce: "Drunken driving is proscribed behavior."

pretense, pretext: A pretense is a false show, an overt act intended to conceal personal feelings: "My profuse compliments were a pretense." A pretext is a motive or reason for action offered in place of the true one: "She was accused of tardiness, but that was only a pretext for sexism."

principle, principal: A guiding rule or basic truth is a principle (a noun): "He followed the principle 'live and let live.'" *Principal,* which can be used as either a noun or an adjective, means first, dominant or leading thing. A memory aid taught to schoolchildren is "The principal is your pal," because the dominant person at most schools is the principal. In the early years of a home mortgage, most of the monthly payments are applied to the interest on the loan, rather than the principal (the dominant amount).

reckless: Heedless or rash. It is reckless (not *wreckless*) driving that often causes automobile accidents.

recur, reoccur: Copperud's study of American usage found that most experts see no distinction between these forms. Of the language authorities he consulted, only one said that *reoccur* suggests a single repetition. The consensus is that *recur* and *recurrence* are preferred.

refute: To argue successfully, to prove to be false or mistaken. *Disprove* is a correct substitute for *refute.* Do not use *refute* if there is any question about the success of the argument. *Deny, contradict, reject, rebut* and *dispute* are appropriate words to indicate that disagreement took place. "He refuted the argument" means that he disproved the argument. "He rejected, denied, disputed, contradicted, rebutted the argument" means that he disagreed with the argument, but it does not mean that he proved the argument wrong.

regardless: Not *irregardless.*

reluctant, reticent: *Reluctant* means that someone does not want to act: "She was reluctant to audition for the play." *Reticent* means disposed to keep silent: "He was reticent about his failed marriage."

remediable, remedial: Something that can be fixed is remediable. Something that is meant to be a remedy is remedial: "The student enrolled in remedial reading."

repairable, reparable: Both words mean that something can be repaired. *Re-*

pairable is used for physical items: "The child's toy is repairable." *Reparable* is used with non-physical things: "I hope that the damage to the group's morale is reparable."

rise, raise: See Rule 31 in Chapter 2.

rye, wry: Rye is grass. *Wry,* from an Old English word meaning "to turn," is used in the sense of twisted, distorted or ironic, as in *wry humor.*

say, said: The most serviceable words of attribution. Other verbs of attribution, including *stated, declared, admitted, screamed, yelled, shouted* and *cried,* have meanings different from *said* and should not be used unless they accurately describe the speaker's demeanor. Sources don't grin, frown, smile or giggle their comments to a reporter.

seasonable, seasonal: *Seasonable* means timely, suitable to the season: "A wool suit is seasonable for winter." *Seasonal* means depending on the season: "Fresh vegetables are seasonal."

shear, sheer: *Shear* means to cut off, as in *shear wool from sheep. Sheer* as a verb means to turn aside or cause to turn aside, to swerve: "The truck sheered from the mountainside." As an adjective, *sheer* refers to very thin, transparent material, as in *sheer curtains.* It can also mean absolute or utter, as in *sheer folly.*

similar to: Not *similar with.*

sit, set: See Rule 31 in Chapter 2.

sleight, slight: *Sleight* means skill with the hands, especially in deceiving onlookers, as in magic: *sleight of hand.* To slight is to treat as unimportant; as a noun *slight* can refer to the condition of being treated as unimportant: "The slight was unintentional." As an adjective, *slight* can mean light, slender in build, frail or fragile, as in *the slight man.*

sniffle, snivel: *Sniffle* means the act or sound of sniffling or, as a verb, to sniff repeatedly. *Snivel* means to cry and sniffle or to complain and whine.

spade, spayed: A spade is a shovel. To spay is to sterilize a female animal by removing the ovaries. *Spayed* is the past tense of *spay.*

stationary, stationery: An object that does not move is stationary. One uses stationery when writing a letter.

strop, strap: The leather band for sharpening razors is a razor strop, not strap.

supersede: To replace or succeed: "The agency issued guidelines that supersede those adopted in 1988." *Supersede* is often misspelled. It is the only word in the English language that ends in *sede.* Three words end in *ceed: succeed, exceed, proceed.* The others end in *cede.*

supposed to: The correct form (not *suppose to*) in the sense of *expected to:* "I am supposed to attend training sessions this week."

tack, tact: In addition to being a short nail, a tack is a course of action or the direction a ship goes in relation to the position of the sails: "He decided to use a different tack to reach his goals." *Tact* means a delicate perception of the right thing to say or do without offending: "Mending the relationship will require tact." *Tactful* is the adjective form, as in *a tactful person.*

teem, team: *Teem* means to be prolific, to abound, to swarm. The present participle form is *teeming,* not *teaming:* "The room was teeming with flies."

tempera, tempura: Tempera is used in painting, tempura in cooking.

temperatures: They get higher or lower, but they don't get cooler or warmer.

tenant, tenet: A tenant is one who pays rent to occupy a building or land. A tenet is a principle, doctrine or belief held as a truth: "Doing unto others as you would have them do unto you is a tenet of Christianity."

that, which: See Rule 18 in Chapter 2.

there: Generally, sentences should not begin with *there,* as in *there is, there was, there were.* Rather than writing "There were four touchdowns scored in the game," write "The team scored four touchdowns." Get to the real subject rather than using a false subject. Examples abound of good writing with sentences beginning with *there,* especially where the idea is to downplay the true subject, but more often in common usage *there* at the beginning is a signal of lazy thinking.

tort, torte: *Tort* is a legal term referring to a wrongful act or damage not involving a breach of contract for which a civil action can be brought: "Libel is an example of a tort." A torte is a rich cake.

tortuous, torturous: *Tortuous* means full of twists and turns, crooked, deceitful or tricky, as in *a tortuous act* or a *tortuous path. Torturous* pertains to torture.

toward: Correct usage in the United States; the British prefer *towards.*

translucent, transparent: When looking through something that is translucent, one can see light but cannot see objects on the other side; one would be able to see through a transparent glass or fabric: "He installed translucent windows in the office to provide privacy."

trooper, trouper: A trooper is a member of the cavalry, a mounted police officer or a state police officer. A trouper is a member of a troop of actors or singers. *Trouper* is also used to refer to a veteran entertainer.

type: Use as a noun, not an adjective. Incorrect: "He is a studious type person." Instead, say "He is a studious type." *Type* with a hyphen is acceptable in technical uses, as in *B-type blood.*

unique: Something that is unique is one of a kind, so expressions like *more unique, most unique* and *very unique* should be avoided.

up: Avoid its use as part of a verb, as in *stood up, beat up, paired up* and *stirred up.*

venal, venial: *Venal* means open to or characterized by corruption or bribery, as in *a venal government official. Venial* means that which may be forgiven or is pardonable, as in *a venial sin.*

veracious, voracious: To be veracious is to be habitually truthful or honest: "A veracious person is not likely to become a thief." *Voracious* comes from a Latin word meaning "devour." It means greedy, ravenous or very eager, as in *a voracious reader.*

viral, virile: *Viral* means of or caused by a virus, which is an organism that causes certain diseases: "He is ill with a viral disease" (not with a virus). *Virile* means of or characteristic of a man's ability to function sexually. Alternatives to virile that can refer to both sexes include *energetic, vigorous, strong, dynamic* or *bold.*

waist, waste: *Waist* is correct for referring to part of the human body: "He put his arm around her waist."

wangle, wrangle: To wangle is to get or cause by contrivance or tricks: "Can you wangle an invitation to the party?" To wrangle is to argue or quarrel. As a noun, *wrangle* means an angry, noisy dispute. A wrangler is a ranch hand who herds livestock, especially saddle horses.

well-known, widely known: Journalistic usage prefers *widely known* to describe someone whose name or work is known by many people: "The actor Paul Newman is widely known, but few of his fans have ever met him, so they do not know him well."

who's, whose: See Rule 17 in Chapter 2.

wholly: Entirely: "The incorporated village was wholly within the city."

wreak, wreck: *Wreak* means to inflict: "The storm will wreak havoc on our new plants." To wreck is to damage.

Index